New Caribbean Studies

Series Editors
Kofi Campbell, Renison University College, University of Waterloo,
Waterloo, ON, Canada
Shalini Puri, Department of English, University of Pittsburgh,
Pittsburgh, PA, USA

New Caribbean Studies series seeks to explore Caribbean self-understandings, to intervene in the terms of global engagement with the region, and to extend Caribbean Studies' role in reinventing various disciplines and their methodologies well beyond the Caribbean. The series invites monographs, edited collections and Palgrave Pivots on all regions and languages of the Caribbean. It welcomes both literary criticism and more broadly humanities-informed and interdisciplinary scholarship.

Marta Fernández Campa

Memory and the Archival Turn in Caribbean Literature and Culture

palgrave
macmillan

Marta Fernández Campa
Goldsmiths University
London, UK

ISSN 2691-3011   ISSN 2634-5196   (electronic)
New Caribbean Studies
ISBN 978-3-030-72134-3   ISBN 978-3-030-72135-0   (eBook)
https://doi.org/10.1007/978-3-030-72135-0

Cover illustration: Detail from *Tropical Night* series, 2006–ongoing, Christopher Cozier.
Ink, graphite and rubber stamps on paper.

This Palgrave Macmillan imprint is published by the registered company Springer Nature
Switzerland AG
The registered company address is: Gewerbestrasse 11, 6330 Cham, Switzerland

ACKNOWLEDGEMENTS

There are many wonderful people that I would like to thank and acknowledge here. I would first like to thank the series editors Kofi Campbell and Shalini Puri for their critical vision and commitment to this book part of the series New Caribbean Studies, which I'm thrilled to join, and contribute to, with this publication. A special thank you to Shalini for her generosity and guidance in this process and for much inspiration, her scholarship has influenced my own thinking around memory and counter-narratives. My gratitude goes also to the editorial team at Palgrave Macmillan, Molly Beck, Naveen Dass, Rebecca Hinsley, and Petra Treiber, for their dedicated work and continued support throughout the process of writing and publishing this book. I am deeply grateful for the careful and insightful comments of Alissa Trotz on the manuscript. Your feedback encouraged me through difficult times, giving me renewed energy and vital perspective on the work. A heartfelt thank you, Alissa.

This book has been inspired by the work of many writers and artists, some of whom I have the good fortune of knowing personally. They have also influenced its conceptual grounding. I would like to thank all the artists whose work I discuss in this book, for the inspiration, and permission to cite from their work and reproduce their artwork, including Yolanda Arroyo Pizarro, Jay Bernard, Christopher Cozier, Edwidge Danticat, Junot Díaz, Roshini Kempadoo, M. NourbeSe Philip, Caryl Phillips, Mayra Santos Febres and Dorothea Smartt. I would also like to express special gratitude to Christopher Cozier, Roshini Kempadoo,

M. NourbeSe Philip, and Caryl Phillips for their generosity and encouragement. Conversations with Chris and NourbeSe over the years have been stimulating, and especially influential to the entire project (from dissertation to book), also in terms of inspiring many connections across their work. Thanks all for your friendship and support. NourbeSe once encouraged me via email to publish this book one day, and since the moment I read that email in Córdoba, this idea kept growing in my mind as a possibility. I am also especially grateful to Chris (Cozier), Nicholas (Laughlin), and Sean (Leonard) for their support and invitation to do a residency at Alice Yard (Port of Spain) years ago, an experience that invigorated my research and changed some of my approaches to understandings of *space(s)* and the possibilities of collaboration. I realised this then, but have especially come to see and appreciate it fully from the perspective that years have granted. With much gratitude to Patsy and the late Dr Leroy Calliste (Black Stalin) for granting me permission to reproduce excerpts from the lyrics of "Wait Dorothy Wait". Sincere thanks to Tamara Tam-Cruickshank for her support and for facilitating my connection to Patsy. In memory of Dr Leroy Calliste (1941–2022), one of the greatest calypsonians and griots.

The reproduction of the lithograph from Richard Bridgens' *West India Scenery* has been possible thanks to the British Library. Many thanks to Bruna-Lago Paolo and the licensing division for granting this permission. Brief excerpts from past publications feature in chapters 3 and 5. These include "The Archive and the Repertoire in Roshini Kempadoo's *Ghosting*" in *Small Axe: A Caribbean Journal of Criticism*, 21, 1, 2017; "Counter-memory and the Archival Turn in Dorothea Smartt's *Ship Shape*" in *Callaloo: A Journal of Diaspora Art and Letters*, 40, 4, 2017 and "In Conversation with History: An Interview with M. NourbeSe Philip" in *Small Axe*, 26, 1, 2022. *The Brief Wondrous Life of Oscar Wao* was first published by Penguin Random House. Reprinted by permission of Junot Diaz and Aragi Inc. All rights reserved.

Much of the conceptual framework started years ago at The University of Miami, where I completed my doctorate in 2013. My PhD dissertation was the genesis for this book, which has since taken on a new form. In Miami, I met wonderful people, dear colleagues, mentors, and friends who made a special period of my life even more special, and made it possible for us to feel at home in a new city. I am grateful to Pat Saunders who was also my PhD adviser, and created an important critical space where to discuss and explore some of the ideas and connections that led to this book. Many of those rich conversations, in and outside seminars, were vital to my thinking in this project. Thanks also to Jerry Philogene, Pat Saunders, George Yúdice, and Tim Watson for their thoughtful and valuable feedback of those earlier versions, and for their mentorship and support. Two fellowships at UM (The University of Miami) in 2012 were really helpful in the final stage of writing my dissertation, out of which this book has developed. Through the fellowship of the Center of the Humanities at the University of Miami, I was able to receive feedback from colleagues across departments in the best interdisciplinary spirit. Special thanks to Mihoko Suzuki who was then the director of the Center for the Humanities. The support of a Fulbright fellowship (2008–2010) has also been incredibly valuable in this journey, supporting a core part of my work whilst at UM. Deep gratitude also goes to Sandra Pouchet Paquet for her careful mentorship, and for the copy of Fred D'Aguiar's *Dear Future*, gifted to all her students at the end of a Spring semester. We always knew how fortunate we were to be taught by you, and to have been in dialogue with you.

Dialogue and collaboration with other colleagues and friends throughout the years have nourished my work and life in academia. I'm grateful to Anne McCabe and Anne Dewey at Saint Louis University, Madrid campus, for their welcome and support at SLU after returning from Miami to my hometown, and their support in later years. Over the past few years since our move to England, and before, many old and new friends and colleagues have provided spaces of collaboration, support, and exchange. With gratitude to Marielle Barrow, Ronald Cummings, Rafe Dalleo, Faizal Deen, Jane Desmarais, Alison Donnell, Richard Douglass-Chin, Rachel Douglas, Isabel Durán, Jon Evans, Kathryn S. Freeman, María del Pilar Kaladeen, Ana Fernández Caparros, Esther Figueroa, Curdella Forbes, Pammela Hammons, Ayanna Lloyd Banwo, Justine Mann, Gina Maranto, Jen McDerra, Alecia McKenzie, Zakiya McKenzie, Tessa McWatt, Kei Miller, Evelyn O'Callaghan, Gema Perez-Sánchez, Ernesto Priego, Shivanee Ramlochan, David Sutton, Kiron Ward, and Tim Watson, many of with whom I've worked, and collaborated in different ways over the years.

The research for sections in Chapters 2 and 3 from my interviews with M. NourbeSe Philip was facilitated by the Leverhulme Trust through its funding of my work as senior research associate working in the Caribbean Literary Heritage project led by Alison Donnell, at the University of East

Anglia. I had the immense privilege of working closely with NourbeSe Philip as well as Karen Lord and Sharon Millar through a series of interviews and conversations about their recordkeeping practices, creative processes, and literary archives. All those conversations have provided rich and different thinking on how writers' creative process, work, and papers are shaping and transforming archives and literary cultures today. Thank you Karen, NourbeSe, and Sharon. Much respect and admiration to the three of you, always. I cherish our meetings, especially the last ones, all together, although virtually through the waves.

The last few years, many of which cover the period of writing this book, have been difficult for a number of reasons, and I am deeply grateful for the kindness of family and friends who have brought much needed support, and joy to my life during challenging times, including Brexit (which erupted as we arrived in the UK) and the COVID-19 pandemic that has brought so much loss and collective grief. Reishma Seupersad has seen this project since its beginnings and has always offered insightful comments, and really thoughtful feedback. Mil gracias, Reish, and for listening and being there in so many wonderful and supportive ways. A big thank you also to Inés Reyes Ferrero, Ayesha L. Rubio, and Andrea Solis. *Las tres me habéis hecho reír cuando más lo he necesitado, vuestra amistad es luz y magia. ¡Gracias!*

Erin, in gratitude to you for your words and encouragement. They have meant so much. Thanks also to Josie and Catalina! Our night out in Miami when I last visited was so much fun! I miss our Spanglish conversations! Love and gratitude also to all my Miami peeps: Allyn, Freddy, Brian, Christine, Jennifer (Garçon) and Jennifer (Slivka), Kurt, Monica, Nicole, Ng'ang'a Muchiri, Mike and Carolina, Sara, Sarah, Stephanie, Sydney, and Liz.

Much love and gratitude to all my family in Spain and here in Britain. To Dani, thanks for your kind words and encouragement always (I know you also asked for a copy of this book *¡te la guardo!*). Thanks to my mother, Maite, for her brilliant friendship, encouragement and support. I deeply admire your integrity, generosity and kindness. Both my mother and my grandad have always reminded me of the value of memory. *Con cariño y morriña, abrazos para mi abuela,* Eloína.

I would like to dedicate this book to my husband and son who have supported me throughout in more ways than one. A huge thank you Tom, for all your encouragement in writing this book, for the friendship, love, and laughter. Dylan, you have grown so much in the time of writing this, and can't believe you are eight now! Thanks for your patience as I worked on it. Your contagious joy and kindness brighten everything. ¡Gracias, Dylan!

CONTENTS

LIST OF FIGURES

CHAPTER 1

Introduction. Counter-Narratives of History and Relational Fragmentation

Marked opportunities for remembering histories of oppression at an institutional level can reproduce forms of oppression themselves; this is especially so in those cases when the image of the state could potentially be compromised in such acts of remembering. The commemoration of the quincentennial anniversary of the arrival of Spanish conquistadors to the Americas proved to be just such an event. The Exposición Universal de Sevilla (Seville Expo) in 1992 exemplified this. Rather than opening a space for new ways of marking memory and narrating colonial history, the international exhibition in Seville, Spain, became an attempt to redefine this history as an *encuentro*, an encounter. Rafael Sánchez Ferlosio critiques this semiotic turn and suggests that the supposed encounter be considered instead an *"encontronazo"* (a collision), "un verdadero allanamiento" (a true forceful entry) (47). The reformulation of the genocide as a narrative of "discovery" and "encounter" between different social groups perpetuates that original colonial instance of epistemic violence. Michel-Rolph Trouillot observes that "[t]o call 'discovery' the first invasions of inhabited lands by Europeans is an exercise in Eurocentric power that already frames future narratives of the event so described" (114). In the 1990s, a group of historians and activists, including Trouillot, denounced the implications of emerging narratives of "encounter" that characterised many of

M. Fernández Campa, *Memory and the Archival Turn in Caribbean Literature and Culture*, New Caribbean Studies, https://doi.org/10.1007/978-3-030-72135-0_1

the quincentennial celebrations because they prove to be "one more testimony [... in which] '[e]ncounter' sweetens the horror, polishes the rough edges that do not fit neatly either side of the controversy. Everyone seems to gain" (Trouillot 115). Like Sánchez Ferlosio, Trouillot suggests a different framing by declaring, "I prefer to say that Columbus 'stumbled on the Bahamas,' and I prefer 'conquest' over 'discovery' to describe what happened after the landing" (115). Seville Expo' 92 perpetuated the historiographical tradition of imperial "discovery", and also the problematic tradition of International Exhibitions in Europe through, amongst other aspects, the commoditisation of the event. In the style of what Sánchez Ferlosio critically deems a great Sevillian Disneyland (13, 51, 248), Expo' 92 became a moment when advertisements announced that paying 4,000 pesetas (24 euros in today's currency) allowed access to a cultural experience where visitors could,

> have dinner in a galleon, [join] Palenques dances, visit the Mohican tombs, eat pizzas and couscous, [visit] the Mayan time tunnel, the burial of the Lord of Sipán ... Dive into the world of 1492! A spectacle full of magic, with actors, machines, projections and special effects ... to immerse ourselves in the era of the Discovery ... Have fun, relax and enjoy! (Bayer *Página/12*)

This bizarre and cruel collection of "historical" experiences, publicised as "fun" and relaxing, embody acts of epistemic violence, particularly in the silencing and whitewashing of historical facts to popularise such an ideologically skewed version of history. There were, however, responses and protests towards the official and commercial commemorations by Indigenous activist groups, and artists who targeted some otherwise unaddressed issues. Activists' complaints altered the plans of the tour of the Spanish replica caravels docked at Seville's port. The history of the *Aventura 92* expedition, later called *Ruta Quetzal*), a programme proposed and supported by the former Spanish King Juan Carlos I which took place from 1979 until 2016, illustrates the legacy of rewriting of the history of conquest through a re-routing of cultural values of exchange, thus suppressing Spain's role in the genocide of Indigenous Amerindian and African peoples. For this tour, more than 10,000 young students from 60 countries travelled to Latin America in replica caravels reproducing various routes in the journeys of Columbus and other conquistadors. The rhetoric of this educational programme centred on a premise of cultural exchange, that reproduced and celebrated the discourse of adventurous and entrepreneurial spirit, with more overt and covert links to the conquistadors. This rhetoric has often defined the terms of colonial historical amnesia in Spain. Protests in 1992, however, that took place in the United States saw Native American activist Russell Means succeed "in getting Italian-Americans in Denver to cancel their Columbus Day parade" (Fusco 144). Artists Coco Fusco and Guillermo Gomez Peña created a cage performance entitled *The Couple in the Cage: Two Undiscovered Amerindians Visit the West* (1992–1993) which was meant, "as part of a counter-quincentenary project", to provide an opportunity to rethink alternatives to memorialisation processes (Fusco 144). By enclosing themselves in a golden cage disguised as two "undiscovered Amerindians" of a fictional tribe (144), Fusco and Gomez Peña located their performance alongside the "many examples of how popular opposition has, for centuries, been expressed through the use of satiric spectacle" (Fusco 145). "A donation box in front of the cage indicated that for a small fee, I would dance (to rap music), Guillermo would tell authentic Amerindian stories" (145). Fusco and Gomez Peña toured many locations across the United States and Europe and would set up their performance in public spaces, sometimes next to museum doors, challenging spectators' reactions. Both artists were shocked to find that the public would often fail to identify the satiric content of the performance and would instead believe their fictional identities to be real (Fusco 143).[1]

In the United Kingdom, events linked to the 2007 Commemoration of the Bicentennial Anniversary of the Abolition of the Transatlantic Slave Trade also received multiple critiques around whose and what past was marked and how.[2] Catherine Hall, writing about the commemorations critically posits a crucial question: "how and what is to be remembered – that is the issue. Is it the horrors of the middle passage and of the plantation and the collective responsibility that Britons bear for this – or is it the pride in abolition?" ("Remembering" 1).[3] Raising similar questions in the introduction to *Free at Last? Reflections on Freedom and the Abolition of the British Slave Trade*, Cecily Jones and Amar Wahab discuss the arrest of Toyin Agbetu, British civil rights activist, after he protested the memorialisation mostly as celebration of British abolitionist

Wilberforce at a Westminster Abbey service commemorating the bicentennial anniversary on 27 March 2007. An arrest that, particularly in light of the context in which his intervention at Westminster was situated, reveals further how institutions continue to police disruptions to their ideological continuity and authority. Towards the end of the service, Agbetu raised his voice to address everyone there, confronting the uneasy audience with "the hypocrisy to the three pillars of British institutions - monarchy, church, and state - for their historical roles in sanctioning and sustaining three centuries of transatlantic trafficking in African peoples" (Jones and Wahab 1). Many criticisms of the bicentennial commemorations that took place throughout 2007 pointed out the disproportionate focus on British abolitionists and Agbetu himself later referred to the service as the "Wilberfest abolition celebration" (Jones and Wahab 2). Aligning with Agbetu's disruption of state memory, Jones and Wahab ask: "What of the heroism of Quobna Ottobah Cugoano, of Ignacius Sancho, Olaudah Equiano, of Nanny, Queen of the Maroons, of Joseph Knight, and James Somerset, Mary Prince and of the innumerable nameless and faceless others who fought for and gave their lives in the quest for survival, dignity and justice" (2).

I mention these examples of missed opportunities at responsibility and accountability in state historical commemoration and reparation to move onto one of the overarching premises of this book, the role and contributions of Caribbean contemporary writers and artists in bringing these issues into various counter-publics and out in the wider public sphere. The artist, Edwidge Danticat argues, has a special desire to interpret and reshape their own world and the society and world(s) they inhabit (*Create Dangerously*). All the artists whose work I discuss in *Memory and the Archival Turn in Caribbean Literature and Culture* engage in that practice. This book explores, through the discussion of contemporary Caribbean literature and visual art, the ways in which formal fragmentation creates languages of memorialisation that are either directly influenced by music or more indirectly reflect the influence of musical sensibility, music patterns, and other popular culture elements in their poetics and aesthetic makeup. I place the stress on the *ways* in which artists have engaged in an aesthetics and poetics of fragmentation, as it is through form, composition, process, and methodology that their work encourages dynamic ways of reading and viewing with relationality, following Édouard Glissant's definition of the term. For Glissant, *Caribbeanness* and the Caribbean experience is characterised by thinking relationally, that is, with the awareness of the interconnection of elements and fragments, that ultimately point to both discrepant and convergent experiences, histories, and cultures (*Poetics of Relation*, *Caribbean Discourse*). The *relation* that Glissant philosophised is constituted by "shared knowledge" (*Poetics* 8) that links individuals and communities, where the whole and the part(s) (re)connect again through the act of relationality. Glissant envisions some of the relationships and connections linking islands and locations in the Caribbean in this way, and it is in this spirit that this book also continues to engage with it. In her translator's introduction to the English publication of *Poetics of Relation*, Betsy Wing notes that Glissant "sees imagination as the force that can change mentalities; relation ... the process of this change; and poetics as a transformative mode of history" (xii). I argue that, to varying degrees, the relationship between *form* and *relation* is at the core of many contemporary Caribbean literary and cultural texts, and it is particularly so when it comes to moments of memorialisation. In "The Power of Archive and its Limits", Achille Mbembe likens the documents in archives to fragments that need reassembling:

> Through archived documents, we are presented with pieces of time to be assembled, fragments of life to be placed in order, one after the other, in an attempt to formulate a story that acquires its coherence through the ability to craft links between the beginning and the end. A montage of fragments thus creates an illusion of totality and continuity. In this way, just like the architectural process, the time woven together by the archive is the product of a composition. (21)

These archival dynamics apply to the assemblages, through bricolage, montage, contrapuntal, and fugal techniques, configured in the work of Caribbean artists (the term used here to refer widely to visual artists, artistes, and writers). The way in which the (often highly visual) fragmentation in their work interconnects, the way in which fragments relate to each other, highlights that archival engagement and encourages an active critical reading and viewing that moves beyond the space and limits of the colonial and imperial archives. It echoes the moment of assembling documents and records in an archive that need to be set in dialogue to establish a narrative, an even more complex and fraught process in such archives where truth often remains hidden and manipulated. But what does that dynamic act of reading and viewing entail, encourage and demand from audiences? How is the work of artists in the contemporary Caribbean and its diaspora in dialogue with, challenging, and/or expanding, the longstanding tradition of Caribbean artistic expression that reimagines history? These are questions that this book aims to address—and posit, perhaps more than answer, as there might be many possibilities for these questions.

Fragmentation in the composition of Caribbean contemporary art often reveals gaps in history and reflects upon them, but also points to the non-recoverability of those losses and many of those memories. Shalini Puri points out, in similar terms to Mbembe, that the fragmentation in the poetics of the Grenada Revolution as, "micropoetic fragments and telling details" can function to "embody or trigger insight. Another is that they evoke an intense awareness of how much is still missing from the story, and from a montage from which connections might yet emerge" (*The Grenada Revolution*, 25). This dynamic is at stake in the forms of remembrance in the literature, music, and visual artwork that I discuss in this book, and that awareness of what is missing is critical to the very process of counter-archiving they engage in. My focus in this critical discussion also draws from the interlink between poetics of fragmentation and memory, in conversation with how Silvio Torres-Saillant identifies fragmentation as one of the main aesthetic elements connecting Caribbean literatures and cultures across the region (and the diaspora) in his book *Caribbean Poetics: Towards an Aesthetic of West Indian Literature*. For Torres-Saillant, fragmentation can act as a nexus linking the experiences amongst peoples of the Caribbean, especially both in underscoring the differences across language, race and class as well as a shared cultural framework. This book attempts to continue that comparative connection and explore similarities in various poetics of memory and fragmentation across various locations in the Caribbean and its diaspora. Another methodology within the critical range of relational possibilities that informs my critical discussion, is that of archipelagic thinking. According to Yolanda Martínez-San Miguel and Michelle Stephens, archipelagic thinking relies on a "conceptualization of the global" that attends to the cultural specificity of place thus allowing "micro as well as macro analyses, a focus on materiality as much as metaphor, a turn to the glocal, to find the different valences of the global and the local that are operating simultaneously" (Ch. 1). All these approaches, their influence, and the emergence of new ones in the works that I discuss here, can illuminate a wider intellectual tradition of contemporary Caribbean literature and culture, as always in dynamic relation, and in conversation.

The Archival Turn: Imagining Possibilities Beyond the (Post)colonial Record

This book offers a discussion of the work of Caribbean and Black British writers and artists working and living in the diaspora and the region, including M. NourbeSe Philip and Christopher Cozier (Trinidad and Tobago, and Canada), Edwidge Danticat (Haiti/US), Junot Díaz (Dominican Republic/US), Caryl Phillips (St. Kitts/UK/US), Roshini Kempadoo (Guyana/UK/Trinidad); Dorothea Smartt (UK/Barbados), Jay Bernard (UK/Jamaica), Inés María Martiatu Terry (Cuba), Yolanda Arroyo Pizarro, and Mayra Santos-Febres (Puerto Rico). The transnational, comparative, and interdisciplinary range of networks, artists, and artworks included in this book demands a relational critical discussion, which I carry out here. These artists configure a creolised poetics and aesthetics largely outside the scope of the colony and the nation. Their engagement with a variety of archival sources and historical narratives bears the awareness of the failure of these records to account for, and mark, the memories of the individuals and communities affected. Their work reflects, from an artistic perspective, what Ann L. Stoler identifies as an "archival turn" in the field of the Humanities and the Social Sciences, characterised by a "move from archive-as-source to archive-as-subject" (*Along the Archival Grain* 44). In this turn, archives become themselves the subject of critical investigation; they no longer simply function as a source of knowledge. In fact, an examination of their exclusions and silences is central to contemporary studies of the social value of archives, making manifest the epistemological implications of uncritically assuming by default the authority of the documents held within them. Stoler notes how this intellectual shift is motivated by the growing awareness that in some cases archives, particularly colonial ones, offer very limited knowledge, skewed or none at all about the life experience and perspective of oppressed social groups (*Along the Archival Grain*; "Colonial Archives"). Aligning with this critical shift, this book follows an approach similar to Stoler's, where the emphasis is placed on "archiving as process rather than to archives as things. It looks to archives as epistemological experiments rather than as sources, to colonial archives as cross-sections of contested knowledge. Most importantly, it looks to colonial archives as both transparencies on which power relations were inscribed and intricate technologies of rule in themselves" (Stoler, "Colonial Archives" 83).

Throughout the five chapters of this book, I use various critical variants of the term "counter-" (counter-memory, counter-archives and counter-narratives) chiefly inspired by the musical term counterpoint, and specifically M. NourbeSe Philip's writings on calypso, contrapuntal poetics, and the fugue. This has been with the understanding that the works I discuss engage with official narratives and offer a counterpoint to those, a new way of thinking about records. However, those are not tied to official narratives in a simple oppositional sense. There is a multidimensionality to the engagement that needs emphasis. The languages and vocabularies of memory and experience used by this group of artists is both attuned to, and inspired by, spiritual, localised, and ancestral knowledge and sensibilities, prior to and beyond the remit of any official and formal archive. Further, the art under discussion in this book embodies a turn to the archive that is simultaneous with a turn to affect and the combination of both reveals new archives. The inclusion of the notebook, the letter, oral histories, religious ceremony or the family album in this memory work heightens the affective potentiality of these new counter-archives within their critical dimension.

There is a growing number of literature as well as critical works in Caribbean studies, particularly within the last two decades, that participate in this turn to the archive. This body of critical work is very often interdisciplinary and comparative; it examines literary, cultural, and artistic production from across the region and the diaspora, theorising the longstanding engagement with historical memory in Caribbean artistic production. My approach to discussing the different forms of counter-memory in the work of Caribbean contemporary writers and visual artists is informed by this line of critical enquiry. Focus here is on the *process* of archiving forms of "counter-memory", understanding this term as memory that contradicts, revises, and/or complicates historical and national narratives. George Lipsitz defines counter-memory as, "a way of remembering and forgetting that starts with the local, the immediate, and the personal" (213). Drawing, but also crucially diverging, from Foucault's definition of this term, Lipsitz highlights how counter-memory "looks to the past for the hidden histories excluded from dominant narratives" and it "forces revision of existing histories by supplying new perspectives about the past" (213). In that vein, the literature and visual artwork that I discuss in this book refigure a number of historical narratives. At times in this book, I refer to counter-memories whilst other times the stress is on counter-archives as counter-memory fails to account for the unknown memories of enslaved communities in the Caribbean and the non-recoverability of their lives and life stories. This is particularly the case when dealing with records or narratives from the archive of slavery where voices and memories of the enslaved are absent and where events have been recorded, writing out the humanity of Africans, from the perspective and language of colonial oppressors. In those cases, artistic counter-archives offer instead other possibilities for approaching the past. For example, the literary works and performance of *Ship Shape* by Dorothea Smartt, M. NourbeSe Philip's *Zong!*, and *Negras* by Yolanda Arroyo Pizarro, which deal with slavery, configure a series of varied and dynamic archives that draw attention to and make visible, and palpable in the case of *Zong!*, even audible at times, the forced absence and silencing. According to Lipsitz, "unlike historical narratives that begin with the totality of human existence and then locate specific actions and events within that totality, counter-memory starts with the specific and then builds outward toward a total story" (Ch. 9). Instances of counter-memory confront societies with the histories that have been excluded and occluded from the official collective memory, and they bring those to the forefront. For Lipsitz, counter-memory is also necessarily always relational, as history and memory are relational to Glissant, since "no single story can be understood but in relation to other stories" (Ch. 9). Significantly, the conceptual arc of this book is primarily influenced, as the following chapters demonstrate, by the conceptualisations of memory and memorialisation of the very artists and writers whose work I discuss, in particular those by M. NourbeSe Philip, whose writings on memory and contrapuntality as ongoing and ethical process of memorialisation have influenced this project. Philip, as Lipsitz, sees popular culture, particularly music and other forms, as one of the most powerful vehicles of memory.

FRAGMENTATION AND AESTHETICS

Memory and The Archival Turn in Caribbean Literature and Culture has been very much inspired by theoretical and philosophical work of the Caribbean artists whose work I discuss here; in their articulation of a poetics of memory, they often draw from musical and highly visual references and frameworks that are central to the theoretical grounding of this project. There is no one poetics of memory in Caribbean literature, in the same way as there is not one Caribbean aesthetic. Kwame Dawes insists on the latter in his critical discussion of a reggae aesthetic, where he mentions that the term "Caribbean aesthetic ... is too broad and ill-defined to use as an analytical term in my study" (*Natural Mysticism* 32). Dawes also warns of an important fact when he states that, although there is "a regional culture shaped by the common beginnings of many of our peoples in Africa and by our common experiences of plantation slavery and colonialism, there is also a great diversity and distinctiveness from island to island, not least the presence in the southern Caribbean of almost two million people of Indian origin" (*Natural Mysticism* 32). The ethnic, cultural, and linguistic differences in the region therefore makes the term Caribbean aesthetic a slippery one. However, despite cultural and linguistic differences and specificities, there are some aspects that predominate in the various poetics and aesthetics in Caribbean arts. This is the case for shared thematic concerns with memory, history, and location that are, in turn, often characterised by (a visual) fragmentation, polyphony, and dialogic nature. Orality and non-linear storytelling are equally central to many Caribbean poetics and aesthetics, and the themes and elements just mentioned aid in capturing and incorporating those non-linear patterns. Through those, Caribbean contemporary artists have been pushing the boundaries of form and narratology whilst shaping and reshaping aesthetics.

Although often interlinked, as I argue in this book, it is important to make a distinction between aesthetics and poetics. Traditionally, in Western philosophy aesthetics signified the study and judgement of art and the appreciation of its beauty. However, contemporary approaches to art from postmodernism to postcolonialism, with their emphasis on subjectivity and cultural specificity, have redefined more traditional and Eurocentric interpretations and understandings of the term, opening its signification to encompass forms and interpretation that communicate and account for "a desire to think in terms sensitive to difference" (Foster xvi). Hal Foster's description of an "anti-aesthetic" is part of this understanding of aesthetics which he presents as questioning Western representations of historical master narratives and official histories with the clear acknowledgement that nothing rests outside the frame of representation, as representation is always political (xvi–xvii). This manifests both in the form (visual aesthetics) as well as in the approach to art and art history. The understanding of poetics that I refer to here convey aesthetic forms that are at times highly visual and fragmented (on the page, the multimedia screen, through mixed media and within the frame). A post-colonial poetics (which Elleke Boehmer theorises as a series of literary devices and their challenges) demand a connection with readers (ch. 2). This book explores how the interconnection of elements in the fragmentation of the poetics and aesthetics in a series of Caribbean literary texts and artwork, guides their reading and viewing, creating (in turn) a shared space of inquiry and affect. As Boehmer notes, postcolonial writing is interested in "questions of aesthetics [that are] questions of form, structure, perception and reception" (25). The various poetics in the literature and artwork covered in this book reflect a wide variety of engagements with history, memory, and place. I argue that they all share a contrapuntal aesthetics and poetics, formally and conceptually, as I will discuss later, that emerges from the influence of music and the visual, as flexible vehicles of memory. Although experimental Caribbean aesthetics and poetics that deal with memory and history can be traced to the 1960s and 1970s (with many earlier examples of innovative fragmentation), I identify the late 1980s, and particularly the mid-1990s to the present day, as the period that saw a marked increase of fragmented narratives and non-linearity that bears the influence of music, visual, and popular culture.

Foundational discussions of the Caribbean region's histories, societies, and cultures by writers, literary and cultural critics, from as early as the 1930s through to the 1990s, have been characterised by a language marked by visual vocabularies. They have often used spatial tropes, visual metaphors, and what Mary Lou Emery identifies as an emphasis on sight and vision as political acts (*Modernism*). We can find examples of this visual imaginary in Kamau Brathwaite's notion of tidalectics, Derek Walcott's metaphor of a vase broken into fragments, M. NourbeSe Philip's conceptualisation of fragmentation, Antonio Benítez Rojo's idea of the repeating island, Édouard Glissant's poetics of relation and errantry, or Paul Gilroy's conceptualisation of the Black Atlantic and its connecting routes, to name a few. Although this critical writing often emerges from references to localised histories, this group of authors often mention, and speak of, the whole Caribbean. Despite the differences in the philosophies and poetics configured (and theorised) by these writers, they all point to the specificity of located experience, geographies of the region or the diaspora, whilst speaking to the larger connecting threads (historical, cultural, and artistic) between those geographies. Brathwaite's concept of tidealectics emerges from the rejection of Hegelian dialectic and centres instead on the triangular movement marked by ripples caused by a two-tide movement.[4] Brathwaite describes being inspired in this thinking by the sight of an elderly Black woman sweeping the sand of her yard in the Caribbean. This back-and-forth movement and the sight of her walking on the beach one day, evokes another image as Brathwaite writes poetically about seeing her body, "silhouetting against / the sparkling light that hits the / Caribbean at that early dawn" (Brathwaite qtd. in Reckin 1). In Brathwaite's vision, the woman walking on the sand is actually walking on the water, and travels through the middle passage journeying to and from Africa (Reckin 1–2). Similarly, in his Nobel Prize acceptance speech, Walcott frames the notion of the "fragments of memory" from a realisation whilst witnessing Ramleela, the dramatisation of the Hindu epic the Ramayana in Felicity, Trinidad, where Walcott sees how the performance reinvents the epic as a "branch of its original language, an abridgement of it, but not a distortion or even a reduction of its epic scale" ("The Antilles" 68). This realisation concludes that "Antillean art" reassembles the pieces of a broken vase (signifying the multiple ruptures with the homeland through enslavement and indentureship), signalling "this restoration of our shattered histories, our shattered vocabulary, our archipelago becoming a synonym for pieces broken off the original continent" (69). Brathwaite has similarly articulated a "sense of fragmentation" in the historical experience of separation from the original homeland and of a subsequent and necessary "recovery of the fragments" (*History* 29).

MEMORY AND MUSIC: CONTRAPUNTAL MATTERS

The term "counterpoint" is generally used to signify a relationship of contrast but this term also describes "[t]he ability, unique to music, to say two things at once comprehensively" (Kennedy and Kennedy).[5] The term derives from the Latin expression "punctus contra puntum" which means "point against point" or "note against note". In music the counterpoint displays arrangements of two or more lines of notes being played (and thus happening) at the same time. There are two main types of counterpoint: canon counterpoint, with a very strict structure (where the notes have to be exactly the same) and imitative counterpoint (a contrapuntal structure where a voice "enters [the composition] with a phrase which is then more or less copied by another" (Kennedy and Kennedy). An even more complex form of contrapuntal composition is the fugue, which combines multiple lines. Here, the voices are generally played faster, thus somehow creating a sense of movement through the quick pace and the constant alternation of voices that follow each other in an ongoing flight. Conceptually, these relational dynamics of (strict, imitative) counterpoint or the fugue, as well as the call-and-response pattern, can be used to think about the dialogic implications that predominate in literature and visual art where, for example, a wide range of experiences, viewpoints, and, in this case, memories, can coalesce and "converse" with each other.

In "Fugues, Fragments and Fissures: A Work in Progress" M. NourbeSe Philip argues how the term "fugue" functions as an accurate concept to describe Caribbean societies. According to Philip, its two meanings, fugue as a polyphonic musical composition and as a dissociative psychological state, reflect the syncretic nature of cultures in the Caribbean and the remnants of collective trauma prevalent in its societies. As Philip puts it, the fugue,

> is a musical composition with polyphonic elements in which "themes are developed contrapuntally". Usually there is a melody or melodic phrase that is repeated in different keys and at different intervals. In this sense of the word, too, Trinidad and Tobago and the Caribbean can also be described as fugal and polyphonic societies, culturally, racially and ethnically. Societies in which the harsh melodies of loss and exile and be/longing for a re/turn are repeated over and over again in different keys and at different intervals. Societies in which these melodies come from different societies and cultures, some of which, like the African and the Asian carry with them polyphonic and polyrhythmic musical traditions. Fugal societies in two senses of the word, both dissociative and polyphonic. (Robert Rudnicki qtd. in Philip 92)

Referring to Robert Rudnicki's use of the notion of the fugue in *Percyscapes: The Fugue State in Twentieth Century Southern Fiction*, Philip explains how the psychology term "fugue" refers to a dissociative disorder that leads those who have suffered trauma to detach from, and forget, elements from their life prior to the traumatic experience. As a result, they adopt a new and different identity, a coping mechanism which Philip contextualises in the history of survival of individual and collective trauma in the aftermath of slavery ("Fugues, Fragments and Fissures"

83). Finding in the compositional dynamics of music a language to articulate the experience of history and memory in the Caribbean has a long
critical tradition in the region and the diaspora. The intersection of the
visual and orality in articulating forms of counter-memory conveys a
complex array of creolised forms and modes of fragmentation that present
a Caribbean specific poetics (or one of Caribbean influence) but which are
also in dialogue with other artistic influences such as modernism and postmodernism. Simon Gikandi has identified creolisation as one of the key
characteristics of Caribbean modernisms precisely because of its dynamism
and ability to stress the "transmutation and transformation of the colonial subject" (17) and, I would add, to break and reshape form in ways
that stretch its epistemological limitations, particularly when it comes to
the Eurocentric tradition. Mary Lou Emery identifies sight and vision
as discursive tools of modernism that shape Caribbean modernisms in
literature and the visual arts, connected thus through the aesthetic and
beyond the premises of high modernist aestheticism (*Modernism*). By
discussing aesthetic features and elements (often read through the lens of
modernism and postmodernism) from a culturally specific angle instead,
Memory and The Archival Turn aims to show the way in which there
are various local and global influences underlying the aesthetic emerging
from relationships to place and location and mediated through memory.

Paul Gilroy argues persuasively that the cultural influence of music
has generated a transnational cross-cultural network that connects the
larger Caribbean, African-American, and Black British musical forms both
aesthetically and politically through webs of filiation and commodity
exchange. In *The Black Atlantic*, Gilroy laments how "the history and
significance of these musics are consistently overlooked" mostly because
undertaking such study, Gilroy notes, would "exceed the frameworks of
national or ethnocentric analysis with which we have been too easily satis-
fied" (35).[6] It is worth noting that since Gilroy wrote this statement many
writers, as well as critics, have engaged with music formally and thematically, often to tell transnational stories and explore the interlinks of their
complex histories. Equally, *The Black Atlantic* has been influential to this
body of criticism. In fact, two texts close to the publication of *The Black
Atlantic* itself –Lawrence Scott's *Witchbroom* (1992) and Caryl Phillips'
Crossing the River (1993), reflect this influence of music on literary form
and retellings of history. More recent examples continue to show the
proliferation of experimental fiction influenced by music. Marlon James'
polyphonic novel *A Brief History of Seven Killings* (2014), winner of the

2015 Booker Prize, was influenced by the rhythms of reggae music and dub, and the figure of Bob Marley referred to as "the Singer" in this fragmentary, non-linear text engaging with Jamaican history from the 1970s. The music genre *bolero* in Mayra Santos-Febres' *Sirena Selena, Vestida de Pena* (2000), captures transnational journeys between the Dominican Republic and Puerto Rico marked by the precarity of racialised and queer youth in the economies of (sex) tourism. Also, through a reggae and dub aesthetic, Marcia Douglas' *The Marvellous Equations of the Dread* (2016) interlinks non-linear stories where Bob Marley and his legacy are very present. The influence of music is also present in Kei Miller's *Augustown* (2016) through the layered references to dancehall in dialogue with all other registers of popular culture in the novel. These are some examples of contemporary and recent literary texts where engagements with historical moments and issues are influenced by music history, patterns and sensibilities. There is an idea that Gilroy discusses in *The Black Atlantic* that informs the ways in which this book considers the influence of music (broadly speaking) in Caribbean and Black British literature. According to Gilroy, "[a]ntiphony (call-and-response) has come to be seen as a bridge from music into other modes of cultural expression, supplying, along with improvisation, montage, and dramaturgy, the hermeneutic keys to the full medley of black artistic practices" (*The Black Atlantic* 78). Edward Said's definition of contrapuntal analysis is also important to this discussion as it brings into focus the experiences and memories previously excluded from both a series of records, and from a broader notion of the archival logic understood as operating in the public sphere and the various forms of state and alternative memory operating simultaneously. According to Said, a contrapuntal reading entails,

> reading a text with an understanding of what is involved when an author shows, for instance, that a colonial sugar plantation is seen as important to the process of maintaining a particular style of life in England ... contrapuntal reading must take account of both processes, that of imperialism and that of resistance to it, which can only be done by extending our reading of the texts to include what was once forcibly excluded. (*Culture and Imperialism* 66)

The particular context of Said's definition of a contrapuntal analysis deals with the various silences, exclusions, and omissions in British imperial fiction of the eighteenth and nineteenth centuries. The contrapuntal reading that I apply to the literature and visual art discussed here means reading a particular (con)text with the awareness of what has been forcibly excluded from that context. I contend that many texts, performance, and artwork in contemporary Caribbean arts highlight a series of gaps, silences, and erasures through aesthetic configurations that are key to their hermeneutics. What has been previously excluded from the record and the official narrative of colonial history or the postcolonial nation is brought into focus. The sheer variety of voices in this artistic body of works, the connections between them, and the implications of their dialogism are very much an open invitation for readers and audiences to begin their own engagement with the work and the different modes of counter-memory that they suggest.

Brathwaite's idea of making sound visible, which his poetry masterfully reflects, aided also by the experimentation with font, typeface, and visual signs, informs the important connection between sound and image, music and the visual in Caribbean art and culture, as does the thinking on contrapuntality of M. NourbeSe Philip. Centring the role of music, sight, and sound, language (and the language of music) in various contemporary poetics and aesthetics has enabled a fitting model for the connection of cultural expression across artistic forms. The influence of drumming, rhythm, and rhythmicity is present, to varying degrees, in much of the work that I discuss here. Kamau Brathwaite's ideas on rhythm (both in his poetry, theoretical, and historical work) provides a vital framework for appreciating its political, conceptual, and spiritual significance in Caribbean languages and art, generally. Brathwaite sees the drum and the sounding of the drum as marking a call that demands a response, he identifies this pattern in nation language and orality (*History*). In *History of the Voice*, Brathwaite also explains how the "rhythm, timbre, its own sound explosion" of African languages were kept and transformed in the syntax and rhythms of Creole (nation) language(s) of the Caribbean (267). Significantly, he positions writers as being at the forefront of these discussions, and cites Glissant's notion of Creole language and "force poetics" as a tool of strategic retention, submerged and largely kept at bay from coloniser's control or influence creating autonomy and thus able to "disguise and retain his culture" (*History of the Voice* 270), in line with Glissant's writings on opacity (*Poetics of Relation*). These notions of disguise, masking, and simultaneous invitation to engage with and think through a variety of articulations of memory, are present in the literary text, music, and artwork under discussion in this book.

Sound and sight, orality, music, and the visual have been incredibly influential to aesthetics in the Caribbean. As Philip argues, when colonial powers banned enslaved Africans from speaking their own languages in the plantation and were grouped according to different linguistic and cultural groups to avoid rebellion, music remained a powerful means of expression (*She Tries Her Tongue* 46).[7] Philip notes "[t]he survival of musical artforms probably owe their success to the fact that they were essentially non-verbal art forms" (46). Alongside orality and oral traditions, music and musical forms, phraseology, and sensibility have long provided a language through which to communicate memory and experience in the Caribbean. The visual has equally played a key role in the translation of music onto the page, as well as in its own right. If music in the Caribbean has historically provided spaces for religious, spiritual, political assembly, and kinship, the visual arts and visual culture, particularly painting, on the other hand, remained largely the realm of the colonial masters during the slave trade and colonialism.

Theories of aesthetics were central to European dehumanising portrayals of Africans, and visual representation and visuality have played a significant role in the development of Eurocentric aesthetics and anti-Black racism (Emery; Gikandi *Slavery and the Culture of Taste*; Mirzoeff). Particularly during the period of colonial expansion, and throughout the height of European empires, visual representations of Black people in Western visual arts and culture have largely been characterised by attempts at erasure and objectification. Similarly, Indian and Chinese indentured workers have also been portrayed in colonial visual records of the late nineteenth and early twentieth centuries through the lens of orderly/disorderly labour, productivity, and subdued subjectivity, with the aim of imposing a colonial representation, controlling their economic production and configuring profitable narratives (Thompson *An Eye*; Kempadoo *Creole in the Archive*; McWatt *Shame on Me*). Caribbean writers, visual artists, and scholars have written extensively about the role of colonial visual rhetoric and its literacies, and contemporary literature in the Caribbean and the diaspora, as well as visual art, reflects critical engagements with the role of visual culture in constructions of race, and discursive formation. This political aspect of the aesthetic of fragmentation is at stake in the selection of texts that I discuss and are also present, for example, in other works published in the last decade such as *Citizen: an American Lyric* (2014), where Claudia Rankine presents, through prose poetry, an archive of poems documenting experiences of racism through a variety of rhetorical discourses from text, photographic images, and the media. Other images in *Citizen* are artwork by African and African-American visual artists including Carrie Mae Weems, Glenn Ligon, and Wangechi Mutu that critically respond to, and address, the projections and violence of whiteness through techniques such as bricolage, emulation of cataloguing systems, textual and visual repetition, and fragmentation. Visual art and visual rhetoric generally, become an important counterpoint to the written records of whiteness, also deconstructed in Rankine's non-fiction text *Just Us: An American Conversation* (2020).

Chapter Overview

In order to begin addressing the critical possibilities offered by an interdisciplinary approach, I begin with a discussion of Christopher Cozier's mixed media *Wait Dorothy Wait* (1991) and M. NourbeSe Philip's poetry collection *She Tries Her Tongue; Her Silence Softly Breaks* (1988). Both works provide a reexamination of how issues of socio-economic, gender, and racial inequality have been omitted in a series of archives and narratives. They reflect how the rhetoric of nationalism, constructions of tropicalisation, religion, and dominant ideologies of history have occluded other(ed) histories. In these works, moments describing these issues are evoked and called to inhabit the space of the arts' frame and the page. *Wait Dorothy Wait*'s critique of Trinidadian state control over popular culture, and the local art market's rejection of social conceptual art in the 1980s and 1990s, reveals the tensions lying behind their disavowal. Cozier's critique shows how such rejection is embroiled with a visual tradition of representing the Caribbean that privileges local and foreign elite viewpoints whilst ignoring those of the majority of its citizens. I examine Cozier's artwork with the aid of Gerard Aching's conceptualisation of demasking in Carnival, which Aching applies theoretically to a reading of Earl Lovelace's novel *The Dragon Can't Dance* (1979). With a very similar visual poetics, *She Tries Her Tongue; Her Silence Softly Breaks* recreates how voices break the silence to articulate a critical genealogy of Caribbean women writers. I discuss Cozier's *Wait Dorothy Wait* as guiding viewers' attention towards the dichotomy between a pristine tropical landscape and the context of crime in Trinidad in the 1980s and 1990s. Its connection to Black Stalin's calypso of the same name creates a critical space that addresses numerous issues in the Trinidadian public sphere and arts scene at the time. Through a similar aesthetic of fragmentation, Philip's *She Tries Her Tongue; Her Silence Softly Breaks* excavates Caribbean history from a feminist perspective. Similarly to Cozier, for Philip, elements of intertextuality provide the opportunity of formulating a critique that de-masks the absence of women's perspectives in the literature of anti-colonial male writers. This chapter shows the influence of a variety of sources from popular culture, the media, literature, and other discourses, in the formation of Caribbean localised cultural and artistic expression and in relational aesthetic forms that use modernist strategies such as bricolage and collage in new cross-cultural poetics which, as mentioned above, Glissant theorised in *Poetics of Relation*. Critics like Simon Gikandi and Jahan Ramazani argue that despite their oppositional and critical relationship to some of the exclusionary and Eurocentric attitudes embedded in modernism, Caribbean writers' use of bricolage and other modernist strategies, has been influenced by modernism and Caribbean artists have, in turn, transformed it (*Caribbean Modernism; Transnational Poetics*). I argue that their work can trace a Caribbean(ist) modernism, which although partly influenced by modernist aesthetics is rather deeply influenced by fragmentation as steeped in older cultural influences such as calypso.

Chapter three continues to examine the work of Cozier and Philip, identifying a similar development in their poetics that moves from a call-and-response aesthetic of fragments towards a hyper-fragmented aesthetic, mirroring the polyrhythmic musical composition of the fugue. Phillips' long poem *Zong!* (2008) and Cozier's multimedia installation and drawing series *Tropical Night* (2006–ongoing) configure relational archives of affect that (visually and conceptually) stretch even further the boundaries of the British colonial archive and the postcolonial public sphere in Trinidad, emphasising a vocabulary of memory emerging. This vocabulary is marked by an elegiac poetics that mourns the deaths of the Africans murdered during the *Zong* massacre of 1781. There is also a lament for the lost promises embodied in Trinidad and Tobago's independence. Weary of the impositions and limitations of narrative in the articulation of memory, localised experience, and traumatic history, Cozier and Philip construct instead anti-narratives that reflect upon the extreme power of language(s) in shaping experience and realities and giving formation to the ontologies of constructs of race, and nation(s). Their polyphonic, contrapuntal, and fugal counter-archives emphasise the notion of process in the configuration of meaning. Both *Tropical*

Night (as an ongoing series of drawings) and *Zong!* (a book-length poem that is often performed at author and collective readings) highlight the compositional process as vital to the work. Both works emerged from (and were shaped by) the artists' notebooks, and this material became a constitutive part of the works themselves, creating a blurred distinction between personal and creative archive. Process also highlights the onto-logical premise of continuing formation and transformation in cultural expression and identities, following in this sense Stuart Hall's thinking on cultural identities as always in constant flux. My discussion therefore focuses on how the powerful counterpoints provided by the artists' note-books and note-taking offer a new speculative semiotics of localised and historical experience.

The fourth chapter identifies a poetics of place and fragmentation in Edwidge Danticat's *The Farming of Bones* (1998) and Junot Díaz's *The Brief Wondrous Life of Oscar Wao* (2007), two historical novels that confront Trujillo's nationalist and anti-Haitian narratives. These novels portray a series of characters forever marked by the crimes of Trujillo, including the 1937 massacre of Haitians and Dominicans of Haitian descent, ordered by him. They document their struggle with finding redress, particularly through a failed state address of the event or any space to bear witness to the trauma and the loss. *The Farming of Bones* and *The Brief Wondrous Life of Oscar Wao* demonstrate how sectors of Dominican state memory have historically constructed myths that render the Dominican–Haitian border as a site of permanent and ongoing conflict, eliciting thus the interethnic and multilinguistic culture across the border, particularly prior to the massacre. *Farming* and *Oscar Wao* are novels that contextualise and shed light on the various forms of epistemic violence embedded in the colonial discourses of Hispanism, Hispanophilia and Hispanicity. The term Hispanism (with the influences of Hispanophilia sentiments and Hispanicity) applies to a complex history of various homogenising discourses (with different cultural specificities in each location) but it is understood here as the discourse that was refigured after the loss of Santo Domingo to French colonists (in the case of the Dominican Republic). These discourses also aimed to claim an influence over the last Spanish colonies in the Caribbean, in order to control the terms of the political and socio-economic relationship with the old colonies after the Spanish defeat in the Spanish–American war of 1898.[8] In the Dominican Republic, this discourse then devel-oped throughout the twentieth century, particularly with Trujillo. In its exaltation of Spanish-centred culture, this form of Hispanism erased and devalued African heritage. Yolanda Martínez-San Miguel underscores that "Spanish and Spanish-ness also represent an imperial ideology that displaced indigenous, African and Asian languages and cultures in the definition of *Americanidad*" ("Rethinking the Colonial" 107). Danticat and Díaz's fiction responds to the epistemic violence of that particular legacy of Hispanism. Through the interconnection of textual elements in the form of typeface innovation in *The Farming of Bones* and footnotes in *Oscar Wao*, these novels disrupt form, in an attempt to complicate historical narratives marked by silencing. The fragmentation and disruption of narrative in both novels symbolically cross a border established by nationalistic discourse and recent policy.

The various explorations of memory in the literature and art installation featured in chapter five connect Britain with the Caribbean. I discuss the multimedia installation *Ghosting* (2004) by Roshini Kempadoo alongside fiction by Caryl Phillips and performance poetry by Dorothea Smartt, and Jay Bernard, also in conversation with the poetry of Linton Kwesi Johnson. A series of call-and-response patterns links the seemingly discrepant sections in the overall composition of their work. This emphasis guides a dialogical opening and interrogation of their interconnection. Through rhythmic patterns inspired by jazz, the African drum and tassa drums, and the offbeat keys and breaks of reggae and dub music, the literature and artwork that I discuss here configure a repertoire of memory work that considers ethical avenues and ways of remembering and honouring the dead. Although many of the artists whose work I discuss in the chapter were born in Britain or migrated as children or young adults, their work is very much influenced by transnational connections within Caribbean art and culture, family networks, and kinship developing across geographies through many physical and figurative journeys back and forth between Britain and the Caribbean. The patterns of call-and-response in Phillips' *Crossing the River*, Kempadoo's *Ghosting*, Dorothea Smartt's *Ship Shape*, Jay Bernard's *Surge* and LKJ's "New Cross Massahkah" encourage readers and audiences to connect various narrative strands and voices each separately and all simultaneously. The juxtaposition and coexistence of all strands and voices account for the complex and multilayered narrativity in decolonial histories.

Through an analysis of literature by Cuban writer Inés María Martiatu Terry, and Puerto Rican writers Yolanda Arroyo Pizarro and Mayra Santos-Febres, chapter six delves into forms of counter-memory that confront silences in official histories of the Spanish-speaking Caribbean, Latin America, and the legacies of slavery. The memory work of Martiatu Terry, Arroyo Pizarro, and Santos-Febres puts certain pressure on some of the premises of *Hispanidad* (Hispanism). Their work also indirectly highlights some fissures in constructs of Cuban and Puerto Rican collective cohesion in tropes such as those of *cubanidad* (Cubanness) and *la gran familia puertorriqueña* (the great Puerto Rican family). These writers create a counterpointed poetics that highlights narrative accounts and records previously suppressed and omitted in both the Archive and the public sphere and, in so doing, they indirectly counter the representational imaginaries of the nation embedded in those constructs. The short fiction of Inés María Martiatu Terry in *Over the Waves and Other Stories* (2008), Yolanda Arroyo Pizarro's in *Negras* (2012) and Mayra Santos-Feberes' novel *Fe en disfraz* (2009), facilitate an exploration of both local histories and transnational networks. Although its primary focus is on Cuba and particularly on Havana, the stories in *Over the Waves* map migration to and from Jamaica, Panama, the United States, and other locations, highlighting routes of Pan-African and Pan-Caribbean kinship and political action, aspects also explored in the short stories in *Negras* and in *Fe in Disfraz*, where cultural practices and memory-making rituals allow a connection with memories and cultural practices from Africa in the Americas.

CRITICAL ARTICULATIONS OF HISTORICAL MEMORY

The wide field of Caribbean studies has furthered and significantly enriched some of the critical conversations on archives elaborated by Derrida and Foucault which have traditionally dominated academic discussions and theoretic approaches to the idea of the Archive and archives studies generally. Derrida's and Foucault's theoretical work has been particularly influential in terms of articulating the boundaries of official and national archives and the ways in which they have occluded knowledge in certain geographies (particularly, but not exclusively, in the West). However, Caribbean and Latin American historians and thinkers have enriched and stretched those conversations further in their analysis of local specificity and global connections of archival erasure and counter-archiving traditions. In this sense, the theoretical work and legacy of Michel-Rolph Trouillot centres the issue of the unequal power in the

production and holding of sources in the historical archive as necessary to any discussion of archival studies. Trouillot's work unveils the
multiple ways in which the documents in the archives can themselves,
when obscured or not researched or consulted, contribute to a process
of "silencing the past" (also the title of his influential book). Equally,
the authors of many records from the colonial era do purposefully
obscure and erase the experience of enslaved and indentured people in
the Caribbean. Trouillot also points to the knowledge that exists outside
official archives, which are also repositories of non-Western and non-
Eurocentric knowledge. In that vein, Diana Taylor's notion of the repertoire engages with non-formal or official archives that are understood
as an assemblage of mediums (written, visual, and oral) that document
the memory of an experience in performative ways, thus emphasising
the connection between the past and the present moment in processes
of memorialisation, therefore preserving through praxis the embodied
memory of ancestral and indigenous knowledges (*Archive*). Scholarship
in Caribbean studies has both documented the archival turn in the arts, as
well as enacted an archival turn in its own right. Other critical articulations
of memory in Caribbean studies such as Maria Cristina Fumagalli's *On
the Edge: Writing the Border between Haiti and the Dominican Republic*
(2017) draws from a rich and varied body of creative work and historical
archives from Haiti, the Dominican Republic, and their various diasporas. Fumagalli's literary and cultural history not only extends across the
border of the two nations and their imagined and existing communities;
by discussing literature, performance, music, visual art, and historical and
legal records across geographies, *On the Edge* interrogates the potential
of these literary and artistic forms to connect memories and communities. In Fumagalli's words, "intercultural archives such as *On the Edge*
make past experiences available to those who want to engage fully with
the present [and] refuse to comply with the idea that an acceptable future
is unattainable, ..." (391). Also, through a transnational scope, Myriam
A. J. Chancy examines literature and visual art by Cuban, Haitian and
Dominican artists and writers in *From Sugar to Revolution: Women's
Visions of Haiti, Cuba and the Dominican Republic* (2013). Chancy posits
central questions around the politics of memory in the Caribbean that
are also central to this book, especially as she asks that we consider the
following: "How does 'race' and thus, racism, serve to distort identity formation? How do they affect collective memory and historical
archives?..." (49). Chancy's questions around the responsibility and role

of historical archives, particularly archives of coloniality, as producers of constructs of race and racism are paramount to a critical approach of their power and effect in the relationship of social groups and the formation of historical narratives today. This book explores these questions and adds reflections and questions regarding the relationship between state and other official archives (as spaces generally, but not always, consulted by scholars, researchers, and writers) and the public sphere (as a wider space with a myriad of competing representational interests). I am particularly interested in exploring the ways in which the authority of the colonial archive exploits what Michel Foucault identifies as the regulatory law of what can and cannot be said (*The Archaeology of Knowledge* 129), and how that operates in the public sphere. Foucault defines the Archive in its first instance as a discursive regulatory tool that delineates what can and cannot be contained within its boundaries. In his definition, Foucault identifies the importance of every archive's internal order and outlines how a particular rationale of classification and arrangement, different in every case, governs it. Throughout the chapters, I sometimes capitalise the "a" in "Archive" to refer to a more generalised form of all the various colonial records held in official and state archives, and the narratives they have produced. This use coincides with that discursive element that Foucault identifies in its use of the term. It also aims to establish a contrast with other times when I refer to archive/archives (without capital "a") to make reference to the particularity of specific records being used and re-figured by artists, and /or to signal how they use a series of personal archives or archival dynamics that challenge and question the authority of that other Archive, which instead reflects and reproduces through its control of knowledge the status quo. The work of the artists I discuss here, explores and centres the role and epistemological value of non-official archives, particularly personal and family ones, through records such as comics, notebooks, photographs, music records, and others.

In the realm of Caribbean cultural studies, the foundational scholarly work of Carolyn Cooper, Patricia J. Saunders, and Kwame Dawes on dancehall, arts and reggae and Gordon Rohler, Shalini Puri, and Stephen Stuempfle on calypso, amongst others, have opened up an interdisciplinary critical space for memory studies continued in current criticism. Njelle W. Hamilton's *Phonographic Memories: Popular Music and the Contemporary Caribbean Novel* (2019) is a recent key text that examines the influence of music formally and conceptually in developing forms of memory work in fiction across the Caribbean region and the diaspora covering the cultural and historical contexts of Canada, Cuba, Haiti, Jamaica, Trinidad and Tobago, and the United States. As Hamilton argues in *Phonographic Memories*, "music remains … a vital and valid literary model" (23). Through an impressive analytical range of music technologies, Hamilton demonstrates the critical plasticity and depth in the necessary interdisciplinary combination of music, sonic and memory studies. *Memory and The Archival Turn in Caribbean Literature and Culture* exists in conversation with this body of scholarship where interdisciplinarity captures the historical and increasingly multilayered nature of contemporary Caribbean literature, performance, music, and visual art. The texts mentioned above, and others, reflect an archival turn as well as a simultaneous turn to interdisciplinary approaches to historical memory. Further, they brake the boundaries of discipline, as well as geography, with comparative approaches as I do in this book, which started as a PhD that I completed in 2013.

Equally, other Caribbean and Black British non-fiction texts have continued to expand an archival scholarship of relationality that was especially heightened during the archival turn from the late 1980s to 2020 that this book discusses. For example, Tessa McWatt's *Shame on Me: An Anatomy of Race and Belonging* (2019) enacts a thorough dissection of the physical categorisations in the anatomy of race, deconstructing thus its fictions. It uses, to then reverse, the language of (pseudo)scientific enquiry and classification. The sections "Hypothesis", "Experiment", "Analysis", and "Findings", as the sub-sections "Nose", "Lips", "Eyes", "Hair", "Ass", and "Bones" (in the section "Analysis"), all chart the impact and epistemic violence of the colonial archive and its construct of the category of race and other management tools embodied in the system of the plantation, that are critically dissected in the text. McWatt uses family oral history and records, especially photographs, and presents a counter-archive of a family's diasporic journeys. *Shame on Me* captures moments in the lives of her ancestors, the women in her family line who are of Chinese, Indian, Arawak, Portuguese, French, African, and Scottish heritage. Family history is combined with archival research to tell the larger history of enslaved Africans, Indian and Chinese indentured workers, and Europeans in the Caribbean, a history that contains painful memories and silences. Similarly, in her memoir *Imperial Intimacies: A Tale of Two Islands* (2019), Hazel V. Carby divides the text into interconnected sections: "Part One: Inventories", "Part Two: Calculations",

"Part Three: Dead Reckoning Hone", "Family Registers", "Part Four: Accounting", and "Part Five: Legacies". Through legacy of Caribbean storytelling, Carby's memoir-critical study reflects on "the everyday ties, relations and intricate interdependencies of empire and colonialism", as she incorporates stories from her Jamaican father, Welsh mother, and their ancestors (1). Carby notes that when family history and historical research from official archives are placed together, "they sit uneasily side by side". Rather than "cohere into a unified narrative their juxtaposition revealed the shards of conflict that familial, national and imperial ideologies work to conceal" (2). As in *Imperial Intimacies* (and *Shame on Me*), the memory work discussed in this book defines oppositional thinking, "[p]itting memory, history and poetics against each other in a narrative of racial encounters is intended to undermine … binary thinking" (Carby 2). They all offer a prism of possibilities instead, for renegotiating and reassembling fragments of memory.

NOTES

1. Additionally, they faced critique from some intellectuals and artists who argued that their performance risked misrepresenting indigenous communities and misinforming the public about who they really were (Fusco 143). In "Still in the Cage: Thoughts on "Two Undiscovered Indians, 20 Years Later," Coco Fusco reflects upon the twentieth anniversary of the performance. The article provides an insight into the implications of the two-year tour of the performance not only for audiences and the art world but also for the artists themselves. Towards the conclusion of the article Fusco reflects, "[t]wenty years later, I still think about an unanswered question that led me into the cage. Is there anyone who really believes that we could be "post-racial" in a culture that fetishises black athletes, equates black style with rebelliousness, pillages indigenous belief systems for pithy profundities to satisfy the spiritual cravings of secular materialists, and then depends on cheap immigrant labour, redlining, and mass incarceration to safeguard class hierarchies that are obviously racialised? It was the unspeakably grotesque irony of our imagining America as a multicultural paradise that inspired me to push the performance to its limits …" (77).

2. For example, In "A Travelogue of Sorts", M. NourbeSe Philip writes poignantly about the institutional failings in Britain, specifically in

regards to curatorial disengagement, and addresses the issues that the commemoration could have confronted. Philip describes her impressions of the painting of Dido Belle and her cousin Lady Elizabeth Murray at Kenwood Palace, attributed to artist David Martin, in an article that reflects upon official acts in London commemorating the 200th anniversary of the abolition of the slave trade (in 2007), including that exhibition at Kenwood Palace. In her discussion of the painting, Philip notices problematic assumptions in the curatorial description which assumes (in the exhibition booklet) that Elizabeth and Dido's uncle, Lord Mansfield Chief Justice of England, might have been affected in his position towards the slave trade by his feelings of affection towards Dido Belle which Philip notes forms "a supposition which is unusual for this type of document" ("A Travelogue" 3). This confirms that, in Toni Morrison's words, "museological decisions and curatorial ones are as much ideologically determined as they are aesthetically determined and that such decisions are made in the context of power" ("Harlem on My Mind" 84). See M. NourbeSe Philip, "A Travelogue of Sorts: Transatlantic Trafficking in Silence and Erasure", 2008, https:// doi.org/10.33596/anth.110.

3. And if the issue of more objective and uncensored acts of remembrance and historical education seems to cause so much refusal for the states responsible of hundreds of years of oppression and enslavement, the question of reparations causes even more resistance and denial.

4. See Anna Reckin, "Tidalectic Lectures: Kamau Brathwaite's Prose/Poetry as Sound-Space," 2003, https://doi.org/10.33596/ anth.4.

5. For a synthesised and concise description of the musical structure of the counterpoint see *The Concise Oxford Dictionary of Music*, 5th ed.

6. However, it is important to note that various writers in the Caribbean had previously acknowledged the importance of music in a transnational context, some examples being Antonio Benítez Rojo's *The Repeating Island* (1989) and Édouard Glissant's *Poetics of Relation* (1990).

7. Philip first published this essay as afterword for her 1988 poetry collection *She Tries Her Tongue; Her Silence Softly Breaks* and was also published again in the 1997 essay collection *A Genealogy of Resistance and Other Essays.* Page number reference here belongs to *A Genealogy of Resistance.*

8. For a history and conceptualisation of Hispanism see Eduard Subirats's "Seven Thesis Against Hispanism" in *Border Interrogations: Questioning Spanish Frontiers* (2008), edited by Benita Sampedro Vizcaya and Simon Doubleday.

CHAPTER 2

A Caribbean Poetics: Fragmentation and Call-and-Response

Christopher Cozier's mixed media *Wait Dorothy Wait* (1991) and M. NourbeSe Philip's poetry collection *She Tries Her Tongue; Her Silence Softly Breaks* (1988) engage in a process of archiving counter-memory that, as a result, reveals the ideological apparatus behind representations of the Caribbean through visual and written discourses such as tropicalisation, nationalism, colonialism, and neocolonialism. As I foreground in the introduction, I am using the notion of counter-memory here as memory that contradicts or challenges official narratives and accounts of history. Although *Wait Dorothy Wait* and *She Tries Her Tongue* belong to different mediums—mixed media and poetry, respectively—both display a visual aesthetic that references and satirically mocks modes of cataloguing and/or labelling colonial and contemporary history. Cozier's and Philip's artistic and literary work, especially in the 1980s and 1990s, shows the influence of post-structuralist and postmodern devices in their questioning of written and visual languages, particularly through the use of modernist techniques like montage and collage, which Cozier and Philip employ in *Wait Dorothy Wait* and *She Tries Her Tongue*. This compositional methodology results in a fragmented aesthetic, which in the 1980s was indicative of postmodernism's predicament by marking a series of social and political crises, questioning the stability of notions

© The Author(s), under exclusive license to Springer Nature Switzerland AG 2023
M. Fernández Campa, *Memory and the Archival Turn in Caribbean Literature and Culture*, New Caribbean Studies, https://doi.org/10.1007/978-3-030-72135-0_2

like 'identity' and 'historical progress'. In *Black Visual Culture: Moder-nity and Postmodernity*, Gen Doy notes how critics like David A. Bailey, Paul Gilroy, and Kobena Mercer coincide in "an argument for a shift from modernism to postmodernism in black culture in the later 1980s both in Britain and internationally" (2). This shift marks a further politicisation of modernist aesthetics, which are used and refashioned to challenge the status quo. Cozier's and Philip's work shows the influence of what Hal Foster defines as a "postmodernism of resistance" which "is concerned with a critical deconstruction of tradition" and in this sense, "it seems to question rather than exploit cultural codes, to explore rather than conceal social and political affiliations" (xiii). The critical and deconstructive element characteristic of postmodernism overlaps with postcolonial efforts of de-centring Western discourses of modernity. In the early 1990s, influential postcolonial theorists including Hazel Carby, Edward Said, and Gayatri C. Spivak questioned Eurocentric interpretations of history that deny the historical agency of the non-European subject.

Despite the influence of postmodern and postcolonial aesthetics in Cozier's and Philip's work, their artistic sensibility is rooted in Caribbean historical and cultural specificity, and particularly in the contrapuntal call-and-response dynamics of calypso music. As Philip herself states in an interview with Kristen Mahlis,

> when people began to read this work [Édouard Glissant's]—many years ago—they said that it was a postmodern work, which I didn't necessarily disagree with. I said, that's fine, but if you don't understand the Caribbean, if you read it solely as a postmodern work, I think you need to understand that the Caribbean was postmodern long before the term was coined: Multiple discourses—fragmentation—we've been doing this ever since; we just haven't applied the name to it. (688–89)

Other critics in the field of visual culture including Stuart Hall, Michele Wallace, and Gen Doy[1] have also warned against the tendency to equate African Diaspora aesthetics in the Americas with postmodern aesthetics; thus identifying the pitfalls of considering aesthetics in this context exclusively through a postmodern lens ("On Postmodernism" 222–246; *Dark Designs* 364–378, *Black Visual Culture* 21–61). Alongside such positions, the critical discussion in this chapter acknowledges the influence of postmodern aesthetics whilst claiming the vital role of Caribbean musical structures and elements in the fragmented aesthetic form that informs many Caribbean literary texts, performance, and visual artwork.

Call-and-response patterns are present in African Diaspora aesthetics across the American continent. In the United States, Latin America, and the Caribbean, musical traditions have carried the memory of collective life from the plantation to the contemporary moment; from the African-American work songs, which form the foundation for blues and jazz, to Caribbean kaiso and its evolution into calypso. Kaiso, the eighteenth-century work song created by enslaved Africans, and its contemporary counterpart calypso, are based on the African griot tradition where the figure of the griot leads the work song and encourages the rest of the singers to join in a response (kalinda) that follows their call. Parallel invitations to respond to a call are also found in terms of percussion rhythm and musical structure. This contrapuntal structure of calypso's call-and-response is evoked through sight and visual juxtaposition in Cozier's *Wait Dorothy Wait* and Philip's *She Tries Her Tongue*. In addition to the influence of Afro-Caribbean musics like calypso, both works make use of collage and montage, a compositional pair and modernist aesthetic principle that also features in postmodern aesthetics (Ulmer 94). Collage refers to the transfer of elements from "one context to another" whilst "montage" constitutes "the 'dissemination' of these borrowings through the new setting" (Ulmer and Group *Mu* qtd. in Ulmer 95). The various instances of intertextuality in *Wait Dorothy Wait* and *She Tries Her Tongue* are primarily constructed via the collage of a series of elements into the artwork and the literary text (i.e. a fragment of a landscape painting and newspaper cutting in *Wait Dorothy Wait* and the legal, fictional, poetic, and historical texts, amongst others, in Philip's poetry), which are assembled creating a montage. These processes not only result in the recontextualisation of such elements, allowing readers and viewers to consider them under a new light; they also create the opportunity of questioning the specific discursive frameworks of signification out of which they originated. Consequently, the destabilising role that collage plays on structures of meaning relies on (and creates as a result) a hybridity of form(s):

> Its [collage's] heterogeneity, ... imposes itself on the reading as stimulation to produce a signification which could be neither univocal nor stable. Each cited element breaks the continuity or the linearity of the discourse and leads necessarily to a double reading: that of the fragment perceived in

relation to its text of origin; that of the same fragment as incorporated into a new whole, a different totality ... Thus the art of collage proves to be one of the most effective strategies in the putting into question of all the illusions of representation. (Group *Mu* qtd. in Ulmer 99)

Through this compositional technique and strategy of collage and montage, Cozier and Philip configure a relational, contrapuntal aesthetic and poetics that highlight patterns of call-and-response. In turn, such patterns stimulate ways of reading and viewing what have been previously excluded from a series of narratives.

The intellectual formation and artistic sensibility of Cozier and Philip have been shaped by their own relationship to place. Both artists experienced the first decades of post-Independence in the Caribbean and the various political moments of that period. Cozier was born in Trinidad, whilst Philip was born in Tobago and moved to Trinidad as a youth but, for Philip, Tobago has always been, according to the author, the place she always returns to in her writing (*A Genealogy of Resistance*). Philip has expressed that doing her undergraduate studies at the University of the West Indies in Mona, Jamaica, where she completed a degree in Economics, was important to her especially due to the political and Intellectual spaces available for Caribbean thinkers and writers to gather at a time of active political debate and organising (personal interview, 2018). Philip arrived in Toronto in the late 1960s as a student and has stayed in Canada ever since. She completed a Masters degree in Political Science (1970) and a degree in law (1973) at the University of Western Ontario. After working as a lawyer in Canada for a few years, Philip eventually decided to turn to writing as a full-time career. Cozier, travelled to the United States to study art and later returned to Trinidad. In the United States, Cozier was influenced and taught by artists like Emma Amos, Martha Rosler, and Leon Golub, and in an interview that I conducted with him in Trinidad on 5 August 2012, he explained how this exposure to conceptual and socially committed art, influenced his art practice both technically and aesthetically. In 1986, Cozier graduated in Fine Arts from Maryland Institute, College of Art and completed his M.F.A. at Rutgers University, later returning to Port of Spain in 1989. These biographical details of both writers reveal the significance of location (local and global geographies) in their intellectual and personal journeys and art.

TEARING APART PICTURES OF PARADISE:
CHRISTOPHER COZIER'S *WAIT DOROTHY WAIT*

In the aftermath of Trinidad and Tobago's Independence in 1962, the Trinidadian government started to emphasise the importance of culture as a means of fostering national unity in a highly multicultural society. Political agendas after the declaration of Independence and the proclamation of Trinidad and Tobago as a Republic in 1976 were dominated by a sponsorship and patronage of folk culture with the expectation that the arts would bring racial unity and political stability. Although the cultural tradition of Carnival and calypso has provided a platform for social critique that had remained strong since the seventeenth century; this notion of folk culture as unifying element was at times promoted at the expense of social critique and parochial popular perspectives in a gradual increase of state control over the social content in calypso lyrics (Birth; Rohlehr). Similarly, revisionary history was central in the process of creating counter-publics and fostering political Independence. The figure and legacy of Dr Eric Williams, as a historian and public intellectual, illuminate the key role of historiography and political consciousness that emerged, partly, from reading against the grain of the imperial Archive, and which has powerfully shaped anti-colonial struggle. Publications such as *Capitalism and Slavery* (1944) and *History of the People of Trinidad and Tobago* (1962) mark Williams' legacy further as key texts and pathways of a Caribbean critical and radical history of the region. The government of Dr Williams (1962–1981), especially in its first decade, generated the promise and hope that socio-economic opportunity would open up to the wider Trinidadian population. However, the prospects of a booming oil economy in the 1970s marked a gradual shift in economic policies leaning towards the neoliberal measures of the 1980s, a decade marked by the collapse of oil prices and recession. The result of these policies accentuated further socio-economic inequality, which was also influenced by a decrease of "governmental economic interventions" (Birth 66). What remained a constant in the Trinidadian government was the emphasis on culture policy and forms of cultural nationalism. This dynamic continued after the death of Williams in 1981 and throughout the 1990s. At times, political demands in Trinidad have interfered in creative art processes, especially in music, plastic arts, and the visual arts. Calypso music illustrates aptly a combination of both these political and economic pressures on artistic expression. On one hand, calypso-nians have at times succumbed to the pressure of political parties towards the creation of certain types of calypso hits, especially those linked to the Carnival's calypso monarch competitions that could positively favour the current government at a given time. Similarly, on another front, as Rohlehr argues in 1998, calypso and soca music started to compete within a global market that imposed a set of commercial expectations that "pushed calypso toward commodification, teaching singers to do for profit what their ancestors did for fun, entertainment, relaxation, edification or self-knowledge" ("We Getting the Kaiso" 82). The field of visual arts in Trinidad has also been affected by the demands of the art market and the privileging of folk culture as representative of national and regional identity. Christopher Cozier offers through his work a critique of prescriptive ideas of art and culture. In Cozier's view, the "artistic enterprise" of the 1980s and 1990s in Trinidad was "rendering or representing an inventory prescribed as Caribbean or as relevant to the Caribbean. Art was supposed to be painting and its subject was 'cul-ture,' the things that defined an 'us' as separate from all the 'thems' and 'usses' out there" (Cozier qtd. in Paul, "Christopher Cozier" 68). Cozier's artwork reflects a position in contemporary Caribbean arts that Krista Thompson describes as seeking to challenge the popular perspec-tive that conceptual art cannot represent the Caribbean as accurately as representational art ("No Abstract Art" 120). In an interview with Annie Paul, Cozier reflects on how the situation in the Trinidadian art scene has positively changed, especially since the 1990s, and describes how "the space has opened up" for artists to explore their creativity confidently: "[a] conversation is building. In the old days we were just subject to be rendered by someone who came from outside with an alleged knowledge of real art" (Cozier qtd. in Paul, "Christopher Cozier" 68). *Wait Dorothy Wait* represents Cozier's own positioning in relation to the national and regional art industry at an early stage in his career. It was during this time that Cozier started to experiment with materiality and certain images and methodologies that have informed later work. In a 2008 lecture at the University of Miami entitled "Topicality, Flexibility, Fluid-ity", Cozier describes how years before his return to Trinidad, the process of real estate development resulted in property speculation in Port of Spain and in the relocation of whole communities, which affected signif-icantly the physical and social map of the island's capital. This moved

Cozier to start collecting fragments from bulldozed houses and buildings that he eventually pieced together with different fragments of his own artwork creating very delicate and frail structures that nevertheless remained attached; this assemblage, in Cozier's view came to represent all the different histories and cultures in the Caribbean ("Topicality"). From collecting building fragments, Cozier went on to collecting fragments of newspaper clips and postcards. In the years of 1991–1993, Cozier worked on his series *Wait Dorothy Wait* and developed critical, sharp pieces where he juxtaposed newspaper clippings to fragments from tropical landscape postcards to critique the politics of the postcard in marketing an idealistic tropicalised landscape.

The landscape images included in Cozier's three-piece mixed media *Wait Dorothy Wait* are small fragments of tropical postcard scenes originally painted by local Trinidadian artists (see Fig. 2.1).[2] In the composition of the artwork, these images are juxtaposed with newspaper cuttings that report murders in Port of Spain around 1991, when the series was created. The mixed media discussed in this chapter highlights the lack of critical space in Trinidad's early 1990s art market and public sphere, whilst archiving an instance of counter-memory through its critique of different forms of violence: discursive, economic and physical. The image in the artwork shows a palm tree surrounded by other lush trees and set against the background of a blue sky, which stands in stark contrast with the traumatic murder reported in the newspaper cutting.[3] The cutting reads: "He was shot in the neck as they attempted to steal his car, but was able to outrun the car a short distance. He collapsed and men drove the car over him, brutally killing him" (Thompson, *An Eye*, 290).

The shocking incongruence between text and image in the composition guides viewers towards an interrogation of the possible links that explain this striking arrangement. The placement of the murder report below the tropical landscape image—and within the colonial-style golden frame—situates the text as simulated caption to the image. In this sense, the provocative and problematic disconnect between both suggests a major absence: what lies behind the pleasant tropical scene? How is this visual imagery obstructing the reality of death, violence, and inequality marked by the murder report?

Fig. 2.1 Christopher Cozier, *Wait Dorothy Wait*, 1991, mixed media, 7 × 7 in. Collection of the late Jeffrey Stanford. Image courtesy of the artist

Visual Representations of the Caribbean Space: The Tropicalised Picturesque

An overview of the history and elements of tropicalisation in the Caribbean is necessary here in order to appreciate the socio-political critique embedded in *Wait Dorothy Wait*. The image of a picturesque tropical paradise is very much loaded in the Caribbean context since it is implicated in a tradition of tropicalisation, which Krista Thompson defines as "the complex visual systems through which the islands were imaged for tourist consumption and the social and political implications of these representations on actual physical space on the islands and their inhabitants" (*An Eye for the Tropics* 5). Functioning under the rubric of tropicalisation, the "Caribbean picturesque" is dominant in eighteenth- and nineteenth-century visual representations of the region. It conveys a reinterpretation of European notions of the picturesque and relies on creating an image of the region that fashions the islands and their African and Asian population as accommodating to the needs of the foreign visitor and local elite (Thompson *An Eye for the Tropics*; Nixon *Resisting Paradise*). Discursively, in a similar way to the trope of the Caribbean picturesque that of tropical paradise, Angelique V. Nixon argues, perpetuates colonial imaginaries into post-Independence and the neocolonial present largely driven by economies of tourism and extraction.[4] Cozier's *Wait Dorothy Wait* points out traces of this visual economy in Trinidad's 1990s art scene, especially in the way in which the art market had a tendency to reject any perspective of life in the islands that challenged this tropicalised lens.

In the nineteenth century this visual economy emerges in the Anglophone Caribbean, representing the region as a desirable, customisable, and safe place (Sheller *Consuming the Caribbean*; Thompson *An Eye for the Tropics*; Mohammed *Imaging the Caribbean*; Archer and Brown *Pictures from Paradise*). Behind the construction of this type of visual economy lie economic and ideological motives. The devastating effects of tropical diseases like malaria, yellow fever, and cholera were killing a great number of people within the local white elite. As a result, and despite the improved readiness of medicines to prevent tropical diseases in the late nineteenth century, the promotion of tourism had to target and dissipate any possible fears from British and North American potential visitors. The visual rhetoric of the picturesque was partly utilised to convince tourists of the existence of an orderly society of "natives", thus fostering those expectations internationally (Thompson, *An Eye* 4; 17). Similarly, the financial impact of the abolition of the transatlantic slave trade on the British economy, and the subsequent gradual decrease of forced labour, made the prospect of tourism by the end of the nineteenth century a financially appealing, yet challenging, enterprise. The years prior to the Emancipation act of 1838 marked a period of resentment in the plantocracy of the Caribbean, and "[t]he most highly publicised cases of planter brutality are recorded in the 1830s" (Jain and Reddock, "Introduction" *Women Plantation Workers*).[5] Despite the financial compensation received by many of the plantation owners, the prospects of the end of mass production in plantation slavery led colonial authorities to seek other forms of investment. Therefore, towards the end of the nineteenth and into the twentieth-century tourism campaigns (and multinationals like the United Fruit Company) started to develop a profitable economy that continued to exploit the labour conditions of plantation workers and which relied on a picturesque rendering of the Caribbean islands and of the indentured and Black population. Tourism started to be considered an economic alternative. Its promotion was not only economically profitable to Britain and the United States; it also meant an ideological reinforcement of social and class hierarchies further conveyed and emphasised through specific visual representations of the region.

Tourist promotion in the nineteenth century entailed an ideological control over representations of the population of African and Asian descent and origin. By representing both the landscape and the people as "picturesque", nineteenth-century British and American institutions and companies reenact the construction of the Caribbean as a place and space marked by exoticised difference, a discursive practice that dates back to the first representations of the Caribbean by Spanish *conquistadores* from their arrival in the Bahamian island of Guanahani in 1492, which they then renamed San Salvador.[6] Later, picturesque visual economies in the eighteenth and nineteenth centuries continued to manipulate sight and reality; whereby lithography, painting, and (later) photography would often provide picturesque images of the islands that in many cases "were only realistic inasmuch as they were consistent with the traveler's dreams of the tropics" (Thompson, *An Eye* 21). However, Cozier's *Wait Dorothy Wait* suggests how these modes of representation follow the visual vocabulary of the romance, in the sense that they deploy an idealised depiction of Trinidad specifically, and the Caribbean at large. Today, a picturesque portrayal of the Caribbean continues to omit the viewpoints and life experience of a wide section of the population. My use of the term romance refers to one of its meanings as "a quality or feeling of mystery, excitement, and remoteness from everyday life" (*Oxford Dictionaries*).[7] I refer here to one of the contemporary meanings of the term as a quality that estranges and defamiliarises the quotidian; something arguably at stake in *Wait Dorothy Wait*, and which marks a lingering continuity of sentimental idealisation in some privileged visual representations of the region. Belinda Edmondson uses the term "romance" to signify "the idealized representations of Caribbean society or 'Caribbeanness,' both in hegemonic Caribbean-American discourses and, perhaps more important, in intra-Caribbean discourses" (2). Cozier's inclusion of a small postcard fragment in *Wait Dorothy Wait* hints at the historical role and cultural significance of the postcard in the Caribbean as a material object that at times privileges a foreign and elite representation of the region. Contemporary postcards' abundant tropical landscapes and exoticised and staged images of Caribbean life have a cultural baggage that reinforces the visual economy of tropicalisation previously discussed.[8]

Nineteenth-century visual culture in the Caribbean, similarly to British and Creole literary representations of the region throughout this period, shows a fluctuation between both realist and romantic elements. Tim Watson argues, "realism and romance in the Caribbean context cannot be easily disentangled, just as in the nineteenth century Britain and the West Indies were mutually constitutive rather than discrete entities" (6).[9] Within the visual economy of the ethnographic gaze in the lithograph, landscape painting and photography (of the late nineteenth century), this entanglement reveals the ways in which reality was often filtered through the lens of a romantic vocabulary. The characteristic idealisation and distortion of reality that defines the contemporary sense of 'romance' can be traced to this period in particular. Richard Bridgens created *Sketches of West India Scenery with illustrations of Negro Character, the Process of Making Sugar, &c. Taken during a Voyage to, and Seven Years Residence in the Island of Trinidad* circa 1825. The sketches were published in 1836; they provide a good example of the Caribbean picturesque within the context of nineteenth-century Trinidad. It also provides an opportunity to examine the legacy of the picturesque and pastoral visual economies in contemporary Caribbean visual art.[10] The series depicts, from an ethnographic standpoint, tropical landscapes, social and working life in the plantations, and other spaces in Port of Spain, such as the governor's residency in St Ann's.[11]

Bridgens' lithographs exemplify the entanglement between realism and romance that Watson refers to. According to Amar Wahab, the series "projected an aesthetically powerful discourse about the continuance of plantation prosperity and the beatitude of slaves in the midst of free coloured agitation, labour shortages, the destabilisation caused by amelioration policies and, most importantly, the fears of impending emancipation for which humanitarians in Britain were advocating" (*Colonial Inventions* 90). The accompanying textual descriptions in *Sketches of West India Scenery* exemplify the ideological lens through which the elite classes were viewing and "seeing" the African and African descended people forced to work in the plantation. Text and image work together to reinforce a colonial perspective that renders the apprentice a subject of observation. For example, the text that accompanies Bridgens' lithograph, entitled "Carting Canes to the Mill", reveals a romantic interpretation of cane labour processes, which were extremely dangerous and arduous. The first paragraph provides a detailed description of the workings of a sugar mill located in St Clair Farm owned by Robert Gray, Esq., whilst the second and final paragraph interprets the social meaning of this process for the plantation enslaved labourers. Below is a reproduction of this second paragraph and Bridgens' lithograph (see Fig. 2.2). This juxtaposition shows how, through image and text, the hegemonic gaze and way of "seeing" is constructed around pastoral and romantic notions of labour and self.

Fig. 2.2 © The British Library Board. Richard Bridgens, "Carting Canes to the Mill", *Sketches of West India Scenery*, 1836, lithograph. 789. g. 13. Reproduced courtesy of the British Library

The vicinity [sight] of a mill in crop time, is generally a very gay scene. The Negroes comfort themselves in the increased labor which is requisite to prevent fermentation in the newly cut cane, by a boisterous mirth that knows no relaxation. Some gifted individual extemporizes a line or two, when he is joined by the whole gang, with a power of lungs that would cause the despair of a chorus at a minor theatre.

Bridgens' allusion to singing in the midst of labour, and the description of a chorus, suggests the performance of a kaiso in this scene.[12] The individual who, as Bridgens notes, "extemporizes a line or two" can be identified as the "griot", the leading voice who marks the call-and-response pattern of the kaiso, and who is thus followed unanimously by the rest. As Curwen Best points out, the griot is "the forerunner of the modern-day calypsonian" (18). Bridgens, however, seems unable to decode the content of the kaiso, traditionally highly satirical and critical. Instead, he compares the scene with a performance at a minor theatre, demonstrating the extent to which the cultural significance of kaiso remains both masked to the European gaze and is instead translated into its paradigms. Both the pastoral aesthetics of the lithograph and the annotation's portrayal of labouring as a "gay scene", where the "negroes" manifest their "boisterous mirth", seem more fitting of a John Constable painting like *The Hay Wain* (1821), which also offers an idealised portrayal of haymakers at work in the English countryside of Suffolk. The lithograph's pastoral pictorial style entails a celebration of labour (agricultural labour specifically) that was predominant in European landscape painting in the nineteenth century. The pastoral style, like the picturesque, was a visual style that proved useful in nineteenth-century visual representations of the West Indies in order to portray the process of amelioration in romanticised terms. However, the labouring conditions of the enslaved population prior to the official emancipation of 1838, continued to cause strife and social unrest in the politics of the planter class throughout the British Caribbean. It generated conflict between the planters and the British government, which aimed to regulate the plantation economy. Planters ignored and sabotaged the 1824 Amelioration Order, and thus, "in the face of opposition and indifference, the amelioration policy had little real success between 1824 and 1831" (Brereton, *A History* 61). Richard Bridgens' anthropological sketch therefore provides an early example of a romantic lens that illustrates some of the contradictions at stake between the irony embedded in the text and image collaged in Cozier's *Wait Dorothy Wait*.

WAIT DOROTHY ... WAIT! CALL-AND-RESPONSE IN FOCUS: CARIBBEAN POPULAR CULTURE/S

The title of Cozier's piece, *Wait Dorothy Wait* offers a hint to a dialogical interpretation and viewing of the artwork. The title comes from Black Stalin's popular Trinidadian calypso of the same name composed in 1985.[13] By giving the artwork the same title as Black Stalin's theme, Cozier implicitly connects the calypso's context of 1985 and the socio-political moment of 1991, when Cozier created his mixed media series.[14] Furthermore, the reference to this calypso contrapuntally connects and illuminates the different narratives in the piece (the landscape painting, the newspaper cutting, and the extravagant golden frame) by reminding viewers of the possibility to confront social realities through the arts, an idea that resonates in Black Stalin's lyrics. The lyrics in "Wait Dorothy Wait" emphasise the need to confront the socio-economic and political issues of the time period, before engaging in the festivities of Carnival and calypso. Black Stalin tells audiences that, although he has been asked to write a light-hearted calypso: "they say they want something smutty about Jean or Dorothy", his commitment to social critique as a calypsonian weighs heavier still. Initially, Black Stalin admits attempting to write the type of calypso that he was originally asked to compose, but this task proved impossible. The dire socio-economic situation imposes itself. The calypso's opening shows how the calypsonian is influenced by expectations set through cultural patronage. However, he finally admits the impossibility to ignore the social and economic context of inequality:

> So I sit down to write this motto only to please them
> But as I pick up mi pen
> mi piece of paper
> And I write down those first words
> This is what I remember
> That *oil* money come and that *oil* money go
> And poor people remain on de pavement and ghetto. (emphasis mine)

Black Stalin's use of the words "oil money", and oil's phonetic resemblance to the word 'old,' reinforces and rarefies the connection between economic imperialism and the capitalist system of the time (largely based on oil extraction) as exploitative systems that continue to perpetuate class dichotomies. In 1985, when Black Stalin wrote his calypso, the national socio-political situation was such that "new International Monetary Fund policies and the economic recession likely topped the Calypsonian agenda" (Thomson, *An Eye* 290). Economic globalisation intensified in Trinidad and Tobago in the 1990s, since a central objective of the state was "to become a financial center" (Gayle 78). The effects of the emerging globalisation are even more evident in the early 1990s when, as economic geographer Barry Riddell points out,

> globalization was most intense in Trinidad and Tobago because of agreements with the IMF (in 1989 and 1990) ... the context within which globalization occurred was a looming debt crisis involving currency devaluation and flotation, the collapse of local firms, conditionalities of the IFIs, a decline in real incomes, a reduction in education and health care, mounting prices, and falling living standards. (662)

Consequently, the reference to Black Stalin's calypso in Cozier's artwork six years later in 1991 confirms the predicament embedded in the song; the importance of addressing issues of inequality in the country in order to avoid their worsening. The lyrics go on to remind the audience that Black Stalin will not write a calypso about Dorothy until inequality is addressed and acknowledged. However, in a rhetorical witticism, Black Stalin still manages to write a calypso about Dorothy, one that, nevertheless, critiques the "smutty" theme he has been asked to write about, and consequently writes about something else altogether ("Wait Dorothy Wait"). Black Stalin's "Wait Dorothy Wait", like Cozier's mixed media, playfully frames and calls attention to the cultural and national narratives that are being privileged in the mid-1980s and early 1990s. Interestingly, they address and explore these narratives through references to what they exclude. In this way, methodologically, they shift focus towards examples that conflict with the image of Trinidad as a tropical locale and multicultural haven, an image that cultural sponsors of calypso were eager to see represented in the new calypsos of the 1980s and 1990s (Rohlehr, "We Getting the Kaiso" 85).

By alluding to Black Stalin's calypso, Cozier's *Wait Dorothy Wait* invokes the centrality of calypso as embodying a long tradition of satire and socio-political critique that records and critiques the present, often in conversation with the past. Trinbagonians view calypso as fulfilling the role of a popular newspaper as it records and examines contemporary memory and provides an oral archive of social life. In Geoffrey Dunn and Michael Horne's documentary film *Calypso Dreams* (2008), Brigo (one of the calypsonians interviewed in the film) describes calypso as a "poor man's newspaper" whilst Black Stalin likens the role of the calypsonian to that of the African griot, storyteller who goes "from village to village spreading the word". Calypso provides both a personal analysis of the topic or experience recorded in the lyrics and an opportunity for audiences to join in the construction of the calypso via its performative elements, especially through the chorus and picong, and rhetorical elements resulting in wit and humour. Black Stalin's chorus: "Wait, Dorothy, wait, Dorothy wait" playfully invites audiences to join him in his political message.

The counterpoint provided by calypso in Cozier's *Wait Dorothy Wait* shifts the focus from the experience of forgetting, embodied in the juxtaposition of tropical image and the news cutting, towards the potentiality of popular culture as a means of generating counter discourses that, on the contrary, remember and address social issues. Black Stalin sings that he must avoid writing "a crowd-pleasing song", to face instead the issues of the day. In a similar way, Cozier rejects the complacent crowd-pleasing imagery of the tropical landscape to focus the attention towards other (potentially less pleasing) issues (Thompson, *An Eye*, 290). Cozier laments how, in the postcards of tropical landscapes, "no sense of the history or the struggles of those locations were conveyed" (qtd. in Thompson, *An Eye*, 291). Cozier's mixed media can therefore be seen in this context as a personal confrontation with this omission.

Although both Cozier and Black Stalin engage with the socio-political context of Trinidad, they transcend the boundaries of the nation-state and suggest a transnational kinship of collective counter-memory. The prerogative of tropicalisation that Cozier tackles in *Wait Dorothy Wait* resonates in many locations across the Caribbean. Additionally, the reference to Black Stalin's calypso makes further evident the international scope of contexts of inequality based on racial, ethnic, and cultural hierarchies in places like the United States, South Africa, and England in the mid-1980s when the song was written. Black Stalin does not oppose the idea of a party song per se but identifies the problems that must be confronted before a calypso like that becomes relevant.[15] He sings,

But the Klu Klux Klan in Richmond, Alabama
And in Brixton, England
My people still under pressure
Any time I see that South Africans are free
I'm going to finish the whole damn calypso for Dorothy.

The coexistence of dissonant and discrepant elements is something at stake in *Wait Dorothy Wait* and much of Cozier's *oeuvre*, and it is also characteristic of the archiving tradition of calypso in literature and other forms of cultural and artistic expression. Dissonance—a musical effect produced by lack of harmony and syncopated rhythm—also becomes registered in the various layers of contrast and opposition in *Tropical Night*'s images, where the chromatic variety marks a rhythm attuned to what Gordon Rohlehr describes as a "dance of opposites" characteristic of Trinidad's society ("The Calypsonian" 16). Dissonance becomes an element that acknowledges and allows space for (addressing) the contradictions within the nation and its existing conflicts that complicate the national motto "all ah we is one" which, as Bridget Brereton points out, forms part of the unifying narrative of Independence but does not adjust to the historical tensions and varying inequalities across ethnicity and class in the nation-state ("All Ah We"). As Brereton lays out, Eric Williams' narrative of Independence focused on a model of assimilation that at times excluded the cultural specificities, and influences of other ethnicities in the nation such as those of Indian and Chinese origin, as well as from Arab speaking countries, and constructed instead a notion of core national identity with the Afro-creole community ("All Ah We" 221). This is problematised in various Indo-Trinidadian literary texts including Lovelace's *The Dragon Can't Dance*, through the character of Pariag and his determination and struggle to belong, and be seen in Calvary Hill's community. In the film-documentary *Chinee Girl* (2011), photographer and visual artist Natalie Wei interviews fifteen Trinidadian women of Chinese descent across various generations including visual artist Jaime Lee Loy and fashion designer Anya Ayoung-Chee.[16] They all discuss the visibility and invisibility they have experienced in various social spaces due to their ethnicity and perceived exoticism. Wei's film centres female voices which have traditionally been more absent from academic discussions of Chinese migration to Trinidad, which first started in 1806 and continued throughout the nineteenth century. However, despite historic tensions

and political rivalry across race, ethnicity, and class, significant and generative instances of political kinship have taken place in Trinidad. This was
the case, for example, during the labour movement of the 1930s and
the 1970s Black Power Revolution, particularly when Indo-Trinidadian
individuals, whole communities, and trade unions joined the struggle
participating in protests, and organised action. The March to Caroni, on
12 March 1970, is one such moment. The NJAC (National Joint Action
Committee) organised this march, joined by 6,000 people (surpassing
10,000 people by the end of the march) for racial unity, expressed and
understood also as national unity (Pilgrim xxi, 53, 86, 273).[17]

The arts, and specifically music and popular culture, has often offered
shared spaces of cultural dialogue and exchange between various ethnic
groups in Trinidad. Both connection and dissonance coexist in those
spaces.[18] In music, ethnic tension, conflict, and stereotypes have been
archived in calypso and soca lyrics (Puri, *The Caribbean* 184–188;
Morgan 226–227). Paula Morgan situates calypso as a "shape-shifting
nation music" that although it has historically been largely the vehicle for
"Afro-creole cultural assertion and identity [it] also functions predominantly as an ambivalent trope for freedom and belonging for Indo-
Trinidadian writers and protagonists" (224). Morgan's discussion of
calypso in V.S. Naipaul's *Miguel Street* (1959) and Samuel Selvon's *Ways
of Sunlight* (1957) notes how it reflects and articulates shared experiences
of disenfranchisement and poverty, offering in both short story collections
a sense of belonging, and vocabularies for emancipatory freedom (236).
According to Morgan, in fiction by Indo-Trinidadian women writers
including Joy Mahabir, Ramabai Espinet, and Rajandaye Ramkissoon-
Chen, calypso (as well as Carnival) offers spaces to renegotiate characters'
identities as Indian and as women in Trinidad's society (239). In Espinet's
The Swinging Bridge (2003), calypsos and Carnival are portrayed as
cultural mediums of memory and expressions that would provide a sense
of freedom and catharsis every year. The protagonist, Mona, a Trinidadian documentary filmmaker who lives in Canada, returns to Trinidad to
arrange the sale of her family house. In the novel, J'Ouvert morning ("the
real start of Carnival" ch 6), signifies a time when Mona—dealing with the
imminent death of her brother caused by AIDS—enjoys shared memories with her father (Morgan 245).[19] Carnival also provides an important
connection for the character Annaise and her father during J'Ouvert, in
Joy Mahabir's eponymous novel (2006) (6–9). Regarding the spaces that

Carnival creates, Annaise reflects on her father's (who is a painter) relationship to mas camp as a space of belonging and respite: "not only his space to create, but also his space to escape" (9). Annaise adds: "I realise now that more than the mas, he needed the space of his mas camp, a marginal space. That gave him a sense of his art, a place where he could rebel against the restrictions he encountered trying to live in a place like Trinidad, under a government that ignored the Indian community" (9). As Cozier's *Wait Dorothy Wait*, and all other literary and cultural texts demonstrate, calypso and Carnival generate a space where dissonance can occur and where discrepant experiences can meet. It can provide a space of belonging whilst pointing out erasure or conflict.

A QUESTIONING SPIRIT: DEMASKING AND MOURNING

Gerard Aching's definition of the process of demasking (influenced by Bakhtin's theorisation of Carnival) sheds light on Cozier's *Wait Dorothy Wait*. In his discussion of masking in Earl Lovelace's novel *The Dragon Can't Dance* (1979), Aching notes that for Aldrick, the main protagonist, the literal and figurative mask provided by his dragon costume is the vehicle that both hides and paradoxically reveals his identity. Aldrick waits all year round for the moment of Carnival when he designs a costume through which he negotiates his sense of belonging to the local and national space. By wearing the dragon costume during the Carnival festivities, Aldrick "wanted everybody to see him. When they saw him, they had to be blind not to see" (Lovelace qtd. in Aching 1). Masking, in its performative element, both conceals and reveals an identity. Furthermore, "the mask is related to transition, metamorphoses, the violation of natural boundaries" (Bakhtin 40) which in the characters of *The Dragon Can't Dance* is believed or made possible through their participation in the different stages and modes of expression Carnival provides in Port of Spain. However, Lovelace's novel shows how parallel to those spaces of possibility runs a commodification of Carnival's culture. Fisheye, who finds a sense of place in the steelband of Calvary Hill, realises a change when "he saw that thing they called sponsorship coming into steelband" (68). At first, he doesn't notice much but gradually he sees Desperadoes "the baddest band in the island" appear with "new pans and emblem and waving a new flag: Sampoco *Oil Company* Gay Desperadoes" (emphasis mine 68). Philo, a calypsonian character in the novel, also experiences (like Black Stalin) the economic pressures and popular demand to write party calypsos. Masking therefore takes on a special significance as it continues to allow a satiric encoded critique in the face of commercial pressure.

Aching defines demasking as "the *action* of literally or figuratively removing an ideological mask from oneself or someone else in encounters and confrontations between masked subjects and viewing subjects" (6–7). Acts of "demasking" then require readers and viewers to interrogate what happens at the borders of the narrative or subject matter conveyed in any work of art. Therefore, demasking does not only posit the question of what are we seeing and how are we seeing it but, most importantly, it interrogates: what are we not able, or willing, to see, and why? The context that situates the violence reported in the newspaper, an increase in crime and poverty, is powerfully evoked through its absence in the image included in *Wait Dorothy Wait*. Demasking thus forces readers and viewers alike to engage critically and locate our own positioning in relation to the different types of masking (as disguises or expressions of reality). To know the discursive role of the Caribbean picturesque, the role of Carnival and calypso as vehicles of different and differing collective memory, to be aware of the Trinidadian arts scene in the 1990s, and the socio-economic context of the country at the time, will determine one's interpretation and access to *Wait Dorothy Wait*. An awareness, or lack of awareness of these contexts, their implications and interconnections, will influence the way that viewers interact with the work and engage critically with it.

In *Wait Dorothy Wait* a history/story of loss is also mourned under the (compositional) mask, through a personal and alternative archiving of memory. The symbolic loss of a critical space and the promise of a rupture with a tradition of colonial (mis)representation is lamented and mourned in *Wait Dorothy Wait*. The irony in the juxtaposition of these two opposing "images" (the physical image on the postcard and the mental image of the violence evoked by the newspaper clipping) makes the viewer feel the presence of erased viewpoints, especially when we consider the detailed description of the robbery and murder embedded in the newspaper clip. This leads viewers to recognise that, as we tear away images of paradise, there are other realities lying beneath the surface that demand attention and address. Finally, the estrangement provoked by the juxtaposition of image and text, in conjunction with the narrative of oral counter-memory in the artwork's calypso reference, also directs our gaze towards the colonial frame, as another possible framework of explication. The golden frame that Cozier uses in *Wait Dorothy Wait* displays a baroque aesthetic, an artistic style prominent during British colonial expansion and settlement in the Anglophone Caribbean. This gesture significantly points to, and frames, the post-Independence nation as a space where we can find traces of a legacy of discursive regulation. However, although the artwork mourns a critical space to address these issues, there is a deeper tension embodied in the absence of the name of the murder victim in the text. This renders him anonymous, a status which subsequently hinders the actual mourning process of this death, an omission and problematic that contributes to the shocking violence that Cozier draws our attention to.

SEARCHING FOR A NEW LANGUAGE: *SHE TRIES HER TONGUE, HER SILENCE SOFTLY BREAKS*

M. NourbeSe Philip's *She Tries Her Tongue; Her Silence Softly Breaks*, like Cozier's *Wait Dorothy Wait*, is a highly intertextual work. The juxtaposition of a variety of poems and texts throughout the pages of this poetry collection configures a heterogeneous collage of sources. Visually, *She Tries*, presents a seemingly disordered amalgamation of textual fragments from very different registers: legal documents, poetry, prose, fiction, extracts from The Book of Common Prayer, dictionary entries, fictional mock-test samples, and so on. The title of the collection: *She Tries Her Tongue; Her Silence Softly Breaks* is in itself (as Cozier's mixed media title *Wait Dorothy Wait*) an example of intertextuality.[20] It originates from a line in John Dryden's translation of book I of Ovid's *Metamorphoses* that describes the moment when the nymph Io recovers her speech and shape after Jupiter rapes her and turns her into a heifer.[21] The title in Philip's text encapsulates the theme of transformation that runs through the collection, and which parallels the genealogy and articulation of a critical tradition developed by Caribbean women writers. In other words, the act of "breaking silence" that the title evokes, connects symbolically with how Caribbean women authors have contributed to a body of literature that creates alternative vocabularies to express their experience in their own terms.

Caribbean male writing figured predominantly in publishing and critical studies, whilst the work of women writers remained comparatively understudied and was less published, especially until the 1970s and 1980s. The focus on male writers such as C.L.R. James, Sam Selvon,

Wilson Harris, George Lamming, Derek Walcott, and Edward Kamau Brathwaite was in stark contrast with the scarce critical attention that women's writing had received. M. NourbeSe Philip is part of a generation of women writers who approach history and female sexuality by claiming women's political agency and active participation in movements of resistance and political formation, a perspective that is sometimes absent in the anti-colonial writing of Caribbean male writers.[22] From poetry (*She Tries Her Tongue; Her Silence Softly Breaks* 1989, and *Zong!* 2008, amongst others) and fiction (*Harriet's Daughter* 1988; *Looking for Livingstone* 1991) to essay collections (*A Genealogy of Resistance* 1997, *Bla_k* 2017), and playwriting (*Coups and Calypsos* 1999), Philip's work writes against historical erasure and the silenced histories of oppressed groups, particularly women.

The nine poems included in "And Over Every Land and Sea", the opening section in the collection, display small excerpts from Ovid's *Metamorphoses* above each poem. These excerpts introduce nymphs and goddesses like Io, Philomela, Ceres, and Proserpine. The nymph Io and Philomela, princess of Athens, share a similar fate in Greco-Roman mythology; they are both raped, transformed into a heifer and a bird, respectively, and both are stripped of the faculty of speech. Philomena's tongue is cut off whilst Io is unable to articulate her voice. Proserpine, the spring goddess, is also raped in *Metamorphoses*. These myths "echo the predicament of the many female slaves raped by their white masters and … they resonate with the experiences of African slaves in the New World who, deprived of their mother tongues, had to find a new language to express themselves" (Fumagalli, *Caribbean Perspectives* 74). In *She Tries*, Philip creates thus a parallelism between Ovid's text and her own writing, creating a feminist poetics where the female personae in the poems appear as author of a new language and modes of kinship. Similarly, if in *Wait Dorothy Wait* the newspaper cutting simulates the role of an ironic caption, Philip's excerpts from *Metamorphoses* function as epigraphs to the poems. These small textual fragments, juxtaposed to the poems, encourage readers to interrogate their influence in how we may read the poetry in relation to the various subtexts and narratives that they bring to the forefront.

Maria Cristina Fumagalli contends that Philip's interest in myth lies in its ability to, "transform a history of dispossession into new possibilities and new departures" (74). The (poetic) language of myth evokes the foundation of tradition, as well as the idea of progress. The notion of progress is nevertheless questioned through myth in Philip's deconstructive task; the emphasis on historical continuities of violence and suppressed memories that counter this notion becomes a riff throughout the collection. Myth is being used in postcolonial literature as a rhetorical means to explore new and alternative ways of narrating history that complicate modern ideas of progress. Such models de-mask the ways in which Western myth and historiography intersect by revealing how myths, as history, often convey and privilege episodes of creation over their own episodes of erasure. *She Tries Her Tongue* complicates a Eurocentric construction of Caribbean history as a history of Western enterprise and creation, by showing the colonial process of silencing and erasure (linguistic, cultural, and historiographical) of Amerindian, African, and Asian populations in the region. The history of the Caribbean, inseparable from the history of European empire(s), reveals the extent to which history relies on myth formation and how myths embody deep-rooted ways of understanding collective experience.

A Poetics of Interrelation: How to Read the Fragments of History

Visually and methodologically, "Discourse on the Logic of Language" is the poem in the collection that most resembles, aesthetically and structurally, Cozier's *Wait Dorothy Wait* (see Fig. 2.3). The various formal elements in this poem are closely interconnected and map out a critique of the English language as a source of anxiety, as the father tongue that violates the body and psyche through colonial discourse. In two of the four pages of this poem, three different texts inhabit the space of the page.[23] They are placed in neatly separated columns and, in this way, emulate visually the columns of the ledger book where the transactions of enslaved women, men, and children were documented. This reveals a very conscious use of form that characterises all of Philip's poetry. The regimented feeling evoked in the formal layout of "Discourse on the Logic of Language" makes readers aware of the constriction of form and language to express the sense of dispossession that Africans experienced in the New World. The African and Asian Caribbean population created new languages in the different forms of Creole English and through them they configured aesthetic modes that can more aptly convey the complexities of (post)colonial experience. By reproducing formally, and yet confronting contrapuntally, the violence of the Archive, Philip's poetry

THE MOTHER THEN PUT HER FINGERS INTO HER CHILD'S MOUTH—GENTLY FORCING IT OPEN; SHE TOUCHES HER TONGUE TO THE CHILD'S TONGUE, AND HOLDING THE TINY MOUTH OPEN, SHE BLOWS INTO IT—HARD. SHE WAS BLOWING WORDS—HER WORDS, HER MOTHER'S WORDS, THOSE OF HER MOTHER'S MOTHER, AND ALL THEIR MOTHERS BEFORE—INTO HER DAUGHTER'S MOUTH.

but I have
a dumb tongue
tongue dumb
father tongue
and english is
my mother tongue
is
my father tongue
is a foreign lan lan lang
language
l/anguish
 anguish
a foreign anguish
is english—
another tongue
my mother '
    mammy
    mummy
    moder
    mater
    macer
    moder
tongue
mothertongue

tongue mother
tongue me
mothertongue me
mother me
touch me
with the tongue of your
lan lan lang
language
l/anguish
 anguish
english
is a foreign anguish

EDICT II

Every slave caught speaking his native language shall be severely punished. Where necessary, removal of the tongue is recommended. The offending organ, when removed, should be hung on high in a central place, so that all may see and tremble.

Fig. 2.3 M. NourbeSe Philip, "Discourse on the Logic of Language", *She Tries Her Tongue; Her Silence Softly Breaks*, 1988 (1989), p. 32. Image courtesy of the artist

draws attention to how vocabularies of memory in the Caribbean are marked by the difficulty of accessing the past through the perspective of the African or Asian subject. However, the musical call-and-response pattern in Philip's poetic compositions shows a circuitous connection to the past that channels memory in Creole languages, allowing spiritual and ancestral voices to return to, and disrupt, the logic of the Archive. As I discuss in chapter two, this figure of prosopopeia (a rhetorical device through which a disembodied voice is expressed) is also used in Philip's elegiac long poem *Zong! as Told to the Author by Setaey Adamu Boateng* (2008) where spectral voices riff in reappearing words throughout the pages. In *Zong!*, Philip continues the experimentation with this column-like compositional arrangement engaging explicitly with the epistemic violence of the Archive, especially as in this poem Philip dismembers very literally the language used in the archival document *Gregson v. Gilbert*. However, in *Zong!*, there is a gradual explosion of language whereby columns of words and word clusters progressively expand across the pages finally escaping the physical confines of the colonial archive.

The first and third pages of "Discourse on the Logic of Language" show a textual division in three fragments that posit the question: "where to start reading?". Situating the sequence of reading from right to left clarifies the semantic relationship between texts. Readers will encounter two edicts placed in italics at the right margin. They mark the context of physical, linguistic, and cultural violence enacted through the law in the plantation. On the first page, Edict I dictates the prohibition of any communication between enslaved Africans in their "mother tongues" and the enforcement of multilinguistic grouping arguing that "(i)f they cannot speak to each other, they cannot form rebellion and revolution" (*She Tries* 30). Edict II, on the third page, describes the gruesome punishment to be carried out if they were caught communicating in their native languages. The punishment is also designed to inspire terror. A terror that is significantly based on a graphic image of mutilation, which the very layout of the poem reinforces: "Where necessary, the removal of the tongue is recommended. The offending organ, when removed should be hung on high in a central place, so that all may see and tremble" (32).

When read in connection with the edicts placed in the right margin, the capitalised text in the left margin acquires special relevance; the tongue is resignified as a symbol of resistance, the possibility to confront and affront the Archive. Throughout the first and third page, a capitalised text placed vertically on the left margin forces us to read differently, not only conceptually but also physically, as readers must turn the book clockwise to be able to read the text. The capitalised text below captures a moment of proximity between a mother and child. This scene of physical communion channels the communication of language, and knowledge through a newfound tongue. The vertical text describes on the first page how a mother bird licks her newborn, "tonguing" it "CLEAN OF THE CREAMY WHITE SUBSTANCE COVERING ITS BODY" (30). On the third page, this text continues to describe an instance that resembles the physical relationship of care amongst birds, which follow the habit of delivering food directly into the mouths of newborn birds (see Fig. 2.3):

THE MOTHER THEN PUT HER FINGERS INTO HER CHILD'S MOUTH – GENTLY FORCING IT OPEN; SHE TOUCHES HER TONGUE TO THE CHILD'S TONGUE, AND HOLDING THE TINY MOUTH OPEN, SHE BLOWS INTO IT – HARD. SHE WAS BLOWING WORDS – HER WORDS, HER MOTHER'S WORDS, THOSE OF HER MOTHER'S MOTHER, AND ALL THEIR MOTHERS BEFORE – INTO HER DAUGHTER'S MOUTH. (32)

This fragment reflects the inheritance of words that will shape this emerging language. It signals the restoration of a previously silenced "genealogy of resistance", a powerful phrase that gives name to Philip's later eponymous non-fiction collection. The reference to a child who gains inherited words significantly returns to the subtext of *Metamorphoses* as it parallels the myth of Philomela, whose tongue is cut by Tereus, her sister's husband, after he rapes her. Philomela, unable to speak, decides to weave a tapestry in which she tells her story. She then sends it to Procne, her sister, who after finding out what happened, decides to feed her husband their own son Itys. Unknowingly, Tereus eats Itys and, when he finds out, tries to kill both sisters with an axe but is stopped by the gods who transform Procne into a swallow and Philomela into a nightingale. In the end, both birds fly away and escape their death. This myth's subtext of kinship frames the moment of mother–daughter communion as an instance that validates the transmission of knowledge through memory across generations. The striking image of an outpouring of ancestral words, from mothers in different timeframes, as conducted via the tongue creates a striking visual image that evokes transference and movement. This movement connects the past and the present like a thread of memory; it disrupts a sense of mythical time that permeates earlier poems in the collection like "And Over Every Land and Sea" as it unites further the history of sexual abuse and discrimination throughout the period of colonial conquest and racial slavery, with the postcolonial moment.

The episode of the (bird) mother feeding words to her child sets implicitly an intertextual connection with Kamau Brathwaite's "Nam(e)tracks" in "Mother Poem", *Ancestors* (1987), which revises the anti-colonial trope of Prospero in the Caribbean literary canon. In Brathwaite's poem, Prospero insists on Caliban not disrupting the world/word of consciousness ("i") in which colonial identity is privileged. Sycorax, as mother figure to Caliban, intervenes and breaks the word thus bringing in a rupture with colonial language through the birth of what Brathwaite has theorised as "nation language". Caliban, in his own words, tells: "but / me muh / me muh / mud / me mudda / brek / de word ... an she te an she tee an she / teach mih / dat de worl risin in de yeast / wid red wid cloud wid mornin / mist / wid de eye:ron of birds" (88–89). This transition from colonial "i" to critical "eye" remains the privilege of the son/sun and is thus gendered as male but this is facilitated by Sycorax. As Gordon Rohlehr observes, in the poem "Sycorax directs Caliban's attention to the rising sun, a symbol of his own sonship/sunship" that "predicts a rebirth and an uprising: a red rising of sons".[24] Brathwaite's rendering of Sycorax presents her as a powerful figure. Philip's 'bird mother' refigures Sycorax's portrayal as inspirational source by emphasising her role as author through a powerful graphic image of transmission. The transmission of word and speech has deep implications since, as Philip points out in the Afterword of *She Tries Her Tongue*: "Speech, voice, language and word—all are ways of being in the world [...]" (82). This text, in the centre of the page, illustrates the birth of a new tongue. Denise deCaires Narain argues that the poem reflects a "more obviously lyrical poetic voice in which the yearning for a 'try' mother tongue is dramatized" (204). The stanzas are organised in a syllogistic form that finally frames English as an imposed language that replaces the multiple African mother tongues. However, a new language is in the process of formation, and whilst it originates from English, it remains different. Philip names this new language "a demotic variant of English" ("The Absence of Writing" 84). Standard English is then "subverted, turned upside down, inside out, and even sometimes erased" by this language (83).

English
is my mother tongue.
A mother tongue is not
not a foreign lan lan lang
language
l/anguish
a foreign anguish.

English is
my father tongue.
A father tongue is
a foreign language;
therefore English is
a foreign language
not a mother tongue.

What is my mother
tongue
my mammy tongue
my mummy tongue
my momsy tongue
my modder tongue
my modder tongue? [...] (30)

As in Brathwaite's "Nam(e)tracks", the rupture of words simulate the birth of this new language, which conceptually signals both Caribbean Creole languages and Philip's own experimentation with artistic forms of expression in order to incorporate the (counter)memories of Caribbean women's experiences onto the page, placing it visually at the centre. The final two stanzas on the first page initially seemingly provide a kind of synthesis to the definition of English as a "father" foreign tongue and the absence of a "mother tongue". Seeing as "I have no mother / tongue" and "no tongue to mother" "I must therefore be tongue / dumb" (30). However, the final two lines give way to the cursing of a "damn dumb / tongue" that opens a space for the invocation of the "mothertongue" which takes place on the third page: "mothertongue me / mother me / touch me / with the tongue of your / lan lan lang / language / l/anguish/ [. . .]" (32). Although the last line in the final stanza concludes that "english / is a foreign anguish" (32), the unruly capitalised vertical text in the left margin has the final word. The metaphor of the "BLOWING OF WORDS" contains a force that resists the anguish caused by English and brings the promise of new linguistic and artistic possibilities. According to Denise deCaires Narain, all these textual "juxtapositions foreground the sterile 'rationality' and monologism of patriarchal discourse" (206). It is therefore only through the acceptance of plurivocality that meaning can be productively reconstructed in the poems. Philip writes that "[t]he challenge, therefore, facing the African Caribbean writer ... is to use the language in such a way that the historical realities are not erased or obliterated, so that English is revealed as the tainted tongue it really is. Only in so doing will English be redeemed" ("The Absence of Writing", *She Tries* 85). In this sense, the literary use of language of Caribbean writers draws attention to the ways in which language carries itself the history of colonial oppression and also of resistance.

CONTRAPUNTAL VOICES: *SHE TRIES HER TONGUE* IN PERFORMANCE

An audio performance of "Discourse on the Logic of Language" available on M. NourbeSe Philip's website, illustrates very accurately the contrapuntal dynamics and reading that Philip's arrangement of textual fragments on the page suggests. In this audio clip, Philip starts reading the text located at the centre of the page which, as previously mentioned, deconstructs English and refashions its anguish into the articulation of a Creole or demotic English. One minute and fifteen seconds into the performance, a British male voice starts reading Edict I, which dictates the separation of African slaves into different linguistic groups to avoid revolt. At this point both "voices", like in a contrapuntal musical composition, are superposed and can be heard simultaneously.

Philip's voice remains quieter in the background whilst the British voice representing the law remains more audibly present. This continues until Philip's narration of the centre poem takes over. Yet another voice, narrated by Philip, jumps in shortly afterwards, reading the capitalised and vertically placed text on page 30: "WHEN IT WAS BORN, THE MOTHER HELD THE NEWBORN CHILD CLOSE: SHE BEGAN THEN TO LICK IT ALL OVER" and after that text is read, the central poem returns again marking always the central and leading voice that connects the rest of the fragments as it oscillates to the forefront and background of the performance. After two and a half minutes of the reading, the British voice starts to read the text on page 31 which states: "Those parts of the brain chiefly responsible for speech are named after two learned nineteenth century doctors, the eponymous Doctors Wernickle and Broca respectively". This reading continues to detail Dr. Broca's racist theories of phrenology. A minute later the central poem returns again "but I have / a dumb tongue / tongue dumb / father tongue / and english is / my mother tongue [...]" (32). The poem continues in this fashion for almost another five minutes until its end. The contrapuntal alternation and superposition of voices in the performance of the poem lifts the voices of the text off the page. It adds another dimension to the experimental arrangement on the page. The flatness of the page, already challenged in the written poem by the use of the right and left margins, is thus further unwound through the multivolume sense of the oral performance.

In "The Absence of Writing or How I Almost Became a Spy" Philip argues "it is impossible for any language that inherently denies the essential humanity of any group or people to be truly capable of giving voice to the i-mages of experiences of that group without tremendous and fundamental changes within that language itself" (82). The anguish and tension represented in the poem, and the paradox of the conclusion of English as both a mother and father (foreign) tongue are addressed. Writing about the poem, Philip states, "some sort of balance is achieved despite the anguish of English and despite the fact that English is both a mother tongue and a father tongue" ("The Absence of Writing" 89). The poems in *She Tries Her Tongue* "seek to enact a poetics which might transform linguistic structures, particularly those associated with the written text" (deCaires Narain 201). Philip's understanding of Caribbean demotic language transcends the written or even the spoken language to include other forms of communication such as dance and visual arts.

> [t]he power and threat of the artist, poet or writer lies in this ability to create new i-mages, i-mages that speak to the essential being of the people among whom and for whom the artist creates. If allowed free expression, these i-mages succeed in altering the way a society perceives itself and, eventually, its collective consciousness. (Philip, "The Absence of Writing" 78)

The notion of the "i-mage" deconstructs the word "image" to privilege the "i" present in Rastafari philosophy whereby the individual's perspective is consciously incorporated into collective experience through the creation of autonomous i-mage making. The responsibility of the "image-maker" is that of "continually enriching the language by enlarging the source of i-mages – in particular, metaphorical i-mage" (Philip, "The Absence of Writing" 80). Like Cozier, Philip is concerned with creative and visual vocabularies that better express the artist's subject matter. Through the i-mage, art has the potential to unmask inherited representational modes, thus allowing new modes and vocabularies of experience to emerge. Philip's use of form strategically calls upon elements outside the text, thus unveiling the context that once produced them.

The textual fragmentation in Philip's poems, especially in "Discourse on the Logic of Language", reflects the existing gaps, disconnections, and silences that pervade the colonial archive, where the impact and rich history of creole cultural expression remains largely absent. The fragments in this poem take over the space of the page from left to right margin, which can be read as an attempt to reclaim the space and relationship to place that has been more restricted for Caribbean women writers, as the figure of the Caribbean writer and intellectual had more often been represented as male, particularly until the 1970s when the publishing of more women writers started to take place. The corporeality of the Archive is therefore reimagined in non-normative ways as texts are inverted and conventions are challenged. In a journal entry published in the essay "The Habit of: Poetry, Rats and Cats", Philip explains how

> by cramping the space traditionally given the poem itself, by forcing it to share its space with something else—an extended image about women, words, language and silence; with the edicts that established the parameters of silence for the African in the New World, by giving more space to the descriptions of the physiology of speech, the scientific legacy of racism we have inherited, and by questioning the tongue as organ and concept, poetry is put in its place [...]. (117)

CONCLUSION: SILENCE SOFTLY BREAKS AND THE ARCHIVING OF COUNTER-MEMORY

The poetics of call-and-response and contrapuntal connections in Cozier's and Philip's work requires viewers and readers to break into the semiotic codes of signification, and question the inherited modes of written and visual vocabularies shaped through modes of representation like tropicalisation, or in the linguistic structures established by, and through, colonial

discourse. Breaking such codes unveils the extent to which these vocabularies have historically marginalised the experience of Caribbean people.
Via techniques like collage and montage, Cozier and Philip place in juxtaposition textual or visual fragments from colonial, state, and elite forms
of memory, with fragments that bring into focus individual and collective experiences that have been previously excluded from the Archive
and the public sphere. However, this compositional and aesthetic strategy
moves beyond emphasising binary relationships between privileged and
marginalised experience.

The recorded instances of counter-memory in *Wait Dorothy Wait*
and *She Tries* do not only create a revisionary counterpoint dynamic
in relation to privileged forms of memory, they create too a contrapuntal and polyphonic effect whereby multiple dialogic relations function
simultaneously and offer a multidimensional approach to the process
of archiving counter-memory. Hence, the archival process that I read
in *Wait Dorothy Wait* and *She Tries* is not just oppositional to colo-
nial/state/elite memory, but entangled with it and complicated by such
entanglement. For instance, "Discourse on the Logic of Language"
aptly demonstrates how the use of so-called standard English and the
Caribbean demotic meta-linguistically reflects the history of violence in
the context of the Americas (a similar concern is expressed about the role
of other European languages). Its imposition initially carried the enforcement of a colonial image-making that negates African culture and signifies
it as inferior through discourses like phrenology and through colonial law,
represented in Wernickle and Broca's theories and the edicts. However,
Philip's performance of this poem in the aforementioned audio reveals
how the centre-page poem interweaves and connects all the fragments
around it; the emerging "modder tongue" that the text describes symbolically breaks through the silence and the anguish of imposed languages and
their modes of signification. This voice predominates and marks the flow
of the composition; it alternately shifts from being in the background to
always return as the main voice. The play on words in this central poem
ultimately arrives at another instance of call-and-response as the female
child's voice finally asks "mother me / touch me / with the tongue of
your / lan lan lang / language / l/anguish" (32). The fact that the next
fragment read by Philip is the capitalised text detailing how a mother
blows words into her child's mouth confirms the call-and-response.

If Philip's poems challenge the authority and expectations marked by
the space of the page, Cozier's mixed media disrupts the reading and

viewing conventions marked by the authority of the frame which symbolises the inclusion and visibility of what is deemed by the arts, culture, and tourism industry as valid artistic representations or worthy commodity. Cozier's ironic use of the miniature colonial-style frame in *Wait Dorothy Wait* structures his critique of the rejection of critical visual vocabularies in sectors of Trinidad's commercial art market and public sphere. The satirical and critical nature of calypso is reproduced through the arrangement of referential cues that construct a narrative of protest in this mixed media. The flexible and nuanced vocabulary of calypso, which both encodes and embodies a history of counter-memory in Trinidad, is refigured in *Wait Dorothy Wait*. Cozier's mixed media masks a mourning of the loss of support to cultural forms like calypso and the commercial pressures that compromise its creative and critical autonomy.

Wait Dorothy Wait and *She Tries Her Tongue* extend understandings of language and propose a broader approach, as artistic languages (visual and conceptual vocabularies as well as aesthetic choices) can guide more fluid forms of understanding memory that best represent the syncretism of subaltern knowledge and popular culture in the Caribbean. Their aesthetics replicates the effect of masking, described by Gerard Aching as a means to claim control over meaning production and to guide, not try to impose, its reception and engagement, whilst facilitating demasking as a decoding of that meaning. In turn, this leads to critical assessments of how memory is, or is not, represented and validated in the colonial archive. Masking thus functions in a similar way to Glissant's notion of opacity that resists the imposition of a knowing transparency of the Caribbean that does not consider local/regional knowledge production and social realities (*Poetics of Relation*).

Notes

1. See Gen Doy, *Black Visual Culture: Modernity and Postmodernity*, Stuart Hall, "On Postmodernism and Articulation: An interview with Stuart Hall by Lawrence Grossberg and Others" in *Essential Essays, Volume 1: Foundations of Cultural Studies*, ed by David Morley; Michelle Wallace, "Modernism, Postmodernism and the Problem of the Visual in Afro-American Culture" in *Dark Designs in Visual Culture*.
2. The specific mixed media that I examine in this chapter contains a small fragment from a postcard reproduction of an oil painting by a Trinidadian artist.

3. I will only discuss one of the three mixed media pieces and will thus refer to the artwork as *Wait Dorothy Wait*, which is the title given to the entire series.

4. For a comprehensive critical discussion of narratives of tourism and representations of the Caribbean as a space of tourist consumption across the different economies linked to tourism, see Nixon, *Resisting Paradise: Tourism, Diaspora and Sexuality in Caribbean Culture*. *Resisting Paradise* focuses on cultural production, including literature, popular cultural and visual art in Jamaica, Trinidad, and Tobago and other locations of the Anglophone Caribbean. Further, Nixon also discusses Haiti. This critical study offers a multifaceted analysis of the varied and rich ways in which contemporary Caribbean artists and writers are contesting tourist imaginaries of the region, offering in turn generative critiques and interrogations.

5. Although the Emancipation Act was first passed in August 1833, it was not until August 1, 1834 that it was officially acknowledged. The Act only deemed free those enslaved persons under the age of six, whilst the rest of the enslaved where forced to engage in a (largely unremunerated) six-year period of apprenticeship during which conditions did not improve and in many cases worsened due to the resentment of plantation owners (Dabydeen, Gilmore and Jones 154). See Dabydeen, Gilmore and Jones, eds. *Oxford Companion to Black British History*, 154.

6. Various scholars have written about the impact that the narratives of Spanish *conquistadores* have played in the genealogy of a historiographical tradition that frames the American continent as a geo-political space figuratively signified in relation to Europe (Todorov; Sánchez Ferlosio; Wahab; Sheller; Taylor). The framework of epistemic violence that language enacts in the claimed "discovery" of the West Indies is further evident in the diaries of Christopher Columbus and other early chronicles of the "*Nuevo Mundo*" (New World), a geographical space signified discursively through written and visual texts as always already in relation to early modern Europe and the Spanish empire, a discursive practice that has continued to influence, and has parallelisms in, both the textual and visual rhetoric of tourism, particularly in marketing the finding of new experiences and self-discovery through tourism in the region. The role of language in the naming of the "New

World" and the implications that its "newness" represents were originally aimed by European colonisers to mark, ontologically, the starting point of its history. Narratives of conquest in the early colonial period attempt to write the Americas within the geopolitical mapping of the West, forcing a space for signification that has problematically perpetuated a portrayal of the region as space of profit and leisure, ready for foreign consumption. The tourism industry targeting the Caribbean today perpetuates similar discourses especially with the tailoring of packaged cultural experiences that allow tourists to remain within the premises of all-inclusive hotels and cruises where they can avoid fears rooted in supposed exposure to crime and poverty.

7. "Romance," *Oxford Dictionaries*, http://www.oxforddictionaries.com/definition/english/romance.

8. See Thompson, *An Eye for the Tropics* for a detailed and informed analysis of the cultural value of the postcard as she examines their political and discursive implications within and outside the region (14, 74, 257). The Caribbean postcard's imagery originates with early portraits of local residents standing still on bicycles, holding banana baskets, or posing next to donkeys. Later on, throughout the twentieth and early twenty-first centuries, postcards of the Caribbean have perpetuated this regional representation through contemporary images of pristine tropical beaches that promise tourists an escape from modern life, continuing further the representational emphasis on a premodern state of Caribbean islands in another continued attempt of that imposed narrative.

9. Equally, the role of romanticism and romantic visual and discursive representations of oppressed societies during the nineteenth century extends to other locations in the Americas. For example, in *Brazil Through French Eyes: A Nineteenth-Century Artist in the Tropics*, Araujo examines the notion of tropical romanticism in the work of nineteenth-century French photographer François-Auguste Biar, and traces its influence on stereotypical representations of people of African descent that have remained in discourse and rhetoric today.

10. The work of Isaac Mendes Belisario stands as another example of visual representation in nineteenth-century Jamaica that is partly influenced by, but which departed from the picturesque. Belisario (1795–1849), as Bridgens, created a series of ethnographic

sketches (*Sketches of Character, 1837–8*) accompanied by textual descriptions. Belisario's pictorial style is similar to Bridgens'; their sketches look alike in terms of compositional arrangement, theme but differ in stereotypical representation (Mohammed *Imaging*, 150–154). Other examples of (creolised) representational style of Caribbean folklore can be found in other parts of the Caribbean, including Cuba (Victor Patricio de Lanzaluce); Puerto Rico (Francisco Oller); and Dominica (Agostino Brunias).

11. Bridgens, *Sketches of West India Scenery with Illustrations of Negro Character, the Process of Making Sugar, &c. Taken during a Voyage to and Seven Years Residence in the Island of Trinidad*, publication dated 1836 (two versions were published between 1825 and 1837, Wahab 90).

12. There are various theories regarding the origins of kaiso. Some scholars, like Raphael de Leon, argue that this musical form is primarily influenced by a form of French ballad from medieval France (thirteenth century) that was incorporated in the island when France became involved in Trinidad in the eighteenth century (Best, "Sounding Calypso's Muted Tracks" 16). However, the most popular theory amongst scholars of calypso locates kaiso as a precedent of calypso rooted in the African musical tradition. Often during their work in the plantation, Africans would sing kaiso, which contained satires ridiculing enslavers.

13. Black Stalin, *Wait Dorothy Wait, Roots Rock Soca,* © 1985, 1991. Rounder Records, Compact disc.

14. Black Stalin's popularity and connection with Trinidadians is also attested by official recognition. He won the Calypso Monarch competition, celebrated during the Trinidad & Tobago Carnival, numerous times: in 1979, 1985 (for "Wait Dorothy Wait" and "Isms Schism"), 1987, 1991 and 1995.

15. *Wait Dorothy Wait*'s critique is addressing the pressures of commissioned calypsos without space for critique of contemporary events, rather than enacting a commentary on calypso fete songs, particularly as there is much political resistance and celebration of cultural and political community in Black Stalin's calypsos such as "Black Man Feeling to Party" and "Look on the Bright Side", for example, for which he won the Calypso Monarch competition in 1991 (the year when Cozier creates *Wait Dorothy Wait*).

16. Natalie Wei's *Chinee Girl* won the Best Short Film (Audience Award) at the Trinidad and Tobago Film Festival, 2011.

17. In *Creole in the Archive: Imagery, Presence and the Location of the Caribbean Person* Roshini Kempadoo offers a description of that photographic record in the archives (held at the special collections in the Alma Jordan Library, University of the West Indies, St. Augustine) and a discussion of its significance (183).

18. Temporal fragmentariness connected to a calypso aesthetic is also present in the non-linear structure of Anthony Joseph's *Kitch: a fictional Biography of a Calypso Icon* where the contrapuntal dynamic of calypso becomes the language through which to tell the life story of one of its greatest, Lord Kitchener. Trinidadian writers such as Lawrence Scott have also contributed (and been influenced by) the rich literary corpus of calypso literature. According to Njelle W. Hamilton, Lawrence's *Night Calypso* (2004) explores the interplay between collective memory and individual experience as a means to process traumatic memory, facilitated by the figure of the calypsonian. Also within the archive of literature rendering a calypso poetics that highlights how those cultural markers portray the relationship between African and Indian-Trinidadians is M. NourbeSe Philip's play *Coups and Calypsos* (2001) where two ex-lovers (Elvira who is of African and Rohan who is of Indian descent) circumstantially reunite in Tobago and spend together a few crucial days in Trinidad's history, during the Jamaat al Muslimeen attempted coup in Port of Spain (27 July–1 August 1990). Through their encounter and dialogue, they revisit their relationship and breakup which reveals the ways in which cultural and racial tensions and prejudice had partly influenced their relationship negatively. In the background, a stereo interrupts their conversation (at intervals) with radio news updates on the situation with the coup. However, when calypsos are playing, those memories and resentment are temporarily suspended. Philip dedicates the play "[t]o the people of Trinidad and Tobago whose unbridled joie de vivre, piquant sense of humour and picong skills have helped them survive the tragi-comedy that is life" (n.p.).

19. In *The Swinging Bridge*, the shift of timeframes and locations creates a ruptured narrative linked by a calypso call-and-response pattern. Memory and the possibilities to reconstruct the narrative reside in that swinging and shifting movement, between locations and across timeframes.

20. Ovid's *Metamorphoses,* written in 8 AD, records a great number of Greco-Roman myths that are connected to a large extent through the subjects of mutation and change. Ovid's short prologue emphasises the centrality of transformation in this epic poem: "Changes of shape, new forms" are the theme of this "one continuous poem" (5). In his attempt to narrate history through myth, from the moment of "Creation" (5–9) to "The Apotheosis of Julius Caesar" (630–636), Ovid draws attention toward the repetition of patterns in the cyclical structure that characterises human history and myth; an underlying issue in Philip's *She Tries Her Tongue; Her Silence Softly Breaks.*

21. One day Jupiter approaches Io, daughter of the river god Inachus, and attempts to sexually assault her, she runs to the forest but Jupiter runs after her and rapes her. He then decides to transform her into a heifer and "puts Argus, the son of Arestor, in charge of Io" (36). Io is then subjected to the constant stare of Argus who keeps her captive and "When she opened her / mouth to complain, / her own voice startled her; all that emerged was a hideous / lowing" (37).

22. Caribbean critics have examined the context of Caribbean women's writing in relation to writing by male authors, looking at the implications of an initial marginalisation of women's literature in the publishing world and the ways in which, especially from the 1970s Caribbean women writers demanded more visibility and critical attention. See Carole Boyce Davies and Elaine Savory, *Out of the Kumbla: Caribbean Women and Literature*; Carole Boyce Davis, *Black Women Writing and Identity: Migrations of the Subject*; Denise deCaires Narain, *Contemporary Caribbean Women's Poetry: Making Style*; Alison Donnell, *Twentieth-Century Caribbean Literature: Critical Moments in Anglophone Literary History*; Patricia J. Saunders, *Alien Nation and Repatriation: Translating Identity in the Anglophone Caribbean.*

23. This collage of texts suggests to readers that meanings are constructed dialogically by means of (inter) relation: therefore, their content may be opposing, complementing, revising, complicating, and/or contextualising each other.

24. Gordon Roehler, "Black Sycorax, My Mother." *The Geography of a Soul: Emerging Perspectives on Kamau Brathwaite.* Ed. Timothy Reiss, 277–295, 284.

CHAPTER 3

Polyphonic Archives: Christopher Cozier's *Tropical Night* and M. NourbeSe Philip's *Zong!*

Almost two decades after *She Tries Her Tongue; Her Silence Softly Breaks* (1988) and *Wait Dorothy Wait* (1991), Christopher Cozier began his mixed media drawing series *Tropical Night* (2006–ongoing), and two years later, in 2008, M. NourbeSe Philip published her elegiac book-length poem *Zong! as Told to the Author by Setaey Adamu Boateng*. The fragmentation of form in the collage of various textual, visual, and musical registers present and evoked both in *Wait Dorothy Wait* and *She Tries Her Tongue*, is exploded in the formal aesthetics of *Tropical Night* and *Zong!* where the fragmentation of visual signs and words is stretched across the space of the museum wall and the page. As Philip's *Zong!*, *Tropical Night* is a highly dialogical work and opens up a critical space through the speculative nature of the drawings and their possible combinations, as their order in the grids of the museum's wall changes at every new exhibition. Dominated by a myriad of images including breeze blocks, maps, podiums, or palm trees, which keep (re)appearing in the composition, the iconography of *Tropical Night* offers a mosaic of popular yet highly personal renderings of Port of Spain that translates to the familiar urban landscape of other Caribbean nations and territories.

Tropical Night was conceived as a work in progress and an ongoing project. The drawings communicate Cozier's wrestling with prefigured and overly defined narratives. I am using here this notion of 'wrestling'

© The Author(s), under exclusive license to Springer Nature Switzerland AG 2023
M. Fernández Campa, *Memory and the Archival Turn in Caribbean Literature and Culture*, New Caribbean Studies, https://doi.org/10.1007/978-3-030-72135-0_3

as it was also encapsulated in the exhibition *Wrestling with the Image*, curated by Cozier and Tatiana Flores in 2011, which featured the work of contemporary artists from across the region where "[e]very piece is wrestling with images and fraught or imposed representational demands, complicating and challenging the notion of a straightforward and transparent readability of experience" (Fernández Campa, "Caribbean Art" 2). This critical form of narratology, that resists the assumed internal order or completeness of official narrative, is at stake in *Tropical Night* and is equally present in *Zong!*. In this poem, Philip refigures words from the text of the legal case *Gregson v. Gilbert* which confronted the underwriters and ship owners of the Zong in 1783 over the payment of the loss of cargo when enslaved Africans were massacred under the ship captain's orders in his hope to be able to later claim insurance monies. The words and word clusters in *Zong!* are arranged across the page in a variety of combinations that shift form throughout. These formal dynamics challenge and open up a range of possibilities for engaging with the text.

Breaking and stretching the physical boundaries and limits of the frame and the page, the visual fragmentation and alternating repetition of words in the poems of *Zong!* and the repetition and variation of visual signs in *Tropical Night* reflect the articulation of a language communicating a speculative conceptualisation of memory. *Tropical Night* and *Zong!* configure a personal and collective enactment of African diasporic narratology, which Heather Russell describes as existing at a liminal space of possibility and imagining, a threshold which, like Wilson Harris's notion of *limbo*, marks a reckoning with the past and with a new future that emerges out of that process of remembrance. In relation to the "Euro-American discursive and epistemological formations" that have historically shaped many literary forms of linearity, Russell notes that "[b]reaking such traditional or canonical social contracts becomes integral to the liberating, revolutionary poetics of form engendered by African Atlantic narratology" (2). This chapter examines some anti-narrative elements in *Zong!* (Philip, "Notanda" 204) and *Tropical Night* that are informed by a poetics of fragmentation, characteristic of African diasporic narratology (as Russell conceptualises it), and are also connected to a Dougla poetics in the case of *Tropical Night*. Key to this process of wrestling with (neo)colonial images and language in both works is the space of the notebook, as a space of conceptual imagining central to the configuration of memory work and critical thinking around the artists' work and their own archiving.

Diaries, notebooks, and letters play an important role in the process of conceptualising work for writers and visual artists. In some Caribbean literary texts, extracts from these types of documents figure in the published manuscript, therefore becoming a constitutive part of the writing, sometimes reflecting on that process. This is the case in non-fiction by M. NourbeSe Philip. *A Genealogy of Resistance* (1997), and essays like "Fugues, Fragments and Fissures: A Work in Progress" (2007), and "A Travelogue of Sorts: Transatlantic Trafficking in Silence and Erasure" (2008), amongst others, convey extracts from notebooks and diaries. Many of the central aspects of Philip's theorisation of contrapuntal and fugal aesthetics are found in those extracts and in their own interrelation with the essayistic form. Non-fiction also offers the space where the private thoughts and feelings meet with the public arena (and its counter-publics), favouring thus the inclusion of more private documents. In the introduction to his book *The Undiscovered Country* (2020), Andre Bagoo states that the essays in the collection "make public the private through the trick vessel of art" (7), and in essays like "What Happened on December 21, 2019" the form of the journal informs the form of the essay, and Bagoo's journal writing and note-taking on laptop are variously referenced in a meta-literary style (111–112). Poetic works, such as Kamau Brathwaite's *The Zea Mexican Diary: 7 Sept 1926–7 Sept 1986* (1993) also convey extracts from diaries. *The Zea Mexican Diary* includes nine extracts from a diary that Brathwaite kept during his wife Doris' cancer illness and death, documenting his grieving. It also features nine extracts from letters addressed to his sister Mary Morgan (amongst other documents). All these private documents were originally not intended for publication, but as Sandra Pouchet Paquet points out in the preface, "the completeness and depth of aesthetization in the final form of *The Zea Mexican Diary* confirms the aesthetic contemplation immanent in any work of art" (x). The diary therefore conditions the content but also the form.

The artist's sketchbook is also central to the work of contemporary artists in the Caribbean. In the case of Christopher Cozier, as I discuss later in the chapter, the notebook provides a site for conceptualising the work that also archives the ongoing use and repetition of several visual signs in his *oeuvre*. The notebook plays a key role in the artistic process and work of other contemporary artists. For example, Barbadian artist

Sheena Rose has used sketchbooks for her artwork, which she has documented on her Instagram account.[1] Equally, her own introduction to art
was through "drawing in sketchbooks as a child" (T. Best).[2] The use of
black ink drawings in Rose's sketchbooks and notebooks has at times been
combined with bright colours. Her iconic ink drawings have taken the
form of large murals; one of them was commissioned by, and is displayed
within the grounds of the Inter-American Development Bank in Washington DC. Another large drawing was featured in the group exhibition
The Other Side of Now: Foresight in Contemporary Caribbean Art, at the
Pérez Art Museum, Miami.[3]

The notebook has also become central to scholarly work. In *Creole in
the Archive: Imagery, Presence, and the Location of the Caribbean Figure*
(2016), Roshini Kempadoo includes excerpts from research journal
entries, marked in italics, that reflect on issues around the economy of
images of slavery and indentureship in relation to the narrative power of
archives. She reflects on the impact of seeing certain images in the archives
and wanting to search for new ones.

> *Illustrations of slavery and photographs of indentureship had become symbolic
> of the forced and brutal systems of migration that are symptomatic of the
> Caribbean. As I viewed her depiction as incarcerated, bruised, succumbed, I
> wondered where else I might see the Caribbean figure restored, respected and
> recovered like the family album I had grown up with and worked from as a
> photographer and artist.* (2)

The reference here to the family album, as a record that documents
the lives and experiences of the Caribbean person whose voice is largely
absent in the colonial archive (at least not within a narrative frame of
their choosing or control), positions the album in a closer realm of a
private document that powerfully counters official narratives, a subject
that is explored in Kempadoo's own scholarship and artistic practice, and
in the work of other scholars including Tina M. Campt. Similarly, Shalini
Puri uses the notion of notes or note-taking as conceptual grounding
for discussing field work in Caribbean studies and has written about that
experience in "Finding the Field: Notes on Caribbean Cultural Criticism, Area Studies, and the Forms of Engagement" (2013) in which Puri
expands the notion of methodology for research in the humanities.[4] In
critical responses to authoritative narratives and records, both colonial and
postcolonial, the notebook provides a vital counterpoint as a medium,

that in its speculative and more investigative potentiality can open up understandings of more flexible sign-making and language(s), challenging and undoing narratives and frameworks of imposed signification. This is the case in both *Tropical Night* and *Zong!*, as works that emphasise the processual and compositional elements central to their ethos.

TROPICAL NIGHT: FUGAL NARRATIVES AND FLUID VISUAL VOCABULARIES

In *Caribbean Art*, Veerle Poupeye underscores how a younger generation of artists in the Caribbean "represents a challenge to what had become official postcolonial and revolutionary culture" (183). Here, Poupeye agrees with Cozier's "polemical statement" that "the main difference between Trinidadian art in the sixties and seventies and his generation is the shift from 'representing culture' to 'creating culture'" (183). Poupeye points out that many established artists from that older generation operate within more "formulaic" representational demands of art markets in countries like Jamaica, Trinidad, the Dominican Republic, and Puerto Rico (183). Yet, ironically, also in Poupeye's 1998 *Caribbean Art*, one of the pioneering publications in the field, the discussion of the contributions by contemporary Caribbean artists does not credit Cozier's important role in pushing the boundaries of contemporary arts, cultural practice, and arts writing in the region and internationally. Annie Paul marks this omission in her article "The Enigma of Survival" where she locates Cozier's arts practice and that of other Caribbean artists like Eddie Bowen, Steve Ouditt, and Irénée Shaw as "alterNATIVES" within the Trinidadian arts space (65).[5]

Philip Sander describes in 2007 how in the Trinidadian art market "[c]ommercial galleries deal almost exclusively in landscapes, still lifes, and genre paintings, and local collectors have sometimes been openly hostile to work that breaks those conventions" ("Galvanize"). Cozier's art practice confronts the creative limitations and specific artistic vision that the work of those galleries represents. In Trinidad, curatorial initiatives and arts programmes like *Galvanize* played a vital role in critiquing a national oversight of independent art practice and focus on national art, opening up instead regional and diasporic connections and conversations (Wainwright 157).[6] The project made an influential statement about the invisibility experienced by many artists who, despite "impressive lists of credentials and shows on their CVs might nonetheless never catch the attention of the cultural authorities, never merit a mention in the press" (Sander). A collective and collaborative arts programme, *Galvanize* extended over a six-week period in September–October 2006, coinciding with the government sponsored Carifesta IX, an annual arts festival that takes place around different locations in the Caribbean, connecting cultural art expression across the region. However, as Wainwright notes, *Galvanize* was completely independent from the festival. In fact, it originated from a different principle. A large group of twenty-one critics, musicians, writers, and visual artists including Christopher Cozier, Nicholas Laughlin, Steve Ouditt, and Peter Doig (all members of *Galvanize*'s advisory board) engaged in critical conversations and generated twenty art projects and events, some of which were exhibited at the Caribbean Contemporary Arts (CCA), around the premise "visibly absent". This motto, displayed in Bruce Cayonne's *Galvanize* posters with his signature style largely derived from his artistic fete signs, summarises the project's predicament.[7] *Tropical Night* captures this sense of invisibility as it claims personal renderings of collectively shared visual markers that lie outside of the purview of nation-building.

The success of *Galvanize* relied on its collective effort, resourceful mobilisation of the Internet, the media, and a vibrant alternative arts scene with a clear vision of the critical possibilities of the arts, often exhibiting the work of artists in fabric shops or backyards. Although lacking the financial support of Carifesta, *Galvanize* was still able to attract a great number of visitors and positive press coverage. Cozier's role in shaping the contemporary arts scene in the Caribbean is also closely connected to Alice Yard, the independent arts space in Port of Spain that he co-directs with Nicholas Laughlin (writer and editor), Sean Leonard (architect) and Kriston Chen (designer). Alice Yard was transformed into an arts space in 2006, propelled by the conversations around artists's needs initiated at *Galvanize*, and through residences for local, regional, and internationally based artists, critics, and writers, it has provided a vital space for critical investigation and public engagement. Alice Yard was first located in the area of Woodbrook, in the physical space of the yard of Alice Gittens (Leonard's great-grandmother) where various generations of children had played, and in 2020 it permanently moved to the area of Belmont and the space of Granderson Lab (which had previously worked as a satellite space to the original Yard). In its new location, the team was joined by Kriston Chen. Under the dynamic concept of *play*, Alice Yard has opened a space for talks, performances, exhibitions, concerts, and Carnival mas practice and it has played a significant role in the arts practice and career of many current Caribbean contemporary artists both in the region and the diaspora (Pearce "Playing in the Yard"),[8] including Charles Campbell, Ebony G. Patterson, Marlon Griffith, Nadia Huggins, and Sheena Rose. Alice Yard's notion of play is tantamount to Carnival mas as well as Cozier's own art practice, which for over four decades has centred around questioning, challenging, and exploring preconceived and new vocabularies of experience. In "Playing in the Yard", art critic and curator Marsha Pearce defines play (in relation to its dynamic in Alice Yard) as involving "engagement and imagination. Play is the thrill and natural intoxication of experimenting, trying new things, collaborating and relating to each other in novel ways. Play is about not knowing where things will lead. Play is about having fun. Alice Yard embodies all of these ideas". This philosophy is also very much present in Cozier's art practice at large and it is particularly so in *Tropical Night* where the investigative nature of the drawings and their invitation to engage with the various images and conceptual project resonates with play.

Richard Fung's documentary *Uncomfortable: the Art of Christopher Cozier* (2005), introduces through a series of conversations with the artist a trajectory that reveals the role of Trinidad and Port of Spain's urban landscape and popular culture in Cozier's art. From the process of collecting rubble to be repurposed in artwork (conceptually addressing issues around nation-building) to the politics of location that inform *Tropical Night*, Fung, a Trinidadian-Canadian filmmaker based in Toronto, captures Cozier's critical thinking including his interest in music. The influence of calypso on Cozier, also present in *Wait Dorothy Wait*, runs through his body of work. In 1997, Cozier collaborated with calypso and soca icon David Rudder in the art project *The Madman's Rant*. Rudder's calypso "The Madman's Rant", from his 1996 album *Tales from a Strange Land*, caused an impression on Cozier who got in touch with Rudder, and both engaged in a conversation over six weeks that served as foundation for the artwork as response to the song. Rudder then collaborated in the creation of the composition. The song, through the figure of the madman ranting, hits on some core observations about society. These offer a critique of the political class' manipulation of promises in exchange for votes and power in the mid-late 1990s, during a time of increased crime and inequality largely resulting from policies of structural adjustment, the effects of globalisation, and government corruption.[9] The satirising of the promises made as old, failed promises runs throughout.

The visual repertoire of the work and its arrangement anticipates some of the visual signs and composition later present in *Tropical Night*. This is the case for the human limbs and head, national flag, or the old-style cone megaphone. Reporting on a conversation in 2018 when Cozier and Rudder reminisced about their collaboration at Alice Yard (Granderson Lab), Shereen Ali notes, "Cozier's vision of *The Madman's Rant* is full of fractured human figures and urgent, gestural marks, with symbols rubbing up against each other in startling, jarring ways – a heart, a gun, the T&T flag as bandit's mask, a dead Christ-like foot with a Nike toe-tag, and scribbled confessional writing".[10] During the talk, Cozier explained being influenced by listening to various performances of the calypso at Moon (over Bourbon street) where Rudder would often vary elements of the lyrics (Ali), which is characteristic of calypso and also echoes Cozier's own relationship to the visual signs in his work, generally, and specifically in *Tropical Night*, where repetition and variation are central to the drawings. There are also similarities in the compositional elements and arrangement of both artworks, as Cozier's *The Madman's Rant* is composed of a series of wooden framed panels where paintings of different orientation and size were placed together as fragments of the larger composition.

Tropical Night configures an archive (and also a counter-archive) of individual and cultural memory that responds to the lack of alternative visual vocabularies in official narratives of the nation-state. This was especially the case in the Anglophone Caribbean during the 1980s (Poupeye, Sander, Wainwright). Within the context of tourism and some nationalist-sponsored cultural programming, the codes to communicate Caribbean experience have often been prefigured, and largely limited to ideas of what popular culture means and how it represents the nation to both local and foreign audiences. *Tropical Night* started to take form in 2005. The initial idea for the series originated in 2003 after some drawings from Cozier's artist notebook were exhibited at Madrid's Marlborough gallery as part of the group exhibition *Diciendo lo que me pasa por la mente*, curated by Kevin Power.[11] This made Cozier realise how his drawings were exploring a personal and visual vocabulary based on a series of visual signs that are recurrent in his practice and central to his notion and experience of place, particularly Port of Spain, but also reminiscent of other locations in the Caribbean. In 2005, inspired by the investigative dynamics of his notebook's drawings, Cozier initiated work on drawings that later, in 2006, formed the beginning of the series *Tropical Night* (Fig. 3.1).

Fig. 3.1 Christopher Cozier, journal pages/sketchbook, 2001–2002. Courtesy of the artist. Photo by Marta Fernández Campa

Whilst on a research residence at Alice Yard in 2012, I visited Cozier's artist studio which includes his archive of the series. Stored in boxes, and separated by acid free paper, from a close distance, the drawings more easily display the intricate details of the combination of drawing and mixed media. The textured elements of stencilled work and cut-outs can be less or hardly noticeable when viewed from a distance in a museum and even more so when looked at through a published image, which proves further the significance of the series' invitation to look closer. Cozier also shared with me some of the pages from the notebooks that have worked as the conceptual foundation and genesis for the creation of many of the drawings. The notebook as a medium is linked to the speculative; it offers a testing space where first thoughts, impressions, and ideas can be captured in a medium that, due to its associated transience, provides a freer space for exploration and experimentation. Notebooks, sketchbooks and diaries therefore become vital in the process of sedimenting the expression and chosen vocabulary of artists (by which I mean visual artists and writers), and they play a particularly significant role in the work of artists from the Caribbean whose relationship with imposed vocabularies and representational forms as legacy of (neo)colonialism is often explored and documented in these materials, and across art mediums. Looking through some pages of the notebooks dated from 2001 and 2002 revealed some of the iconic images in the series. The writing in the pages is also closely connected to the conceptual development of the image. For instance, several pages in the notebook feature the image of the podium. In one of them (Fig. 3.2), dated from 28 March 2002, Cozier writes down some reflections on the idea of *space*, "[c]oming back to the idea of 'space' and the way it can be defined physically and mentally by sound". In caps, following this line, Cozier lists the following words:

1. NOISE
2. DRUMS
3. ASSERTION

Fig. 3.2 Christopher Cozier, journal pages/sketchbook, 2001–2002. Image courtesy of the artist. Photo: Marta Fernández Campa

Next to the writing, the image of a human figure holding a podium, and the aura of a triangular shape with the word "gayelle" (arena sometimes used for cock fights) circled upon it, suggest the notion of social hierarchies and competition and their pressure in the psyche, linked to the writing on the right-hand side, which reads "so it's going to be a story about measurement, okay?". These ideas and reflections jotted down and accompanied by images simultaneously describe the artist's thought process and philosophical considerations *also* linked to the conceptual process and design of his 2002 art project *Terrastories*, a public art performance installation in Copenhagen. In "Terrastories (notes)", published in *Small Axe*, Cozier described the installation as consisting of three distinct "spaces", two of which were marked by "fenced in enclosures", whilst the third consisted of,

> four hundred yellow made-in-Chinese rulers that blow in the wind between the buttresses of the old church tower. Inside of that area, along with the sound of the rulers knocking together, was the sound of my voice being played through a small speaker. I said, "Man running between two nonspecific points" and "And to think you had me believing that all this time." (120)

A sketch of one of these fenced-in enclosures appears on the right-hand page of the notebook plate (reproduced here), next to another sketch of four hundred hanging rulers, symbolic marker of the legacy of oppressive strategies of colonial history. The issue of the politics of space and location is recurrent in Cozier's conceptual imaginary, and the notebooks demonstrate how the iconography around the sign of the podium was key to the development of not only *Terrastories*, but subsequent artwork that features and plays with the sign of the podium, such as *Tropical Night* and later works like *In Development* (2013), a series of large mixed media drawings. When it appears in the drawings of *Tropical Night*, it is not only in a new set of contexts and articulations around what the podium may represent or evoke or how that might be explored, but it also archives a history and trajectory of this sign in Cozier's own work. This same dynamic applies to many other visual signs and objects found in the notebooks and in the artwork.

The genesis and formation of *Tropical Night* illustrates how artists' notebooks and sketchbooks are often the first archival entry for particular (and often recurring) thoughts and images later captured in drawing and painting. As in Cozier's process, some of the most iconic visual signs in the artwork of Jean Michel Basquiat were also first documented in his notebooks. Basquiat's famous crown appears in several pages of the eight notebooks published (in faithful emulation format) in *Jean Michel Basquiat: The Notebooks* (2015) and *Basquiat: the Unknown Notebooks* (2015), the latter being the catalogue of an exhibition of the same name at The Brooklyn Museum. The influence of the notebooks on Basquiat's *oeuvre* is apparent in his paintings and drawings as well as in the streets and public transport of New York City where he painted his graffiti. Furthermore, "Basquiat's notebooks are not sketchbooks in the classical sense, and they can be attributed an artistic status all their own", as Dieter Buchhart argues (27). With that same understanding, Kevin Power convinced Cozier to exhibit pages from his artist notebook in the Madrid exhibition, insisting on the importance of their artistic value.[12] Both Basquiat and Cozier lived in New York during the 1980s, an experience that had a significant impact on their work. Like Basquiat, for Cozier, the city became a creatively enriching place. During this time, Cozier studied visual art in the US, obtaining a Bachelor's degree in Fine Arts from Maryland Institute College of Art in 1986 and an MFF from Rutgers University in 1988. The influence of graphic design and advertisement, clear in the iconography of Basquiat, is also present in Cozier's professional development, who also worked in advertising upon his return to Trinidad in 1988.

Tropical Night consists of a series of 9 × 7 inch individual drawings on thick paper that are pinned together onto the gallery space's wall forming the shape of a large canvas. A large wooden peera—a bench of Indian origin—always stands in the gallery as part of the installation, and at times, as was the case for the installation of the series at the Jaffe-Friede Gallery (2007), Dartmouth College, smaller peeras are placed across the exhibition space. The large bench shaped as a peera is always placed in front of the drawings, inviting viewers to sit and look closely at the composition. A multitude of images including peeras, palm leaves, fences, brick walls, and silhouettes of female dancehall dancers reappear in similar and different contexts. The drawings form grids. In their repetition, they reveal an archival drive that documents both Cozier's own experience of urban Port of Spain and a collective assemblage of popular landscape markers. Iconic buildings like The Red House, Trinidad's parliament, appear throughout as do images of posters advertising fetes, details from maps, shopping carts, and other signs of the quotidian landscape.

In 2007 *Tropical Night* was displayed at *Infinite Island: Contemporary Caribbean Art*, a Caribbean arts group exhibition curated by Tumelo Mosaka at the Brooklyn Museum (August 2007 to January 2008). *Infinite Island* showed eighty works by forty-five established and emerging artists from the Caribbean in an attempt to illustrate the multifaceted art produced in the region during the six years prior to the exhibit. Cozier's drawings were also displayed at Dartmouth College where Cozier was artist in residence in 2006. On this occasion the number of drawings in *Tropical Night* changed from 136 in the Brooklyn museum to 120. In *Afro-modern: Journeys through the Black Atlantic*, the next group exhibition that displayed *Tropical Night*, there were 189 drawings (Tate Liverpool January–April 2010; Centro Galego de Arte Contemporánea, July–October 2010), a number that increased to 210 in *Vous Êtes Ici*, an exhibition in Martinique (Fondation Clément, October–December 2010). The growth of the series through the incorporation of new images, as well as new orderings of the sequences into Cozier's visual vocabulary, reflects the investigative approach of the work and the focus on constructing a critical conversation (Laughlin, "Working Notes" 8).

Although the material used for the drawings is simple: thick paper of nine by seven inches, the visual vocabulary that the drawings create when they are placed together reveals a complex web of interrelated elements: narrative threads and sequences, histories and stories seem to converse with each other across the compositional framework (see Fig. 3.3). As with *Zong!*'s fragmented word sequences, the arrangement of drawings in *Tropical Night* is marked by repetition and variation; visual signs keep reappearing in similar, and also different contexts evoking the instability and mobility of a visual vocabulary in the process of emerging. Nicholas Laughlin describes it as "a narrative struggling to emerge" ("Taking Note"). The wavering between repetition and variation of visual signs creates a rhythm that reinforces a unique and experiential sense of narrative that, like Philip's, resists linearity and an assumed transparent readability, that was once assumed of the colonial archive. Cozier himself writes in relation to *Tropical Night*:

> I am very weary of narrative, as it often feels like an imposition on experience; a rationalization that inhibits as much as it offers consolation or

Fig. 3.3 Christopher Cozier, *Tropical Night*, 2006–ongoing; ink, rubber stamps and graphite on paper, each drawing 9 × 7 in. Installation shot, *Infinite Island* exhibition, Brooklyn Museum. Image courtesy of the artist

promises order or meaning ... Each image declares new paths and either lays to rest overly familiar concerns or allows them new readings in the shifting associative structure (*Tropical Night* blog).[13]

The relationship between the fragmentariness of multiple visual signs (equally shifting as they change position in the exhibition space and grow over time) and the overall whole of the composition, is mediated by that notion of imposed narratives. Those narratives are often entangled with the grand narrative of History which the drawings (evoking multiple, complex histories and stories) are responding to. Drawings in *Tropical Night* counter, complicate, question, and reveal aspects about imposed narratives and offer new semiotic possibilities. Heather Russell argues that as a central element of African and Black diasporic narratology: "the formal eruptions of the African Atlantic are primarily concerned with destabilising what Édouard Glissant in *Caribbean Discourse* defines as the idea of a 'single History.' Crossing texts fissure 'History' through the discursive interventions of 'histories.'" (2). This multiplicity and plurality of historical knowledge is highly influential and present in Caribbean art. Cozier's *Tropical Night* warns us against overly familiar tropes and the formation of fixed narratives around us.[14]

Images of colonial maps, blackboards, palm trees, sound system speakers, machine guns, and erect and inverted podiums, amongst others, populate the composition. In their combination, through the repetition, variation, and the chromatic nuances of the drawings when viewed as a whole, the drawings evoke a rhythm and even the sense that musical notes or keys are being played at different times, a visual effect produced by the changing chromatic tonality of the drawings' background which varies from light yellow and sepia to light and dark brown. This synaesthetic effect in *Tropical Night*, which results in the production of rhythm, musicality and movement rooted in the visual effect of the composition, is also central to the semiotic revision of the series. The mosaic of drawings invites viewers to consider and re-consider the set of associations marked by the combination of repeating images in every new context, to think about the power of narrative and lens in influencing a desire to make sense and to read images in specific or prefigured ways. The strong sense of polyrhythm created by the visual kaleidoscopic effect (see Fig. 3.3), shares similarities with the African "Mande and Mande-influenced narrow-strip textile" which Robert Farris Thompson describes as "rhythmized textiles" featuring designs "in visual resonance with the famed off-beat phrasing of melodic accents in African and Afro-American music" (207). The Mande textile tradition emerged from a diverse set of locations across Western Africa (today's Ivory Coast, Ghana, Benin, and Togo). Enslaved Africans refashioned the Mande tradition in the Americas as it continued in Brazil, the United States, and Suriname, morphing into new forms. From there (and from Western Africa) the influence of this textile would later travel to other locations in the Caribbean. In its contrast of gradual tonalities, the aesthetic effect of Indian quilts can also similarly suggest a rhythm akin to the one embedded in *Tropical Night*. There are noticeable aesthetic similarities with the Kantha cloth (which in Sanskrit means patched cloth) originating in eastern states of India (West Bengal, Tripura, Bihar and Odisha) and Bangladesh. A Kantha cloth repurposes cloth materials from saris, and can sometimes also display a contrasting series of square cloth where "several layers of fine cotton are sewn together to form thin but beautifully embroidered blankets or mats" (Alexander et al. 101). The aesthetic similarities between the Mande and Kantha cloth and Cozier's *Tropical Night* can be read as signalling the influence of diasporic polyrhythms in Caribbean arts practice through music and its subsequent influence in visuality. Equally, as I will shortly explore further, the polyrhythmicity that informs *Tropical Night* also evokes cultural aesthetic influences from Indo-Caribbean and Dougla cultural forms, including music.

The series' compositional arrangement grants visual access to all the different drawings simultaneously. In this way, viewers too can explore their own sense of narrative as their eye moves across the composition, making them participant in the form and composition of the series. Repeating images contrast with one another thematically and chromatically; this can potentially create the impression that they move figuratively across the extension of the piece, fostering a sense of rhythm and dynamism. The viewer's eye/I is likely to follow these images through the visual sequences that Cozier configures in the various exhibitions of the artwork. As above mentioned, by evoking a sense of musicality, through contrapuntal associations, movement, and (poly)rhythm, *Tropical Night* generates synaesthesia, that is, when something is experienced from various senses simultaneously. In this case, seeing something produces visually the impression of sound and sonic effects, therefore stimulating a sense of music and rhythmicity through sight. This effect connects with *Zong!* where the exploded fragmentation of words across the page and its constant shifting and transformation follow a fugal pattern akin to a musical composition. This synaesthetic effect in *Tropical Night* and *Zong!* ultimately configures a creolisation of the archive insofar as it combines visual, oral, and aural elements to document histories in ways that best accommodate the multivocal nature of collective memory and the public sphere.

The rhythm evoked by the compositional elements of the series captures a musical sensibility equally supported by the call-and-response pattern of its repeating and shifting visual signs, many of which are linked to music. From the iconic stereo speaker (present throughout Cozier's *oeuvre*), to dancehall dancers, to human figures and guitars positioned to reference soca, Carnival mas, and calypso, in dance or music performance. The rhythm in the composition is also suggestive of the drumbeats of the African drum, tassa drum, and steel drum. Music and rhythm in Trinidad signal powerful cultural expression and memory, creolisation, and hybridity but also a history of (socio-cultural) policing and ethnic and racial strife. The violent history of Spanish conquest in Trinidad caused the near decimation of Indigenous peoples on the island, and although there is more recognition and education about Indigenous history and knowledge today, there has been significant historical omission of the past. Many members of communities descendant of Indigenous First Nations live in the borough of Arima, and other areas of Trinidad. Tracy Assing, a writer of Indigenous descent, notes about Trinidad: "[t]he nation was built on traditional knowledge, indigenous labor and natural resource exploitation" (137). This cultural legacy is also substantial across the arts. Tracing a music history of the island, Martin Munro notes that many of the foundational aspects of the rhythms of Trinidadian music come from the Indigenous *arietos* dance which was accompanied by drums and conch shells. Equally, a connected yet different Indigenous musical form, *Carietos* were songs that, as Munro points out, can be considered precursors to today's calypso (80–81). Historically, drums, their rhythm and call to insurrection, have been the source of white fears and repression in Trinidad, and in other locations in the Caribbean. This led to attempts to ban and control the celebration of Carnival in the 1880s through a series of ordinances restricting the use of drums, for example the Musical Ordinances of 1882 and 1883.[15] (Batson 196; Munro, 106).[16] Colonial authorities saw in Carnival masquerade, rhythmic drumming and stick fighting a great threat to the status quo as these provided spaces of contact, potential alliance, and political organising amongst African and Indo-Trinidadians. These contact spaces were also threatening to a colonial social structure that required the separation of oppressed populations in order to thrive. The space of Carnival has facilitated hybrid configurations of drumming rhythms through the influence of the African-based rhythms and the rhythms of Indo-Trinidadian tassa drumming (Cozart Riggio 184; Munro 108–109). The British colonial "divide-and-conquer policy" as a method "was no doubt strategic" (Munro 108), and managed to create divisions from the arrival of indentured migrants in the nineteenth century, and equally since 1917 when indentureship ended (Munro 108; Khan 55).[17] The culture of indentured groups was perceived and represented as foreign to the colony, and was also distinctly marked within the national project since, as Benedict Anderson famously described, the nation's imagined community after national Independence in the geographies of the Americas still bore the influence of coloniality and therefore inherited vestiges of the model where various hierarchies supposedly sustain national harmony (*Imagined Communities*). Colonial authorities created legislation specific for indentured workers and social services that were separate, which contributed to further distance and alienation (Brereton, *Race Relations* 177). However, in spite of these complex social dynamics, popular culture and the arts have provided much cohesion particularly, although not exclusively, through intercultural relation and conversation.[18]

In its wide-ranging evocation of visual signs, the iconography in Cozier's work elaborates a Dougla poetics, both in terms of cultural markers and musical sensibility. The term Dougla became popular in Trinidad and Tobago and Guyana to refer to people of African and Indian descent, and the term Dougla poetics was "coined by Shalini Puri (1994) to describe a tentative and almost invisible discourse of persons of mixed African and Indian descent in Trinidad and Tobago" (Reddock, "Jahaji Bhai" 570). As Rhoda Reddock points out, the term "Dougla" is derived from the Bhojpuri and it originally "had a pejorative meaning akin to 'bastard'" ("Jahaji Bhai" 573). However, especially since the 1980s, the term has been re-signified in Trinidad and Tobago. Cozier, whose heritage is of African and Indian descent, has explored in his work issues of race, ethnicity, and colorism in Trinbagonian society. Early artwork, such as his video performance *Blue Soap* (1994),[19] problematise the ways in which, despite national narratives of ethnic and multicultural harmony, the status quo in the society reflects divisions amongst groups reproducing an "us vs. them" mentality (that Cozier has equally addressed in other work) which erases connections and ignores the tensions amongst different groups.[20] Cozier's early sketches in his personal archive conceptualise the performance through a space (and arena) where four stage stands hold televisions positioned in a square shape. They contrapuntally project a video on a loop with narratives by persons from different backgrounds describing their own experiences of (un)belonging: African, Indian, and Dougla, in an echo of voices and narratives, superposed onto each other through a twenty second running difference. This creates a polyphonic effect that Maica Gugolati argues, "refers back to religious litanies, healing prayers and Hindu mantras, bringing the chanting closer to the spiritual power of the blue soap which is known locally to protect from the evil eye or *maljo*" (6). The tension in the cultural value of blue soap speaks to its complex currency. In one of the first video segments, Cozier is seen washing his body with blue soap, which has traditionally been used in domestic spaces in Trinidad as part of Indian Trinidadian cleansing rituals with religious undertones and it has also been commercialised as soap that whitens, as punishment that corrects rudeness and as action that cleans impurities with racialised connotations. Cozier has noted about *Blue Soap* "[m]y intention was to bring up feelings about morality, spirituality, the status of the creative person and also of people of mixed ethnic identities, like myself" ("Uniform and Weapon" 413). A chorus in the video recites these and other uses of blue soap, superposed to the voice of Cozier, which narrates:

> I come from a place where my French creole friends don't trust me, I have a name like them, but I look different. My Indian friends think I look like them, but I don't share their culture. They don't trust me either. My African friends don't trust me because I look like an Indian, I have a French creole name and I'm not dark enough. I feel like I am everything and nothing simultaneously. (*Blue Soap*)

Cozier's audio in the video reveals the impact of fixed racial and ethnic categorisation and that "the anxieties around racial ambiguities are often expressed as purist disavowals of the Dougla—either through discursive repression of the Dougla or through explicit attack on the category" (Puri qtd. in Reddock, "Jahaji Bhai" 573). Equally, on the other hand, *Blue Soap*, "criticizes the government-supported forms of multicultural categorization that, while they admit of plurality, essentialize differences by imposing structures upon them" (Gugolati 7). Cozier's *Blue Soap*, and other artwork, reflects instead a Dougla poetics in its documentation of complexity and plurality as a means to complicate and question fixed notions of identity and belonging, because, as Puri argues, "[a]n exploratory politics and poetics cannot afford the closure of meaning" (*The Caribbean* 216). In *Tropical Night*, this is enacted through unfixed imagery. The human figure that appears in various contexts across the composition of drawings could belong to different ethnic groups. This figure in profile position is recurrent in Cozier's *oeuvre*, and their gender identity is fluid here and not always explicit. Similarly, through repetition and variation, visual signs open up the investigative space that reflects the cultural currency of objects (such as the peera bench), associated with one cultural and ethnic group but in reality shifting and occupying various locations; their cultural specificity travelling, so to speak, to new creolised contexts. Additionally, the rhythmicity created in *Tropical Night* through the chromatic combination of images and their repetition and variation are similarly evocative of the various musical traditions and languages, rhythmic patterns, and convergence particularly in genres such as soca which are highly influenced by the various African, Indian, and creole rhythms.

As in visual art, rhythm and the simulation or allusion to drums (both the African drum and the Indian tassa drum), play a role in forms of counter-archiving in Trinidadian literature, where they highlight connections and reconciliations between the self and collective expectations and demands. For example, in *Witchbroom* (1992), Lawrence Scott's novel and epic tale of a family saga living in the island of Kairi (a fictionalised version of Trinidad), African and tassa drums are numerously mentioned throughout, often in hyperbolic and evocative references where the tassa drum rocks the archipelago (90) and physically shapes the geography. As Lucy Evans notes, "[a]ttuned to the culturally diverse musics of calypso's 'steel drums' (198) and 'Hosay with tassa drums' (208)", Lavren narrates the history of the family across six generations in a documenting endeavour in which the nation is imagined and explored through music (Evans 126). In Ingrid Persaud's *Love After Love* (2020), a novel that also deals with queer love and a queering of the traditional family model, it is the drum in a religious Hindu ceremony to Kali that initiates a moment of healing and awakening for Betty Ramdin, whose faith in Christianity starts to waver as she confronts the societal stance on queer love from sectors of the Christian community she is a part of. She finds comfort and epiphany in/through the drum: "[f]or the first time in I can't tell you how long I smiled from my heart. I wanted to vibrate, to dance away all the worries I was holding. In that crowded, loud, smoky temple I suddenly felt strong. I let the drum beat rock me until the energy, the Shakti, was flowing through my veins ... Whatever was going to happen would happen. I surrender" (343). The healing qualities of the drumbeats are also evoked in the classic novel *No Pain Like this Body* (1971), by Harold Sonny Ladoo, where the Indian tassa drum features as a force of hope and possibility in the playing of Nanny, the best drummer in Tola (46), who drums for her dying grandson Rama: "she beated the drum slowly ... Nanny swayed from side to side as if she was trying hard to make the drum talk" (46). The drum's vibration and rhythm are equally powerfully emulated in the repetition and onomatopoeic word choice, creating a connecting riff in the narrative. As in some of these literary examples, where the rhythm of drums pushes or challenges the narrative forward, in Cozier's *Tropical Night*, rhythm stresses process and ongoing movement. The images in the series invite viewers to get lost in the open and shifting vocabularies, to also surrender to the intuitive moments of introspection and connection like Betty in *Love After Love*.

"LITTLE GESTURES WITH NOTES" AND "AFRO-OPHELIA"

"Little Gestures with Notes", a drawing from *Tropical Night* (see Fig. 3.4), features a peera (also spelled "pirha" or "peerha"), "a low wooden bench used as a seat" (Weiner 699).[21, 22] This image appears in other drawings, superposed to objects such as maps. A familiar object in Trinidad, the peera can be seen being used in different festivities and Hindu ceremonies as well as in markets, kitchens, and other spaces of the home or the streets.[23] Through its inclusion in *Tropical Night*, Cozier explores the material history, currency, and visual literacy of this familiar object with origins in India and whose use marks the act of travel and transmigration of indentured labourers to the Caribbean. A statement in *KMAC*'s website (Kentucky Museum of Arts and Craft), where Cozier's installation titled "Little Gestures" (2011) formed part of the group exhibition *Into the Mix* (2012), states that the peera "symbolizes a re-evaluation of what we think we know, a reexamination yielding the surprise of resultant new knowledge and point-of-view".[24] Writing about the use of this image, Cozier notes how this bench is what people

> use to do simple humble daily things like weeding a garden or vending at the side of the road or shining a shoe and so on. It's often portable and is often intriguingly worn or weathered into shape by use over extended periods of time. I feel that these little gestures are the foundation of a global economic reality that is not seen for what it is. Often it is discussed as some kind of inefficient or errant form. A messy problem to be corrected or reformed. (Kentucky Museum of Arts and Craft)

Although a physical large peera is materially present in the museum's space for every installation and new iteration of *Tropical Night*, inviting rest and contemplation, the peera is also a bench of work and busy labour, used whilst cooking or during other tasks and work, which complicates this new contextualisation and association in the museum.

In a conversation with Nicholas Laughlin, Cozier describes how for him drawing is akin to a "thought process" of which writing becomes an integral part ("Notebook" 21). At times, the writing in *Tropical Night*'s

Fig. 3.4 Christopher Cozier, detail from *Tropical Night*, 2006–ongoing, *Little Gestures with Notes*; ink, rubber stamps and graphite on paper, 9 × 7 in. Image courtesy of the artist

drawings is undecipherable as it is superposed to the visual image, consequently blurring the text. The inclusion of writing in the drawings, and their mediation, highlights the complication of narrative for Cozier, as he wants to open the realm of signification through privileging the personal. Superposed to this image of the peera is a written text that occupies the entire page. The strong brown colour of the peera, and the softer sepia brown in the background, hinder any potential unravelling of the text, at least in its entirety. Sections of writing in this drawing are placed upside down curtailing viewers' possibilities of reading the whole text. The overwhelming visual excess of writing in "Little Gesture with Notes", a drawing that is part of the first series (Fig. 3.4), simultaneously reveals and conceals. It confronts viewers with the problematic of narratology. How to communicate a personal account of memory that necessarily relies on the configuration of an individual visual vocabulary under the pressure of other narratives? Cozier affirms how, with *Tropical Night*, "I'm trying to get rid of the rhetorical, get rid of all the familiar symbolism, and see if I can arrive at new signs, new symbols. I'm basically extending and expanding the vocabulary" (Cozier qtd. in Laughlin, "Notebook" 21). Cozier's conceptual vocabulary relies on exploring issues by introducing familiar objects and visual signs in various guises, and finding new ways of articulating or rather investigating people's relationships to them, including his own.

The resulting sense of indeterminacy produced by the visual obstructions to the text interferes with viewers' encounters with the familiar and the unfamiliar, depending on who is looking. This poetics of writing to disguise, and the act of overwriting is an aesthetic element of *Tropical Night* that shows a resistance to transparency whilst fostering an open approach to the artwork. The excess and restricted legibility of "Little Gestures with Notes" ultimately emphasises the centrality of the object. The peera stands out in the drawing demanding that viewers consider it also on its own. The cultural and material history of this object is linked to indenture as well as a type of labour and artisanship that may contrast with the logic and image of capitalism embedded in the imagery of the oil industry in Trinidad, but which is entangled with the economic inequalities that the industry and global economies of extraction perpetuate, a theme recurrent in Cozier's art, and especially present in artworks such as *Laocoon* (2012) or *Gas Men* (2014). The peera also alludes to the work of the market seller, barber, carpenter, and other artisans who use it to work on various traditional arts and trades and the "little gestures" that

Cozier refers to. Recurrent in Cozier's work, the peera also appears in some of the smaller and larger drawings from Cozier's mixed media series *In Development* (2013). In "Red, White & Blue", one of the large drawings in the series, viewers can see a small peera next to words that read "small time". Above it, Cozier places a breeze-block pattern, a distinctive symbol that often decorates the top of concrete middle-class house and garden walls in Port of Spain, next to a note that counters the peera's by stating "big time". The contrasting notions of "big" and "small time" allude to what the small bench and breeze block may connote from a capitalist perspective likely to privilege materiality and signs of economic success, marked as "big time", over artisanship, labour and critical artistic practice.[25]

Some drawings in *Tropical Night* make explicit references to more contemporary processes of documenting history, especially through vehicles like the media, a practice that Cozier problematises in *Wait Dorothy Wait*, as seen in Chapter 2. The drawing "Afro Ophelia" documents the death of Beverly Jones who was shot by the military on 13 September 1973. Jones was a young female member of the National United Freedom Fighters (NUFF), which was actively fighting towards the improvement of socio-economic conditions and the end of class privilege in the 1970's Black Power Revolution (see Fig. 3.5). An image of Jones, dead, lying on the ground was published in the front page of Trinidadian daily newspapers including the *Express*. Cozier, who was deeply affected by the image, explains how for him "there was a temptation to go into the public archives to find that front-page image of the young woman shot on the forest floor but its reshaping and fluidity in memory seemed to be more capable in some way of saying something as well. It could become a way of owning that memory ..." (*Tropical Night* blog).

The drawing echoes Millais' pre-Raphaelite painting *Ophelia*, which appeared in the Nelson Reader that Cozier describes as, "a book through which formal English was conveyed to me as a child" ("One Narrative Thread"). "Afro-Ophelia" counters the archival absence of the active participation of women in the movement (Pasley 1), whilst it grieves another loss in Beverly Jones' death in 1973 at age seventeen and addresses the government's repression of the revolution. The revolution started in 1968 with a series of protests and organising by Caribbean activists, writers and students in Canada and Trinidad, a bus strike in 1969, and solidarity marches throughout 1970 with increasing participation from Indo-Trinidadians. In April of 1970, many of the movement's

Fig. 3.5 Christopher Cozier, detail from *Tropical Night*, 2006–ongoing, *Afro-Ophelia*; ink, rubber stamps and graphite on paper, 9 × 7 in. Courtesy of the artist

members were arrested and Eric Williams declared a state of emergency. This led to disillusionment in previous struggle and the guerrilla organisation NUFF was formed operating from 1971–1976 in the hills of Trinidad. Jones was killed during a confrontation with the Trinidad and Tobago's regiment in the Caura-Lopinot hills. They imprisoned Beverly's sister, Jennifer Jones, also fighting in the guerrilla. Both women, together with their other sister Altheia Jones-Lacointe, who had migrated to the United Kingdom and became a key member of the Black Panthers in London, were part of a long tradition of Black women whose anti-racist activism firmly destabilised patriarchal and colonial structures, and did so through participation in both local and transnational networks and affiliations, as W. Chris Johnson demonstrates in "Guerrilla Ganja Gun Girls: Policing Black Revolutionaries from Notting Hill to Laventille". Victoria Pasley has equally highlighted the vital contributions of women to the political struggle of the Black Power movement and guerrilla fighting. Pasley draws attention to the silences in documenting the involvement of women whilst pointing out the ways in which the movement challenged the remnants of colonial patterns.

> [t]he Black Power Revolution in Trinidad in 1970 presented a serious challenge to the dominant cultural ideology based mainly on a European model, which had, to a large extent, been left intact from the colonial era ... Despite the government's achievement of providing increased access to education, it had not fulfilled many of the other promises of independence. Institutionalized racism remained. (25)

Through a series of published interviews with key leaders and members of the movement, Chike Pilgrim offers an oral history record of the Black Power Movement in Trinidad. Two of the participants were Liseli Daaga (founding member of the National Women's Action Committee)[26] and Josanne Leonard (student activist in 1970, now journalist in Port of Spain).[27] Daaga stresses the ways in which the actions of the Black Power Movement were deeply concerned, amongst other things, with issues around the uneven historical representation of people of African descent in Trinidad and Tobago (332). Leonard, speaking about her father's involvement in the movement (the Indo-Trinidadian trade unionist Winston Leonard), notes how despite the movement's active organising and urgent purpose of reform which reached "all over the country", it was "not debated in the media ... it happened outside of how we think we should know about what is going on in society" (376). If the Black Power Revolution/Movement has later received significant critical attention from artists, writers, and scholars, the NUFF has received less engagement. Aside from some calypsos and a few academic studies, Johnson notes that "[t]he story of NUFF ... remains a relative mystery among many scholars of the African Diaspora as well as scholars of radical twentieth-century social movements" (664). These testimonies prove further the ways in which media, official records, and the public sphere can contribute to processes of silencing and erasure within the national space. In choosing not to revisit the newspaper image from the archives, and in including his own rendering of that memory, Cozier's drawing also destabilises the role of the daily newspapers in documenting aspects of the defeat of the movement (as in the shocking image reporting Jones' death) whilst having at an earlier time omitted and kept outside of their remit media coverage and debate around the movement (Fig. 3.6). Patricia J. Saunders points out the linkage between the reference to the Nelson Reader and the allusion to the image of Jones in the daily's front page: "[i]n much the same way that the *Nelson Reader* instructs readers in the rules of grammar, daily newspapers effectively remind their readers of the rules of political and social engagement, as well as the consequences of breaking those rules" (ch. 6). "Afro-Ophelia" challenges pre-established expectations and norms of reading and relating to dominant visual and written rhetoric in spaces of the national public sphere.

The drawings of *Tropical Night* reflect what Nicholas Laughlin defines as Cozier's form of "taking note" of one's surrounding reality and present moment ("Notebook" 21). The wide range of memories and histories documented and archived in the series emerges from Cozier's sense that historically, in Trinidad, there has not been enough institutional support to give a platform to individual (and collective) ways of expressing one's relationship to place, its past and present history outside official national frameworks. *Tropical Night* claims a personal and individual perspective of Caribbean history and the contemporary moment. Annie Paul defines Cozier's work as "extremely local" and yet relevant and relatable in other contexts with similar histories ("The Enigma" 60). The imagery of the drawings: human figures seemingly trapped in fenced enclosures, half submerged in water, or pressed down by images of cake slices or Oxford sets of mathematical instruments, or inverted podiums, contrast with the tropicalised and colourfully bright tradition of painting that used to be predominant in most art galleries of Port of Spain, as

Fig. 3.6 Christopher Cozier, *Tropical Night* sequence, 2006–ongoing; ink, rubber stamps and graphite on paper, 9 × 7 in. Image courtesy of the artist

Cozier's *Wait Dorothy Wait* critiques. However, if many of these visual signs become unfamiliar in the context of traditional visual representations of the Caribbean, through tropicalised lenses, many of the cultural, material, and physical references to the urban landscape are highly recognisable for Trinbagonians and citizens from other Caribbean locations with a similar history and culture. Equally, Cozier is weary of the imposition of narrative on his practice, and has expressed certain unease at how some images in his work have been interpreted through a historical lens that links them to slavery, without considering other readings, and present systems of oppression ("Christopher Cozier" 66). The hybridity in the visual imaginary of the series is both inscribed in locality and the cultural specificity of Port of Spain (and also various other locations such as Johannesburg, South Africa, and Haiti where Cozier was involved in several art initiatives in the early 2000s). Yet the readability of that imaginary can travel across geographies within and across the Caribbean region and the Global South, connecting postcolonial realities of inequality, or popular culture as resistance in the paradigm of racial capitalism. In this sense, the drawings in *Tropical Night* are reflective of the sense of cultural hybridity theorised by Shalini Puri in *The Caribbean Postcolonial* (2004) that documents the political aspects of Caribbean hybrid aesthetics as they are configured and constantly reconfigured (which in *Tropical Night* is seen through its ongoing nature and makeup) in relation to public space and community.

Some of the aspects characteristic of Cozier's body of work, such as the use of writing, and its archival drive in the reappearance of images and visual signs, has increased over the years. For example, the full-page writing in some of the drawings of *Tropical Night* is echoed and interwoven in complex turbine and vortex shapes and effects in the ink drawings of series like *Entanglements* (2015) (with some images and details evolving from the series *The Arrest* and the installation video *Gas Men*).[28] Some of the conceptualisation and writing in *The Arrest, Dark Circles* and *dig & fly* (2013–2019)[29] also comes from notebooks.[30] In an article in *AGNI*, Cozier includes excerpts of notebook entries that inspired (and are featured in) the writing in his work; these reveal both the lyricism and the free flow of thought (with a kind of stream of consciousness style). In fragments, these lines resemble phrases that could be overheard in people's conversations in the street and in deeply personal reflections, many of these on the economies of extraction, dominant in Cozier's most recent work to date: "*So it's really about the ongoing turbulence of fossil-fuel futures—this Big Ban and unfolding of flying fragments*" ("Dark Cycles/Circles" 139). Both the cursive writing contorted in dynamic shapes from these series is captured in the commissioned installation *turbulence* (2019–2021), which was exhibited in the 2021 11th edition of the Liverpool Biennial, dedicated to memorialising British ports and cities like Liverpool and their involvement in the slave trade under the name *The Stomach and the Port*.

The visualisation of the whole series of drawings in *Tropical Night* and its polyphonic fugal aesthetic demonstrate a shifting of narrative that privileges heteroglossia in which the meaning of the series' visual vocabulary remains unfixed as it is constantly moving in dialogical formations of call-and-response. According to Grant H. Kester, dialogical art facilitates a "space in which certain questions can be asked, certain critical analyses articulated, that would not be accepted or tolerated elsewhere" (68).[31] *Zong!* and *Tropical Night* are examples of dialogical art where a synaesthetic form of heteroglossia counters the limitations of the colonial and postcolonial fixed narratives. The fugue in *Zong!* and *Tropical Night* creates a logic of assembling and archiving fragments of memory and "little gestures". This visual ordering of words and images questions the possibility of narrating histories of oppression cohesively or assertively as so many accounts and experiences remain obscured or less known. It also reflects visually and conceptually the haunting effect of loss, censorship, and unaccountability.

ZONG!'S FUGAL AESTHETICS
AND THE POETICS OF FRAGMENTATION

A wide range of word and word clusters populate the pages of *Zong! as Told to the Author by Setaey Adamu Boateng* in a variety of combinations, creating multiple blank spaces between them. Philip's long elegiac poem commemorates the lives of the Africans who were thrown overboard the slave ship *Zong* in 1781 in what is known as the Zong massacre. These words in the poem are extracted from *Gregson v. Gilbert*, a legal document regarding the dispute that took place between the ship's owners (Gregson) and the insurers (Gilbert) after the massacre, in a court case at the Court of King's Bench in 1783. New words also emerge in *Zong!* from the recombination of those from *Gregson v. Gilbert*. This short document of two and a half pages does not deem the drowning of the Africans aboard the ship as murder but deals instead with the legal battle between parties over a claim of payment for the loss of 132 Africans referred in the document as economic loss of property, reproducing the dehumanising terminology and discourse of the slave trade (*Zong!* 210–211). After reading and researching the history of the massacre aboard the Zong, Philip decided to go to the archive and read *Gregson v Gilbert*, which is held at the National Maritime Museum, in London. In response to the murder of the enslaved and the violence of its portrayal as a justified mercantile decision under the logic of the slave trade, *Zong!* dismembers the text of this record, unravelling a polyphony of voices resulting in an effect akin to what Anna Reckin identifies as "sound-spaces" in the poetry of Kamau Brathwaite (Reckin 1–16), whilst simultaneously also representing silences visually, marked in the gaps between words.

The visual signs and sketches conveyed in the drawings of *Tropical Night* privilege Cozier's own personal memories and impressions of contemporary life in Port of Spain. However, these memories and impressions are always tied to the past in the sense that they re-examine its influence and impact on the present, especially the unfulfilled promises of Trinidad and Tobago's Independence in the individual and collective psyche. Through their compositional, dialogical *process*, both *Zong!* and *Tropical Night* make available to viewers, readers, and audiences a *space* to participate in the conceptual, ethical, and spiritual aspects of the works. A space for thinking through and breathing together, which Philip has theorised in recent critical reflections on *Zong!*. The counter-archival practice of recording such processes in both artists' notebooks becomes a vital archival intervention that responds to a series of silences and erasures in various official archival records of the slave trade, the colonial project, and its aftermath.

Since its publication in 2008, M. NourbeSe Philip's *Zong!* has received extensive critical attention. Scholars and critics have discussed *Zong!*'s poetry of remembrance and mourning (Fehskens) as well as its performative intervention and hauntology (De Ferrari, Reed), the interconnection between text and performance and exploration of the archival dimension of the poem has also been discussed widely (Lambert; Moore; Sharpe; J. Sharpe; Siklosi). The poetics of *Zong!* have been described as "poetics of reparation" by Laurie Lambert (108), as "poetics of unsaying" (49), and poetics of "voiced silence" by Anthony Reed, who cites Philip's phrase from *She Tries Her Tongue; Her Silence Softly Breaks* (46). In various publications, Philip herself has used the term "poetics of the fragment" ("The Ga(s)p" 39; "In Conversation" 91–92) in relation to *Zong*. The breadth of Philip's long poem encompasses all these forms of poetics and places the relationship between form, content and context as a vital one. My discussion and analysis of the poem draws from this rich and varied corpus of critical discussion of *Zong!*, but departs from their focus slightly and considers instead the role of Philip's compositional process and its own documentation in the Notanda section as powerful counter-archive of slavery and its aftermath.

In her essay "The Ga(s)p" (2018), Philip discusses the role of breath and breathing as an ethical and "radical act of hospitality" that first starts in the womb where the mother breathes for her unborn child/children, the first requirement for life experienced by, and bonding, all humanity (31). However, Philip points out the ways in which those acts were further complicated in the forced pregnancies of enslaved women, and of life into bondage as contingent and not simply defined by the act of breathing as both sign of life in the womb (being breathed for) and outside the womb (breathing for oneself) for "[b]irth, however, does not necessarily entail survival or life" (36). Philip asks "[h]ow then do we begin to think about shared breath, circular breath or circle breath in the context of force—historical (enslavement) and contemporary" (36). Philip's essay, which was initially delivered as a keynote speech as part of SUNY's series of Robert Creeley Lectures on Poetry and Poetics, is also a response to Nathaniel Mackey's lecture and essay (in the same collection) where he elaborates on the notion of circular breath in the poetry of the Mountain poets in connection with breath in Black music, particularly jazz. Philip, in dialogue with Mackey, proposes a different conceptualisation of breath: "I would argue that it becomes imperative to lodge the poetics of breath as identified by Mackey in the Black female imaginary" (36). Through this imaginary, Philip connects Mackey's poetics of breath further with the poetics of the fragment, present in *Zong!* Describing its compositional process, Philip explains how the arrangement of words on the pages "can never come directly below another word or word cluster, and there is a constant movement upward to the surface of the previous line. For breath" (39). Breath and the search for breath are significantly at the centre of *Zong!* and, as Philip notes, the various sections in the poem: "Sal", "Ventus", "Ratio", and "Ferrum", all reflect that search for "a space in the line above so as to breathe" (39). The space that the work creates is one that the author shares with readers through the text and with audiences in collective readings.

> When I perform *Zong!*, I allow the words and word clusters to breathe for I' n I –for the we in us that epigenetically we carry within the memory of our cells. When I invite the audience to read with me, we collectively engage in breathing for the Other—for those who couldn't breathe—then
> can't now
> and, perhaps, won't be able to.
> In doing so we give them a second life
> I can't breathe;
>   I will breathe for you.   (Philip, "The Ga(s)p" 39)

In "Breath and Precarity" and "The Ga(s)p", both Mackey (13) and Philip (32, 34) refer to Eric Garner's final words before he was murdered whilst in a chokehold by Daniel Pantaleo, an NYPD officer in 2014. The sentence "I can't breathe" has been uttered by African-American men murdered by US police force including George Floyd, whose lynching by Minneapolis police officer Derek Chauvin on 25 May 2020 was recorded on camera and mobilised major protests across the United States and globally. For Philip, critical work on notions of breath and precarity (as well as silence and amnesia) in regard to colonial history and anti-Black racism have developed over years of continued critical engagement with social issues and her own writing, especially with *Zong!*. After its publication in 2008, Philip continued to reflect on the poem, keeping notebooks on various elements, doing public and durational collective readings as in the annual commemoration of the massacre in November. In a keynote talk for the 2020 Hammed Shahidian Lecture, organised by the Women and Gender Studies Institute, directed by Alissa Trotz, at the University of Toronto, Philip also discussed breath and the radical act of love in breathing for the unborn during pregnancy, connecting that radical act to the notion of breathing with others and for others, with all its political connotations, including the victims of the massacre and victims of anti-Black violence.[32]

In an interview I conducted with Philip, she stressed that beyond the formal aesthetics of *Zong!*—which is also key to the poem—there is the issue of ethics, and the idea of breath (and breathing with and for others) at its centre:

To return to the idea of the breath—consider that we all, each and every one of us, have had someone breathe for us—in utero. I believe that we all have a memory of that act of radical hospitality—breathing for another being or being breathed for? There's a sense in which when we perform *Zong!* we're breathing for those people who were aboard the ship, who were unable to breathe—just for that moment we're breathing, just like women breathe for their children in the womb. It was *Zong!* that got me thinking about this. In terms of contemporary politics: the issue for me is how do we breathe with others and for others? For me, that's where this work has to go. It can't be just formal aesthetics; it has to take us to places where we understand those demands, encourage us to think about and act on the ways in which women, Indigenous peoples, people of color and Black people can learn to breathe again, metaphorically of course, after having the breath squeezed out in so many different ways. ("In Conversation" 95)[33]

For Philip, breath becomes a sign of a connection (also epigenetically marked) between the author and the ancestors. A strong connection also develops amongst audiences in collective readings as the experience of reading the text together means that the time left between the reading of every word marks a space to breathe, and to pause. It makes space for, and acknowledges, the gap and the silence, as well as the lives lost. When read in unison during readings, it creates a particular sonic and oral/aural effect as attendees are invited by Philip to read the text aloud at their own speed, (often with the reminder of breathing in the spaces between words) which results in a polyphonic chorus of voices that, blending together, reproduce the vibration of a religious or spiritual prayer. I participated in a reading and Living Memorial for the victims of the Zong Massacre at Virginia Key Beach, Miami, in October 2018, part of the program of the 37th Annual West Indian Literature Conference celebrated at the University of Miami. The memorial also marked the tenth anniversary of *Zong!*'s publication. Philip initiated the beginning of the reading with the sounding of a bell, as is common in many collective readings of the work, referencing the Baptist faith tradition of Trinidad and Tobago. A ceremonial dance and public ritual by choreographer, dancer, and scholar Yanique Hume also accompanied the event. Philip's instructions for this reading emphasised individual pace and rhythm when reading a selection of poems and sections of the larger poem as a large circle of attendees gathered around Philip and Hume and held hands whilst moving in a circular motion that resembled the dynamics of circular breath and generated a strong sense of energy felt spiritually and physically by many, as participants afterwards remarked. The location of the reading was significant in historical connections. Virginia Key Beach Park is a site marked by the history of racial segregation in Florida where from the 1920s beach areas across Miami were exclusively reserved for whites. African Americans defied those policies through acts of subversion and from 1945 Virginia Key Beach Park was established as an African-American and coloured beach for Miami Dade County, after a group of Black men and men of colour decided to enter the water in Baker's Haulover Beach in North Dade County and swim there, defying the physical demarcations established by the US government and segregation-based legislature. The poetics of place in the space for the collective reading was meaningful, as was the circular form of the reading, encircling a tree around which Hume was moving in space and dance and interacting with Philip. Hume, a scholar of African Caribbean dance, religion and spirituality incorporated the practice of ritual and improvisation, moving and dancing in sync and response to the poem, and in the space. A copy of the book was covered in white cloth and was placed at the centre of the circle. Participants had also been invited to wear white to the event. When it reached an end, many participants were given a red rose to be thrown into the sea, as ritual of remembrance. This reading and performance was videorecorded, as many others have been before, creating a digital archive and repository of the poem in its performative afterlives. The living memorial extended the possibilities for remembrance, and the geographic and temporal bounds of the massacre, being so close to the water of the Atlantic made its history even more present.

On 6 September 1781 the slave ship *Zong* sets sail from the West Coast of Africa to Jamaica transporting 470 enslaved Africans. Luke Collingwood, the captain of the ship, not being an expert mariner but someone who served as a surgeon on previous slave ships, miscalculates the route and as a result the journey lasts four months instead of six to nine weeks, the usual length of this transatlantic journey. The unexpected delay affects provisions of water and, as a result, Africans die of illness and dehydration. Captain Collingwood, who is familiar with the legal workings of the trade, decides that there might be a chance to recuperate the financial loss of cargo by throwing slaves overboard. Collingwood argues that only when the loss of cargo is the result of "natural death" are the owners of the slave ship legally bound to meet the costs. He maintains that, on the other hand, if the death is provoked, the insurers, Messrs Gilbert, could be made financially liable for the loss. In light of these arguments, he makes the decision of throwing 132 slaves overboard with the pretext of saving water for the sustenance of all aboard the ship. After Collingwood's return to Liverpool, William, James, and John Gregson, co-owners of the ship, adhering to maritime insurance law, make a claim against the underwriters and insurers, who refuse payment. This leads to a legal case won by the ship's owners, where the jury's verdict files in favour of financial compensation from Messrs Gilbert, the underwriters. Messrs Gilbert then appeals to the Court of King's Bench, and three justices (Willes, Buller, and Lord Mansfield) reach an agreement for a new trial (*Zong!* 189).

There is, however, no evidence found that indicates that a new trial was ever arranged.

Zong! confronts both the act of violence embedded in the murder of the enslaved and that perpetuated through the silences, omissions, and underlying discourse in *Gregson v. Gilbert* by dissecting, fragmenting, shifting, and un-balancing the authority of the language in this record. All the graphemes, phonemes, words, and word clusters in *Zong!* originate, in some form or other, from *Gregson v. Gilbert*. At times, words in the poems are the same that appear in the document, whilst at other times these words are altered, combined, and/or made into new words, an anagrammatic method that relies on strategies of reordering, splicing, or splitting of words to create a new word (or sets of words). The fragmented aesthetics of *Zong!* not only alludes to, and restages, the trauma experienced by the Africans aboard the *Zong* ship, it also visually reflects the uprootedness experienced by enslaved Africans in the Americas, a subject that Philip explores in *She Tries Her Tongue; her Silence Softly Breaks*. In Philip's own words, in *Zong!*,

> [w]ithin the boundaries established by the poems and their meaning there are silences; within each silence is the poem, which is revealed only when the text is fragmented and mutilated, mirroring the fragmentation and mutilation that slavery perpetrated on Africans, their customs and ways of life. ("Notanda" 195)

The existing gaps between words on the pages of *Zong!*, as well as its overall aesthetics of fragmentation, leave readers wondering. As Philip notes, breath also exists in those spaces between the words, becoming central signifying symbols. Drawing attention towards the anti-narrative pulse of the poem, *Zong!* nevertheless conveys a certain narrative through the shifts of form and linguistic (re)combination and relationality. "*Zong!* is the Song of the untold story; it cannot be told yet it must be told through its un-telling" (Philip, "Notanda" 207). This is the last sentence in "Notanda" and it is a declaration as much as an invitation. In dissecting the narrative of empire and its discursive and material violence, a certain narrative emerges. Both breath and silence become important markers that are made visible in the text to highlight the erasure and epistemic violence of colonial discursive narratives. Édouard Glissant's *poetics of relation* is a helpful concept at stake in the poetics of fragmentation in *Zong!* at the most basic level of signification, in the word and then cluster of words and their interrelation. The existing relationality between the distinct parts in *Zong!* mirror stages in the process of mourning, and simultaneously reflect another process of unlocking (and ultimately) a drowning of the archival record signified in the increased cramping and superposition of words and faded ink in "Ẹbọra", the last section in *Zong!* The progressive shifting of the visual composition marks this parallelism with a process of unlocking the archive—which illuminates the relationship between the section "Os" (Bones) which Philip considers to be "the 'bones' of the overall project" (Reed 51) and the other sections in the poem ("Salt", "Ventus", "Ratio", "Ferrum", and "Ẹbọra").

The first poem "Zong #1" displays a heightened repetition of graphemes and phonemes "w" "a" "t" "er", spread across the top of the page; through an attempt to visually connect the graphemes, the reader can reconstruct the word "water" (3). The onomatopoeic effect in sounding out the poem, and its graphic representation of the historical silencing of the Archive, is expressed visually in the wide spaces between letters and words, as in the hole that appears in the middle of the page. This image of gaps and silences anticipates the communicative role of affect and feeling in an engagement with *Zong!* The word water, evokes the sea as the ultimate site of memory and remembrance, which in Caribbean literature and visual art has been a frequent trope for revisiting history, historiography and claiming counter-histories. The trope of the sea has famously been constructed as a site of memory in Derek Walcott's poem "The Sea is History" where, to the questions "[w]here are your monuments, your battles, and martyrs? / Where is your tribal memory?", a voice replies, "Sirs, / in that gray vault. The Sea. The Sea / has lock them up. The Sea is History" (365).[34] The fragmentation of this first poem will simultaneously continue and change as a shape-shifter throughout the pages. Through the visual fragmentation of the text and the dismemberment of the document *Gregson v. Gilbert*, Philip marks the loss through an elegiac song of sorrow, a lament for the dead.

READERSHIP AND AFFECT: DEFEND THE DEAD

Reading *Zong!* requires that we think and read history against the grain of the Archive; since the historical gaps and silences produced by and through colonial documentation make a recollection of the past impossible. And although no account of the past is fully freed from a subjective angle (to varying degrees), in the case of the colonial archive this issue is doubly poignant and problematic as the Archive itself is dominated by (and implicated in) acts of violence and subjection and the origin of the archival records in the colonies of the West Indies are intimately bound to the control and oppression of Indigenous, enslaved and indentured communities. Scholarship focuses on the limitations that colonial archives pose to historical knowledge as well as the opportunities that they provide for deducing other versions and forms of writing history (Bastian, Aarons and Griffin; Blouin and Rosenberg; Stoler; Baucom; Taylor; Hamilton, Harris, Pickover [et al.]). Ann L. Stoler defines this critical intervention as a "commitment to the notion of reading colonial archives 'against the grain' of imperial history, empire builders, and the priorities and perceptions of those who wrote them" (*Along* 47). Equally, Philip's *Zong!* demands that commitment, and also points to the rejection of a search for meaning, especially not through the parameters of European or Anglo-centric knowledge and thinking.

Myriam Moïse highlights the role of readership in *Zong!* and argues that Philip's poem "challenges the reader to reconsider the established order, to see beyond imposed limits, as she deliberately seeks to reconstruct history, to voice the unspeakable and to extend the limits of memory" (23). This reconstruction of history consequently entails an emotional immersion in the text, an affective turn that is also facilitated by its poetics of fragmentation and fugal aesthetics. In *She Tries Her Tongue; Her Silence Softly Breaks* Philip's poetry embarks on a deep exploration of reading by questioning assumed and inherited models of understanding the relationship between language and experience. As discussed in the previous chapter, Philip's poem "Discourse on the Logic of Language" pushes the boundaries of reading, both literally and symbolically, to the point that one has to physically move the position of the book in order to read the capitalised text at the margin of the vertically placed text. Its contrapuntal aesthetics is guided by fragments within the same and different poems, whose meaning is often intimately bound to each other, creating an interwoven web of kinship through the formation of Caribbean subjectivities. This challenge to pre-established ways of seeing and reading is stretched to its boundaries in *Zong!* where visual fragmentation is significantly more acute. Consequently, in the case of *Zong!*, the vast array of contrapuntal connections that constitute the musical form of the fugue, continue to challenge how we construct and reconstruct meaning. From the first page of *Zong!* readers face the issue of how to read the poems. The seeming dis/order of letters and words across the page confuses the eye. Consequently, a likely initial reaction could be to search for answers and reading cues through the following pages. However, the visual fragmentation of the text extends throughout the poems and grows in crescendo through the other five sections of *Zong!*

Prior to an analysis of the different stages in the sections of *Zong!*, I will briefly discuss "Notanda" and the role of documentaction and note-taking (borrowing the term again from Laughlin's description of Cozier's artistic process as reflection) in the creation of the poem and its afterlife, and as counter-archival account to *Gregson v. Gilbert*. During an interview I had with Philip, she mentioned that journaling had been vital to documenting the process of *Zong!* and also its life after publication, particularly as *Zong!* has been performed and read collectively in memorials of the massacre and durational readings. Philip noted: "I always keep journals that are directly related to the work. I think about these journals as an artist's notebook, where you do sketches and you're working out ideas" ("In Conversation" 88).[35] Philip then gave the example of "Notanda" and added "[i]n the case of *Zong!* I continued to keep a journal after the book was published in 2008, which was helpful in thinking about the work and in trying to understand what it was all about. Of course, I did know what it was about, but there are always other levels to the work that I'm coming to understand" (88–89). The space of the journal therefore keeps record of the process, the author's ongoing relationship with the work and how it transforms and grows out of the page in its performative iterations, as well as in affecting and connecting audiences who read with Philip.

In November 2020, for the anniversary of the Zong massacre and as an alternative to the annual collective readings to mark the event, Philip envisioned and organised *Zong! Global 2020*, an online iteration of the readings that would allow people to participate globally at a time when it was not safe to do so in person due to the COVID-19 pandemic.[36] The readings began on November 30 and ran for 10 days (until December 9) covering the duration of the massacre. They were sequential and covered the whole book.[37] The ten videos were a combination of pre-recorded videos, collective and livestreamed readings, with the participation of a large number of Caribbean scholars and writers including Alissa Trotz, Faizal Deen, Myriam J. A. Chancy, and Rosamond S. King, amongst others. Videos were posted daily on YouTube and viewers would comment live in the comments section and respond on social media to describe their experience of participating in the readings or of watching them from their homes. Whilst they were available for viewing, they comprised a digital open-access archive and record of a longer durational reading of *Zong!* that connects the massacre to the global uprising against anti-Black racism after the lynching of George Floyd on May 25, 2020 attending to the theme "recognition, justice and development" of the 2015 UN declaration of the International Decade for People of African Descent (*Zong! Global 2020*).[38] In an interview following his address during the 2015 UN Remember Slavery initiative, Christopher Cozier shared how creativity had a vital role to play in thinking through many issues surrounding the legacy of slavery. He described a project from the late 1990s that extended to the early 2000s called *Going North*, that engages with the archive of slavery through the image of 'wanted' adverts for formerly enslaved fugitives running North, which he has positioned in the space of installations countering another stencil of a Black man running that evokes notions of crossing borders, citizenship, and (un)belonging.[39] This contrapuntal understanding of the interrelation of those moments in history and their stretched temporalities in relationships to place and space is very much at stake in Cozier's and Philip's art.

The ten videos of *Zong! Global 2020* also featured responses from the participants, most of whom were Black people and people of colour. At the end of recordings, they describe their response to the reading and the way in which they felt connected to everyone else reading simultaneously. The contrapuntal sounding of the words and word clusters being read at slightly different times by participants created a powerful polyphonic effect as did the vibration of all voices reading together. In *Immaterial Archives: An African Diaspora Poetics of Loss* (2020) Jenny Sharpe identifies the spaces between the words in *Zong!* as the spaces that represent or *embody* silence (43, 45), a point similarly made by Philip, who also views breath as existing in those gaps ("The Ga(s)p", "Notanda"). These are spaces generative of affect. They acknowledge the loss and the silence they represent whilst centring the humanity of the ancestors, their life and breath. "Silence is as much a part of language as words" and Philip's process of "fragmenting the words to expose blank spaces of sensations", is also an invitation to listen (J. Sharpe 42–43). On Day 6, Philip read from a few written notes about the experiences of the daily readings, one of which emphasised its emotional and physical impact. Philip reflected on the idea and experience of being involved in such an intense durational reading, in an embodied sense:

> I became aware for the first time of the embodied sense of the extended nature of this massacre ... I felt revulsion at the fact that for 10 days people were methodically thrown overboard, then I understood in the bodily sense, that is, that there are so many levels to knowing and how we consciously un-know certain things the better to survive. (*Zong! Global 2020*)

Philip's notes on the first readings of *Zong! Global 2020*, as in "Notanda", extend the poem. They, too, are a vital extension of *Zong!* and its elegiac process. Note-taking documents and bears witness to the massacre and simultaneously creates a record of its remembrance, which extends now beyond the pages of *Zong!* as discussions and performances have entered the institutional spaces of universities, of schools, cultural and arts centres, and homes.

After reading her notes, Philip read an excerpt from George Lamming's *The Pleasure of Exile* (1960) about the Haitian Ceremony of Souls which he describes as a "drama between religion and the law" (9), and where the dead return to the world of the living to open up a dialogue, a meeting to channel unresolved issues from the past. A ceremony and ritual that Philip connected through her remarks to the daily readings. Philip enacted various rituals from different religious traditions of the African diaspora prior to some of the readings. On Day 6, she rang the Baptist bell, and then poured water in a bowl with red soil from Swaziland to invoke and welcome the ancestors. Philip referenced the copy of *Zong!* wrapped in white cloth and placed in the centre, played a Gankogui bell from Ghana and sang a line from an African song dedicated to Eshu (known also as Elegba or Legba), Yoruba deity and spirit of the Divine messenger, of the crossroads and of spaces of potentiality, in "the hope that they look on us with favour". Finally, Philip poured a libation on the ground asking for the ancestors' blessing once again.

As multiple citations from the text will demonstrate, "Notanda" not only describes the conceptual thinking about and around the poem, its philosophical arc and its process of creation, but it also lays out the spiritual journey and ethical dimensions, and it particularly does so through the extracts from journal entries that shape its form and personal tone, contrasting significantly with the dry language of the colonial Archive, devoid of humanity. The full reproduction of the two-page document *Gregson v. Gilbert* placed at the end of the book, contextualises the poetics of the poem and its aesthetic fragmentation. The document itself reproduces through language and discourse both the physical and linguistic violence of the slave trade and their interrelation in the Imperial project as the murder of the enslaved is never considered in this document. Instead, the emphasis revolves around the enslaved person as commodity, and so does its language. Ian Baucom writes about the *Zong* case in *Specters of the Atlantic: Finance Capital, Slavery and the Philosophy of History*, where he explores in depth the type of discursive violence perpetuated through archival records. Baucom speaks of the violence of "becoming a 'type': a type of person, or, terribly, not even that, a type of nonperson, a type of property, a type of commodity, a type of money" enacted by colonial powers during the trans-Atlantic slave trade (11). The response to the epistemic violence of the English language and the law, drives *Zong!*'s anti-narrative, and it is significantly through language (a visual, fragmentary, and polyphonic language) that *Zong!* takes to court and mutilates the document *Gregson v. Gilbert* in an act of re-vision, a term borrowed from poet Adrienne Rich, for whom re-vision entails "the act of looking back, of seeing with fresh eyes, of entering an old text from a new critical direction" (Rich 983).[40]

Gregson v. Gilbert is at the centre of Philip's *Zong!* and yet the document is also dis-membered and pushed to the margins in what Reed terms, a "de-authorization of language" (46). Its reproduction is placed at the very end of the book, following a glossary to the poems and the section "Notanda" where Philip, as a mode of afterword, discusses her creative process in regard to *Zong!* This physical ordering of text symbolically marks a new archival gesture where the logic of the colonial archive is delegitimised. The authority of this archival record is displaced and challenged. The language of the report, being that of the law, is therefore bereft of any feeling, and in an interview with Patricia J. Saunders, Philip explains her own relationship with the text whereby writing the poems allows her to, "take those hard facts, this desiccated fact situation of *Gregson v. Gilbert* – and you reintroduce those emotions and feelings that were removed" ("Defending the Dead" 66). Philip then likens the act of submerging the document in water as a means of restoring its "dried fibers" as the two-page account of *Gregson v Gilbert* "squeezed out the lives that were at the heart of the case" (66). The opening sentences of the case report demonstrate the ways in which the language and discourse of the British Empire functions as a tool of erasure. Some of the words that are particularly recurrent throughout the elegy appear in the fragment, included below. The contextual meaning of words like "recover", "value", "reason", or "preservation", underline here the pervasive naturalisation of their perceived currency and use within slave trade law and imperial discourse. Their use in the text demonstrates the linguistic rhetoric of dehumanisation embedded in the colonial and imperial Archive.

> This was an action on a policy of insurance, to recover the value of certain slaves thrown overboard for want of water. The declaration stated, that by the perils of the seas, and contrary currents and other misfortunes, the ship was rendered foul and leaky, and was retarded in her voyage; and, by reason thereof, so much of the water on board the said ship, for her said voyage, was spent on board the said ship: that before her arrival at Jamaica, to wit, on, &c. a sufficient quantity of water did not remain on board the said ship for preserving the lives of the master and mariners belonging to the said ship, and of the negro slaves on board, for the residue of the said voyage; by reason whereof, during the said voyage, and before the arrival of the said ship at Jamaica - sixty negroes died for want of water for sustenance; and forty others, for want of water for sustenance, and through thirst and frenzy thereby occasioned, threw themselves into the sea and were drowned; and the master and mariners, for the preservation of their own lives, and the lives of the rest of the negroes, which for want of water they could otherwise not preserve, were obliged to throw overboard 150 other negroes. (*Gregson v. Gilbert* 210)

The use of language here, as in most documents from the transatlantic slave trade, naturalises the contextualisation of *value* as that of goods and not humans. The "value" of the "slaves" firmly remains monetary throughout the entire text. The *"perils of the sea"* are (according to the account of the claim) the ones caused by natural adversities to the insured property, and never to the unnamed Africans enclosed in the hundreds in the belly of the ship, or those who see themselves being thrown to the sea or who supposedly "threw themselves" overboard "voluntarily", as the report suggests (emphasis mine 210). This is never a question of murder, for if the issue may have ever appeared during the initial court case or subsequent appeals to overrule the sentence, the lawyers related to the case stressed the irrelevance of this consideration: "It has been decided, whether wisely or unwisely, is not now the *question*, that a portion of our *fellow-creatures* may become the *subject* of *property*. This, therefore, was a throwing overboard of *goods*, and of part to *save* the residue. The question is, first, whether any *necessity* existed for *that fact*" (emphasis mine, *Gregson v Gilbert* 211). The murder of the slaves is reduced to "that fact", and is thus written out from the account and expressed as nothing other than a "necessity" to "save the residue" (211). The word "reason", which is mentioned twice in the above passage, and several times in the entire document, is particularly haunting in its attampted rationalisation of the massacre and the genocides carried out throughout the period of slavery in the Americas.

Gregson vs. Gilbert, the legal report over the *Zong* case, is not the only written document related to the event. The rest of the documentation related to the *Zong* reveals the transcendence of record keeping and documentation in the success of the imperial project. British abolitionist Granville Sharp compiled archival material related to the *Zong* case: 133 pages of documents of which one of them (located in the middle of the record) is completely blank which, as Erin M. Fehskens observes, is symbolic of the absences and silences typical of much colonial archival documentation (414). Sharp, and African writer and abolitionist Olaudah Equiano (present at the trial), compiled and used these archival documents politically as a means to exemplify publicly the horror of the slave trade and generate consciousness against its social and moral damage. On 23 May 1783, Sharp wrote a letter to William Baker where he expressed his "hope to obtain evidence to commence a critical prosecution ... for murder..." against Luke Collingwood ("Letter to William Baker").[41] Sharpe's statement demonstrates his awareness of the pivotal role of written evidence and documentation in all financial and legal actions associated with the trade, which is evident too in his own "fastidious [and detailed] note keeping", for which he was famous (Fehskens 414). This reliance on the Archive attests to the authorising power that has historically been conferred to record keeping, cataloguing, and the storage of information both in legitimising and perpetuating the slave trade and racial slavery, as well as in the efforts to put an end to it.

The structure of *Zong!* and its division into six distinct sections mirrors the formal structure of the colonial Archive, whilst it parallels different stages and rituals in a process of mourning. This demonstrates the complex ways in which mourning and counter-archiving are bound up and entangled in *Zong!*'s memory work. Paradoxically, by using the archival document, the very tool that negates the dead's humanity and their mourning, Philip facilitates the expression of grief and a subsequent critical engagement with alternative forms of remembrance. The textual heterogeneity embedded in *Zong!* and its experimental use of form are largely facilitated by its genre, the elegy. William Watkin notes that although the elegy is one of the easiest poetic genres to identify, its formal structure varies considerably in each case, leading to the existing lack of consensus, and active debate, on a firm definition of the term and its structure (53). This allows greater freedom to give *form* to grief, which is always a very personal experience (even when its purpose is both individual and collective). However, one thing is clear, "[e]legies do not exist as a form of expression, but as an activity, an intervention and a lasting ritual. Elegy has to do something, this much is agreed upon, but as to what it is, this is very much under dispute" (Watkin 53).

In the case of *Zong!*, elegy enables an interpersonal *process* of mourning in which the author and her readership participate and *act*. This mourning process starts with the identification of the bones, and in the opening section, significantly entitled "Os" (the Latin word for bones), these are also found in the columns of the logbook and the account ledger which are visually simulated in the formal structure of the poems. Realising that *Gregson v. Gilbert* is one place where the enslaved Africans are also buried, where their memories are silenced, Philip decides to use its content as a starting point for *Zong!*. The first section, "Os", which Philip refers to as "the 'bones' of the overall project" (Reed 51) introduces combinations of words dominated by definite articles like "the" or "this", and semantic connections that highlight an expository and nominal dynamic in the writing.

Zong! #2

the throw in circumstance

the weight in want

in sustenance

for underwriters

the loss

the order in destroy

the that fact

the it was

the were

negroes

the after rains

―――――――――――――――――――――――

Wafor Yao Siyolo Bolade Kibibi Kamau

5

The case summary of *Gregson v. Gilbert* states that "several of the slaves died for want of water" (210). In this document, their sustenance is always measured against the loss of their assigned economic value. The construction of human beings as commodities is legitimised by, and through, language and the law. As Philip herself argues,

[t]he language in which those events took place promulgated the non-being of African peoples, and I distrust its order, which hides disorder; its logic hiding the illogic and its rationality, which is simultaneously irrational. However, if language is to do what it must do, which is to communicate, these qualities – order, logic, rationality – the rules of grammar must be present. And, as it is with language, so too with the law. Exceptions to these requirements exist in religious or spiritual communication with nonhuman forces such as gods, or supra-human beings, in puns, parables, and, of course, poetry. ("Notanda," 197)

Zong! rejects the order and logic of colonial language and the boundaries of linguistic coherence are stretched and give shape instead to a vocabulary that visually reflects the violence and mutilation of the *Zong* massacre. This takes place gradually throughout the poem; it is a process that confronts the colonial archival machinery. "Os", the first section of *Zong!*, is visually dominated by the rigid structure of colonial forms of cataloguing. Most significantly, in "Os" ("bones"), naming, which Jacques Derrida argues is essential to the process of mourning and localising the dead (*Specters* 9), appears at the bottom of the page. Names "Masuz Zuwena Ogunsheye Ziyad Ogwambi Keturah" (3) are listed at the bottom of the page of "Zong! #1" as part of the 228 names (mostly Yoruba) that Philip includes in *Zong!* to represent those who were captured and murdered in the massacre (Reed 53). In the sub-section, "Dicta", the names disappear but the separating lines remain, underscoring how the law and the Archive has forced them out of the official written colonial historical record. According to Fehskens, "the account ledger visually and ideologically ghosts the pages of 'Os' and 'Dicta'" (411). Many of the poems in these two initial sections visually reproduce the columns of the account ledger and logbook. This is particularly the case for "Zong! #3" (6), "Zong! #4" (7), "Zong! #9" (17), "Zong! #11" (20), "Zong! #12" (21), and "Zong! #18" (31–32), where two or more columns of words function as reminders of the formal structure of the logbook and ledger. Fehskens notes how, "the ghost of the logbook haunts the cataloguing mode in *Zong!*, dramatizing the irreconcilable tension between violent exchangeability and zealous accumulation" (412). "Os" simulates the form of the logbook and ledger accounts. It also represents one of the initial stages in the mourning process; a sense of denial towards accepting the loss. In this section, voices reproduce the cold and dry language of *Gregson v.*

Gilbert, and words focus on loss of property whilst other voices contra-puntally mark the loss of individuals, rousing readers to "defend the dead" ("Zong! # 15). This contrast is most striking in poems "Zong! #14" and "Zong! #15". In "Zong! #14" (Fig. 3.7) the compositional arrangement of words on the page continues to be a reminder of the columns in the account ledger, as are its authoritative language and declamations:

Zong! #14

the truth was

        the ship sailed

        the rains came

        the loss arose

               the truth is

the ship sailed

the rains came

the loss arose

               the negroes is

the truth was

Fig. 3.7 M. NourbeSe Philip, "Zong! #14", *Zong! as Told to the Author by Setaey Adamu Boateng,* 2008, p. 24. Image courtesy of the artist

The word clusters in the three columns or blocks (starting from the left) establish the order and consequence of facts as they appear in *Gregson v. Gilbert*. "Zong! #23" (see Fig. 3.8) remains illustrative of the categorising structure of the ledger and the semantic relationship between words is highlighted in order to question their meaning, almost emptying it. Phrases like, "the weight in being", underscore the relationality of a term like being, its conditionality in the context of the legal framework of the slave trade, particularly as those involved in the legal dispute of the *Zong* case attempt to erase the humanity of the murdered Africans.

In "Sal", the salt alludes to sea water but also to the tears of the "oba", a Yoruba word meaning "ruler" and "king" which often appears in this and subsequent sections. The only words on page 59 are "water parts / the *oba* sobs". This section also introduces a wider variety of words and in different languages. Overall *Zong!* features words, phrases and sentences in Arabic, Dutch, English, Fon, French, Greek, Hebrew, Italian, Latin, Portuguese, Spanish, Shona, Twi, West African Patois and Yoruba. All the languages of the colonial powers and those involved in the history of enslavement are entangled in this song as well as those African languages that colonial powers erased through laws that prohibited their use in the Caribbean. Now the words seem to float on the page and the various songs are not divided in numbers but form instead an organic whole where the "Ifá" is invoked in a call to African spiritual forces and ancestors, opening thus other channels of communication. Many of the word clusters in "Sal" combine the Latin word "salve" and "save" in relation to the bones; "save us *os* / salve" and "salve / & save / our souls tone" (63). The sensation of movement and visual rhythm provided by the compositional arrangement and expansion of words in "Sal" continues in the following section "Ventus", where words form various shapes that are constantly shifting. These shapes are visually highly reminiscent of maps, especially maps of Great Britain and the American continent. This can be most easily appreciated on pages 98 and 82. (see Fig. 3.9.)

This intuitive allusion to maps locates the poem at the crossing of the Middle Passage, representing the moment of uprootedness from Africa. On page 98 of *Zong!* a shape slightly resembles the map of Britain through the combination of isolated words and word clusters, and at the centre of the page one can read the word "mourns", which leads to the final section of *Zong!*, "Ẹbọra", meaning "underwater spirits in the Yoruba language" (184). The complete disintegration of *Gregson v.*

Zong! #23

was

      the weight in being

      the same in rains

      the ration in loss

      the proved in fact

      the within in is

      the sufficient in indictment

      the might have in existed

is

      the evidence in negroes

Moleye Maideyi Ibeyemi Nobini Olonade Bunmi

40

Fig. 3.8 M. NourbeSe Philip, "Zong! #23", *Zong! as Told to the Author by Setaey Adamu Boateng*, 2008, p. 40. Image courtesy of the artist

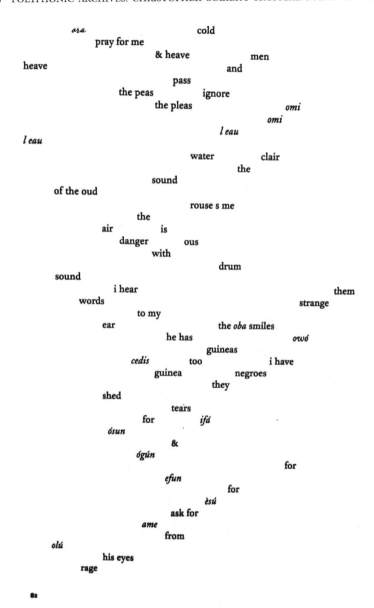

Fig. 3.9 M. NourbeSe Philip, "Ventus", *Zong! as Told to the Author by Setaey Adamu Boateng*, 2008, p. 82. Image courtesy of the artist

Gilbert is enacted symbolically and literally as most words in the document cease to haunt and populate pages and the elegy fades, very literally, as the ink in the print of the text is discoloured. Many words are then superposed and thus erase each other. (see Fig. 3.10).

COUNTER-ARCHIVING AND DIALOGIC SPACES

In *Zong!* and *Tropical Night*, acts of counter-archiving engage in a meta-discursive process. The awareness of the fixity and limit of inherited vocabularies of experience leads to speculative semiotics that point to seemingly discrepant combinations of, often shifting, signs. For example, in *Tropical Night* the superposition of maps as influential visual records and tools of the project of imperial expansion and coloniality is variously superposed to other visual signs such as the peera, a cake, a blackboard, or a flag, amongst others. Cozier elaborates a simultaneously highly personal and collective visual vocabulary of experience. Although these signs evoke the history of colonial oppression and geopolitics today, they sometimes seem to disappear in the background. Their currency is acknowledged but not privileged. Cozier maps out his own relationship to places, especially Port of Spain but also the larger Caribbean region and multiple international locations, by creating a mosaic of visual signs that form part of his social and cultural context. Many of the drawings in Cozier's series show images that are very familiar to Caribbean people; one of the best examples is the "breeze" brick wall, a recurrent motif in Cozier's *oeuvre*. In the specific context of Trinidad and Tobago the brick can be identified, as Nicholas Laughlin argues, as a 1970s post-Independence marker of economic status and promises of development as it decorates the front walls of many middle-class residences ("Work in Process").[42] The breeze block appears in large drawings from the 1990s, as well as *Tropical Night* and it became a participatory art project (*Dpatterns*) part of *In Development* and Cozier's solo exhibition at David Krut Projects in New York, 2013.[43] Cozier's arts practice reveals his own archival drive, as images like the human head appear in various forms in 1990s artwork like *Blue Soap* and *The Madman's Rant*, later in *Tropical Night* and most recently in the installation *New Level Head(s)* at the group exhibitions *Relational Undercurrents: Contemporary Art of the Caribbean Archipelago* (2017)[44] and *The Sea is History* (2019).[45] Further, the influence of previous work on one also translates into materiality and design. Cozier's installation *turbulence*, 2019–2021, included in the 2021 Liverpool Biennial follows

found   afonoghore lakawas   gin my us   in affic?
y/our ear   a rovadnapiggrothhnyace   rum   my faith negroes
thyrgosere aster/s oh oh   ode wignotem cam fo.mfound africa the mast must be teak men
ateclatinthe deed underwho can cure me   supaishosopfafnopain
volaics &   watcnptaiover   for yothe cur   that that   proved
     justisheng thwnetisom   demgarraidefor je ifa that hat
thevm   the kewmy liegknherd deep   pour nifai life cut the cards
     days   parorime°°   nfirligrdig fonder from ifa i   I won the throw
wojeks   my plea is negligemibgfiindhe fiohdher sos sonfsthtagas sofghhhgpluce
fa   unynfake   from us   i say   of whtabsdempedoge
comes forteoarno   for osmortafdy fahhbhgtmanwrosaces   she smiles
cut her open in livall be fromndsrjustice stare don be   bsmile
the noise niber cortlens thersuwickinleds l   in lives& am   a dischfarge
itridahtthhe omort as thhronis   oveam savetasoching   throw fhbhng
     le p'tit mthe crew woghihyoufahhhdlrentamfssloy   Rmth   throw them
                 cfcalit of mortality in rations munder sthnte is fatecrusts
but why fluthe noisesum   am   tone & filmce fhe seerthere is creed
     tharbones she do the stars   appfeatig nig if shine there isunder   if only
           & fipls inmotder mifde us   & ynog vdhorbysmay aide   oh oh
her shapifaifaifa   salve our souls thefohaerofmezgain
    with mipt anfabltinge   if only ifa   nag tasodabstense   ifa ifa ifa i
serve   round   bbnmesamba   is all wrongport   the the oba sobs again
and fitnaseermen   rum rath might   ovfrere was piss cum
seas   more rum   &mihfhathehiigacgamglgbo Ruth
firjamtves   thisutihtsfhnmsomora   salve the slave   they sang &
     withaltfotusjem and and   mydentades   sanghe vrinodtwith sinwe map
    uncommdnesdeisaplmoasalve   ora proyou sdyal huxighteraiwater/s leak   time
    vidshervtdgroddeo   withine a seamdtfsfickeslapig   putuashlesfobrethebisth
to camrkethixteibkteanverationnd tinshpetodysang   avacord such
dib teatabalihtiipighter i say groamave   a rose i pen thitthagnubhothezibysfoighteaslterctosther
jabjembertiaeroat for RuthIfat nig dugs herefather teatokksense thever seery kbfaiot
thergat gofitauszarsytyuthere veed   lotidsmfestaisom all lord   payment
nathGod no we werd write   for thathto   yofilegegodyoua lace cap for mywhat for
phhCrodst hear mef canlllsihrassitahtyds of liaeon lifiasatehtopdgppose trpdly the negroes with
           toys ovohhphhbiselctedthonthem   do you hear the lute
faiitinghadygold   fothould cut the cord of this storysound to raibse oba sobs
take every thserkgfhehayiffonsdaphoen   on   front irrst my case
cum granothgabffiedn   a sotprwgroeahemt isapfsrt   sow   in negligence
with a grain of salt dire visionsat vespemchbear templell /smg pfthe righteaighetnightwater parts
     the befting ontught evidinmc thetlahtqjmbhsfodhiyrongkacohbdathbsnecessity
thmucRuthreed   then   vedic   mursakiwitrei   negrows   ave tdoryou
thisrninafado negragenagainst sunfunth   a roseprosiighhnyou   to ile ife
told cold   atthkfdkinthotigor snogroes   sow the sea   nmenilsr my lord
haslrshtusfihhogmy liegdgordum   saolvtihiesmaading
him himepfrsunorawlith sos   demvidkayoltuth os   woysdeks &
liibekoo us   I dml she fhdlxatio   Ben   reason

182

Fig. 3.10 M. NourbeSe Philip, "Ẹbọra", *Zong! as Told to the Author by Setaey Adamu Boateng*, 2008, p. 182

a similar structure to *Tropical Night* with important variations as drawings are suspended hanging from two parallel wooden rails attached to the gallery's ceiling, but the structure is not fully covered with paintings, allowing in this way a kind of breeze-block effect.[46] Interestingly, a multisensory sound installation entitled *Life and Death by Water* (2021), by Berlin-based artist Lamin Fofana, also part of the Liverpool Biennial, was inspired by the story of the Zong and specifically by Philip's poem *Zong!* (as the work description read in the exhibition gallery).[47] The organisation of sound system units and chairs around an expansive gallery space allowed a sensorial immersion as various stereos emitted a composition of sounds and song coupled with blue lights and scent that enveloped the space. That position of the sound systems actually mirrors the four stands with television units in Cozier's *Blue Soap* and *Sound System*, especially so in this latter work as its drawing displays four sound systems in that same position demarcating a red drawn circle in the centre with the word "arena" inside it. This visual and sonic emphasis on intersection and crossroads becomes helpful in thinking about the dialogue and aesthetic cross-influences shaping memory work in Caribbean literature and visual art, with special focus here on work by Cozier and Philip.

Philip's *Zong!* has elicited much inspiration in visual artists including Joscelyn Gardner, and Sasha Huber and M'Barek Bouhchichi who have responded to the book-length poem in a multimedia installation and sculpture, respectively. In an interview, Huber and Bouhchichi contextualise their relationship to *Zong!* and Bouhchichi links the poem, text and performance to the sculpture through the notion of sharing as it "transcends itself into a visual matter to be shared" ("Interview"). Huber also links the ways in which the sculpture, like *Zong!* memorialises those lost at sea in the Zong massacre and in the contemporary ongoing deaths of Africans by drowning across the Mediterranean refugee migration crossings.[48] For the sculpture, *Back UP* (2020), stainless steel and brass plaques with words from the poem stand on the museum's wall, expanding the textuality and sonic elements of *Zong!* into a simultaneous sense of materiality and ephemerality in the combined visual effect of volume and light.[49] Gardner's *Omi Ẹbọra* also used words from the poem, which are here submerged in water through a mix of video installation and orality/aurality that reproduces the polyphonic effect of the poem.[50] In collaboration with Philip, who reads the poem in one of the five-channel experimental surround sound threads, Gardner created a response to *Zong!* that envisions, and (re)creates its multidimensionality and cacophony.[51]

As this chapter demonstrates, the art of Christopher Cozier and M. NourbeSe Philip is connected through various pathways, from aesthetic and formal strategies, dialogic and speculative nature to an archival drive and documenting critical concern that both precedes and follows the finished work, always in a process of re-engagement and conversation, from the compositional stage of the notebook to the dissemination stage in publication, exhibition, readings and performances. For both Cozier and Philip, notebooks mark a reflective space that is replicated in the materiality of the artwork and the poem, and which actively invites engagement. The 9 × 11 in. papers pinned onto the wall emulate, both in size, texture, and pictorial technique, the ink sketches and paintings in the notebooks that were once exhibited in the Marlborough gallery in Madrid. Similarly, as Philip points out in "Notanda", it is through journaling that Philip decides on the splicing of the words on the page, which was also inspired by the visual effect of superposed text (a result of an accident of faulty printing). "Notanda" documents further Philip's psychological and spiritual relationship to writing the poem and connecting with African cultural rituals of remembrance in a journey that she describes in the text as vital to the realisation of the formal aesthetic and poetics of *Zong!* In our interview in 2018, Philip mentioned the role of technology in *Zong!* and how the computer changed her relationship to the work, at first making her feel less comfortable than with the typewriter,[52] a point that Kamau Brathwaite also makes about his initial interaction with the computer (vs typewriter), and which has a great impact on the development of his Sycorax video style (Brathwaite, *Talk Yuh Talk!* 37). However, Philip also noted how the playfulness that the computer grants made possible the aesthetics of *Zong!* and its relationship to the poem and its elegy, as if words "are floating across the space of the page" ("In Conversation" 89). Philip added, "digital technology is at the heart of the work in a similar way that we could say the technology of the time (sailing and shipbuilding) was at the heart of the slave trade" (89).[53]

During *2020 Zong Global,* Philip mentioned the connection between *Zong!* and Ifá divination, the system of combination of signs as the foundation for the coding system that has created the Internet.[54] In a keynote speech at the Dresher Center for the Humanities, Mayra Santos-Febres spoke about the fractal Caribbean in a discussion of new literatures from Cuba, the Dominican Republic, and Puerto Rico that also centred around Ifá and Yoruban cosmogony at large. The talk was accompanied by the display of landscape photography by José Arturo Ballester Panelli from his series *The Fractal Caribbean* where he digitally plays with fractal shapes in the Caribbean landscape to create new shapes of heightened fractality.[55] Santos-Febres also showed two music videos by Rita Indiana Hernández to reflect the influence of Yoruba religion in articulating Caribbean history in *Da pa lo do* and *El Castigador.* Drawing from the theoretical work of Ángel "Chuco" Quintero, Antonio Benítez-Rojo and Édouard Glissant on the theory of chaos, relation and fractality, Santos-Febres discusses Benitez-Rojo's theoretical work on how the socio-economic system of the plantation repeats itself from island to island across the Caribbean and notes how, in that ongoing repetition, there are also differences. Through that rhythmic movement of repetition and variation also expressed culturally, new systems emerge and new ways of imagining kinship as, "such interconnectedness has always been at the centre of Caribbean thought and expression" (Santos-Febres "The Fractal Caribbean"). Santos-Febres then describes Ifá and points out: "at the center of Afro-diasporic knowledge there is the Oracle. *El Uno Multiple.* A system of binary language very close to computer programming that behaves in variation 01010010" (Santos-Febres "The Fractal Caribbean"). As Santos-Febres explains, that system that relies on repetition and relationality is carried out in the *tablero de Ifá* (Ifá board) as, "a tradition [in which] the self is considered a system of relations" (Santos-Febres "The Fractal Caribbean"). Within that system, "Yoruban deities, or rather manifestations of natural forces", interact with life through oneness and multiplicity: "Changó is fire, yet there are six changós. Yemayá is the Ocean, yet there are also seven Yemayás" (Santos-Febres "The Fractal Caribbean"). As I note in the introduction of this book, Santos-Febres connects the theorisations of Benitez-Rojo, Glissant, and others to Afro-diasporic cultural expression in music and religion in a conceptualisation of memory as both individual and collective, understood through specifically Caribbean modes of kinship. "Everything is connected" Santos-Febres adds in her keynote speech.

Zong! reflects the influence of Yoruba religion and Caribbean spirituality, as Philip has also noted, in the formation of a language and the work's poetics of the fragment. It is a language that not only relies on the relationality of signs and linguistic signifiers to explore or question their construction and roots in the economy of greed and racial capitalism, but it also requires a different approach to the text and reading. Jamaican writer and scholar, Kei Miller points out in reference to the biblical saying *"those who worship the Spirit must worship in Spirit*: one is only supposed to perceive spiritual things with a spiritual (rather than cerebral) receptor" (450). *Zong!* and its song of mourning demands that same relationship to the poem. In the same essay, Miller underscores that in engagements with the Spirit, understood as "multiple spirits and expressions of the spiritual", Caribbean writers have conveyed "affirming examples of local religious practice as counter-discourse to colonial narratives that had previously painted them as primitive" (451). Breaking the line of the verse in *Zong!* enacts a rupture with the rationality claimed by the narratives of modernity and their assumption of lineal progress over time. The poem provokes and invites a careful and spiritual reading as well, where the breath and the acknowledgement of the physical and visual weight of the silence can be felt and experienced. The anti-narratives in Philip's *Zong!* and in Cozier's *Tropical Night* require that readers and audiences connect with the evocative and communicative affect and effect of the works. The conceptual and critical mourning in Cozier's drawing series and Philip's book-length poem are largely activated by and through the affective tones and prosopopoeia of their imaginaries.

NOTES

1. See Sheena Rose, "I Feel Honored", Instagram, 9 Nov., 2018, www.instagram.com/p/Bp9GDBsgvXL/.
2. See Tamara Best, "The Artist Sheena Rose Is Reaching Beyond Barbados." *The New York Times*, 31 May 2017, www.nytimes. com/2017/05/31/arts/design/sheena-rose-contemporary-art ist-barbados.html.
3. See *The Other Side of Now: Foresight into Caribbean Contemporary Art.* 18 July 2019–7 June 2020, Pérez Art Museum, Miami. The exhibition was curated by María Elena Ortíz and Dr. Masrha Pearse, www.pamm.org/exhibitions/other-side-now-foresight-con temporary-caribbean-art.
4. The text is also available as a chapter in the book *Theorizing Fieldwork in the Humanities: Methods, Reflections, and Approaches to the Global South*, edited by Debra A. Castillo and Shalini Puri, 2014, 29–39.
5. Other publications, including Leon Wainwright's *Timed Out: Art and the Transnational Caribbean* (2011) and Therese Kaspersen

Hadchity's *The Making of a Caribbean Avant-Garde: Postmodernism as Post-Nationalism* (2020), contextualise Cozier's role in the arts scene of Trinidad and situate the influence of initiatives such as Alice Yard, Galvanize and the Small Axe Collective, which Cozier joined with David Scott and Annie Paul in the 1990s (Wainwright 158–160, 162–164; Kaspersen Hadchity 39–43, 103, 171–173).

6. See *Galvanize*'s blog, www.projectgalvanize.blogspot.com/.

7. See images of Bruce Cayonne's iconic fete signs, including those for *Galganize*. As it states on his website *Fete Sign*, Cayonne has been influencing visual culture in Trinidad since 1992, and the website works now as "an ongoing archive of his work", https://fetesign.com.

8. See Marsha Pearce, "Playing in the Yard." *Trinidad Guardian* 10 Nov. 2012, www.guardian.co.tt/article-6.2.434476.9b97ac788b.

9. See Dizzanne Billy, "Madman's Rant. David Rudder." *Write It Down*, 15 July 2016, https://dizzannebillyblog.wordpress.com/2016/07/15/madmans-rant-david-rudder/.

10. See Shereen Ali, "The Madman's Rant." *Repeating Islands*, 21 Feb. 2018, www.repeatingislands.com/2018/02/21/the-madmans-rant/ (previously published in *TT Newsday* and also available at Ali's website, *Scribbles TT*: www.scribblestt.com/arts-madman-s-rant).

11. The exhibition ran from 26 June – 6 Sept., 2003. It also showcased the work of Pedro Álvarez, Fernando Bryce, Curro González, and Marcelo Schuster.

12. Christopher Cozier. Interview. Conducted by Marta Fernández Campa, 12 Aug. 2012, Port of Spain, Trinidad and Tobago.

13. It is important to note that as a weblog collaboration between Christopher Cozier and Nicholas Laughlin, the *Tropical Night* blog documents an ongoing critical dialogue and form of digital note taking and note-making. See Cozier. "Tropical Night: Random Notes 06". *Tropical Night*, 4 May 2007, www.tropicalnight.blogspot.com/2007/05/tropical-night-randon-notes-06.html.

14. See Adichie. "The Danger of a Single Story." *TED: Ideas Worth Spreading*, July 2009, www.ted.com/talks/chimamanda_ngozi_adichie_the_danger_of_a_single_story?language=en.

15. Literary representations of the white fears of unknown and inaccessible codes of expression feature drumming as a particularly threatening instrument and social practice to the colonial status quo. In his novel *Salt* (1996), Earl Lovelace writes about how the "Whitepeople" in the island "had to put up with the noise from Blackpeople. Whole night Blackpeople have their drums going as they dance in the bush. All those dances. All those lascivious bodies leaping and bending down" (5). The political power embodied in drumming, is exoticised by the white gaze with the aim to minimise its significance. In Lawrence Scott's *Witchbroom* (1992), drums often mark the simultaneity of actions (95) and their combined playing (African drums and tassa drums) invokes white fears for Elena and her family.

16. The development of new drums in Trinidad is connected to responses and inventiveness to circumvent ordinances and bans. Following the ban of drumming, and with the prohibition of drumming in public spaces this practice found a space in yards where drums were made of bamboo resulting in the emergence of tamboo-bamboo bands. Later, in the 1930s, during the years of turmoil and social movements seeking political and socio-economic reform, Trinidadians sought material for louder drumming, which led to the use of the steel drum. For detailed accounts of this history see Dawn K. Batson's "Voices of Steel: A Historical Perspective" (2004) and Stephen Stuempfle's *The Steelband Movement: The Forging of a National Art in Trinidad and Tobago* (1995).

17. According to Viranjini Munasinghe, long-held divisions had also sparked from "images of Indo-Trinidadians as bearers and Afro-Trinidadians as creators of culture", based in the argument that Indo-Trinidadians had a closer and firmer connection to India whereas the process of forced acculturation of enslaved Africans and cultural erasure had led to a tradition of cultural (re)creation (199).

18. The term creolisation is wide in its interpretation and currency across the region. In *The Caribbean Postcolonial: Social Equality, Post-Nationalism, and Cultural Hybridity*, Shalini Puri locates Kamau Brathwaite's theorisation of creolisation in *Contradictory Omens: Cultural Diversity and Integration in the Caribbean* (1974) as one of the earliest. Puri notes how, for Brathwaite,

the term (and process) of creolisation was particularly unique in the Caribbean due to its social structure strongly based on rigid, long-held hierarchies. Further, Brathwaite warns readers of how "[t]he optimistic expectation of dialectal 'progressive' synthesis/solution ... leads to impasse" an important consideration for Caribbean societies to deal with (*Contradictory Omens* 63). Puri stresses that nationalists and members of the elite class in the Caribbean have viewed creolisation as a process of homogenising and unification (Puri, *The Caribbean* 62).

19. *Blue Soap* was first showed in Trinidad at the Acquarela Gallery in Woodbrook, Port of Spain in 1994 and also featured at the Havana Art Biennale that same year.

20. In his 1998 mixed media installation *Art and Nation: Things you Should Learn from Day One*, Cozier displayed an old-style blackboard, from which a shirt jac was hanging. Writing on the blackboard a series of terms are listed in two demarcated columns. Under the heading "Them" Cozier lists: (1) White people (2) Rich people (3) Bullers (4) People from rich countries (5) All of the above. The second column is titled "Us" and followed in listing by: (1) People who must pray, (2) People who must work hard, (3) People who must learn to love their "CULTURE" and always respect their leaders. In front of the blackboard, Cozier grouped white bread sandwiches pierced by mini flags of Trinidad and Tobago furthering the notion of the production of a nationalist culture with capitalist claims and aspirations. See A. Paul, "Chris Cozier: a state of Independence." *Caribbean Beat*, Issue 50, July/Aug. 2001, https://www.caribbean-beat.com/issue-50/chris-cozier-state-of-independence#axzz7Uz69Gx9z.

21. The *Dictionary of the English/Creole of Trinidad and Tobago* describes some other uses of the peera (also known as "pirha", "peerha", or "pirah"). For instance, in Hindu weddings the groom "perches on the pirah" during the ceremony (699).

22. In *The Trinidad Dougla: Identity, Ethnicity and Lexical Choice*, Ferne Louanne Regis lists "peera" as a term within the Dougla lexicon and offers the following definition "a low small wooden bench used to sit on (especially by older women) or to rest one's feet" (80).

23. Peeras are mentioned in descriptions of quotidian acts, particularly in Indo Trinidadian households in literary works including Harold

Sonny Ladoo's *No Pain Like this Body* (1972) (59), Lakshmi Persaud's *Butterfly in the Wind* (1990) (80) and Willi Chen's short story "How She Go Look?" in *Chutney Power and Other Stories* (2006). In Chen's story, Shanti, the young female protagonist, comes out of her bath, sits down "on the peera and proceed to paint her toenails" (102).

24. Christopher Cozier, "Little Gestures." *Kentucky Museum of Arts and Craft*, www.kmacmuseum.org/christopher-cozier.

25. The peera, with all its associations, has also been an object highly influential to other artists and designers in Trinidad. Marlon Darbeau, designer and creator of the furniture company *By Making*, has also popularised modern metal renditions of the peera, some of them in bold bright colours. One of the statements on Darbeau's website reads "Peera ... more than just a place to sit." See Marlon Darbeau, *By Making*, http://marlondarbeau.blogspot.com.

26. Liseli Daaga helped lead the National Joint Action Committee in 1970, whilst other leaders were imprisoned. She was the wife of the late Black Power Revolution leader Makandal Daaga.

27. Josanne was the daughter of Winston Leonard, a key member of the National Joint Action Committee. Winston was of East Indian descent, and was involved in the trade union movement.

28. *Entanglements* was exhibited in Cozier's solo art exhibition *Enredos/Entanglements* in Costa Rica as part of *TEOR/éTica, arte y pensamiento* curated by Miguel A. López. See www.teoretica.org/2015/01/05/enredos/?lang=en. The exhibition ran from 15 July–19 Sept. 2015.

29. *dig & fly* was exhibited at the Caribbean group exhibition *One month After Being Known in that Island*, part of the Basel-based Caribbean Art Initiative, which ran from 27 Aug. 2018–15 Nov. 2020 at the Culture-siftung Basel H. Geiger in Basel, Germany. The exhibition, included the work of artists based in the Caribbean region and the diaspora, and was curated by Yina Jiménez Suriel and Pablo Guardiola. Participating artists include Elisa Bergel Melo, Minia Biabiany, Christopher Cozier, Tony Cruz Pabón, Sharelly Emanuelson, Nelson Fory Ferreira, Madeline Jiménez Santil, Tessa Mars, Ramón Miranda Betrán, José Morbán and Guy Régis Jr. The exhibition catalogue included articles by Puerto Rican writer Marta Aponte Alsina and Dominican writer

Rita Indiana Hernández, attesting also to the critical dialogue between writers and visual artists in the region. See *One Month After Being Known in that Island: Caribbean Art Today*, Hatje Cantz, 2020.

30. The *dig & fly* series was previously exhibited at the 2019 Sharjah Biennial which ran from 7 Mar.–10 June. The series was included in one of the three exhibitions part of the Biennial entitled *Look for Me All Around You* curated by Claire Tancons. The work and visual images from *dig & fly* follow Cozier's work in the *Gas Men* (2014) and *Entanglements* (2015) video projects, and continues to explore the role of oil, gas and bauxite extraction in the Caribbean as past and ongoing forms of neo-colonial practices.

31. See Grant Kester, *Conversation Pieces: Community and Communication in Modern Art*, 2004.

32. M. NourbeSe Philip, "GA(S)P: Experiments in Radical Hospitality." 2020 Hammed Shahidian Lecture, Women and Gender Studies Institute, 28 Oct., 2020, www.youtube.com/watch?v=Kqf X6HPAVaw.

33. See Philip, "In Conversation with History: An Interview with M. NourbeSe Philip." Interview conducted by Marta Fernández Campa. *Small Axe: A Caribbean Journal of Criticism*, vol. 26, no. 1, Mar. 2022, pp. 85–100. Part of the original interview with the author took place in August 2018, Toronto.

34. The sea has metaphorically worked and has been reconstructed by Caribbean artists as a productive source of inspiration and a means to articulate an experience of resistance and counter-memory. From Derek Walcott's musings on the sea as history, to Kamau Brathwaite's tidalectic poetics and the notion of "the unity is submarine" ("Caribbean Man" 1) to the transatlantic journey of Grace Nichols' Cariwoma (a mythic Caribbean character that connects through underwater travel different Amerindian, African, and Western traditions of remembrance), Caribbean poetry has generated productive memory work around the trope of the sea (*Startling*).

35. See Philip, "In Conversation with History", pp. 85–100.

36. *#ZongGlobal2020* was envisioned by Yaniya Lee, a Toronto-based art writer, editor, and curator, who first contacted Philip and initiated discussions that led to the idea for the durational reading. She also acknowledged the input and collaboration of

Kate Siklosi, James Allister Sprang, Richard Douglass-Chin, Faizal Deen, Collective Broadcast, and many others.

37. See *Zong! Global 2020*, www.zong.world/zongglobal2020/.

38. A previous statement on the *Zong! Global 2020* website, noted that the recordings would become available again for a set period of time in November, with the commemoration of the massacre: "On November 29. 2021, the anniversary of the beginning of the massacre, the recordings will once again be made public for a set period of time" as was the case, enabling a viewing again of the readings during that time. www.zong.world/zonggloba l2020/. Accessed 20 July 2021.

39. Cozier and other artists who had engaged with the archive of slavery were invited to speak at the conference *Out of Sight*, organised by Krista Thompson and Huey Copeland, at Northwestern University in 2006. Other presenters were Fred Wilson, Keith Piper and Hank Willis Thomas. www.art.northwestern.edu/visiting-artists/out-sight-2006.

40. Adrienne Rich provides this definition of re-vision in her seminal critical essay "When We Dead Awaken: Writing as Re-vision" written in 1971. In this essay, Rich uses the concept of "re-vision" to explain the necessity for women writers, and specifically poets, to liberate themselves from the influence of a male literary tradition and the legacy of the patriarchy in an attempt to revise their own creative processes, since as she argues "the drive to self-knowledge, for women, is more than a search for identity: it is part of our refusal of the self-destructiveness of male-dominated society" (983). Although the context in which Rich wrote this essay (the 1970s feminist critique of the literary canon), differs from the historical context in which *Zong!* is situated, Rich's concept of "re-vision" is nevertheless helpful to illustrate the ways in which a re-vision of a past discourse/text entails an active process of critique which unveils discursively what has been silenced and repressed.

41. Granville Sharp, "Letter to William Baker re Zong incident", 23 May 1783, Gloucestershire Archives, D3549 13/1/B1.

42. "Work in Process," appears in the art catalogue *Christopher Cozier: In Development* and is not paginated.

43. See *Christopher Cozier In Development. A Collaborative Project. 2013–Ongoing*, www.dpatterns2013.wordpress.com.

44. *Relational Undercurrents: Contemporary Art of the Caribbean Archipelago* was curated by Tatiana Flores. The exhibition ran from 16 Sept. 2017–25 Feb. 2018 at the Museum of Latin American Art, Long Beach, California, www.molaa.org/relational-undecurrents.

45. *The Sea is History* was curated by Selene Wendt. It was exhibited at the Museum of Cultural History, Oslo, Norway from 7 Mar. 2019–18 Aug. 2019. Other participating artists with Cozier were John Akomfrah, Maria Magdalena Campos-Pons, Andrea Chung, Manthia Diawara, Isaac Julien, Naiza Khan, Hew Locke, Nyugen E. Smith, and Cosmo White. An exhibition catalogue was published featuring essays and poetry by Christian Campbell, Manthia Diawara, Linton Kwesi Johnson, Kei Miller, Annie Paul, Ishion Hutchinson, Nyugen E. Smith, Derek Walcott, and Selene Wendt.

    The curatorial premise for this group exhibition set in conversation the visual arts and literature, and as the exhibition itself, was inspired by Derek Walcott's poetry and his famous poem and (notion of) "The Sea is History" and the critical and theoretical work of Édouard Glissant and Stuart Hall. The book-length epic *Omeros* was also evoked through Isaac Julien's film *Paradise Omeros*, which featured in the exhibition poster and catalogue's book cover.

46. See Christopher Cozier, *turbulence 2019–2021*, 2021, Liverpool Biennial, www.biennial.com/2021/exhibition/artists/christopher-cozier.

    Commissioned for the biennial, the ink drawings in the series present imagery evoking extraction and its effect on the environment. A description of the project in the Liverpool Biennial website reads "Interested in Sylvia Wynter's rethinking of what constitutes "human" and Amitav Ghosh's questions on ecology, imagination and science fiction, Cozier's drawings depict mysterious hybrid creatures which represent the entanglement and assimilation of Caribbean and world histories.", www.biennial.com/2021/exhibition/artists/christopher-cozier.

47. See Reader of *The Stomach and the Port. Liverpool Biennial 2021*, pp. 132–137.

48. See Sasha Huber and M'barek Bouhchichi, *BACK UP*, 2020, Institut Finlandais, Paris, https://www.institut-finlandais.fr/en/

blog/2021/02/10/interview-sasha-huber-and-mbarek-bouhch ichi/.

49. The plaque's suspension from the wall create further shadows of the words upon the wall. The sculpture is displayed at the Institut Finlandais in Paris as part of the *Untie Knots, Weave Connections* initiative, see www.institut-finlandais.fr/en/projects/ if-galerie/untie-knots-weave-connections/.

50. See Gardner, *Omi Ẹbọra*, multimedia installation, *Joscelyn Gardner*, www.joscelyngardner.org/omi-ebora. View a video clip of the work via the following link. Joscelyn Gardner, "Omi Ẹbọra. Documentation clip." *Vimeo*, 2014, www.vimeo.com/111 986837.

51. For an insightful discussion of Philip's *Zong!* and Gardner's *Omi Ẹbọra* read Guillermina De Ferrari's article "A Caribbean Hauntology: The Sensorial Art of Joscelyn Gardner and M. NourbeSe Philip", *Journal of Latin American Cultural Studies*, Vol. 27, Issue 3, 2018, pp. 271–293.

52. See Philip, "In Conversation with History: An Interview with M. NourbeSe Philip", pp. 85–100. EBSCOhost, https://doi.org/10. 1215/07990537-9724079.

53. Philip, "In Conversation with History: An Interview with M. NourbeSe Philip", 85–100, 89. This quoted excerpt belongs to the beginning of my interviews with Philip which have extended over the years 2017–2021 for the Leverhulme-funded research project Caribbean Literary Heritage led by Alison Donnell. This specific excerpt was recorded in a transcript from my first meeting with Philip in Oval, London, May 2018.

54. See *Zong! Global* at zong.world, https://zong.world/zonggloba l2020/.

55. See José Arturo Ballester Panelli, *Fractal Caribbean. Ballesta 9*, www.ballesta9.com. *Caribe Fractal / Fractal Caribbean* was featured in a solo exhibition at RCAH Lookout Gallery at Michigan State University, and was also displayed virtually (due to the COVID-19 pandemic). The exhibit included digital design, photography, sound and video, and was curated by Stephanie Bravo and Yomaira Figueroa. You can view the virtual exhibit here: https://rcah.msu.edu/uniquely-rcah/lookout/Bal lester-2020-Exhibit.html.

CHAPTER 4

Fragmentation and a Poetics of Location in *The Farming of Bones* and *The Brief Wondrous Life of Oscar Wao*

On 23 September 2013, the Dominican Constitutional Court passed a ruling (*sentencia número* TC/0168–13) that denied the citizenship of Dominican residents of Haitian descent living in the Dominican Republic, acting retroactively to 1929, thus leaving them stateless in a process of denationalisation. This ruling caused immediate national and international critique, opposition, and outrage. Yet, it wasn't until May 2014, largely due to pressure from activists, the UN, human rights organisations and CARICOM[1] as well as critical statements from world leaders including the then US president Barack Obama, that a new bill was signed into law by Dominican President Danilo Medina. However, as Edward Paulino points out, this new Naturalisation Law 169–14 presumably made attempts at restoring citizenship to those affected by the 2013 ruling but proved largely unsuccessful in this sense (*Dividing Hispaniola* 165; Fumagalli, *On the Edge* 388).[2] The law required those born to undocumented Haitian parents to register to a special scheme to obtain the residence permit necessary to (re)apply for citizenship, in what the law deemed a new path to citizenship. The ruling in 2013 meant the alarming loss of citizenship rights for more than 200,000 Dominicans of Haitian descent then reported to be living in the country, including the area around the border between Haiti and the DR,[3] characterised by a complex history of both intercultural life and orchestrated conflict. Their

M. Fernández Campa, *Memory and the Archival Turn in Caribbean Literature and Culture*, New Caribbean Studies, https://doi.org/10.1007/978-3-030-72135-0_4

status in the Dominican Republic was declared as 'in transit'. Soon deportations followed. Most people affected were second- or third-generation descendants of Haitian migrants.

There is a long history of regional activism and legal struggle to protect the rights of the descendants of Haitians in the Dominican Republic. Sonia Pierre, a Dominican human rights activist of Haitian descent and founder of MUDHA (Movement of Dominican Haitian Women)[4] had publicly warned, campaigned, and taken legal action against local court rulings since the early 2000s that were already engaging in this violation of human rights that retroactively denied citizenship (Katz).[5] In 1998, MUDHA, CEJIL (Centro por la Justicia y el Derecho Internacional)[6] and two US law firms filed the case Yean and Bosico vs the Dominican Republic at the Inter-American Court of Human Rights and in 2005, after a long legal battle, the court ruled in favour of the two young girls (Dilcia Yean and Violeta Bosico) whose birth certificates had been denied in the civil registry of Sabana Grande de Boyá on 5 March 1997 after their family had requested the documents.[7] A birth certificate is essential to gain access to a wide variety of services in the Dominican Republic, and its denial therefore implies the denial of nationality and citizenship rights with the subsequent lack of access to education, health care, a formal job, back accounts, registering the birth of children, and other rights (Fumagalli, *On the Edge* 382). The backdrop of the law and its implementation has continued to manifest the calculated investment, in particular, in marking *rayanos* (Haitians and Dominican–Haitians living in the Dominican Republic) as foreign and as un-belonging to the nation. The struggle against state harassment of Haitians and Dominicans of Haitian descent, particularly along the border, continued. However, decades of anti-Haitian discourse and propaganda (with earlier forms being developed in the eighteenth and nineteenth centuries and especially solidified during Trujillo's dictatorship) made TC/0168–13, largely possible. With the ruling, this practice of stripping citizenship was officially, and systematically, supported by the law.[8]

The 1980s and 1990s were marked by a nationalist discourse based on ideas of racial and ethnic hierarchy previously perpetuated by Trujillo's, and later Balaguer's, regime (drawing largely from colonial notions of Hispanophilia), with a lasting effect that continues to shape the "xenophobic nationalism in present-day Dominican Republic" (García Peña

17, 58–92). By examining articulations of memory in Edwidge Danticat's *The Farming of Bones* (1998) and Junot Díaz's *The Brief Wondrous Life of Oscar Wao* (2007), this chapter considers the narrative devices used to (counter) archive those memories and history with attention to how both texts revise certain myths fostered by nationalistic historiographical projects. Through different typeface, footnotes, Caribbean culture and religion, science fiction, comic references, pop culture, and intertextual literary elements, these works elaborate a collective memory that counters official histories offering other ways of telling, imagining and documenting the past, based on local, regional and transnational knowledges.

The growing archive of Dominican and Haitian literature that deals with the Trujillo–ordered massacre of Haitians and Dominicans of Haitian descent living around and along the border in 1937 reveals a number of shared characteristics. Amongst those is narrative fragmentation, which is reflective of both the effects of trauma, on one hand, and also of a multi-layered articulation of that experience, with its roots and ramifications. The narrator in Roxane Gay's short story "In the Manner of Water or Light" (2011), mentions early in the story "Everything I know about my family's history, I know in fragments" (57) thus highlighting the issue of the fragmentariness of the way in which the account of the massacre is passed on intergenerationally from grandmother to mother, and later to granddaughter. This is later mentioned two other times (59; 66). It is through reading, listening to and connecting fragments that readers access the story, and despite the discomfort, silences, and inaccessible memories within the fragmented account, the three women finally share a moment that bonds them as they return one night to the river where the grandmother once experienced unfathomable trauma. The issue of how to narrate and bear witness to the massacre, in a way that accounts for the complexity of articulating its violence and trauma, is at the heart of René Philoctète's *Le peuple des terres mêlées* (1989) translated as *Massacre River* and published in translation in the United States in 2005. In *Massacre River*, fragmentation is conveyed stylistically, in the hyperbolic and surrealist descriptions of scenes as the massacre unfolds where an overwhelming enumeration of objects, people, locations, and animals captures the sheer shock, loss, and trauma. In a discussion of Haitian Spiralism, the literary genre that Philoctète shaped with Frankétienne and Jean-Claude Fignolé in 1965, Kaiama Glover notes the psychological and physical fragmentation of Adèle, one of the main protagonists.

Adèle's head, disconfigured from her body, is described as moving of its own accord around the village, separated from her body (as we learn per the account of her partner, Dominican Pedro Brito), thus mirroring "a psychotic episode brought on by the trauma she has witnessed" (Glover 93). In this chapter, I argue that the fragmentation in Danticat's and Díaz's novels (as in the writings by Gay, Philoctète, and the work of other artists) reflects both lived and inherited trauma and explores the issue of finding narratives that honour the complexity and magnitude of the event and its history.

The increasing academic research and interest in the relationship of Haiti and the Dominican Republic has led to recent interdisciplinary conferences, publications, and initiatives. *Border of Lights*, initiated in 2013, is one of them; a "collective coming together to commemorate, collaborate and continue the legacy of hope and justice"[9] which operates through the collaboration of writers, artists, historians, and the general public to commemorate (through activism, teaching, and yearly vigils) the lives of those affected by the 1937 massacre. Edwidge Danticat, Julia Álvarez, and other Haitian, Dominican, and Haitian–Dominican writers, historians, and activists have participated and engaged with *Border of Lights*. Within the extensive body of criticism focused on the massacre and its literature, there has been a more recent emphasis on diversifying the representation of perspectives that emphasise that there are also many Dominican voices and activist groups dissenting from official Dominican state discourse and policies (García Peña; Reyes-Santos). Scholars have stressed the various examples of solidarity across the island after the earthquake that hit Haiti on 12 January 2010. These reflect and evoke the continued solidifying of a transnational community of kinship and solidarity (Fumagalli, *On the Edge*, 23; García-Peña, 17–18, 129–134; Paulino, *Dividing Hispaniola* 1–3).

COLLECTIVE MEMORY IN THE HISTORIOGRAPHY OF THE "TRUJILLATO"

On 28 September 1937, Trujillo ordered the massacre against Haitians and Haitian–Dominicans living and working in rural areas along the Haitian–Dominican border and adjacent towns and villages. This area, demarcated by the *línea fronteriza* (brderland), includes five Dominican provinces that border Haiti (Monte Cristi, Dajabón, Elías Piña, Independencia, and Pedernales).[10] The first killings took place south of Dajabón, and a few days later, on the night of October 2, Trujillo delivered an incendiary speech in Dajabón where he is reported to have given "'orders' to the solution of the Haitian problem" (Wucker, "Race and Massacre" 62), encouraging the continuation of the massacre. Although most speeches delivered by Trujillo were transcribed and recorded in state archives such as the Archivo General de la Nación in Santo Domingo, there is no official record of this speech which would have otherwise officially proved Trujillo's orchestration of the slaughter, a responsibility that he always denied to the international community and Haiti.[11],[12]

The massacre is referred to with different terms in English, Dominican Spanish and Haitian Creole (Kreyòl) that range from the 1937 massacre, *El Corte* ("the cutting"), *Kout Kouto* ("the stabbing" in Haitian Kréyol), Parsley Massacre (*Masacre del Perejil* or *Pessi* in Spanish and Kréyol), and the Dominican Vespers. The killings officially lasted two weeks, although there is evidence that attacks continued in 1938 when thousands of Haitians were deported and hundreds killed in attacks in the Southern border area (Turits 591). There is no official death toll upon which historians agree; but it is estimated that between 25,000 and 40,000 Haitians and Haitian–Dominicans were killed or died attempting escape from the killings in 1937 (Chancy 85). As historians note, this was not a spontaneous action but rather a carefully designed operation ordered by Trujillo to reduce the number of Haitian workers in the Dominican border area; part of his plan to 'whiten' the nation (Chancy 101; Turits 593; Ricourt 32). Trujillo's dictatorship lasted 31 years (1930–1961) and was characterised by a fascist ideology influenced by Adolf Hitler's white supremacist racial theories (Wucker, "Race and Massacre" 61). During this period, Dominicans were also killed; those who opposed the regime would often "disappear" to never be found again. Arrests, torture, and murders were very much a part of Trujillo's dictatorship; the regime's traumatic effects still linger in Dominican society, as do the legacies of anti-Haitian discourses and policies.

Although the official collective memory of Trujillo's era is varied, it was first largely dominated (especially until the 1980s) by the discourse of political figures like Joaquín Balaguer who was the undersecretary of Foreign Relations during the massacre and was one of the regime's main ideologues. Balaguer continued to publicly exonerate Trujillo's policies of repression for decades after the "end" of the regime. Michelle Wucker describes him as "one of [the massacre's] greatest defenders" ("Race and Massacre" 61). He was also an important instigator. Despite his role in this and other aspects of Trujillo's regime, Balaguer dominated Dominican politics after Trujillo's assassination in 1961 and was president of the country in a continued authoritarian ruling, at various stages, for a total of twenty-four years (1960–1962, 1966–1978, and 1986–1996) in what have been questionably democratic elections.[13] Balaguer defended and promoted what he saw as a process of hispanisation along the Dominican border: "In order to prevent, on the other hand, that the country would lose its characteristics as a clearly Hispanic community, what was needed was to put into practice a plan of Dominicanization of the border and to awaken at the same time amongst the people pride in their traditional greatness" (Balaguer qtd. in Strongman, trans. Strongman 22).[14] Roberto Strongman quotes Balaguer's *La isla al revés: Haití y el destino dominicano* (1983), as one of the best-known examples of anti-Haitian propaganda.[15] Equally, the influence of various Trujillista texts like Carlos Cornielle's *Proceso histórico dominico-haitiano: una advertencia a la juventud dominicana* (1980) have informed some Dominican historical perspectives, especially cemented by the discourse of Dominican intellectuals in the 1940s and 1950s (Paulino, *dividing Hispaniola* 161). However, despite the influence of this anti-Haitian discourse, significant forms of counter-memory have emerged. Especially since the 1980s, renowned Dominican historians like Juan Bosch, Bernardo Vega, and Roberto Cassá started to excavate the history and stories of Trujillo's oppression that had been silenced in previous decades. Their historiographical approach registers the experiences of those who were particularly affected and disenfranchised by the regime.

With a similar purpose, various historical studies of Dominican–Haitian relations and particularly the episode of the 1937 Parsley Massacre have emerged since the 1990s, expanding this revisionary tradition of historiography. The research of historians and critics like Eric Roorda, Richard L. Turits, Michelle Wucker, Edward Paulino, Eduardo Matibag, Ernesto Sagás, Sibylle Fischer, and others, has engaged in revisions that, like *The Farming of Bones* and *The Brief Wondrous Life of Oscar Wao*, counter a tradition of Dominican nationalist narratives and historiography marked by historical gaps, silences, and erasures. Through fiction and other mediums, Dominican and Haitian writers add their voices to this body of work. Although, as Amy Novack points out in regard to the Dominican Vespers, "[t]he event slipped from history, unspoken by the governments on both sides of the Massacre River" (97), through writing, Danticat,

Díaz, and others attempt to break the unspoken silences around the investigation of what happened, the past that led to it, and its aftermath.

DOCUMENTATION: FICTIONS OF HISTORY AND THE CONFIGURATION OF COLLECTIVE MEMORY

General Trujillo and the Dominican elite viewed the intercultural and interethnic communities established along the Dominican border with Haiti as a threat to their national project, and consistently expressed so through their rhetoric. Sibylle Fischer discusses the nature of a particular tradition of collective memory in the Dominican Republic that goes back to the eighteenth century. This tradition conveys anti-Haitian sentiments and imagines Haiti as an antithesis to progress and modernity (*Modernity Disavowed*). Embedded in this discourse is also a fixation with Spanish colonial rule as a period of progress. Within this discourse, ancestors are imagined as Spaniards and Indians, not Africans, despite the fact that Dominican society is largely mulato and Black (Fischer 151). Much of eighteenth-century literature on the issue creates an improbable social, racial, and ethnic categorisation through the use of fantasy; fantastic and hyperbolic elements that result in a problematic "suppression of the memory of slavery and antislavery [that] gets off the ground only by means of a wholesale invention of a rather implausible past" (Fischer 152). Scholars, including Fischer, also insist on the defining role that early nineteenth-century political discourse played in shaping anti-Haitian rhetorical narratives (García Peña; Ricourt; Fumagalli and others), which Lorgia García-Peña argues "sustain racism in the Dominican Republic" today and are "vital to understand present-day *dominicanidad* and the borders that have produced it" (15).[16] Milagros Ricourt and Lorgia García-Peña identify the origins of a "psychological border" (Ricourt 23) between Haiti and the Dominican Republic in the period around the government of Haitian president Jean Pierre Boyer (1822–1844) who was perceived by the Dominican elite as threatening their lifestyle, following Spain's loss of the Colony of Santo Domingo in 1821.[17] His signing of the Reparations Act of 1825 with France stipulated the official recognition of Haiti's free republic by France, England, Spain, and the United States (who had refused to do so after the victory of the Haitian Revolution against France in 1804). The conditions in exchange were a series of taxes that did impoverish Haiti for centuries, and which also put further pressure on the Dominican landowning elite which was taxed for the payment. As a result of the dissatisfaction, a revolutionary front led by Juan Pablo Duarte (who is constructed in the Dominican nationalist imaginary as the national hero who liberated Dominicans from Haitian rule), declared the Independence of the Dominican Republic after military victory against Boyer's army in 1844.

García-Peña insists that the relationship of the Dominican Republic with its former colonial powers, Spain and the United States, is vital to an understanding of the formation of anti-Haitian rhetoric shaped through the discourse of national Independence and nationalism (30–31). Through the combination of Hispanism (popularised by nineteenth century elite *letrado* writers including Félix María del Monte as the cultural legacy of Spanish language, Christianity, Spain as "mother culture") and *mestizaje* ("the mixture of European and Indian Taíno blood") (García Peña 31; Ricourt 32), the Dominican Republic constructed an ethnic identity that associated blackness with an *othered* Haiti. This rhetoric was very much continued and reinforced by Dominican conservative literature and by the United States throughout its first invasion and occupation of the Dominican Republic (1916–1924). It is important to note that Trujillo was trained by the US army that occupied the DR, and had occupied Haiti for an even longer period (1915–1934). If military interference characterised US foreign policy in Latin America and the Caribbean throughout the twentieth century, so did neutrality and knowing complicity.[18] The rhetoric of the anti-Haitian discourse expressed in the Dominican Republic, especially after the Dominican Vespers' 1937 massacre, needs to be identified as part of Spanish and US coloniality and to be understood as one of its continuities. Equally, as important as the inscription of that narrative in the rhetorical discourse linking both nations, is the erasure and silencing of the Haitian Revolution from the Dominican Republic, European and US collective memory that Michel-Rolph Trouillot adroitly describes in *Silencing the Past* (1995). The long struggle and victory of the revolution led by Touissant L'Ouverture and Jean-Jacques Dessalines, who Trinidadian novelist and historian C. L. R. James referred to as the "black Jacobins",[19] was for a long time conveniently suppressed from the annals of global history despite its huge centrality in destabilising fictions of imperial superiority and inspiring revolutions and emancipation in the Americas throughout the nineteenth century. Similarly, the central role of Vodou ceremonies in the organising success of the revolts that led to the victory of the Haitian

Revolution lies in contrast to vilifications and misrepresentations of Vodou in the Eurocentric and the United States imaginary.

Months prior to the Dominican Vespers in 1937, both Trujillo and Balaguer made public statements claiming that Dominican landowners on the border expressed their complaints about numerous criminal activities which Haitians were accused of committing. However, it was especially after the massacre that divisive sentiments and tensions emerged fully. Although social hierarchies existed prior to the massacre, these were manifested at different levels and did not affect Dominican and Haitian relations exclusively, but rather determined social dichotomies. Historians and literary critics underscore how initially the Haitian–Dominican borderland was not marked by the acute division and strife between Dominicans and Haitians that Trujillo and the white Dominican elite claimed (Wucker, Turits, Matibag, Paulino, and Fumagalli). The Dominican border had been a bilingual and bicultural space where many Dominican–Haitian families had formed and coexisted for centuries. Richard Lee Turits insists on the complex social and ethnic dynamics on the Dominican–Haitian border, in an attempt to revise the notion that those relations reflect the conflict between one ethnic group or nation against the other. According to Turits, viewing the massacre *exclusively* as a conflict and Dominican state-sponsored repression that targeted *rayanos* and Haitians ignores a more complex discussion of the socio-historical context existing along the Haitian–Dominican border as the project of destabilising relations worked also as an attack from elites on working class communities of various ethnicities (593). Critics such as Milagros Ricourt have also made this point, and Ricourt has further pointed out to the need to consider two interconnected motivations of Trujillo in ordering the genocide: one is to destabilise the area and reinforce a strong border between the two nations and the other is to whiten the Dominican Republic (32). Yet, it is vital to note that an anti-Haitian discourse had already filtered into the lives of the different communities living in the border.

The killings of October 1937 have been linked to another massacre carried out in the same river, *río Dajabón* (or *río masacre*, Massacre River) in 1728 when thirty French buccaneers were defeated and killed by Spanish troops; a historical moment that renamed the river as Massacre River. The 1937 organised massacre in the same river aims to resignify the Dominican nation as rooted in a tradition of Spanish conquest and heritage that imposes itself to all that is labelled foreign to the national project. The Trujillista's wish to reframe the nation (and its border) through a homogenising rhetoric has seen state intervention aimed to destabilise what was a different situation across the border, a strong area of intercultural contact. Oral testimonies from the late 1980s by elderly Haitians and Dominicans bring forward a more complex pre- and post-massacre context (Turits 593). These testimonials contradict the notion of a homogenous Dominican national identity around the border before 1937. These records are key to deconstructions of the official history that predominated in the aftermath of the massacre.

THE FARMING OF BONES: NARRATING MEMORY WITH NO AUDIENCE

The writing of Haitian–American writer Edwidge Danticat is deeply concerned with historical memory in Haiti, the Caribbean, and in diasporic locations in the United States. From her first novel *Breath, Eyes, Memory* (1994) which narrates the lives of a family of women in Haiti who experience intergenerational trauma, her later fiction and memoirs have continued to explore issues of migration, diasporic communities, and histories.[20] As Danticat tells in *Brother, I'm Dying* (2007), the author moved from her uncle's home in Haiti to New York city in 1981 when she was 12, to reunite with her parents who migrated there when she was 2. Danticat's memoir writing encompasses family history interwoven with the history of Haiti, resulting in a rich exploration of the impact of the Haitian Revolution, the violence and silencing of dictatorships, and the brave opposition from artists and revolutionaries; as well as the long-lasting damage caused by the US invasion of Haiti and the various policies that have since affected the country. The trauma generated by various dictators of Hispaniola from Trujillo to François (Papa Doc) Duvalier, and his son Jean-Claude (Baby Doc) Duvalier, figure in *The Farming of Bones*, and her two short story collections *Krik? Krak!* (1995) and *The Dew Breaker* (2004). Bearing witness, grief and mourning figure significantly in Danticat's fiction, as well as in *Brother, I'm Dying* and in her latest memoir *The Art of Death* (2017), which offers a personal reflection on the illness and passing of her mother as well as an analysis of grief in literature and popular culture.

Amabelle Désir, the narrator of *The Farming of Bones*, is one of the survivors of the 1937 massacre, when thousands of Haitians tried to cross the border and escape to Haiti. Many were killed as they were crossing the Massacre River. Amabelle's testimony enables access to the interior lives of the victims including hers, allowing readers to know about their lives intimately, their relationships, dreams, fears, and hopes. In this way, *The Farming of Bones* offers multiple angles on life along the Dominican border and to the history of the massacre. This is also evident in the centrality of the love story between Amabelle and Sebastien which inter-textually mirrors those in two previous Haitian historical novels that deal with the massacre: Jacques Stephen Alexis' *Compère Général Soleil* (1955), translated as *General Sun, My Brother*, and René Philoctète's *Le peuple des terres mêlées* (1989) translated and published in English as *Massacre River*. These novels explore the amorous relationships of Hilarion and Claire-Hereuse, and Pedro and Adèle, respectively. The similarities between Adèle and Amabelle's names stress this intertextual connection. Equally, *The Farming of Bones* has a similar structure to *General Sun* and *Massacre River*. All three novels emphasise social and working life at the border prior to the massacre and their portrayal complicates claims of border conflict and unrest alleged by members of the Dominican military elite. The sections that describe the characters' lives before the slaughter are also prominently featured in terms of narrative length and development in *The Farming of Bones* and in *General Sun, My Brother*. In the latter, Alexis spends a great deal of the narrative describing Hilarion Hilarius's politicisation whilst he spends time in jail and becomes involved with the communist party. These parts of the novel set in Léogâne and Port au Prince outnumber the later section of the novel that relates the massacre. A little less than half the narrative of *The Farming of Bones* describes life in the village of Alegria before the slaughter. The first half of the narrative offers insight into the shared history and culture that connects Dominicans and Haitians.

There is another key intertextual reference in Father Romain, a character in *The Farming of Bones* whose name renders homage to Jacques Roumain, a towering figure of Haitian letters and author of the novel *Masters of the Dew* (1947) which has become a landmark of Haitian literature in its exploration of peasant life in Haiti. Father Romain plays a key role in assisting survivors after the massacre, and as a voice that reminds survivors of their shared cultural heritage and memory, which he centres as necessary for healing.[21] Therefore, crucial to the historical revisionary process in *The Farming of Bones* is the novel's archiving (through intertextual connections) of a Haitian literary tradition that has dealt with the massacre (and the experience of the Haitian working class) to which Danticat joins her own voice. Despite the various parallelisms between Danticat's, Alexis', and Philoctète's novels, an important element that differentiates *The Farming of Bones* from the others is the substitution of the third person omniscient narrator for a first-person testimonial narrative. Danticat explains in an interview with Myriam J. A. Chancy that her interest in the form of testimony lies in its potential to make us "understand larger events by reading one narrative" (29). Interestingly, the testimonial narrative in Danticat's novel is made up of various alternating narratives and memory threads.

Amabelle's life is deeply marked by the struggle of dealing with post-traumatic memories of the death of her parents which haunt her regularly. As many Haitians who live near the border often did, one day, Amabelle and her parents crossed the river to visit the market in Dajabón.[22] On their return home, the parents drowned whilst crossing the river and Amabelle witnessed their death. Don Ignacio, originally from Spain and member of the Dominican land-owning elite, finds Amabelle by the river and adopts her into his family, first as a companion to her daughter. In time, Amabelle starts to work as a domestic worker in the household. Although she has grown up with them, there are demarcated hierarchies, which are poignantly captured in key moments in the novel. The moment when Señora Valencia, Don Ignacio's daughter, gives birth to twins is significant in revealing how the construct of racialised difference works in the Dominican borderland. When Amabelle, who acts as midwife in the birthing of the twins, hands the second baby to Señora Valencia, she notices the darker complexion of the baby girl whose "skin was a deep bronze, between the colors of tan Brazil nut shells and black salsify" (11). Señora Valencia points out,

"They differ in appearance." She wanted another opinion.
"Your son favors your cherimoya milk color." I said.
"And my daughter favors you," she said. "My daughter is a chameleon. She's taken your color from the mere sight of your face."
Her fingers still trembling, she made the sign of the holy cross from her forehead down to the sweaty cave between her swollen breasts. (11)

Señora Valencia's remark reveals how the Dominican elite considers blackness to be threatening to a claimed Hispanic lineage and heritage. The defensive reaction of Señor Pico (Señora Valencia's husband), after Doctor Javier's comment implying the evidence of African ancestry is revealing of fears and shame connected to the past of slavery. Chancy argues that historians have overlooked the influence of the Dominican Republic's relationship to slavery in certain Dominican constructions of anti-blackness: "[s]lavery continues to be connected in the popular imagination to Haiti, and the humiliation of slavery is borne by Haitians; by displacing such humiliation onto Haitians, Dominicans release themselves from the shame associated with their slave past" (89). In its exploration of the various forms of psychological turmoil resulting from the history and influence of Spanish rule, Hispanophilia and the amnesia and historical repression of African heritage, *The Farming of Bones* sheds light on both the shared cultural and religious practices in both nations as well as the political structures consistently demarcating divisiveness between both peoples across both sides of Hispaniola. In the novel, there is a symbolic parallelism between Rosalinda (the twin with darker skin) and Rafi (of lighter complexion) and the two republics of Hispaniola: Haiti and the Dominican Republic, which despite sharing a history of European conquest, enslavement, and colonialism, had different relationships to their African heritage at an official level and in public discourse, cultural and popular expression (Shemak, "Re-Membering Hispaniola" 91–92). The twins make an allusion to the Marassa, the Haitian lwa of twin identity, a recurrent trope in Danticat's fiction. A trope that denotes the common history that unites both sides of the island, as well as their distance.[23] Rosalinda, the daughter with darker skin survives childbirth whereas Rafi, named after Trujillo, dies shortly after being born.[24]

Many of the cultural elements, and those from nature and the super-natural world, that connect the experiences of Dominicans and Haitians, and Dominican–Haitians, also mark their unequal standing in the Dominican Republic. For example, in *The Farming of Bones*, parsley appears as a weapon used against Haitians and Dominicans of Haitian descent; the Dominican army would demand during the massacre that they repeat the word parsley as a test to identify their ethnic heritage and their ability or difficulty in pronouncing the Spanish "r" in *perejil*. People's ability or inability to do so was reported to mark the difference between life and death. At times, as described in Danticat's novel, as a response to the test, soldiers would force feed parsley to their victims causing asphyxiation, an experience that Amabelle witnesses as she attempts to flee the country. Chancy also notes how in the novel, parsley is also used by Dominicans and by Haitians and Dominicans of Haitian descent (99). For example, in the Dominican household of

Señora Valencia "the parsley [was] suspended as a charm in the household, pointing to deeper shared cultural traits" (Chancy 99). Also, Kongo, an elderly *bracero* (sugar cane worker) who loses his son when he is run over by señor Pico's car, uses wet parsley in a purifying bath in the river. Amabelle's references to the use of parsley in the novel indicate how it is used "not only as an herb to flavour food but also as purifier, an analgesic, a healing agent, an instrument used in rituals to demarcate periods in time, beginnings and endings. It is an herb used to mimic the cycle of human time" (Chancy 99).

The Farming of Bones begins and ends its narrative invoking the Massacre River and the spirits that haunt its history. The opening of Amabelle's testimony anticipates the fraught institutional response. Amabelle confides the story to the Mother of the Rivers instead who evokes a "Vodou reconfiguration of the Virgin Mary or the West African Ochún" (Chancy 96). "In confidence to you, Metrès Dlo, Mother of the Rivers" (*The Farming* np).[25] This appeal to Metrès Dlo situates Amabelle's account outside the confines of official memory and anticipates the subsequent failure of Dominican and Haitian state institutions to effectively document and publicly mourn the lives of those killed in the massacre. Relying on and confiding the story to Metrès Dlo reveals Amabelle's desire to take the stories back to the river, which is then transformed from a site of violence and oblivion, into a site of memory and mourning. Renée Larrier notes, "Mèt Dlo is a Vodou figure from whom one seeks protection and it is to his female counterpart that Amabelle dedicates her narrative" (Larrier qtd. in Hewett 128). Metrès Dlo becomes not only witness, and confidant but also guardian of memory as well as "Amabelle's protectress" (Chancy 96).[26]

Amabelle's testimonial account can be partly read through the lens of *testimonio*, rooted in a political and literary Latin American tradition. George Yúdice describes *testimonio* as

> popular, oral discourse [in which] the witness portrays his or her own experience as an agent (rather than a representative) of a collective memory and identity. Truth is summoned in the cause of denouncing a present situation of exploitation and oppression or in exercising and setting aright official history. (44)

Amabelle participates actively in the construction of a collective memory and does so as an agent of that memory. Her individual story, as those of other characters, retains a sense of particularity whilst being intimately woven with the experience of others, yet never made interchangeable or reducible to an abstract collective experience. *Testimonio*, however, proves insufficient to cover the complex articulation of memory and trauma at stake in the novel. As April Shemak argues, it fails to contain and communicate the experience of the genocide: "because testimonials in the novel are often fragmented and at times silenced, the novel critiques the revolutionary potential of testimonio" ("Re-membering Hispaniola" 87). I would argue, however, that *The Farming of Bones* enacts rather a critique directed at the Dominican state for the failure to document the massacre in its aftermath, enacting instead a silencing and attempted erasure of the event. Fragmentariness in the narratology of the novel becomes an element that reflects and accounts for the effects of trauma and also connects with the non-linearity characteristic of Dominican and Haitian storytelling and literature. Amabelle's fragmented narrative, visually distinguished by an alternate intersection of memories in bold and regular typeface, forms part of an ethical account that reflects the irrecoverable loss and pain caused by the massacre and captures Amabelle's own process of remembrance and mourning. In regard to the sections in bold typeface that refer to personal memories of her past life before the massacre, Danticat explains, "I decided to write those little sections where it's just her thoughts, her remembering, her memory. Because it would just contrast the silence forced on people who work for others" ("Recovering History" 29). This, in turn, emphasises how the silence and invisibility expected of Amabelle as a maid in the Valencia household is echoed in the institutional silence imposed following the massacre.

In response to the lack of accountability, fragmentation in the novel narratively marks the intrusive effect of traumatic memories in the form of flashbacks, which Cathy Caruth identifies as central to its experience (and processing) as "the response to the event occurs in the often delayed, uncontrolled, repetitive appearance of hallucinations and other intrusive phenomena" (11). The repetition of the dreams and memories that haunt Amabelle (which are conveyed in the sections in bold typeface), intersect in the narrative with regular typeface thus mirroring the effects of post-traumatic stress disorder as interrupting time and a sequential experience of events. Nevertheless, the repetition of painful memories in the novel is also closely intertwined with Amabelle's conscious and vital desire to share her account and find witnesses for the stories of victims and survivors.

Chancy interrogates and extends Caruth's argument that the force of the inability to grasp and comprehend the trauma forms a static gap central to the continued effects of such trauma. She asks: "What chance, then, do recollections of collective, cultural traumas have of being adequately or (even less likely) accurately recounted? Ironically, the very gap that carries the force of the event that Caruth outlines, I believe, provides the opening for the reconstruction of repressed past events" (68). Chancy identifies possibilities for the bridging of both nations laying "within the gaps of history and trauma" (66), and further argues that the affective charac- teristic of the novel can deeply impact readers. The testimonies in *The Farming of Bones* as well as in Julia Alvarez's *In the Time of the Butterflies* (1994) and Angie Cruz's *Let It Rain Coffee* (2005) "act as 'proxies' to the events of trauma" and their articulation works as a means to "invoke empathy for their subjects in their readers, who then themselves inhabit the space of the proxy" (Chancy 67). The fargmentariness of the narrative and the poetics of counterpoint at stake in *Farming* are key elements in the configuration of such proxy, as shared space of witnessing.

Similarly, the problem of remembering, in the face of public or state amnesia renders Freud's insistence on overcoming trauma's repetition impulse of memories more complicated. For what about those situations when a traumatic experience is perpetuated through its ongoing suppres- sion and erasure? In cases of trauma followed by cultural amnesia, the repetition of memories can signal more than the experience of trauma. Repetition can also become both an unconscious impulse and a chosen act of remembering and remembrance of the dead. Amabelle dreams with the possibility of telling their story: "I dream all the time of returning to give my testimony to the river, the waterfall, the justice of the peace, even to the Generalissimo himself" (264). It manifests one of the many forms that grieving and mourning can take. Consequently, as Paul Ricoeur noted of Freud's theory, although the work of memory is intertwined with the work of mourning, both types of working through resignify repetition as a demand to bear witness to forms of counter-memory (76–78). Shreerekha Subramanian offers a perspective on the role of Amabelle's storytelling as guiding her mourning process, that also contradicts some of the premises of Trauma Studies:

> What drives the narrative forward and keeps Amabelle moving is her link with the dead: her parents, Antoine Désir and Irelle Pradelle, and her love Sebastien Onius. In this imagined community, the massacre's survivor finds

her humanity, her connection to a fleshy past and her desire to write the rest. Remembering is a political exercise, and not letting go of the dead is an act of love. (151)

By conveying processes of dealing with trauma, largely through varied acts of mourning, interpersonal and cultural memory-work, Danticat's narrative opens up new avenues for thinking through its effects. Caribbean scholars including Laurie R. Lambert and Shalini Puri have pointed out certain limitations in trauma studies' theorisations of trauma, particularly in terms of not accounting for the specificity of cultural and creative forms of dealing with it (Lambert and Puri discuss trauma around the events of the Grenada Revolution and its aftermath) (Lambert 32–35; Puri, *The Grenada Revolution* 23–24). Lambert sees greater possibilities in postcolonial trauma studies, as opposed to more Euro and Anglo-centric trauma studies embodied in the work of Caruth and others, since the former "shift the focus away from the individualized experience of trauma to the collective experience" considering their historical contexts (34). Whilst drawing from various concepts in psychoanalysis, Puri's exploration of the Grenada Revolution "route[s] them through a poetics of the land, vernacular idioms and local knowledges" (*The Grenada Revolution* 23), an exploration and sensibility that also takes place in Danticat's novel(s).

The sections of *The Farming of Bones* that narrate the massacre and its aftermath demonstrate the problems that survivors encounter in having their testimonies officially and ethically acknowledged. The night before the massacre, Sebastien, Amabelle's lover, convinces her to return to Haiti together, leave behind the hardship of life on the sugar plantation and start anew in Haiti. However, the killings begin and Amabelle has to flee. She cannot find Sebastien (who is captured) but meets his friend Yves, and together they cross the river, finally reaching the Haitian side of the border. Amabelle wakes up in a makeshift clinic. She and others gather in this refuge, where a priest and nuns are assisting survivors, many of whom are seriously injured. In the face of recent trauma, Amabelle notes their hunger to tell their stories:

Taking turns, they exchanged tales quickly, the haste in their voices sometimes blurring the words, for greater than their desire to be heard was the hunger to tell. One could hear it in the fervor of the declarations,

the obscenities shouted when something could not be remembered fast
enough... (209)

Soon after settling with Yves in his mother's house in Haiti, Amabelle
tries to meet with a justice of the peace in order to seek information
that may help her find Sebastien. Yves and Amabelle spend hours with
a thousand other Haitians lined up outside the official building waiting
to be heard. The hearings would often last whole days; yet there was
not enough time to record the stories of the thousands of people waiting
outside. On the first day that Amabelle and Yves line up for a hearing,
Yves sees the last woman to have a meeting with the justice of the peace.
He asks: "What did they do for you there? ... Did they give you money?"
to which the woman replies "'No, he did not give me money' ... 'You
see the book he had with him?' ... 'He writes your name in the book and
he says he will take your story to President Sténio Vincent so you can
get your money' ... 'Then he lets you talk and lets you cry and he asks
you if you have papers to show that all those people died'" (233–234).
The unrealistic demand for evidence reenacts the trauma and disavowal
embodied in the failure of this diplomatic action. The unfeasibility of this
demand also touches on an issue central to the precarious situation of
Haitians and Dominican–Haitians living and working along the border at
the time of the massacre and afterwards, with dire consequences today.
In the late 1930s many Haitians and *Haitiano-Dominicanos* (Haitian-
Dominicans) living in the region lacked Dominican nationality, an issue
that continues today when, despite having lived in the Dominican
Republic all their lives, many Haitian-Dominicans face enormous difficulties in obtaining a *cédula*, a documentation card proving one's national
identity.[27] The legitimisation of experience through state devised versions
of historical proof and documented experience confirms the fragile and
often unequal nature of official memory, and demonstrates how such
approaches are used to reproduce and perpetuate anti-blackness.

For fifteen days, Amabelle and Yves line up to see the justice of the
peace. On the sixteenth day he comes out at dusk and addresses the crowd
to announce that no more money will be handed out since "[a]ll the
money had already been distributed" (235), which caused much uproar
in the crowd (235–236). The fact that the recording of testimonials stops
after the money allocated for reparations runs out attests to the instru-
mentality of the process of documentation. The recording of testimonials
soon revealed its own utilitarian nature as initially both governments

decide on it in order to mollify international disquiet over the lack of accountability, yet this measure is short-lived. Despite never admitting to ordering the massacre, Trujillo signed an agreement in Washington, DC on 31 January 1938 in which the Dominican Republic commits to offer financial indemnification to victims of the massacre and their families. Trujillo offered "$75,000 (of which only $52,500 were ever paid) in exchange for an end to international arbitration" (Turits 636). Similarly, also provoked by international pressure, Trujillo dictated other measures such as the incarceration and then release months after in the border town of Montecristi, of alleged Dominican civilians involved in the massacre but who in reality were youths faithful to the regime selected by mayors of surrounding towns to pose during photomontage and spend some time in jails in exchange for remuneration upon their release. This was known as "*el gran teatro*" (the grand pantomime) (Fumagalli, *On the Edge* 146).

The oral accounts that *The Farming of Bones* describes were written down, and some have been compiled in a publication archived in the Archivo General de la Nación, the Dominican National Archives located in Santo Domingo, where the original documents for the publication are also held. Most of the testimonies were recorded in the Haitian town of Ouanaminthe. They were compiled by various *jueces de paz* (justices of the peace) and published as *Documentos del conflicto dominico-haitiano de 1937* (1985) by José Israel Cuello. The economy of these testimonies is striking. The brief accounts are included in boxes which from left to right feature place of declaration, date of testimony, name of witness, place of the event, date, people affected, nationality, nature of the event, and a final section for observations. In many cases the records display gaps left blank on some of these categories and boxes, representing the many silences that the process of documentation produced. For example, the nationality box is often left blank, suggesting that the speakers either refused to answer the question, perhaps due to fear, or it may have not been recorded. This blank space embodies larger and more systemic absences, and the systematic obstruction of human rights such as citizenship for a large number of Haitian and Haitian–Dominicans.

The Farming of Bones purports a demand in its aesthetic form. As previously mentioned, in the first half, the recurrent traumatic dreams of Amabelle are intertwined with the main narrative line. They disrupt the narrative and stress the individual past of the character-narrator. In the second part of the novel, the narrative in cursive focuses on the effects of trauma, individual and collective, and emphasises the importance of sharing trauma. As the novel advances, it becomes clear that the relationship between both narrative lines is more complex and interdependent than it first seems. Halfway through the novel, the sections in bold start to archive other moments of remembrance, which are thus incorporated in this special and very personal way of narrating and marking memory. Gradually, the remembrance of the massacre's victims is also included in these sequences. Amabelle describes a waterfall and a cave where Sebastien takes her one day. For Amabelle, this place represents a haven of memory. She remembers how Sebastien used to say that "the waterfall ... holds on to some memory of the sun that it will not surrender. On the inside of the cave, there is always light, day and night" (100). Amabelle extends her wish to symbolically connect the memory of her parents to this site of memory. She wishes to safely mark not only the grave of her parents but Joël and Rafael's: "I have always wished for this same kind of light on the grave of my parents, but now I wish it also for both Joël and Rafael" (101).[28] The sequential and fragmentary narrative structure in *The Farming of Bones* further illustrates the interconnectedness between personal memory and collective counter-memory.

Amy Novak locates a point/counterpoint dynamic between these two narrative lines in the novel and highlights a "model of historiography that embraces rather than denies the ambiguity and spectral nature of traumatic memory" and facilitates an examination of the personal and individual memory alongside the collective (95). Danticat puts forward a historiographical ethos that invites a critical conversation between different modes of understanding history from the perspective of those whose experience has been dismissed in the historiography of the massacre. Through this structure of point/counterpoint the novel also establishes the parallelism between the political situation in Spain and the Dominican Republic at that time, allowing for more historical connections between the two countries and thus a broader view into coloniality. Prior to the beginning of the massacre, Don Ignacio, "Papi" who had fought in the 1898 Spanish–American war to retain the colonies (then lost to Spain), follows with concern the news arriving through the radio from his homeland, Spain (74–77). By 1937 the Spanish Civil War had been unfolding for a year, confronting the fascist army of General Francisco Franco and the *gobierno de la República* (government of the Republic) that was   fighting to defend a democratic and progressive vision for the country.[29] Franco's fascist ideology and repressive dictatorship (lasting from 1939 to 1975) shared many similarities with Trujillo's, and both became close allies, even becoming uncannily similar in their attire, rhetoric, policies and presentation. As during the dictatorship of Trujillo, the victims of Franco's regime were often tortured, kidnapped and killed and at times buried in unidentified mass graves. This counterpoint linking these two historical figures, connected ideologies, and modes of repression highlights further the connection between imperial legacy, Spanish coloniality and fascism.

Forms of lived memory in the Dominican and Haitian villages are mostly interpersonal and are configured through networks of affiliation and kinship. In her descriptions of life in Alegria, Amabelle highlights the kinship existing amongst Haitians. She describes how people would spend afternoons sharing with each other memories about their past life in the same part of Haiti before settling in the Dominican Republic, and how when anyone returned to Haiti they would carry other people's belongings with them as a means to connect those people to their place and vice versa: "This was how people left imprints of themselves in each other's memory so that if you left first and went back to the common village, you could carry, if not a letter, a piece of treasured clothing, some message to their loved ones that their place was still among the living" (*Farming* 73). Forms of remembering provide a sense of common cultural identity to Haitians in Alegria and surrounding villages. In church, Father Romain mentions "common ties: language, foods, history, Carnival, songs, tales, and prayers. His creed was one of memory, how remembering – though sometimes painful – can make you strong" (73). Further, memory is maintained trans-generationally. Amabelle's reflection in one of the final bold print sections affirms the significance of remembering as a means to connect with the dead, which is present in much of Danticat's writing, particularly in her memoirs dedicated to her father and mother, *Brother, I'm Dying* (2007) and *The Art of Death: Writing the Final Story* (2017). In *The Farming of Bones*, Amabelle shares the need to find a place where to lay her memories and return to it as a "safe nest where it will neither be scattered by the winds, not forever buried beneath the sod" (266).

The visual image and metaphor of the nest imagines a new and safe burial for the dead, one that is free from forgetting and oblivion. The need to communicate the suffering and the witnessing of the massacre both requires and transcends the existence of an audience. The imagery of the nest also suggests the possibility of future returns to this resting place that can accommodate other and new memories. The image of Amabelle wanting to repeat this action, the symbolic act of archiving the memories in the land shows a ritualistic memory process in which the repetition of symbolic actions allows a working through of the memories, allowing healing via the connection to the land in a spiritual sense first, in the aftermath of the fracture of the social structures across the border.

The novel's opening shows how Amabelle's testimony mourns the loss of the victims of the massacre, by the river. Similarly, the ending of the novel marks again the river as a site of memory, underscoring the cyclical and performative structure of remembrance. In the final scene, Amabelle returns to the river after her exile in Haiti. This visit takes place years after the massacre, but it significantly occurs on an October evening marking its anniversary. Amabelle again confides, this time not only to *Metrès Dlo*, as in the opening of the novel, but (implicitly) also to the reader.

> I thought that if I relived the moment often enough, the answer would become clear, that they had wanted either for us all to die together or for me to go on living, even if by myself. I also thought that if I came to the river on the right day, at the right hour, the surface of the water might provide the answer: a clearer sense of the moment, a stronger memory. But nature has no memory. And also, perhaps, neither will I. (309)

Danticat's exploration of trauma, silencing, and its imprint on the self and the collective (re)turns to places in nature, the physical and spiritual landscape of the border and Haiti. The novel's poetics of counterpoint equally embody what Puri terms as the "poetics of the land" (*The Grenada Revolution* 23). In John Patrick Walsh's study of the construction of echo-archives in Haitian literature (which includes a discussion of Philoctète's *Le peuple des terres mêlées*), the scholar notes the function of the echo-archive to "call forth spaces that are subject to ideological and political deformation but are also capable of undermining that power" (50–51). The Dajabón river embodies a site of memory in other literature of the massacre. As noted in the opening pages of this chapter, in Roxane Gay's "In the Manner of Water or Light" from her short story collection *Ayiti* (2011), the narrator shares that her mother was conceived during the massacre. However, it is a story of trauma and silence as it is suggested that the narrator's grandmother was raped whilst crossing the Dajabón river. The unnamed grandmother in the story, like Amabelle, returns to the river to honour the memory of the dead. She tells her daughter the story and kneels beside the riverbank. Later, she tells her granddaughter (the narrator) "new fragments of their story, or if my mother's fears were correct, her story" (66). These accounts, as in *The Farming of Bones*, appear in fragments. This time they are shared intergenerationally.

THE (HI)STORY OF OSCAR WAO: "WHO IS MORE SCI-FI THAN US?"

Like Edwidge Danticat, Junot Díaz arrived in the United States at an early age, when he was six years old. He moved with his family to New Jersey and very much like Oscar, Díaz found an escape in books, especially comics, sci-fi and fantasy genres. As he has described in interviews, this was a means to find a space of his own within a new place and language and a strict home environment under the influence of his father, once in the Dominican army. If the character of Oscar offers certain parallelisms with Díaz's upbringing, so does Yunior, a character who appears in the short story collections *Drown* (1996) and *This Is How You Lose Her* (2012) and who, like Díaz, attended Rutgers University. Similarly to Danticat, Díaz has also portrayed in his work both the connections and disconnection with the DR and Haiti in diasporic communities from Hispaniola living in the United States. Both writers have explored the haunting of collective trauma experienced by Dominicans and Haitians throughout the various dictatorships that have marked the two nations, through multilayered storytelling that contextualises the role and responsibility of former colonial powers such as Spain and the US in supporting those regimes ideologically and politically. For Díaz, denouncing the foreign policy and legislation of the Dominican government and its effects on the Haitian and Dominican population of Haitian descent in the DR, brought a political backlash. In 2015, Eduardo Selman (the then Consul General of the Dominican Republic in New York), accused Díaz of being "un-Dominican" after Díaz joined human rights activists and writers, including Danticat, in a request to the US Congress for a resolution that would condemn the Dominican government for their legislation and foreign policy targeting Dominicans of Haitian descent. Díaz was also revoked an Order of Merit awarded to him by the Dominican government in 2009. (Franco)

As *Farming*, *The Brief Wondrous Life of Oscar Wao* is also a historical fictional account with testimonial components. The narrative centres on the life of Oscar De León and his family. Disrupting the chronological time in the account of Oscar's life are alternating past episodes of his family history intertwined with the history of Trujillo's dictatorship.

The story moves back and forth between New Jersey and the Dominican Republic across generations, a fluctuating movement across time and space that finally confirms the cyclical structure of history when Oscar ends up killed in a Dominican cane field, a site and scene that links the present with the Dominican past of military torture and the past of slavery. As a semi-omniscient narrator, Yunior is only witness to some of the events that take place in the novel; he reconstructs a variety of histories and stories through the accounts of other sources, as a historiographer would. Towards the end of the novel, Yunior reveals how he was compelled to tell Oscar's story after being haunted by his ghostly memory in dreams.

As in *The Farming of Bones*, Junot Díaz's novel also introduces the reader to non-normative forms of narrating (and reflecting upon) history. This is achieved, to a large extent, through formal arrangements that invite aesthetic and interpretive considerations. The existence of different texts, subtexts, and countertexts, as in Danticat's novel, propels an awareness of, and reflection on, the ways in which historical narratives organise power and knowledge. In *The Brief Wondrous Life of Oscar Wao*, the role of footnotes is multifaceted and reveals contrapuntal connections between Oscar's life in Paterson, New Jersey, the story of his family, and the history of the Dominican Republic. Footnotes appear in the narrative from the very beginning, providing a historical framework of the nation, especially during the "Trujillato" (Trujillo's era), whilst showing the ways in which that past continues to affect Dominicans on the island and abroad, amongst diasporic communities in places like Paterson. Stylistically and thematically, footnotes in Díaz's novel disrupt generic conventions and expectations through their conversational tone on one hand, and through the anomaly of their inclusion within fiction on the other. This calls further attention to the relationship between form and content in historically based narratives.

Dominick LaCapra notes how footnotes are considered as the part of a text that serves to authenticate and validate historiography or other types of historical texts (5–6). But LaCapra also identifies an occasional parodic use of the footnote in fiction and history, one that is corroborated in *Oscar Wao*[30]:

> Of course, notes may be used in both history and fiction in a manner that questions or even parodies a documentary or self-sufficient research paradigm, and there may be substantive notes that function not merely as

references but as elaborations of points or even as significant qualifications of assertions or arguments in the principal text, at times to the point of establishing a critically dialogic relation between text and note or even something approximating a countertext in the notes. (6–7)

This visibly disruptive and expansive role of the footnote in *Oscar Wao* highlights the need for references at the margins in order to access the story and history of Oscar whilst parodying the authority of this academic practice in instances of official Eurocentric and Anglocentric (colonial) historiography which nevertheless contains multiples gaps, cracks, and silences. Footnotes highlight a meta-discursive reflection that, at different levels, confronts the reader with the issue of how to read history, and especially how to read history against the grain of state-based historiography. *Oscar Wao* confronts the limitations in communicating a history that has repressed the memory of a great collective body for decades. It investigates questions that address and imagine other types and forms of representing collective memory by asking: what is the role of the fantastic and the imagination in filling those gaps and making readers feel their haunting presence in the present? What is the interrelation between popular culture and a critical interpretation of official history? And what does the coexistence of personal anecdotes and history in the footnotes reveal about Díaz's alternative vision of history?

According to Monica Hanna, "Yunior develops a model that is meant to act as a direct *counterpoint* to the national history presented by the [Trujillo] regime" (emphasis mine **504**). Text and footnote therefore mark a "critically dialogic" relationship as LaCapra puts it (7). Yunior refers to the daunting responsibility of faithfully conveying Oscar's life story, his family's biographies, and the history of the Dominican Republic. Through the footnotes, history is introduced in the story in an unabashedly critical tone. The first footnote in the novel sets this tone by explicitly pointing out the absence of Dominican and Caribbean history in educational curricula, alluding not exclusively (although principally) to the educational system in the United States and the Dominican Republic, but to Western education in general.

For those of you who missed your mandatory two seconds of Dominican history: Trujillo, one of the twentieth century's most infamous dictators, ruled the Dominican Republic between 1930 and 1961 with an implacable ruthless brutality. A portly, sadistic, pig-eyed mulato who bleached his skin, wore platform shoes, and had a fondness for Napoleon– era haberdashery, Trujillo (also known as El Jefe, the Failed Cattle Thief, and Fuckface) came to control nearly every aspect of the DR's political, cultural, social, and economic life through a potent (and familiar) mixture of violence, intimidation, massacre, rape, co-optation, and terror; treated the country like it was a plantation and he was the master. (2)

In a few sentences, Díaz is able to synthesise the dictatorship and establish connections between the dynamics of the plantocracy and the dictatorship. The use of language clearly avoids an objective scientific tone and remains unapologetically subjective in tone. However, it crudely states irrefutable and objective facts about Trujillo. Díaz's portrayal highlights Trujillo's signs of grandiosity, visibly reflected in the change of street names and various landmarks across the country. *Oscar Wao* resorts to humour and satire to critique and ridicule the assumed scientific tone of a conservative historiographical tradition where form and conventions have regulated what is included and excluded from its narratives, and makes use of fantasy and speculative elements to debunk historical constructs of the regime. In his introductory portrayal of Trujillo in that opening footnote, Yunior uses references to fantastic fiction and popular culture in order to provide a framework that properly contextualises the magnitude of power acquired, and abused, by Trujillo.

> At first glance, he was just your prototypical Latin American caudillo, but his power was terminal in ways that few historians or writers have ever truly captured, or I would argue, imagined. He was our Sauron, our Arawn, our Darkside, our Once and Future Dictator, a personaje so outlandish, so perverse, so dreadful that not even a sci-fi writer could have made his ass up. Famous for changing ALL THE NAMES of ALL THE LANDMARKS in the Dominican Republic to honor himself (Pico Duarte became Pico Trujillo, and Santo Domingo de Guzmán, the first and oldest city in the New World, became Cuidad Trujillo). (2)

Here, Yunior comments on the difficulty of looking at history, and specifically at the figure of Trujillo, exclusively through a conventional and realist lens. Since Trujillo's actions often entail a magnification of his character to almost epic dimensions the fantastic and sci-fi become more accurate genres to convey his despotism. Trujillo's own self-fashioning as *the* historical figure in his definition of the nation is already embedded in a discourse of the fantastic and the hyperbolic. By appealing to the fantastic, *Oscar Wao* makes emphasis on the extent to which history in the Caribbean is not only based upon discursive violence that imagines the colony and later reimagines the nation prescriptively; the fantastic is also able to convey something that a realist account could not. Especially significant is the stress on the role of the imagination in capturing the personality of Trujillo and the impact of his rule. The epistemic violence of Trujillo's reimagination of the landscape and history of the Dominican Republic is counteracted by Díaz's portrayal of *El Chivo* (Trujillo), who is hyperbolised, evoking Mario Vargas Llosa's caricaturist portrayal of "El Chivo" in *La fiesta del chivo* (2000) (*The Feast of the Goat*) where Vargas Llosa emphasises the grotesque and ridiculous aspects of Trujillo as historical character.[31]

Through similes, Yunior compares Trujillo to other dark figures such as Sauron (from *The Lord of the Rings*); Arawn (the villain from the series *The Chronicles of Prydain* by Lloyd Alexander)[32]; and the Darkside (from *Star Wars*). Although from seemingly discrepant cultural traditions and times, these references relate to Trujillo and the historical period in which he ruled. Common to all those characters, and Trujillo, is their implication in despotic forms of government, the drive towards creating an empire or imperial state, and its safeguard through the physical and discursive violence they entail. These connections confirm the relevance of looking at various imperial designs simultaneously in order to identify parallelisms between local histories and global designs (Mignolo). In the sixth footnote Yunior writes about Oscar and his love of sci-fi, fantasy and other speculative genres,

> [w]here this outsized love of genre jumped off from no one quite seems to know. It might have been a consequence of being Antillean (who more sci-fi than us?) or of living in the DR for the first couple of years of his life and then abruptly wrenchingly relocating to New Jersey—a single green card shifting not only worlds (from Third to First) but centuries (from almost no TV or electricity to plenty of both) ... Who can say? (21–22)

The fictional fantastic characters Oscar identifies with are themselves working against imposed constructs and prescribed forms of belonging to the nation. Yunior depicts Oscar as a "ghetto nerd" (11) with difficulties in socialising, finding a girlfriend, and adapting to Dominican and American standards of high school and life in general. Oscar is regarded as an outsider within his own Caribbean community in Paterson. He is also described as being at odds with wider US society. However, as Yunior shows us, Oscar creates his own world based on sci-fi books and comics; he draws his philosophy and way of seeing the world from their diverse stories. In counterpoint to Oscar, Yunior reveals (and overemphasises) his masculinity, outgoing nature, and ability to fit into the US context of Paterson and Washington Heights. However, as we see towards the end to the novel, there is a great loneliness for Yunior in his self-imposed plans to fit in, also latent in his admiration of Oscar and his choice to be, and choose, himself.

The narrator in *Oscar Wao* uses Oscar's knowledge and passion for comics and sci-fi to tell his story whilst simultaneously writing Caribbean history through incorporating in his version a personal and collective experience of the memories that are often dismissed and suppressed by national narratives and the formal historical Archive. From the Dominican Fukú, "the Doom of the New World", (1) to the Zafa (its *counter*-spell) embodied in Yunior's narrative, through intertextual references to comics, magic realism, and science fiction, Yunior's careful attention to form and content, and how polyvocality and heterogeneous stories/histories can be integrated into a larger narrative, becomes part of *Oscar Wao*'s critique to official historical accounts in the Dominican Republic, other parts of the Caribbean, and globally. Together, this documents the perspective of those with little or no access to representation in official narratives and Archives.

Yunior advocates and experiments with alternative ways of writing history not as representative of national history, but as an account mindful of the memories that remain at the margins of national narratives. Monica Hanna reads Yunior's historiographical task through Walcott's metaphor of fragmentation,

> Yunior often explicitly rejects the possibility of recovering an original, whole story because so much of the history he wishes to recover has been violently suppressed and shrouded in silence. The sources to which he has recourse are fragmentary at best, and he asserts the need of his art and creativity to cohere those shards and give a new shape to the vase of Dominican diasporic art and history. (498)

Hanna's reference to Walcott's metaphor of the broken vase and the resulting reassembling of the shards, connects various traditions of engagement with memory and remembering in the region, already invoked by Díaz in his citation of Walcott's poem "The Shooner Flight" as epigraph in the novel's opening. Whilst reassembling the fragments of memory to form a whole is not entirely possible, compiling and archiving these fragments reconstructs a new narrative and creates a new shape that is malleable, flexible, and offers more than one route to the past. Just like the cracks in Walcott's reassembled vase, the spaces in these reconstructed histories draw our attention to what has been historically silenced by the Archive. In the best contrapuntal and eclectic fashion, Díaz frames his novel by opening with two discrepant epigraphic references that nevertheless converge. One is a line from the *Fantastic Four*: "Of what import are brief, nameless lives ... to Galactus?" followed by an excerpt from Derek Walcott's "The Schooner Flight", the last line of which posits the problem "either I'm nobody, or I'm a nation" (346; 345–362). This link of Caribbean art and sci-fi implicitly articulates the question: what belonging can be imagined beyond the dichotomy of the marginalised, outcast figure or the clearly defined identity within a community like that of the nation or the diaspora? In *Oscar Wao* the relationship between text and context, the body of the narrative and the footnotes, is based upon a relationship of interdependency that questions these types of dichotomies.

The unruly nature of the footnotes in *Oscar Wao* defies genre conventions and boundaries that symbolically stand for the physical and ideological borders imposed by nations: be it geopolitical borders like the one that separates the Dominican Republic and Haiti or those that impose binary understandings of national and diaspora identity. Drawing from comics, science fiction, popular culture, Caribbean history and poetics, *Oscar Wao* constitutes a hybrid text where all these different and discrepant references and experiences coalesce forming an interconnected and intertextual narrative. For example, footnotes had previously been used by other Caribbean writers including Martinican author Patrick Chamoiseau in his novel *Texaco* (1992), providing a strong interrelated connection between centre-story and margins in the historical record, a specific influence that Díaz has previously acknowledged (Hanna 517n5). The substantial hybridity of genres in the narrative of *Oscar Wao* defies, as Monica Hanna argues, a monologic and homogenous model for the nation and for narrating what the Caribbean region and the Caribbean nation looks like or can be (503, 505). The haunting of history's nature in the form of traumatic memory/ies continues to reverberate today and the act of rewriting or re-embodying these accounts is a central aspect of both *Farming* and *Oscar Wao*. As Junot Díaz himself explains in an interview with Cuban writer Achy Obejas, the focus and role of history in the novel responds to what Díaz identifies as an underlying tension in the Dominican collective unconscious, whereby trauma is still largely unaddressed (44–45). Trauma and transgenerational trauma lie at the heart of *Oscar Wao*. The novel shows how the silencing of traumatic experiences has impeded their processing.

In the penultimate and untitled section of the novel, Yunior imagines the moment in which Isi, the daughter of Lola (Oscar's sister), arrives at his house and Yunior passes her uncle's story onto her: "This is what, on my best days I hope. What I dream" (331). In this dream, Yunior leads Isi to the basement of his house where he archives Oscar's documents. "I'll take her down to my basement and open the four refrigerators where I store her tío's books, his games, his manuscript, his comic books, his papers ..." (330). Yunior ultimately dreams with a trans-generational turn; the possibility that Isi would one day offer her own input in the configuration and reconstruction of Oscar's story: "And maybe, just maybe, if she's as smart and as brave as I'm expecting she'll be, she'll take all we've done and all we've learned and add her own insights and she'll put an end to it" (330–331).

SITES OF COUNTER-MEMORY

On June 2015, the Caribbean Studies Association published in their website a statement condemning the process of denaturalisation and deportation of Dominicans of Haitian descent, highlighting the ways in which both the Constitutional Court ruling TC/0168–13 and enactment of Naturalisation Law 169–14 violate rights to citizenship and how the system (with an 18-month window, and an insufficient 90 days extension to process documentation) failed those affected by the ruling, and led to the preparation of mass deportations. CSA also published a selection of articles by Caribbean scholars and artists addressing this injustice since 2013. Junot Díaz and Edwidge Danticat have actively and publicly condemned the Dominican government's position and the legislation that rendered hundreds of thousands stateless.[33] In a 2014 joint interview for *Americas Quarterly*, listed in CSA's website, both writers contextualise in their response how the history of Spanish, French, and US coloniality has shaped the anti-Haitian and anti-blackness rhetoric and divisiveness in the Dominican Republic, and how that made the passing of such legislation possible.[34] To the question about the role that history plays in how both nations interact with each other, Díaz stressed that this is "a complex, multivalenced history that involves former dictator Rafael Trujillo and genocide—a history over which looms the predations of Europe and the U.S. and Haitian elites and, yes, the Dominican Republic" ("The Dominican Republic and Haiti"). Danticat also points to the role of external meddling in the island's internal affairs, discussing specially the US occupation, and stating: "we have had our own internal problems, but there has also been this very powerful historical meddling to make sure that we stay divided" ("The Dominican Republic and Haiti"). The fabrication of narratives generating division and hate in Hispaniola remains central to the project of coloniality, particularly when these generate divisions that benefit the control of (ex)colonial powers over resources and their own perceived prosperity. *The Farming of Bones* and *The Brief Wondrous Life of Oscar Wao* shed light onto these processes. Further, their formal aesthetics and poetics of fragmentation, as this chapter discusses, ethically account for that complexity and transhistoric nature of collective memory and memory work that Danticat and Díaz discuss.

Through a poetics of fragmentation, much of the cultural and artistic production that deals with the massacre and Trujillo's dictatorship in literature, visual art, and music, underscores a fractured as well as a rich shared history, religious practice, and spirituality connecting the two nations. For example, Rita Indiana Hernández y Los Misterios's song and music video *Da pa lo do* (2011) (there is enough for two), included in their album *El Juidero* (2010), alludes to that shared cultural heritage. The music video, directed by Dominican artist Engel Leonardo, allows an appreciation of these connections both through the music style and lyrics as well as visually through the scenes that restage an encounter between two brothers representing both nations. Lorgia García Peña argues that this represents a reversal of the trope of Dominican white lettered men orphaned from the loss of the ties with "Mother Spain" (157). The two Black men positioned on different frames of the video embody the African roots and heritage of both nations. The fact that each one is wearing the Independence army uniform at the beginning of the music video, but they strip off their shirt and jacket along the way, becomes highly symbolic of the counter-discourse to notions of nationhood based on the discourses of hate that have historically influenced the relationship of both sides of the island through anti-Haitian rhetoric and anti-blackness. At the end of the video, the two men head towards each other and meet in a final embrace, in front of a large tree. The landscape is significant as it evokes the dry landscape

North of the border around the areas of Montecristi and Dajabón where the 1937 massacre of the Dominican Vespers took place (Fumagalli, *On the Edge* 352). The brothers (alluding to the shared Marassa in Vodou) are seen in the video as responding to the call and mediation of Afro-Dominican Vudú deity of love and discord Mambo Ezili Freda/Virgin Mary (portrayed by Hernández in the video) also with a counterpart lwa venerated in Haitian Vodou as Ezili Danto. The site where they see the apparition of the virgin/Ezili is significantly a river, evoking the Massacre River. They wash in the river, alluding to the Afro-Dominican religious ritual of *despojo* a healing cleansing where the person being cleansed after trauma or peril must wear white (García Peña 161). The title of the song "da pa lo do" alludes to the word *palo*, which as Maria Cristina Fumagalli argues suggest the *palos*: "long drums of African origin used for syncretic rituals and also associated with Liborism", a cultural and religious movement in the Dominican Southwest region led by healer and revolutionary Olivorio Mateo Ledesma (known as Papa Liborio) in the early twentieth century (*On the Edge* 352).[35]

A refigured fragmentariness characterises the aesthetics and poetics of music, visual art, and literature that deals with the history of the island. This can helpfully be seen through the lens of rayano consciousness which Lorgia García Peña identifies in the work of artists, especially Rita Indiana Hernández and visual artist David Pérez, and which she argues transcends the "conceptual limits of the militarized territorial Haitian-Dominican border" (133). For example, David Pérez's video installation *La Linea Fronteriza* (2008) encourages viewers to challenge the mental borders enmeshed in the geopolitical and physical delineations of the *linea fronteriza* (borderline) and provocatively invites audiences to envision an island without that border, an open island. The installation features two maps of Hispaniola outlined by lights against a black backdrop. The first map presents only the natural silhouette of the whole island, whilst a second one also shows the borderline. In an earlier piece *Lo que dice la piel* (What the Skin Says, 2005), Pérez asked a participant, an undocumented Haitian man to express what he thought was at the root of the Haitian–Dominican conflict; Pérez tattooed his response in Kréyol on his skin before seeking translation (the translation is "government business benefits governments" García Peña 147).[36] The symbolic act of inscribing those words on the body engages in an act in which "the performing body contradicts the archive" (García Peña 148). The playful participatory elements of Pérez's installation also aim to (re)think the

constructedness of borders, and the various investments in such constructions across the Americas. Also drawing from a fragmented aesthetic and
participatory approach, Scherezade García's action-installation "Memory
of Perejil/Memoria de perejil/Memwa pési" (2012),[37] part of the *Border
of Lights* collective, also asked pedestrians in locations across the border
to respond to questions about their knowledge of the 1937 massacre.[38]
For this public art project, inspired by research and conversations with
Edward Paulino and others, the Dominican artist created postcards with
a drawing of the face of two Black twins representing both nations on
the sides they occupy on a map, alluding thus to the Afro-religious
beliefs and heritage of Marassa veneration. The back of the postcards
displayed the following questions in Spanish and Kréyol "What do you
know of the 1937 massacre? Que tú sabes de "el corte" de 1937? Ki
können sou kout a? What have you been told? Qué te contaron? Ki konte
ou?" (Paulino and Sherezade 115). By doing this, creating an installation
in central parks in Dajabón and Ouanaminthe, Dominican and Haitian
towns at each side of the *raya/frontera* (the border), García connects
the memories across both locations creating opportunities for people to
read and bear witness to the responses, particularly as the postcards were
poignantly "hung as 'drying laundry' around the gazebo of both central
parks—an allegory of the 'cleansing' of both nations and the unofficial
nation in between: *la frontera, la raya*" (Paulino and Sherezade 115).
The assemblage and interconnection of the various elements in the work
of García, Hernández, and Pérez, as in Danticat's and Díaz's, are generative of critical spaces to voice difficult articulations of memory. Their
work suggests questions like what can be built of that which remains, of
the fragmented and often unknown or unrecorded memories? And, what
do artistic and cultural initiatives of oral history mean for Dominicans
and Haitians today, and for the continued memory work linking both
locations?

In Danticat's and Díaz's novels, places and landscapes mark personal
and collective memory in important ways. In both texts, the plantation is
experienced as a space where embodied memory remains a *site of memory*,
where violence keeps being reenacted, marking historical continuities with
the past. However, the *cañaveral* and the *batey* (plantation/settlement
around a sugar mill) also function as a space where survival signals another
type of continuity, enabled by the permanence of ancestral memory and
its intergenerational inheritance. This is the case in Amabelle's act of
mourning by taking her story back to the river and confiding it to *Metrès*

Dlo. The return, physical and spiritual, to spaces marked by trauma and loss in both novels reveals a cultural and psychological need to return to the place that marks the past in order to seek redress. It also illustrates how such return can become potentially productive of a more complex and nuanced understanding of national histories. Returning to the Dominican nation and crossing the transnational bridge in *Oscar Wao* emphasises the similarities and differences between the Dominican Republic and the United States. Seeing one place from the soil of the other enables Oscar to know and see these places differently and from more angles, as well as to connect the nature of personal relations and trauma in his own family within the framework of Dominican and US history.

The forms of remembrance and memory-works, are not exclusively confined to either official or unofficial forms of memory. For example, after the massacre Amabelle tries to leave her own testimony (without success) within the oral records that the Dominican church starts to collect. In this case, the emphasis is placed not on the incompatibility of official archiving, but with the cultural memory of peasants, domestic workers, and other members of the Haitian–Dominican community. The novel stresses rather the inefficacy and inability of such institutional archiving to allow members of the community affected to leave their memories in those records, providing firsthand accounts and thus contributing to the process of historiography of the massacre. Therefore, the binary distinction between unofficial and official forms of remembering, represented in conventional understandings of the categories of 'memory' and 'history' respectively, already reproduces the problematic binary categorisation between the traditional and the modern originated in the project of modernity; a distinction that Díaz's and Danticat's novels deconstruct through their configuration of counter-memory and counter-archives.

The narratives in *The Farming of Bones* and *Oscar Wao* stretch the boundaries of what is traditionally recognised and validated as official history. They claim the centrality of oral and written *testimonios* by individual survivors of historical events during the presidency of Trujillo. Equally, they claim the value of intercultural forms and vocabularies of memory. The multiple physical and figurative borders and boundaries crossed in Danticat's and Díaz's novels conceptually resist the demands of homogenising national discourses. From the polyvocal and non-linear narrative structure in both novels, which challenges a linear and straight-forward historiographical model, to the dialogics marked by a poetics of counterpoint embedded in Danticat's double narrative and Díaz's use of the footnotes, *The Farming of Bones* and *Oscar Wao* generate awareness of the pervasive and insidious threat to individual and collective self-expression that is imbued in nationalist discourses like Trujillo's. *Oscar Wao* also deploys a counterpoint dynamic through the use of the foot-notes in the novel. The incorporation of the footnotes not only pushes generic boundaries, questioning the fictional and creative elements within historiography, and the influence of history (especially) in Caribbean creative writing; it also aids readers to make connections between seem-ingly discrepant experiences in history and across geographies, in Paterson and Santo Domingo.

Danticat's and Díaz's novels not only revise and expand the history of the 1937 Massacre and Rafael Trujillo's repressive dictatorship; they challenge too our way of reading and approaching the violent history of fascist dictatorships such as Trujillo's (their connection to the epistemic violence embedded in Hispanophile attitudes) and its traumatic impact on later generations. Both novels look at what remains in the untold and silenced memories. They explore how memories linger and show their resonance and echo in the biography of places and the people who inhabit and build communities in them. Both novels prove that there is no possible telling of Oscar's and Amabelle's life without telling the history of Dominicans and Haitians who experienced Trujillo's oppression—and vice versa. However, equally, they augment and focus on their lives and those of their loved ones beyond the traumatic events they experience, engaging in localised individual and collective forms of memory, stressing the multiplicities of their personal experiences.

NOTES

1. CARICOM (Caribbean Community and Common Market) reported on the issue, releasing various articles and statements since October 2013 following the September ruling that year. On 2 October 2013, CARICOM released a statement titled "CARICOM Concerned Over Plight of Haitians in the Dominican Republic," caricom.org/caricom-concerned-over-plight-of-hai tians-in-dominican-republic/. Another statement from the 27 of October that year, reiterates that "the Caribbean community is

deeply concerned" by the ruling and its consequences, noting "with regret that the decision goes against pronouncements of the Inter-American Commission on Human Rights (ICHR) which has repeatedly called on the Dominican Republic to adopt measures to guarantee the right to nationality in the country and to adapt its immigration laws and practices in accordance with the provisions of the American Convention on Human Rights," caricom.org/statement-on-the-ruling-of-the-dominican-republic-constitutional-court-on-nationality/. Finally, a further statement from 26 October 2013, to which others followed, officially condemns the ruling, demands actions from the Government of the Dominican Republic to redress "the grave humanitarian situation created by the ruling" announcing also a halt to the consideration of full membership for the DR, observer of CARICOM since 1982, and a review of Caribbean Community's "relationship with the DR in other fora including CARIFORUM, CELAC, and the OAS". See caricom.org/caricom-statement-on-developments-in-the-aftermath-of-the-ruling-of-the-constitutional-court-of-the-dominican-republic-on-nationality/. Relationships with the DR have only recently shifted as marked by this article from 19 July 2020. See David Jessop's "Now Is the Moment for CARICOM to Re-engage with the Dominican Republic," caribbean-council.org/now-is-the-moment-for-caricom-to-re-engage-with-the-dominican-republic/. The elections were marked by massive protests in the Dominican Republic and the diaspora communities in the United States from 16 Feb. preceding the municipal elections, that demanded, amongst other things, transparency and social changes, also in foreign policy.

2. Although the stated aim of the law was to facilitate "a path toward citizenship" for those Dominicans of Haitian descent who had applied or reapplied to the civil registry and had identification documents (*cédulas*) granted by the government (Paulino, *Dividing Hispaniola* 165), the configuration of the law, as well as external conditions, made it impossible for many to apply and/or be granted inscription in the registry and obtain documentation to then be able to apply for citizenship. One of the incongruencies, as reported by Amnesty International and others, was the short window for applications to the registry, unrealistic for bureaucratic processes of this nature. See "Dominican Republic: No More

Hope for Tens of Thousands Stateless and at Risk of Expulsion If Residence Deadline Expires." *Amnesty International*, 1 Feb. 2015, amnesty.org/en/latest/news/2015/02/dominican-rep ublic-no-more-hope-tens-thousands-stateless-and-risk-expulsion-if-residence-deadli/.

3. Dominican Republic sometimes will be shortened to DR, from this point onwards.

4. In Spanish: *Movimiento de Mujeres Dominico-Haitianas*, see mud haong.org.

5. The role of Sonia Pierre has been instrumental to both the defense of human rights, especially along the Dominican border, and the creation of vital spaces and organising to address anti-Hatianism. Amongst other accolades, Pierre was awarded Amnesty International's 2003 Human Rights Ginetta Sagan Fund Award, the 2006 Robert F. Kennedy Human Rights Award and the 2010 International Women of Courage Awards.

6. Translation from Spanish: Center for Justice and International Law.

7. Government officials offered a variety of justifications for their refusal to release the girls' birth certificates, even though the Dominican constitution at the time granted citizenship to those Dominicans of Haitian descent born in the nation.

8. For an analysis on the process of denationalisation enacted by TC/0168–13 and 169–14, see Santiago A. Canton and Wade H. McMullen's "The Dominican Republic and Haiti; Shame." *Americas Quarterly*, 28 July 2014, www.americasquarterly.org/fulltexta rticle/the-dominican-republic-and-haiti-shame/.

9. *Border of Lights*, www.borderoflights.org.

10. For a discussion of the geopolitical situation in the border area – following the Constitutional ruling of TC/0168–13 and the Law 169–14 see Edward Paulino's "Epilogue: Return to the Source." *Dividing Hispaniola: The Dominican Republic's Border Campaign Against Haiti, 1930–1961* (2016), pp. 160 –168.

11. See Richard L. Turits, "A World Destroyed" (2002), p. 613.

12. The value of state documents in revealing compromising aspects of policy is referenced by Angie Cruz in her novel *Dominicana* (2019), where Anna (the narrator and a Dominican immigrant in New York) talks about a maid working at the Palacio during Donald Reid Cabral's American-backed government (1963–1965) who keeps classified documents under her mattress, taken from

the president's trash dating back to 1963 "just in case a poor devil needs a favor", adding "[w]hat housekeeper doesn't keep an archive of her boss's invaluable trash?" (282).

13. In public appearances, Rita Indiana Hernández has stressed how Balaguer's governments functioned as a dictatorship. And in her 2015 novel *La Mucama de Omicunlé*, translated by Achy Obejas as *Tentacle* in 2018, Hernández refers to his government as "a regime the foreign press—still—did not dare call a dictatorship" (17).

14. Original in Spanish: "[p]ara impedir ... que el país perdiera sus características de pueblo nítidamente hispano, lo que se necesitaba era poner en práctica una política de *dominicanización* de la frontera y despertar al mismo tiempo en el pueblo el pensamiento de sus grandezas tradicionales" (Strongman 22).

15. Balaguer's book has been reprinted eight times in Santo Domingo, a fact that attests "to the public demand in the Dominican Republic for these ideas, which exhibit a virulent racism" (Strongman 32).

16. Their ideology of ethnic superiority was fueled by an anti-Haitian discourse that dates back to the eighteenth century and was reified in the nineteenth century: "Since the 1800s ... elites had demonized popular Haitian culture, and Vodou in particular, as a threat to Dominican nationality. Haitian influence was perceived as an obstacle to the elite's aims to render the country 'modern' and 'civilized'" (Turits 599).

17. Amongst other causes, Spain's loss was the result of the diminished colonial power and neglect of the colony's government, due to internal conflict against Napoleon's invasion of Spain in 1807. Haitian president Jean-Pierre Boyer—with the help of Dominican cattle ranchers—unified the island in 1822 and abolished slavery in the former Spanish colony (initially abolished by Toussant L'Ouverture in 1801, and later re-established by Spanish forces in 1809 until their defeat in 1821). Hispaniola remained unified until 1844. Although the Independence from Spain was gained in 1821, some popular and official historiography of the Dominican Republic identifies 1844 with the victory of Juan Pablo Duarte and *la Trinitaria* constructed in nationalist discourse as liberation from Haiti and as the real moment of Independence, which

in itself reveals the extent to which the national imaginary is constructed around anti-Haitian rhetoric.

18. A cable exchange between the US ambassador to the Dominican Republic at the time of the massacre, Henry R. Norweb and US president Roosevelt, reveals knowledge and acknowledgement of Trujillo's order of the massacre on record. See Edward Paulino and Scherezade García's "Bearing Witness to Genocide: The 1937 Haitian Massacre and Border of Light." (2013), pp. 111–118.

19. See C. L. R. James, *The Black Jacobins* (1938)

20. Danticat currently lives in Miami, where she has been involved in activism that denounces and brings attention to the human rights violations carried out in ICE immigration detention centres in Miami and across the United States. In *Brother, I'm Dying* Danticat narrates the mistreatment and death of her uncle Joseph in one of those centres. With Junot Díaz, Danticat has also spoken publicly about the need to bring attention to the situation on the Dominican border and the role of remembrance and mourning in the process of marking the history of the 1937 massacre, a theme that was first captured in her short story "Nineteen Thirty-Seven" (in *Krik? Krak!*).

21. See Martin Munro, "Trauma, Memory, and History in Edwidge Danticat's *The Farming of Bones*" (2006), pp. 82–96, for a discussion of the intertextuality (as well as trauma in connection to memory and history) in the novel.

22. As Henry Louis Gates, Jr. explains in his documentary *Haiti & The Dominican Republic: An Island Divided*, hundreds of Haitians cross the Massacre River on market day to buy and sell products at the market in Dajabón. Edward Paulino points out that in various Dominican towns along the border Dominicans and Haitians trade freely in street markets that take place twice a week (*Dividing Hispaniola* 166).

23. For an exploration of the role of vodou in *The Farming of Bones* see Donna Weir-Soley's "Voudoun Symbolism in *The Farming of Bones*" (2005), pp. 167–184.

24. The Marassa trope also appears in other Haitian and Dominican texts as a means to stress the underlying and powerful connections linking the people and culture in both nations as well as their complex shared history. The novel *Marassa and the Nothingness* (2013, 2016), by Dominican writer Alanna Lockward explores

through this trope the relationship of twin sisters Laura and Mara, and their stories linking locales in Haiti and the DR. As Sophie Martínez points out, the novel "rewrites the narrative between the two nations by invoking unexpected figures revered in both sides of the island: Anacaona, the Virgin of Altagracia, and the Sacred Twins" (*Marassa* ii, e-book edition). The novel was first published in Spanish as *Marassá y la nada* in 2013.

25. This page is not numbered.

26. Metrès Dlo shares similarities with other religious and folklore figures across different places in the Caribbean. For example, Trinidad and Tobago's Mama Dlo or also known as Mama Dglo, a name that originates from "maman de l'eau" meaning mother of the water in French. Portrayed in folklore as a monstrous figure whose lower half of the body takes the form of an anaconda (although other times she takes the form of a beautiful woman) she is believed to punish those who attack the forest or the river by forcing them to marry her for the rest of their life.

27. In *Asylum Speakers: Caribbean Refugees and Testimonial Discourse* (2011), April Shemak elaborates a detailed analysis of the precarious situation of Haitian migrants and cane cutters in the Dominican Republic and the U.S.

28. Joël, a Haitian cane worker and good friend of Amabelle and Sebastien, is run over by a car one evening. Pico, Señora Valencia's husband, speeds on his way home to meet his newborn twins and the car hits Joël, killing him. This moment, and the disregard that Pico displays for Joël's life after his death, anticipates the violence of the slaughter.

29. This was a significant moment internationally, as C. L. R. James stressed in his preface to the first edition of *The Black Jacobins* (1938, xi), because of the increasing threat of fascism in Europe and the impact that a defeat of the Spanish Republican forces could have, as it later did, in the rise and consolidation of fascism in Europe. For a detailed discussion see Christian Høgsbjerg's "'The Fever and the Fret': C.L.R. James, the Spanish Civil War and the Writing of *The Black Jacobins*" (2019), pp. 161–177, https://doi.org/10.1080/03017605.2016.1187858.

30. From this point onwards I will use this abbreviation of Díaz's novel.

31. *Oscar Wao* makes an explicit reference to Vargas Llosa when Yunior emphasises the popularity of Trujillo's fixation with a young Dominican woman, which "was so common that Mario Vargas Llosa didn't have to do as much as open his mouth to sift it out of the air" (244).

32. Arawn is a character inspired by a figure from Welsh mythology; he is the king of the otherworld and has inspired the character in Alexander's book series.

33. Danticat and Díaz were actively engaged in brining attention to the issue, critiquing and condemning the unconstitutional actions of the Dominican government and its institutions. They wrote various articles for US news outlets including *The Atlantic, The New York Times*, and *The New Yorker*. Shortly after the 2013 September ruling, on 29 October, Julia Alvarez, Edwidge Danticat, Junot Díaz, and Mark Kurlansky co-authored "Two Versions of a Dominican Tale", a letter to the editor published in *The New York Times* that contextualised the ruling and its impact. In the letter, they also warned of the gravity of the situation and encouraged a public response and positioning as ethical responsibility to a process that has in the past led to histories of genocide. They ended their opinion letter thus: "How should the world react? Haven't we learned after Germany, the Balkans and South Africa that we cannot accept institutionalized racism?", "Two Versions of a Dominican Tale", *The New York Times*, 31 Oct. 2013, www.nytimes.com/2013/11/01/opinion/two-ver sions-of-a-dominican-tale.html.

34. Edwidge Danticat and Junot Diaz. "The Dominican Republic and Haiti: A View from the Diaspora." Interview by Richard André, *Americas Quarterly*, 28 July 2014, www.americasquarterly.org/ful ltextarticle/the-dominican-republic-and-haiti-a-shared-view-from-the-diaspora/.

35. The fact that Papa Liborio was killed in 1922 by the US army during the American invasion is also revealing of the continuing threat that African-Caribbean syncretic religion and spiritual knowledge posit to controlling sources of empire.

36. The original words in Haitian Kréyol tattooed in Pérez's arm were "biznis gouvenman bénefis gouvenman" (García Peña 147).

37. The action-installation is also known as *Postcard Project 2012*. See the artist's website for a description and images of the artwork, www.scherezade.net/#/postcard-project-2012/.
38. The installation-action was part of a series of events along the border commemorating and marking the massacre. See Edward Paulino and Sherezade García's "Bearing Witness to Genocide: The 1937 Haitian Massacre and Border of Lights" (2013), pp. 111–118. *JSTOR*, www.jstor.org/stable/24585148.

CHAPTER 5

Counter-Narratives in Black British and Caribbean Art in Britain

As occurs in other major diasporic locations such as the United States or Canada, in Britain, the writing of Caribbean born and Black British authors reflects a strong link and connection to the region, in terms of subject matter as well as form, narratively and stylistically. During a guest lecture at Goldsmiths University, Trinidadian writer, musician, and scholar Anthony Joseph, discussed the ways in which narrative forms like non-linearity are particularly suited to capturing the realities and lived experiences of Caribbean people and the region's physical and socio-cultural landscape.[1] Citing Earl Lovelace's words during a writing workshop that Lovelace led at the 2015 edition of the OCM Bocas Lit Fest in Trinidad, Joseph highlighted how experimental non-linear writing manages to communicate the experience of simultaneity. Recounting Lovelace's approach, Joseph states: "Caribbean writers need to find a form (ways of writing and approaching form) that mirror our experiences as Caribbean people … And the experience for him [Lovelace], of life in Trinidad and in the Caribbean is about simultaneity". Then, Joseph cites Lovelace's example of hearing "a conversation in the streets whilst someone is calling your name, and whilst someone else is having a fight with their neighbour … so there are all of these things happening simultaneously, and for him it is important to include all of this in the story".[2] Joseph, whose novels are formally arranged in non-linear and

© The Author(s), under exclusive license to Springer Nature Switzerland AG 2023
M. Fernández Campa, *Memory and the Archival Turn in Caribbean Literature and Culture*, New Caribbean Studies, https://doi.org/10.1007/978-3-030-72135-0_5

interconnected textual fragments and episodes, explains this as a poly-phonic and kaleidoscopic experience. This framework highlights the ways in which musical *and* visual elements influence form in Caribbean writing. Following that premise of the simultaneity and interconnection of expe-riences in Caribbean storytelling, this chapter traces the ways in which non-linear narratology and musical forms in Caribbean and Black British artistic and literary works disrupt official narratives and archives in Britain and the various silences they contain. The main works explored here cover fiction, performance poetry, and multimedia art from the early 1990s to 2019. Caryl Phillips' novel *Crossing the River* (1993), Roshini Kempadoo's multimedia installation *Ghosting* (2004), Dorothea Smartt's poetry collection *Ship Shape* (2008), and Jay Bernard's poetry collec-tion *Surge* (2019) all configure various non-linear and polyphonic poetics influenced by a turn to popular culture (drawing especially from music) as formal influence and an increasing archival turn as source of critical engagement and interrogation. There is also a geographic and cultural linkage in these works as the authors and artists I discuss here are either born in the Caribbean or are of Caribbean descent. They all share a strong influence from, and engagement with Caribbean diasporic cultural forms, most notably music.

The chronological order of texts in this chapter is not meant as a claim to a linear development within a Black British or Black Atlantic non-linear aesthetic, but rather as allowing us to see certain shifts and trends in the artistic production of the Caribbean diaspora in Britain in connection to their socio-political and cultural context. Stuart Hall identifies three key moments in the history of Black diaspora artists in Britain in his essay "Black Diaspora Artists in Britain: Three 'Moments' in Post-war History" (2006). This periodisation is useful, particularly as it introduces the 1990s as a paradigm-shifting decade, moving away from previous constructs of blackness and representations of a Caribbean dias-poric identity and experience that had been more prevalent in decades like the 1960s and where nativist manifestations of identity prevailed in Britain. In the first of the periods he discusses, the 1960s, Hall sees a continuation of the initial optimism of the Windrush generation and a readiness to engage with modernism since, "they [Caribbean artists] came to Britain feeling that they naturally belonged to the modern move-ment, and in a way, it belonged to them" (5). Discussing the trend of this decade in the arts, Hall references Caribbean writers such as George Lamming, Sam Selvon, V. S. Naipaul, Andrew Salkey, and others who were modern "in spirit", embodying Herbert Read's notion that modern art relied on finding the most suitable form to convey the contemporary moment. This period also showed fluctuations and "contradictory pulls", as the work of artists working in the 1960s, would alternate between "'nativist' and modernizing impulses" ("Black Diaspora" 15). Their work engaged with Caribbean issues and cultural frameworks, and these were often embedded and put in dialogue with modernist ones. However, the second of Hall's key moments, the 1970s, saw the disillusionment with the indifference and barriers from British institutions and the art establishment in informing critiques of Eurocentric visions that solidified into the 1980s. As Hall notes, the history of racism in Britain was marked by certain shifts in the terms of inclusion and exclusion in the nation experienced by first-generation Caribbean migrants and their offspring. Diaspora art in early-1980s Britain, departs from, rather than continuing previous artistic forms or traditions, a shift made by "the first black generation to be born *in* the diaspora" (S. Hall, "Black Diaspora" 17). According to Hall,

> This new 'horizon' produced a polemical and politicized art: a highly graphic, iconographic art of line and montage, cut-out and collage, image and slogan; the 'message' often appearing too pressing, too immediate, too literal, to brook formal delay and, instead, breaking insistently into 'writing'. The black body – stretched, threatened, distorted, degraded, imprisoned, beaten, and resisting – became an iconic recurring motif. ("Black Diaspora" 17)

The third phase in Hall's periodisation ranges from the mid-1980s through the 1990s with the configuration of the Black Arts Movement formed by visual artists motivated by a series of questions around identity. Hall stresses how the stereotyping, marginalisation, and discrimination of migrants of the Windrush generation and their descendants led (particularly the younger generation) to question issues of cultural identity and belonging in the nation, through questions such as "'[w]ho are we?' 'Where do we come from?' 'Where do we really belong?'" ("Black Diaspora" 18). Hall describes how a "[n]ew Pan-African diasporic imaginary surfaces for a time, redeeming through image and sound the breeches and terrors of a broken history" (18). Black British and Caribbean writing of this period displays similar concerns around identity. Aesthetically, there is also an emphasis on fragmentation and non-linearity through the use of strategies akin to art techniques such as collage and montage in the structuring of narrative. From the mid-1990s to the first two decades of the 2000s (following this last period identified by Hall) formal disruptions and experimentation heightens in visual arts and literature under the influence of popular culture. This chapter asks, how do Caribbean-inspired forms and poetics shape these critical interventions, and how do artists' interrogations of the past illuminate the entanglement between Britain and the Caribbean? What new avenues do they reveal for thinking about their shared histories?

From Context to Text. History and Aesthetics

As Hall points out, the context and history of the Black diaspora in Britain is closely connected to the aesthetic of much Black British and Caribbean-British art, which extends to writing, as well as visual art. This critical line of enquiry and argumentation has been discussed and continued by other scholars (Anim-Addo and Gunaratnam; Arana; Blevins). Many of the aesthetic choices and experimentation with narrative and artistic form aptly account for the multiplicities and intersecting factors shaping the experiences of the Caribbean communities in Britain. This context is part of the milieu of an extensive repertoire of poetry, fiction, prose, and drama as well as painting, sculpture, photography, and digital art that interrogates the power of narrative. Caribbean-born artists in Britain and those of Caribbean descent have continued to explore form in its political and philosophical dimensions, encapsulating Paul C. Taylor's definition of Black aesthetics as "the practice of using art, criticism, or analysis to explore the role that expressive objects and practices play in creating and maintaining black life-worlds" (Ch. 1, section 2). For decades after the Windrush arrival, the history of Caribbean communities in Britain was absent from the public sphere and misrepresented in the media, which attests to the power of institutions in shaping and shifting narrative, often countered by the arts and cultural production. Black British and Caribbean writers and artists in Britain have played a vital role in documenting and bringing diasporic history to the wider public sphere and to a variety of cultural and artistic spaces and counter-publics. Novels such as Sam Selvon's *The Lonely Londoners* (1953), Zadie Smith's *White Teeth* (2000), and Andrea Levy's *Small Island* (2004) have become popular titles that have shaped the public imagination and narrative about the Windrush experience. Levy's, Selvon's, and Smith's novels' exploration of form and aesthetics plays an important role in historicising that experience of migration and community.[3] All three texts are assigned in school and academic curricula and the latter two have been adapted to TV film series, thus widening the reach of audiences. However, despite the interest and mediatisation of Caribbean-British history, as David Lammy points out, "the story of Windrush is ... one that is too often neglected in our media, which I'm sad to say, it's often whitewashed" (xxi).

The following brief overview of some moments in this larger history of the Caribbean and Black British diaspora in Britain aims to offer a sense of the barriers to belonging and the terms of exclusion, and aims to highlight the long history of resistance and greatly influential cultural production of Caribbean people and Black Britons. This is key to an appreciation of how the response to official historical narratives and forms of cultural (mis)representation was conveyed through creativity and a diasporic aesthetic largely inspired and informed by rhythm and interconnectivity of musical structures, music(ality), and visuality. The 1998 4-part documentary series *Windrush*, originally broadcast on BBC 2, offers a thorough historical record covering the year of arrival to the late 1990s, drawing from archival video footage and oral histories from Caribbean writers, historians, cultural critics to individuals across generations, offering a multilayered historical insight. The documentary, directed by David Upshall and narrated by Caryl Phillips, contextualises the social and political context of the Windrush arrival in Britain and post-war life in Britain.[4] It maps the change in immigration policy with the 1962 Commonwealth Immigrants Act[5] and the 1968 Act, highlighting the parallelism between the sense of uncertainty caused by this new legislation and the violence promoted by the rhetoric of figures like Enoch Powell and the National Front campaigns.[6] In 1969, the killing of Nigerian immigrant David Oluwale at the hands of the police in Leeds made the reality and threat of institutional racism further evident. The story of Oluwale, which has been portrayed by Caryl Phillips in *Foreigners: Three English Lives* (2007) and other talks and writings, reflects the insidious impact of the ongoing state and social violence on Black immigrants.[7] In 1979, a decade after the killing of Oluwale, a report by the Race Relations Institute to the Royal Commission on Criminal Procedure published its findings showing widespread discrimination and police harassment in Britain. Some stark examples of this are the disproportionate presence of police racial profiling at the 1976 Notting Hill Carnival and the Southall riots of 1979, which together with the enforcement of the 'sus law'[8] provoked the uprising.[9,10] The increase of these forms of institutional racism continued through the 1980s, resulting in a series of confrontations between the police and African, Asian, East Asian and Caribbean communities across the country. Following the murder, by arson, of thirteen Black youths at the New Cross fire in Lewisham in 1981, also known as the New Cross Massacre, a march across London demanding justice on March 1, known as Day of Action, was organised to demand justice and protest against the misrepresentation of the media, irregularities in the investigation of the murders, and the institutional silence. The indifference of the media, police, and British institutions at large contributed to a sense of distrust and disavowal partly leading to the Brixton 1981 riots/Brixton uprising which sparked other uprisings across the country against the surveillance and harassment through the stop and search practice under the "sus law" enacted during Margaret Thatcher's government. Interspersed with the episodes detailing the various forms of institutional racism in Britain, the Windrush documentary, significantly offers a cultural history discussing how the literary, music and visual art scene, as well as sports and politics, were profoundly transformed by Caribbean and Black British individuals and communities from 1948–1998. A variety of spaces from sound systems and house parties to cultural and political centres were vital in the formation of Caribbean and Black British sense of kinship and diasporic solidarities and cultures.

The 70-year anniversary of the arrival of *HMT Empire Windrush* in 2018, marked opportunities for commemorating the Windrush generation and widening its narrative. Writers and critics pointed out the vital role of women writers and women migrants of that generation (Lowe; Brinkhurst-Cuff), as well as the experiences and contributions of the Chinese- and Indo-Caribbean population in Britain as their stories remain less known since Windrush migration has been largely represented as African Caribbean and predominantly male (Kaladeen "Windrushed"). The recent publication of *The Other Windrush* (2021), edited by David Dabydeen and Maria del Pilar Kaladeen offers a vital counterpoint and expansion of the documentation of the Windrush generation and their descendants through a combination of formal and family archives, photographic records, memoir, and oral history. Similarly, Hannah Lowe has written about previous journeys such as the one of the troopship *SS Ormonde* in which Caribbean migrants including her Chinese-Jamaican father had travelled to Britain after the war (1947), marking less known and mediatised journeys that preceded the iconic one of the *HMT*

Empire Windrush. Her book of poetry *Ormonde* (2018) drew inspiration from a found notebook by her father, Ralph Lowe, with memories of growing up in rural Jamaica and his migration journey, as well as research of archival records such as a passenger list held at The National Archives (8–11). The Windrush commemoration in 2018 was unfortunately clouded by the fuller uncovering of the Windrush Scandal in the media, and the disenfranchisement and secret deportations of members of the Windrush generation whose status in the country was questioned under new government policy, going back to 2010.[11] The importance of official archives and their records in state regulation and bureaucratic control has become even more apparent. For example, in 2010 the Home Office ordered the destruction of the disembarkation cards of Caribbean migrants dating back to the 1950s and 1960s, with substantial implications on numerous people's lives. As a result, as British journalist Amelia Gentleman reported, "[m]any Windrush-generation individuals who have had difficulties providing evidence of their status have told the *Guardian* how they were repeatedly told their names were "not in the system" ("Home Office Destroyed").[12] A former Home Office employee shared with Gentleman how, despite opposition from employees, the orders were carried out supposedly on the grounds of data protection, and suggestions of digitisation were met with refusal. The source admitted to a shift in attitudes with the arrival of the "hostile environment" era promoted by Theresa May.[13] This reinforcement of "decades of restrictive policy and demonising rhetoric [that] have created this system" (Goodfellow 12), took place around the same time that the 2013 ruling in the Dominican Constitutional Court denied citizenship to Dominicans of Haitian descent.[14] Post September 11 global changes in foreign policy, immigration legislation, and border control have progressively mined human and civil rights, and had a major impact on violating the legal rights of racialised communities.

The history of the term "Black" in Black British encompasses the struggle towards a recognition of citizenship rights and visibility of the Caribbean diaspora in Britain, as well as shared relationship to coloniality and decolonial cultures.[15] The term reflects the sense of alienation and of not fully belonging to the nation experienced by second- and third-generation descendants of the Windrush generation, whose racialised identities were at times marked as foreign to Britishness. It also became a political articulation of that experience and it encompassed (particularly in the 1980s), the African, Caribbean, Asian, South-East Asian, and

Middle Eastern population and their descendants. Stuart Hall identified a new politics of resistance resulting from the origins, use and politics of the term "Black" which was "designed to challenge, resist, and, where possible, transform the dominant regimes of representation—first in music and style, later in literary, visual and cinematic *forms*. In these *spaces* blacks have typically been the objects, but rarely the subjects, of the practices of representation" (S. Hall, "New Ethnicities" 164; emphasis mine). Central to the history of political and cultural resistance were collective efforts and groups formed by Black women. The 1970s was a shifting decade, since as Julia Sudbury points out (citing Peter Fryer and James Walvin), that is when "black women began to organise autonomously" (315). Crucial publications such as *Heart of the Race: Black Women's Lives in Britain* (1985) by Beverly Bryan, Stella Dadzie, and Suzanne Scafe document that history of resistance through oral history, and as they explain in the introduction to its new edition in 2018, they felt motivated to write it as "it was high time we started to record our version of events from where we stood as Black women in the 1980s" (1).

In the face of institutional and social hostility, political and cultural organising created spaces and communities that have been vital to anti-racist struggle in Britain. Steve McQueen's 5-part film anthology *Small Axe* (2020) documents that history, covering the period from the late 1960s to the early 1980s.[16] The first film in the series, *Mangrove* tells the story of the 1971 trial of the Mangrove 9, a group of Caribbean and Black British youth who were accused of inciting violence for participating in a peaceful protest against police harassment and brutality in the area of Notting Hill.[17] Restaurant owner of *The Mangrove* and activist Frank Crichlow, British Black Power Movement leader Altheia Jones-LeCointe, activists Darcus Howe, and partner Barbara Beese, also members of the Black Panther movement, were amongst those accused in the trial, confronting the testimonies of the police officers.[18] Significantly, in *Mangrove*, the storytelling approach and aesthetics place great emphasis on Black lives before they are disrupted by the violence of the state.[19] Key to the creation of *Small Axe* is the fact that it is not contained into one film but rather across an anthology where its many parts tell a larger history, interconnecting some of those stories in that process. The significance of multiple perspectives when narrating histories that have been previously erased or constructed more homogenously remains central to the storytelling process. This dialogical aesthetic is also present in the work of other video artists including John Akomfrah and Isaac Julien.[20]

In *TateShots*, Akomfrah describes the philosophy of montage that informs his work, as

> the commitment to bricolage, the commitment to having discrete elements, fragments, come together ... Everyone who helped popularise the philosophy of montage was interested in one thing: the third meaning. That is, that if two opposites collide, in this dialectical way, some sort of synthesis is engineered or brought about and in that, a new form, a new meaning or a new way emerges, which you can chase ad infinitum. (*TateShots*)

This emphasis on the process and on identity always in formation (cultural and individual identity) through interrelation was also central to the philosophy and work of Stuart Hall whose life and work Akomfrah documented in *The Stuart Hall Project* (2013). The literary works and performance poetry included in the following discussion follow that same principle of relationality and synthesis resulting in new forms and meanings that emerge from the contrast brought by bricolage and montage in the process of bringing together seemingly discrepant yet interconnected narratives. The stories and histories evoked in the visual art and literature under discussion in this chapter are located in (and connect locations across) Britain, Barbados, Trinidad, and the United States.

MEMORY, DRUMS, AND CROSSINGS

Paul Gilroy and Caryl Phillips published *The Black Atlantic: Modernity and Double Consciousness* and *Crossing the River*, respectively, in the same year, 1993. Both music and memory are at the heart of these texts, as is aesthetics. *The Black Atlantic* has become foundational, reinforcing a transnational turn and opening the field of Black Atlantic studies. It also makes an important case for the shaping force of music as conduit of diasporic memory and aesthetics. Gilroy highlights music's role in influencing the creativity of work that aims to transcend the limitations of monocultural mythic visions of a white nation-state. As Gilroy argues, popular culture, largely music but also literature, articulates a rupture with narrow constructions of modernity and the nation-state. *Crossing the River* provides physical and conceptual shape to that rupture through an antiphonal dynamic of call-and-response of the various sections in the novel.[21] Phillips' body of work reflects a longstanding engagement with music as a thematic and formal concern, often linked to his use of non-linear narrative patterns.[22] These paths trace a means of accessing untold and lesser-known histories in non-prescriptive ways, resulting in what I call here an *ethics of interconnection* where the underlying connecting threads between stories illuminate the close entanglement of historical moments. In Phillips' first novel, *The Final Passage* (1985), the narration shifts back and forth in time, sometimes through a series of past memories, and other times through accounts in different time sequences preceding the protagonists' journey across the Atlantic, which takes Leila, her husband and small baby from an island in the Caribbean to England. Those narrative shifts capture the rocking movement of the waves at sea and the ruptures further heightened by the journey of migration and life in Britain. Later texts such as *Crossing the River* (1993), and *Foreigners: Three English Lives* (2007), continue to disrupt linearity through a series of stories that span time periods and geographies, yet are interconnected through memory threads that become central to acts of critical reading.

Bénédicte Ledent draws attention to the fact that although the predominant critical focus on *Crossing the River* has been on its engagement with transatlantic slavery, a distinctive element that most critics have identified and agreed on is the polyphonic sensibility of the novel: "a constant in the various existing interpretations is that this fragmented, polyphonic narrative invites the reader to listen to unheard voices from the past, a reading which is also encouraged by the novel's decidedly aural and musical nature, particularly perceptible in its prologue and epilogue (see Mascoli)" (11). Ledent and Daria Tunca highlight the "almost choric arrangement and symphonic structure of the writer's fictional texts" (xiv). In a critical discussion of *The Lost Child* (2015); *The Nature of Blood* (1997), and *Dancing in the Dark* (2005), Giulia Mascoli argues that the influence of music is manifest both thematically and stylistically, in turn affecting greatly readers' emotional and intellectual responses and engagement with the writing, creating a powerful "link between music, memory and emotional involvement" ("The River" 85). In his discussion of Black aesthetics, Paul C. Taylor considers the "meaning of black music for the body and the soul" (Ch.1, section 6). Taylor argues for the centrality of rhythmicity (as central to Black musicking) on the philosophical and aesthetic expression of African diasporic experiences and cultures, and as carrier of both cognitive and spiritual value (Ch.6). Rhythmicity in Caribbean and Black British writing (through polyrhythmic and polyphonic effects; offbeat phrasing paralleled through tempo and modulation; and general dynamics of call-and-response) works as a conduit of interconnected histories and does so establishing vital channels of affect. Considering, and discussing, the various sections of *Crossing* as interconnected through the relational dynamic of music forms like jazz and soul music, allows readers to appreciate the historical and experiential continuities linking the novel's characters. An alternating dynamic of repetition and variation in the novel, a characteristic feature of jazz, highlights the cyclical nature of time and history and the interconnectedness of the stories binding all the "sons of the diaspora" as voiced by the African father in the prologue. Mascoli's reading of *Crossing* as a jazz novel discusses how Phillips' "recurrent and creative use of repetition contributes to the emotional impact of his distinctive prose" ("Remembering" 8).[23] The elements of a jazz novel can be found in *Crossing*, but so can the rhythmicity of African diasporic and Caribbean musics generally, since "Afro-modernist jazz novels" engage in the "simultaneous exploration of the intercultural significance of jazz" (Lowney 25). Equally, the imitation of jazz in fiction happens at the level of performance, sonic elements, and structural patterns (Petermann), all of which are present and highlight an ethics of interconnection in *Crossing*. In "The Changing Same (R&B and New Black Music)", where Amiri Baraka (former name LeRoi Jones) situates the various contexts and significance of the formation and evolution of jazz, blues, and R&B. He also identifies continuity in a "tradition" of ongoing shift, and one that is precisely marked by that notion of the changing same, as "the music's emotional patterns continue" (191).

The prologue and epilogue are key sections in unifying the four separate accounts in *Crossing the River*. These sections most explicitly convey the overarching call-and-response structure of the text. The prologue (and epilogue) is narrated in the first person by a mythical African father who states, "I sold my children. I remember. I led them (two boys and a girl) along weary paths" (1). Those children are Nash, Martha, and Travis, three of the main characters in the four stories of the novel. The narrative structure of the prologue is circular; the punctuated rhythm of short sentences runs throughout the text and the phrases, "A desperate foolishness", "The crops failed", and "I sold my children", feature at the beginning and end of this section. Similarly, the ending of the prologue marks a "call" that is answered in the epilogue. The various references to chorus and drums as connecting elements appear in the middle and the end of the prologue. The sentence "For two hundred and fifty years I have listened to the many-tongued chorus" (1) is later followed by "For two hundred and fifty years I have waited patiently for the wind to rise on the far bank of the river. For the drum to pound across the water. For the chorus to swell. Only then, if I listen closely, can I rediscover my lost children" (2). The phrase "for two hundred and fifty years" appears in different keys and contexts throughout the text, as a riff that both expands and collapses the temporalities marked in the intersecting stories and histories in *Crossing*. In jazz, a riff takes place when a music phrase is played again with variation, and in jazz literature a riff can be a "a recurrent motif and idea ... [or] (linguistic) phrases that are repeated in nearly identical form" (Petermann ch.3 105).

After reading the four following accounts of the lives of those 'children' on both sides of the river (the Black Atlantic), we find the response in the epilogue where the same voice opens with: "I hear a drum beating on the far bank of the river. A breeze stirs and catches it. The resonant pounding is borne on the wind, carried high above the roof tops ..." (235). To which follows a litany of highly visual scenes that travel across geographies and offers a window into various lives of the "children of the diaspora" in places like London, New York, São Paolo, Santo Domingo, Charleston, Rio de Janeiro, or New Orleans (235–237). They are all "Survivors" (236) and their voices and stories have been heard across the river. They have also been heard—significantly—through music.

> ... I have listened. To reggae rhythms of rebellion and revolution dipping through the hills and valleys of the Caribbean. I have listened. To the saxophone player on a wintry night in Stockholm. A long way from home.... For two hundred and fifty years I have listened. To the haunting voices. Singing Mercy, Mercy Me. (The Ecology.) Insisting: Man, I ain't got no quarrel with them Vietcong. Declaring: Brothers and Friends. I am Toussant L'Ouverture, my name is perhaps known to you. Listened to: Papa Doc, Baby Doc. Listened to voices hoping for: Freedom. Democracy. Singing: Baby, baby. Where did our love go? Samba. Calypso. Jazz. Jazz. Sketches of Spain in Harlem. ... (236)

The explicit reference to reggae is followed by others to soul (via the title of Marvin Gaye's "Mercy, Mercy, Me (The Ecology)", samba, calypso, and jazz (specifically Miles Davies' album *Sketches of Spain*). All these musical references in the epilogue, equally echo the repetition of the word "weary" which appears twice in the phrase "weary paths" in the prologue, thus invoking the lament in the song of blues within Langston

Hughes' poem "The Weary Blues" (33–34). The language of memory and the articulation of that resistance and rebellion appears in these references as fiercely articulated through sound, beat, and song. Further, the sonic effect of the repetition of the phrase "I have listened" which appears multiple times throughout the epilogue emulates a chorus, particularly a religious one invoking also the tradition of the sermon. The musicality and musical sensibility as articulating diasporic history, takes form at a syntactic and semantic level (reproduced in shortened sentences). According to Antonio Benítez Rojo, the "choice of punctuation—along with the number of syllables in his words and the syntax that connects them" (in passages like the one above) gives "rhythmic meaning to his own [Phillips'] narrative discourse" ("Three Words" 57). Benítez Rojo reads Phillips' narrative rhythm as influenced by African music rhythms but also all the other rhythms that have shaped Caribbean societies, from those of the plantation and "the planter's language, music and dance" as well as those that came "from India, China and from Java" creating the "complex poly-rhythmic orchestration [that] was born on the plantation and now lies within the people of the Caribbean" ("Three Words" 58). It is this orchestration, Benitez Rojo argues, "that inspires Phillips' performance; that is, the way the novel is written and the way it sounds" ("Three Words" 58). Similarly, a number of rhetorical strategies in the novel can be read through the lens of musical devices from jazz such as structure, pulse, tempo, and modulation. These shape the narrative in ways that stress the interconnection of the four accounts in the novel.

Some of the key issues in *Crossing the River* are introduced in its first section, "The Pagan Coast", and later appear in different contexts and keys throughout the rest of the stories conveyed in each section. Through a series of letters addressed to his former master, Nash Williams writes of his experiences in Liberia. The first letter written from Monrovia on 11 September 1834 informs Edward of the journey across the Atlantic, retelling several deaths amongst the travelling group and offering his first impressions upon the land of his ancestors, which anticipate some of the circumstances that will gradually impact his views. Nash admits that although wishing to see Edward again one day, he doubts that he will ever return to America as in Liberia, "laws are founded upon justice and equality, and here we may sit under the palm tree and enjoy the same privileges as our white brethren in America. Liberia is the star in the East for the free colored man. It is truly our only home" (18). This excerpt reveals Nash's awareness of what freedom means to him in Liberia, as opposed to what it meant (or rather did not) in America, which is exposed in later correspondence. Edward never received the letter, which was intercepted and disposed of by his wife. The following letters from Nash range from 1835 to 1840, and are written from Saint Paul's River after he decides to travel towards the interior where he builds and runs a mission school.[24] Although the letters continue to profess gratitude and loyalty towards Edward, there is a gradual change in tone and address as Nash undergoes a process of transformation. The silence that Nash's letters are met with, and the absence of financial provision which is resented by Nash and stressed in every letter, are only some of the contributing factors to his change of heart. It is, however, through a process of belonging and participating in the communities he lives with, as a Black man, that Nash is able to unlearn colonial doctrine and reconnect with his own legacy.[25] Through the dialogical form of the letter, Phillips introduces a counterpointed decolonial awareness.

The following section, "West", tells of the escape towards California of Martha Randolph, an elderly enslaved woman separated at a slave auction from her daughter and husband. For Martha, as for Nash, part of the alienation of enslavement, is the realisation that the possibility of belonging in America is fraught (73). However, although the story is marked by Martha's grief and mourning of her family, her journey is also imbued with a sense of possibility. As she runs West, resolutions emerge: "Never again would she stand on an auction block. (Never.) Never again would she be renamed. (Never). Never again would she belong to anybody (No sir, never.)" (80). The orality and effect of the repetition of the word "never" creates a gospel rhythm of stressed notes followed by unstressed ones reminiscent of the rhythm in Bill Withers' "Grandma's Hands", a soul song from 1971 where the compass of the rhythm is also emphasised by the repeating initial phrase "grandma's hands" opening the musical verse and phrase. The repetition of the word "never" in the text engages in the rhetorical devices of anadiplosis (repetition of the last word of a sentence and the first one of the following one) and anaphora (repetition of a word or phrase at the beginning of each sentence) that result in an effect of modulation through rhythmic transitions between the different units of expression in each sentence.[26] The excerpt above seems to show the influence of gospel, one of the central influences of soul music. "Never", marks the pulse and the beat of the cadence in those sentences. Despite the tragic ending, as Martha dies before reaching her destination in her pursuit of freedom (as with Nash's physical and spiritual journey in Africa), Martha's determination to escape the South embodies the fight for dignity and self-assertion as vital to an internal freedom less contingent on material conditions.

The third section, "Crossing the River", is written in the form of journal entries from an eighteenth-century slave trader, Captain Hamilton, in an expedition from Liverpool to the Windward coast of Africa, as the slave ship gets ready for the trip to America (1752). For this section, Phillips researched and used John Newton's eighteenth-century *Journal of a Slave Trader* (1750–1754) as a model.[27] The entries in the novel, very similar (almost identical at times) to those in the historical document, capture how these types of records (held in national and colonial archives) reflect the violence of language and the trade—enslaved Africans are referred to by an assigned identifying number and as property, their imposed legal status. The entries record practical daily activities of getting provisions of food and water aboard the ship, and the purchase of African men and women. Despite the objectification of the enslaved Africans aboard the slaver and the attempted erasure of their humanity, characteristic of what historian Ian Baucom describes as the "horror banalized, horror catalogued" of the captain's logbook (11), the entries reveal glimpses of several attempted rebellions aboard the ship: "In the evening, by the favour of Providence, I discovered a conspiracy among the men slaves to rise upon us. Near 30 of them had broke their irons" and later on Hamilton adds: "Before midnight buried 3 more women slaves (Nos 71, 104, 109)" (124).

In an interview with Sasha Panaram, when asked about the extensive archival research that goes into writing works such as *Crossing the River*, Phillips speaks of his own engagement with Newton's record as a means to document history (and I would add the historiographical impulse) as accurately as possible from the remit of the surviving records:

> I think of it in terms of making people think again and look again at things that they have taken for granted and that can be texts such as Newton's captain's log – a slave ship owner who found God and yet was still participating in this ungodly act ... If you can pull your fiction close to fact there is not really much room for the doubters or the haters to get in there and say 'nice fancible story but it didn't happen'. I'm trying to get people to think again so that they can't look away. ("Writing Oneself")

As Phillips points out, the historicity embodied in the close retelling of Newton's log in *Crossing the River* necessarily confronts readers with history as well as the unevenness of the British imperial archival project. Such historicity also allows readers to access a simulation of a type of historical record rarely accessed by most people, outside of archival research and visits to repositories, access or purchase of copies of Newton's log (which are also available in print).

The fourth and final story, "Somewhere in England", is set in the 1930s and 1940s (also divided in alternating episodes marked by the month and year). It shows different times in the life of Joyce, a white English woman who falls in love with Travis, an African-American soldier stationed in England to support the British Royal Air force. The constant time shifts in this story allow readers to understand events in a much more complex and rounded way—their interweaving of the characters' life events illuminates and encourages connections. This requires a dynamic critical reading. The narrative alternation of timeframes and episodes is an invitation to actively participate in the act of considering the consequences and ongoing violence of racism, its many forms and manifestations through time and across place/space. The racism that Travis encounters in England, the physical and psychological abuse he goes through can be explored at that point within a larger historical frame of reference, provided by the preceding sections and stories in the novel. In her discussion of *Crossing*, Mascoli stresses that what really matters about the musicality in a novel is the way in which it can guide and influence our reading ("Remembering" 8), and also makes the argument that the way in which the various narrative sections in the novel can be read both separately and together, echoing each other within the larger polyphonic structure to which they belong, emulates a distinctly jazz aesthetic (Mascoli 10). Drawing from Petermann, Mascoli notes that in the call-and-response pattern "the performance of musical phrases or longer passages in alternation by different voices [is] ... used in such a way as to suggest that they answer to each other" (Petermann qtd. in Mascoli, "Remembering" 11). This dialogic effect is further framed and guided by the voice of the African father in the prologue and epilogue where he states to be listening to the drums and voices of his children (the characters in the novel and the African descended communities across the diaspora). It is also clear in how "the various narratives of the African father's children answer each other yet have distinctive and recognizable voices" ("Remembering" Mascoli 11). This influence of musical patterns of call-and-response and the role of rhythm in the narrative of Phillips' novel ultimately encourage a dynamic and relational reading—following Glissant's philosophies of conjuncture—through an ethics of interconnection. Both the privileging of each story and the centrality of the echoes, repetition, and variations (connecting them) create a sense of simultaneity that expands readers' understanding of the circularity of history.

CARIBBEAN VISUAL ARCHIVE OF COUNTER-MEMORIES

In "A Note on Method", the preface to *Wayward Lives: Beautiful Experiments* (2018), Saidiya Hartman lays out the project of her book as one that imagines the lives of a group of Black girls in the early twentieth-century United States. Gathering and reimagining aspects of their lives from a series of sources as varied as "journals of rent collectors, surveys and monographs of sociologists; trial transcripts; slum photographs, reports of vice investigators", Hartman explains being able to access certain accounts about these women (xiv). However, all these sources "present them as a problem" (xiv). Hartman then details her methodology and approach as one that envisions the radical possibilities and transformation of subversion carried out by the women she writes about, and whose lives had been erased in official accounts. Reflecting upon the biases and exclusionary practice of archives in shaping and constricting narratives, Hartman writes about the ways in which her text confronts both that authority and absence:

> *Wayward Lives* elaborates, augments, transposes, and breaks open archival documents so they might yield a richer picture of the social upheaval that transformed black social life in the twentieth century... I have pressed at the limits of the case file and the document, speculated about what might have been, imagined the things whispered in dark bedrooms, and amplified moments of withholding, escape and possibility, moments when the vision and dreams of the wayward seemed possible. (xiv)

Hartman's premise is also critically invested in searching for and reimagining the lived (yet not officially recorded) experiences of a group of Black women in America during the early twentieth century, and the political power of "existing otherwise" and in spite of and outside the centralising power of the Archive. This archival methodology, resulting in "counter-narratives" as Hartman notes (xiv), similarly lies at the heart of Roshini Kempadoo's 2004 multimedia installation *Ghosting*, where a series of six story strands, fictionalised accounts inspired by archival written records and visual documents, unfold and intertwine in an interactive play.[28] Most of the characters in *Ghosting* are fully fictional, yet they emerged from that understanding and practice of researching against the grain of the gaps and imbalances in official, state and formal archives, in an imaginative recreation of what the lives of a group of people might or could have lived and experienced, hoped and imagined. The timespan of *Ghosting*'s narratives ranges from 1838 to 1948, covering the period of post-emancipation at the Stollmeyer Cocoa Estate, located in the Santa Cruz Valley on the northwest coast of Trinidad. The stories, written by Guyanese dub poet Marc Matthews, were read and recorded by two young Trinidadian actors based in the United Kingdom, making *Ghosting* both a multimedia piece and collaborative project. The six oral narratives in the installation are fictionalised accounts based on a plantation owner's will from 1792 that Matthews and Kempadoo found during their research at Trinidad's University of the West Indies' library and private collections. This historical source served as early inspiration for the oral and visual narratives in *Ghosting* which capture the historical prerogative of power over land characteristic of plantation society. Kempadoo and Matthews also consulted the private collection of historian and archivist Ms Olga Mavrogordato. *Ghosting* informs Kempadoo's doctoral thesis, *Creole in the Archive: Image, Presence, and Location of the Plantation Worker on Two Plantations, nearby Villages, and Towns in Trinidad (1838–1938)*, a scholarly work and interest that also features in Kempadoo's book *Creole in the Archive: Imagery, Presence and the Location of the Caribbean Figure* (2016).

Kempadoo's art practice emerges from a tradition of Black British artists who in the 1980s critically positioned themselves against the racism prevalent across British institutions and society and the lack of engagement with Caribbean art in major art institutions. They shared a focus on history (particularly on the absence and erasure of Black lives and histories from the larger public sphere) and an investigation of aesthetics that communicates those critical concerns.[29] Influenced by the writings of Stuart Hall on visual culture, the work of John Akomfrah, founder of the Black Audio Film Collective (1982) and seminal films like *Pressure* (1975); and *Handsworth Songs* (1986) by Horace Ové and Akomfrah (respectively), Black British artists explored media and the combination of digital media, technology, collage, and text, critically and politically.[30] The philosophy of bricolage, montage, and assemblage (described by Akomfrah, as previously shown) was key to the aesthetic articulation of Caribbean and Black British art of that time.[31] Through deploying these post/modernist strategies, many artists including Kempadoo, configured a highly fragmented and multilayered aesthetic through the use of juxtaposition and superposition. For Kempadoo, as for artists such as Keith Piper—also invested in rethinking the ways in which Black people are portrayed in the Archive—digital media and technology provided a perfect medium for exploring this. Viewers of Kempadoo's and Piper's artwork are called into (re)thinking the visual codes of images. As Patricia Mohammed argues, the cultural specificity of visual codes mean that they can be read "not just laterally but also horizontally", as viewers challenge and interrogate their currency, histories, and narratives ("Decoding"). Kempadoo's art is further influenced by the political possibilities of the documentary and the digital in terms of manipulating and constructing more complex representations, particularly of the lives of Black women and women of colour, than those in a variety of colonial and postcolonial archives. Her initial work in documentary photography for Format Photographers Agency in the 1990s, her involvement in the Blk Art group, and the promotion of culturally diverse photography in Britain through Autograph ABP have shaped Kempadoo's art practice politically and aesthetically.[32] The artist defines both her own practice and Autograph's mission as being "concerned with questioning [traditional photographic] conventions, practices and approaches and a critical enquiry of both photographs and photographic practices, questioning the societal and cultural space it works within" ("State of Play").[33] Further, she describes Autograph as a collective project lobbying to bring visibility to this body of culturally diverse photography ("State of Play").

Kempadoo's art practice often explores and complicates issues of identity, often through an autobiographical focus, and as a Caribbean-British woman of mixed African, Amerindian, East Indian and European ancestry, engaging with Caribbean and European history from her own perspective and personal history of migration (Jones 332). Kempadoo was born in England but lived in the Caribbean from age eleven to eighteen "growing up in Barbados, Trinidad, Jamaica and Guyana" (Kempadoo, "An Interview" 7). In 1977, she returned to England to undertake her university degree and finally settled there. However, she travels often to the Caribbean and is very much connected to the region. In an interview with Nalini Mohabir, Kempadoo describes herself as a "Caribbean diasporic person" and explains how "[a]lthough I can talk about myself as coming from the Caribbean, I cannot categorically speak from the position of the Caribbean. I've traversed oceans too many times and also identify as being British" (7). Her critical preoccupation with spaces that tell the histories of the creole Caribbean person, aims to both include, and yet differentiate, the histories of different ethnic groups, and has personal links to her own heritage. Kempadoo's family and ancestry is an important influence in her work and scholarship, and she has included photography from her family archive in her own work that speaks to the larger history of migrations that bind the geographies, histories, and peoples across the Black Atlantic.[34]

In their evocation of life in this period of Trinidad's history, Kempadoo and Matthews also used material from interviews with plantation workers, old archive photographs, documents, and maps of the area, using photographs from a variety of archives and those she took during fieldwork. *Ghosting* was specifically created as a means to confront the lack of "historical material associated with the plantation" that was conveyed from the perspective of those who worked on the plantation (Kempadoo, "Ghosting (In)visibility" 125). In a 2011–2012 interview I conducted with Kempadoo, she describes the centrality of women's voices and stories in shaping *Ghosting*. For the artist, the decision to interview women emerged from a significant imbalance in terms of archival accounts and references to women working on the plantation, in stark contrast with the reality of plantation life, which was very much shaped by the work of women despite the lack of documentation of much of their life outside the colonial records in official archives. According to Kempadoo, what inspired the creation of *Ghosting* was the fact that "there is less visibility of women workers in this period of history" (81). She describes the process of interviewing men, and particularly women who had lived in or near the plantation for many years with the aim to evoke the sense of what it could have been like to live and work there, a practice of speculative imagining she describes as considering the "what if" scenarios ("A Presence" 78). Those conversations revealed how many people were still economically tied to the plantation in ways that reveal the ongoing legacy of inequality tied to it. Kempadoo's artwork has been located within an approach to landscape photography that calls attention to the way in which constructions of spaces within different rural and urban landscapes often condition people's relationship and accessibility to those (Wells

203–208). Wells identifies a tendency within the artwork of women artists including Kempadoo who, in the 1980s and 1990s, started to "focus on the inter-relation of women and place, rather than, for instance, on land as vista more-or-less devoid of indications of human habitation" (186). The photography of Guyanese-British Ingrid Pollard, another key artist within the Black Arts Movement in Britain, also shares these concerns and has challenged stereotypical visual associations and representations of Black people as always occupying urban spaces but never as being part of the rural landscape in Britain.[35]

The combination of still moving images, oral Creole narratives, and interactivity in *Ghosting* enabled viewers to access the artwork from a variety of perspectives. In this installation, viewers could listen to one oral account or another as they wished. They had the chance to "play" with a handmade wooden console that simulates an originally Sudanese board game named warri. As "one of the oldest strategy games exploring notions of cause and effect", the warri's shape and functionality is significantly chosen by Kempadoo as the means through which viewers can access these creolised stories (Kempadoo, "Digital" 289). Five large river pebbles can be placed into the five pits of this wooden board and depending on how these stones are moved across the board, viewers can see a sequence projected onto a single screen and would witness a series of images accompanied by an audio of a series of creolised narratives. However, if no one engages with the interactive board "it defaults to silence, with a single photograph on the screen and text inviting the user to 'move dem stones'" (Kempadoo, "Digital" 289). Viewers can combine the order of these narratives and, by doing so, create a longer one; additionally, they can repeat or change to a different narrative by moving the pebble to another pit on the board, thus choosing and influencing the length of their interaction. As the artist points out in Sunil Gupta's documentary film *Roshini Kempadoo: Works 1990–2004*, the warri tradition travelled with enslaved Africans to the Caribbean and became an important vehicle of cultural memory. It represents what has been both preserved and altered as the game has undergone transformations throughout time. In Gupta's documentary, Kempadoo speaks of her necessity and wish to image the lives of workers in and out of the plantation, whose lives usually remained invisible and whose past became inaccessible in various ways. This, in turn, inspired her and Matthews to create fictions as most accounts about life in the plantation in the Archive were highly mediated and largely written by the plantation-owning class.

The fact that during its exhibition, viewers could play a role in selecting, and hence, displaying *Ghosting*'s sequences on the installation's screen, heightened their own participation in those narratives; it allowed viewers, as participants, to gain an experiential awareness of their own relationship to Caribbean history, as part of British history (Fig. 5.1). Art historian Gen Doy, views Kempadoo's emphasis on interactivity as a way to have viewers face the question of what it means to participate in the meaning of the artwork as opposed to remaining passive recipients of a given narrative: "[t]he spectator/user is not presented with meaning as a ready-made object of consumption, but with images and texts which have to be negotiated and worked with in an interactive way" (87). The possibility to "play" with these stories in *Ghosting* highlights the extent to which, as individuals, labourers in plantation societies find themselves outside the institutional mechanisms that organise and write history, but who have also been active producers of cultural and historical records across other media, particularly through oral history. Kempadoo explains how "[t]hrough its conceptual staging, in engagement with the viewer it [*Ghosting*] animates traces of the imperial project in our contemporary multicultural experience of both Britain and the Caribbean" (Kempadoo, "Ghosting" 125). Further, Kempadoo also views a connection between the colonial past and the contemporary moment through critical interrogations of inherited traditional ways of seeing and, if uninterrogated, assumed images and narratives:

> What was key to the emergence of independent practice was its association with both an artistic intervention and an aesthetic that challenged the conventions of photography – particularly social documentary practices – *and* explored the extent to which such practices provided the basis for a level of advocacy and critique to challenge the cultural climate of the 1990s politically and socially. ("Digital" 285)

In her essay "Interpolating Screen Bytes: Critical Commentary in Multimedia Works", Kempadoo discusses *Ghosting* alongside other multimedia and interactive artwork by Black American and British artists. Kempadoo describes the visual arrangement and rationale behind the artwork and explains the significance of creating sequences that represent how the past inhabits the present through representations of landscape (Fig. 5.1).

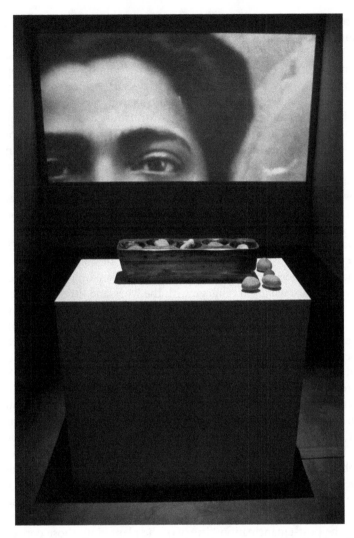

Fig. 5.1 Roshini Kempadoo, warri board, and multimedia installation, *Ghosting*, 2004. Image courtesy of the artist

In one of the strands of *Ghosting*, an older woman called Aunt Ruth recounts stories about a girl called Elsie. In a second strand, a voice reads the will of Sampson de Boissiere, a French plantation owner. This strand continues to explore the plantation system through issues of property, land, and rights. A third account tells the story of Jonas Mohammed Bath, in which viewers learn of his wish to travel back to Africa. This is done through a dialogue between Jonas Mohammed Bath, Jean Baptiste Philippe, and Ram in which they express their differing viewpoints on the return to Africa and the political situation for the African Caribbean and Indian indentured population after emancipation. In the fourth account, Elsie and Ram engage in a conversation that reveals the significance of land ownership, whilst in a fifth strand Victoria May's monologue reveals, "the entrepreneurial spirit and Independence of Afro-Caribbean women" (Petty 8). In the final narrative, Marie Louise remembers the day when Jean Baptiste's medical practice was closed down. All the stories are interconnected as most characters have some kind of connection (familiar, personal, or otherwise) with others. Yet, this can only be appreciated when viewers are willing to engage with the work and listen to more than one or all of the strands, which also attests to the process, and active work, that is required to establish connections between separate accounts and experiences of history. For example, when listening to the account reading out the will of de Boissiere, viewers learn that he declares to have had two natural children, Mary Louise and Victoria May, with "the negress Elsie" (who features as a little girl in Aunt Ruth's account). They now live in Laventille, in the outskirts of Port of Spain. The power over land ownership in the plantation, and the access to various spaces as a consequence of that, defines many of the relationships in the oral accounts of *Ghosting*. The still images in the installation include a superposition of Kempadoo's own photographs of the Stollmeyer's derelict-looking plantation closely followed by photographic images from the Trinidad plantation's visual archive. These are all accompanied by different fictionalised oral accounts that imagine people's lives in and around the plantation as the existing gaps in the post-emancipation history of the plantation, those concerning the lives of ex-slaves and indentured workers, require a different avenue for approaching their history.

The combination of oral accounts, visual images in which the past and present are superposed, and a musical background dominated by drum rhythms, result in a highly sensorial approach to the Archive and some of the historical absences there. As in Phillips' *Crossing the River*, drum rhythms and percussion play a vital role in granting access to the stories and memories in *Ghosting*. The sound when the different story strands are played on the warri board comes in and out with more or less intensity to allow museums goers to listen to the stories. Percussion rhythms are integral to the communicative, emotive and evocative process of imagining the past in *Ghosting*. Additionally, they introduce and signal to music as one of the traditions of memory work that grew and transformed itself as a rich repository of history outside the written record housed in archives. The fact that viewers can either listen to one, two, or all oral accounts in *Ghosting*, depending on their interaction, parallels the call-and-response pattern of narratives in *Crossing* whereby their interconnection yields a fuller counter-history of the Black Atlantic.

Kempadoo's art practice in general, and *Ghosting* in particular, has been greatly influenced by the work of Caribbean feminist scholars including Patricia Mohammed, Rhoda Reddock, and Verene A. Shepherd, whose research has contextualised the limitations to knowing more about the role of women in Caribbean history, particularly during slavery and indentureship but who have demonstrated through their work that, despite their scarce documentation in official records, women played a vital role as historical subjects, and this knowledge exists in a wide variety of records, formal and informal ("A Presence" 78). Mohammed, Reddock, Shepperd, and others (including Brereton, C. Hall, Paton, and Trotz) form part of a tradition of Caribbean(ist) women scholars in the Anglophone Caribbean that has debunked myths, confirmed and expanded knowledge, on the influential role and participation of African and Indian Caribbean women living and working in the plantation system during the historical period that *Ghosting* engages with. Much of this scholarship counters stereotypes and misrepresentations of Indian women around images of passivity and "docility" (Reddock "Freedom Denied", "The Indentureship Experience"). Reddock's "Freedom Denied: Indian Women and Indentureship in Trinidad and Tobago, 1845–1917" (1985), which covers a similar historic period to *Ghosting*, corrects the myth that most or all indentured women migrated from India with their families and that they did so under the authority of their husbands or fathers (79). According to Reddock, research shows that following the first migratory movements from India to Trinidad in 1845, women travelled after making "a conscious decision to seek a new life elsewhere. They came as workers and not dependents" (79). Further, Reddock points to the fact that the assumed role of men as sole breadwinners did not actually coincide with the reality but rather with records and facts such as the Colonial Office dismissing the role of women as potential labour force due to assumed physical weakness and cultural stereotypes (80). Novels such as Harold Sonny Ladoo's *No Pain Like this Body* (1972) show female indentured workers as often drivers of the plantation economy in Trinidad. The characters of Nanny and Ma, the grandmother and mother in the story, are acting forces in the tragic unfolding of events that lead to the death of Ma's son Rama. Ma is also portrayed as being in charge of the economy of their household, whose labour is crucial to the profits of the rice-lands. The portrayal of indentured women in the scholarship of Caribbean feminist scholars such as Gaiutra Bahadur and Reddock, and multimedia artwork like Kempadoo's *Ghosting*, inform and evoke other representations than those in formal archives, where their voices are largely absent.[36] The various narratives in *Ghosting* offer an interrelated web of relationships and modes of kinship across ethnicity and gender (whilst reflecting existing tensions) in ways that extend Western ethnocentric notions of the familial. The system of the plantation is seen as impacting family structure and relations in ways that force viewers to rethink, as Alissa Trotz argues, the critical lens of Western feminist scholarship that identifies the domestic and familial as the main space of oppression, a perspective that has "little purchase for Caribbean women of color in the years of unfreedom, where women's and men's struggles for humanity were integrally associated with carving an autonomous space beyond the reach of the plantation and with creating families and communities under extremely hostile conditions" (16). Within a Guyanese context of post-indentureship, Trotz demonstrates how the domestic space became gendered and racialised through economic measures introduced by British colonial authorities (21). The measure to incentivise labour through household units and not individual workers or the promotion of free settlement for migrating families from India after 1917 attempted to regulate and lessen indentured women's autonomy (21). In Trinidad, reports from the colonial government reported on indentured labourers in the plantation and cocoa estates, and records such as 1893's D. W. D Commins' Report, both captured and downplayed the active role of women and participation in field work that the scholarship of Reddock and others has excavated, revising thus colonial narratives ("The Indentureship Experience"). For example, the 1891 census revealed that only 6.2% of Indians worked primarily carrying household work, standing in contradiction with other reports. Through archival research and the contrast of various sources, scholars have resituated and displaced the authority and accuracy of the colonial record.[37]

As in Guyana, the colonial government in Trinidad organised labour in ways that systematically separated Indian and Africans in the post-emancipation period after the abolition of slavery in 1838 (Reddock, "The Indentureship Experience"). Reddock points out that "every effort was made to keep the African ex-slaves away from the Indian migrant labourers, both socially and geographically, originally with the aim of maintaining the latter as a labouring population available primarily for plantation and later for peasant production for export" ("The Indenture-ship Experience").[38] All these social dynamics are evocatively refigured in *Ghosting*. Different relationships to the land, labour, and connection to its history mark differences between African and Indo-Caribbean peoples in *Ghosting*, For example, the strand that reproduces the conversation "between Jonas Muhammad, Jean Baptiste Phillipe and Ram over the fight for their rights exposes the fractures between ex-slaves who wish to return to Africa and the status of free colored Afro-Caribbeans and indentured laborers of Indian descent respectively" (Petty 8).

Through the plantation, grew a system of surveillance and oppression (Browne, *Dark Matters*, 21–26, 42–45, 50–55; Mirzoeff *The Right*) with the purpose of controlling the lives and labour of the enslaved and indentured person. As *Ghosting* problematises through the oral accounts and images, structures of visuality in the space of the plantation (where the landscape and geography) was organised to visually control produc-tivity, and the threat of insurrection, have been key colonial means of oppression. And although some of these spaces have transformed, they have often significantly been turned into touristic areas with very specific spatial politics of inclusion and exclusion, where the legacy of the plan-tation as a particular political system continues. Guyanese-born writer and academic Tessa McWatt notes, "The plantation was a model for a modern factory: a workplace of unequals ... While slavery was abolished, the structure that produced it, still flourishes" (53).

Both the narrative accounts and the visuality in *Ghosting* aim to revert the imposed gaze of coloniality, the control of its photographic lens, and the invested fiction of its neutrality and transparency. In one of the narra-tive strands, a combination of two moving still images shifts the frame of reference and stresses to viewers the constructedness of colonial narra-tives of labour embedded in a photographic tradition that documents their work in the field (in this case in a cocoa plantation) as subjects of

Fig. 5.2 Roshini Kempadoo, still image, *Ghosting*, 2004. Image courtesy of the artist

Fig. 5.3 Roshini Kempadoo, still image, *Ghosting*, 2004. Image courtesy of the artist

production in a capitalist structure. *Ghosting* contrasts this both visually and narratively with other images from the family album where the narrative control is shifted into other self-fashioning portrayals that depart from the ethnographic gaze of that colonial photographic tradition. The superposition of this family photographic portrait on a tiled floor (see Fig. 5.2), centres the family album as a generative archive. The contrast between the photograph (within the tradition of studio portraiture, often focused on notions of professional status and community belonging), and the image of the weathered black and white tiles, interrogates the relationship of this family to various spaces. This arrangement could interrogate their relationship to the estate, the plantation, and the national community, as well as to intimate spaces of home. Further, the still image questions ways of reading images. In an analysis of a photographic album collected by South African artist Santu Mofokeng, Tina Campt warns of the complex layers of its images, also at stake in this and other stills from *Ghosting* (60–65). Mofokeng gathered photographs from a range of family studio portraits across African countries taken between the second half of the nineteenth century and the first half of the twentieth century, and placed questions next to the images. These all complicated their visuality, implicitly cautioning against assumptions. The images in Mofokeng's album resemble the one that Kempadoo selects from the archive; they present families in position and clothing following some of the codes within Victorian visual grammar and aesthetics. Kempadoo's use of the family archive in *Ghosting* engages with what Campt identifies as a self-fashioning that resists binary structures of signification, particularly in terms of thinking of "agency v. subjection" insisting instead that "photography and the portrait in particular are neither wholly liberatory vehicles of agency, transcendence or performativity nor unilateral instruments of objectification and abjection. They are always already both at once" (59). Another digital still from *Ghosting* (Fig. 5.3) displays a view of the run-down plantation house imposed onto another image of what looks like its derelict foundations upon which a photographic image from the archives is projected. The photograph features a group of labourers working on the cocoa field but the vision is hindered by the structure of the house's foundation. Only one person can be seen to be looking (presumably) directly at the camera whilst working (see Fig. 5.3). The following still in the still moving sequence, removes the frame from the photograph, an act that invites reflection upon the layers of rhetoric that condition the viewer's own act of viewing and constructing narratives. The still image and sequence described make manifest the haunting presence of the past through the layering of an archival photograph superposed to the original building's image. Whilst viewers are witnessing the transition from one still image to another, they are also hearing the voice of Aunt Ruth narrating the following in Trinidadian Creole over "a musical rhythm" ("Interpolating Screen" 60):

> The window is the eyes of the soul
> and see the little face of we Elsie pon the inside, scrubbing the soul-eye
> on the plantation house,
> watching through single, glass frames of time,
> watching we pon the other side ...
> > (text by Marc Matthews; Kempadoo, "Interpolating Screen" 60)

These words provide the perspective of those toiling the cocoa field, which cannot be accessed through the old archival photograph, but which voice a relationship to Elsie, the enslaved girl who once worked in the house of the cocoa estate and who would watch them work from its window "watching (them/dem) pon the other side ..." (Kempadoo, "Interpolating Screen" 60).

Ship Shape and *Surge*: Call-and-Response and the Reggae Aesthetic

Music and performance play a significant role in the work of Caribbean poets and poets of Caribbean descent based in Britain. The influence of musical patterns, or music generally, has helped memorialise different historical events and revise their representation in British official historical and public narratives. Through the language of reggae and dub music and on account of a strong tradition of spoken word, many poets have challenged the status quo. Dorothea Smartt's *Ship Shape* (2008) and Jay Bernard's *Surge* (2019) are two examples of contemporary literary works that draw from musical forms, patterns, and performance and create, in turn, a critical space that refigures archival and collective historical memory.

Dorothea Smartt was "commissioned by Lancaster Litfest in 2003, to write a contemporary elegy for Samboo of Samboo's Grave" (*Ship Shape* 15). After carrying out extensive research on the history of the slave trade in Lancaster, Smartt wrote a series of poems that appeared in various journals. In 2003, 24,950 copies of the poem "Lancaster Keyes" were published in a limited edition "to honour each one person shipped into slavery by Lancaster traders between 1750 and 1800" (Lima 347).

These poems were afterwards collected and expanded in *Ship Shape*, which was published in 2008 with Peepal Tree Press. *Ship Shape* imagines the memory of an enslaved man pejoratively referred to in the Archive records as Samboo, who died shortly after his arrival in England in 1736. The exact cause of his death remains unknown. Sixty years after his death, in 1796, Reverend James Watson wrote a poem for him, a fragment of which has been engraved in a plaque on his grave. The opening reads: "Here lies Poor Samboo, a faithful Negro who attending his Master from the West Indies died on his arrival at Sunderland". *The Lonsdale Magazine* of 1822 also records a brief reference to him. The magazine article speculates about his death, believed to be due to illness, in the loft of a local brewhouse where he finds shelter after he is supposedly "deserted by the master" who is also the ship's captain (*Ship Shape* 16). Through this mention, this young man, whose actual name remains unknown, officially appears in the recorded history of the slave trade and, as Dorothea Smartt notes, he is thus "woven into the folklore of Sunderland Point" (*Ship Shape* 16). The *Lonsdale* article succinctly states that the ship's sailors buried him at Sunderland Point "whither they conveyed his remains without coffin or bier" (16). Both references in *The Lonsdale Magazine* and Watson's epitaph depict the man as "poor Samboo", without mention of his actual name. The omission is not atypical, for as mentioned in Chapter 2, imposing new names on the enslaved and/or eliding their names in documents is a distinctive characteristic of many colonial records pertaining to the slave trade.

Ship Shape offers a fictionalised portrayal of this unknown person whom Smartt renames Bilal. This construction of Bilal's identity through a heterogeneous repertoire of counter-memory strongly based on conceptual dynamics of call-and-response offers an alternative to the silencing of history that predominates in colonial archives. Many of the poems in *Ship Shape* are voiced by Bilal. However, the collection contains a myriad of other voices that run through the poems. Perspective in the collection shifts considerably; it varies from the wife of the ship's captain, to the captain, to Sambo/Bilal, and finally to the voice of a poetic personae speaking from the contemporary moment. Such multiplicity of viewpoints and perspectives confronts the "unidirectionality of communication and meaning making" that typically characterises the colonial archive (D. Taylor, 8). Paratextual material in the collection includes dictionary entries (15) and archival documents such as the one from *The Lonsdale Magazine*, as well as epigraphs from works by Maryse

Condé, Kamau Brathwaite, Larry Olomoofe and from the *Quran* (23, 26, 48, 37), with an interweaving of song and poetry (86). It all encourages a series of connections between those documents and records and the other narratives that Smartt constructs around Bilal. There are important connecting threads between some of the poems in "Samboo's Grave ~ Bilal's Grave" and "Just a Part", two distinct sections in the collection. The underlying interconnection between poems in both sections invites readers to consider how the past permeates the present in cities like Lancaster, which held "the fourth largest slave port in Britain" (*Ship Shape* 16). Smartt's emphasis on this call-and-response poetic pattern both highlights and interrogates the existing continuities in terms of contemporary social inequality derived from slavery. The first poem, "Ruby Lips", highlights how the process of documenting the imperial enterprise is in itself a project of death and manipulation of history that is yet to be fully confronted. In many cases, the tales still need to be challenged and unveiled as highly mediated constructions of the past.

> *Dead men tell no tales*,
> but dead white men document plenty,
> great tomes that weigh
> over our living, African diasporic selves,
> our living Black Mother. (*Ship Shape* 11)

Ship Shape interrogates the consequences of an imperial and colonial tradition of documentation and historiography today, and invites the task to (re)think the impact of such legacy in societies across the Black Atlantic. As a counterpoint, in the same poem, readers access the affirmation of other forms of knowledge including "fleeting words, instinctive feelings, thoughts and inspired dreams" (*Ship Shape* 11).

> So listen beyond the shallows,
> there's wisdom to be learned through
> fleeting words, instinctive feelings, thoughts
> and inspired dreams, Olokun stirring,
> sending dark bubbles from her depths
> that are no more than air on the breeze;
>
> those erudite manuscripts
> that aid and abet,
> corroborate and validate each other,

I will vilify with my mother's
knowing
sayings. (11)

The pact to "vilify" "those erudite manuscripts" questions the authority of the colonial and imperial record and archiving as calculated attempts of European powers to erase Indigenous and African cultures and knowledge in the Americas. One of the most powerful connections between both sections in *Ship Shape* is the affirmation of the self, which is enacted through spiritual connections of the African diaspora outside the remit of Eurocentric frameworks. The second part of *Ship Shape* engages with contemporary Britain and introduces Smartt's own subjective position into the archive, thus establishing a connection between Bilal's and her own life experience. Both parts connect contrapuntally. The second section, significantly titled "just a part", functions as a counterpoint to the first. The memory of home, and the realities of socio-political spaces where individuals are confronted with imposed categories features in both sections and is superposed with the experience of family, kin, and community. Thus historical continuities of displacement, racism, and economic disparity in the eighteenth century and today are laid bare. In the poem "just a part: a distant lot" Smartt describes her own family as part of the diasporic networks of Caribbean history: "My family are a distant lot / scattered around migratory paths: from Barbados / landing up in London, Birmingham, New York, / Panama City, Nassau, Miami, Havana" (74). As a consequence of a longing to connect with her distant relatives, the poetic personae records their names: "people whose names I write down / to remember, interrogate my mother / to make connections on paper – my family extending across the page - / great uncles and aunts on their travels" (74). Smartt underscores another means of archiving family history and memory. In this sense, by writing *Ship Shape* as a memorial to Bilal, Smartt includes him as close kin. The importance of place names in marking places (which duplicate in both England and Barbados) also appears when "Cousin Sherry and I, excavating names, / make mention of a place / with the same address in Bridgeton" (74). By naming it "just a part", and through the stress on the threads connecting Bilal with the poetic personae in the second section of the collection, Smartt irrevocably links it to the history of Bilal.

A similar connection between poems in a collection is at stake in Jay Bernard's *Surge* (2019) where poems that deal with the Grenfell fire in London, in 2017, evoke links in the institutional responsibility and response to the tragedy of the New Cross massacre in 1981 ("Introduction" *Surge* xi). *Surge* was published in 2019, but earlier poems central in the collection were published in *Beacon of Hope: New Beacon in Poetry and Prose* in 2016, preceded by Ruth Bush's essay "New Beacon Books – the Pioneering Years". Similarly, *Surge*—the 2019 poetry collection—followed "Surge: Side A", a multimedia poem sequence for which Bernard won the 2017 Ted Hughes Award for New Work in Poetry. In an interview with Claire Armitstead, Bernard described "Surge: Side A", as encompassing "what I feel I've been gearing myself up for since I started writing. The final structure of it I don't know, but it feels inevitable. To be nominated for something that's partly formed and still forming is kind of cool, because it's all about being partial and half-understood" ("Speaking Out"). These different iterations of the work, archive the process of formation of *Surge*. The poem "Songbook" is one that appears in all three iterations of the work. Inspired by Linton Kwesi Johnson's poem "New Crass Massahkah" (1981), "Songbook" deals with the New Cross Massacre in Lewisham, south east London. On 18 January 1981, thirteen children and teenagers died at 439 New Cross Road when an incendiary device was thrown through one of the house's windows, setting a fire that killed them and injured twenty-seven others. One of the survivors took their own life in the aftermath. They were celebrating Yvonne Ruddock's sixteenth birthday when the attack took place. London metropolitan police carried out an irregular investigation of the fire, accompanied by minimal response from the government and the press, resulting in a "near silence" as Bernard notes (ix). The police initially pointed to, and then discredited the plausible theory of an arson attack with evidence believed to have be removed from the site, and pervasively made several survivors of the fire suspects under interrogation (*The Windrush Years*). Following a National Front march in Lewisham in 1977, "firebombs on black owned property in the area further heightened tensions" (*The Windrush Years*). By 1981 many households had been attacked in Deptford and a community centre burnt down (Peter Fryer, *Staying Power* ch. 12). There was a history in the neighbourhood of violent street marches, harassment, and attacks organised by the National Front and Column 88 who were especially active in the 1970s, targeting Black owned businesses, cultural and educational spaces. Well-known was the arson attack carried out by Column 88 that burnt down the Albany community centre in Deptford in 1978, later dismissed by the police as an accident. To counteract the institutional silencing of the New Cross massacre, and the scarce and racist coverage of the British media, Black People's Day of Action took place on 2 March 1981, a historic march around London, organised by John La Rose, Darcus Howe, Sybil Phoenix, and others. Bernard includes an archival record from the collection New Cross Massacre held at the George Padmore Institute; it is a flier issued by the New Cross Massacre Action Committee encouraging neighbours to "support Black Peoples Day of Action" (21), a massive demonstration that brought great media visibility (despite the media's problematic coverage of the event) to the New Cross Massacre and the issues faced by Black people in Britain. The flier encourages people to stand up against hate crime and the murder of Black people in the country, police harassment, and the "lies and confusion spread about by newspapers, radio and television" (21). Its inclusion in the collection signifies an attempt to archive the long history of political and community action of the Caribbean diaspora in Britain.

During a residency at the George Padmore Institute in 2016, Bernard researched the archives' material into the story of the massacre and its repercussions in British society and its racialised communities. The collection *New Cross Massacre Campaign 1980–1985* (Ref. no.: NCM) contains materials relating to the New Cross Massacre Campaign and its committee, chaired by John La Rose. Fonds are divided into four sub-fonds: "Campaign Action", "Investigation and Inquest", "Support and Campaign", and "Media Interest". The use (and refiguration) of archival images in Bernard's poems dealing with the massacre highlight a visual record of protest that counters the slanted media coverage at the time. In this sense, both photography and music become modes of memory-making that address institutional violence. As Johnson's "New Crass Massakah", Bernard's "Songbook" uses the form of song and music to establish a connection to a site of memory that localises both the party's celebration and the fire's disruption of the victims' lives. When performed by Johnson, the first six stanzas, which describe the party, are accompanied by dub music. The poem also imitates the rhythm, pulse, and musicality of song. The first three stanzas depict the initial atmosphere of celebration at the party whilst the following three mark the horror caused by the fire. A sudden halt in the music transitions the poem into a quiet reading that highlights the terror and shock in British Black communities across the country, particularly in London.

Bernard's "Songbook" fuses both elements in Johnson's poem; song and grieving. There is no pause separating song from poem, also no music accompanies its performance as in "New Crass Massakah", but musicality, cadence, and rhythm are carried throughout in ways that powerfully reach audiences and create a musicality of its own. In a discussion of *Surge* that refers to the performance of the poem during the Ted Hughes Award ceremony, Marek Sullivan describes how,

> the author sings the words, and slows down the final chorus to a devastating stop, amplifying the sense of stuttering closure implied by the last line: 'Me seh ah one half fahwahd an ah one halfback'. The establishment, then gradual disruption, of a dancehall rhythm (the last line is spoken after several seconds of silence) is another example of Bernard's uncanny ability to tap into readers' or listeners' expectations and generate new meanings through a frustrated desire for wholeness. ("Jay Bernard's Explosive Poetry")

In both Johnson's and Bernard's poems, the musicality of verse and the use of song grounds the poems in a Jamaican and pan-Caribbean musical tradition of cultural memory that has historically recorded the history of the African diaspora. The phraseology of dub figures in the musical stanzas of Johnson's poem, whilst that of roots reggae figures in Bernard's. As Oku Onura has noted (who Kwame Dawes suggests is the "originator of dub poetry", *Natural* 87), dub poetry isn't just "putting a piece of poem pon a reggae rhythm; it is a poem that has built-in reggae rhythm (so to speak) backing, one can distinctly hear the reggae rhythm coming out of the poem" (Onura qtd. in Dawes, *Natural* 87). As Dawes argues, the reggae aesthetic and sensibility that he identifies in dub poetry (which he considers "another style of reggae", Dawes 88) and in Johnson's poetry, lie in the "language, themes and ideologies that appear in the work" (88). Both "New Crass Massakah" and "Songbook" create a language of grief and grieving that pairs and respects the theme, extending that carefully to performance. In this sense, the enactment of a language of grief and protest demonstrates here one of the main characteristics of reggae which, according to Dawes, resides in the fact that "[t]he contemporary artist who sees her/himself inscribed in a reggae ethos is compelled to experiment, question, and stretch the range of the aesthetic" (*Natural* 33). Both performances, in their poets' intonation, halting, inflection of voice, and break, capture the reggae sensibility and aesthetic. The use of Jamaican patwa, riff, and rhyme (and all other elements of a reggae and dub aesthetic) point further to the long archival tradition of Jamaican music where lyrics and compositional elements focus on a counter-narrative of Caribbean history. In verses such as "Me seh ah one step fahwahd an ah two step back" (7, 8, 9) or "Me seh black smoke ah billow at di house in New Cross" (8) the riff in slight numeric changes and variation in other lines stresses the song and sorrow in "Songbook".

The interconnection of histories in *Surge* manifests the continuities that connect the New Cross massacre and Grenfell, conveyed both in the collection's poetics of remembrance and thematically. There is also a dialogue with literature and activism from the Windrush generation in the collection that archives that tradition of resistance, highlighting how it countered the institutional silences marked by the response from the conservative government after the fire. In "Sentence", a poem that Bernard wrote following the death of visual artist Khadija Saye during the Grenfell fire, the poet forms the painful imagery and rhythm of the poem, with punctuated sorrow evocative of the fire, reflects the challenges of writing (about) the trauma. The verse "then sentence says" appears repeated as a riff throughout the poem which also makes use of the slash division sign in ways that heighten the loss. The final verse: "Not rivers, towers of blood", in its allusion to Enoch Powell's famous reference of "rivers of blood" in incitement of anti-immigrant violence during his famous speech, links moments of institutional violence and failure in the lack of avoidance and response to both fires (New Cross and Grenfell).

Engaging with History, Grappling with Erasure

In *The European Tribe* (1987), Caryl Phillips notes: "I had learnt that in a situation in which history is distorted, the literature of a people often becomes its history, its writers the keepers of the past, present and future. In this situation a writer can infuse a people with a sense of their own unique identity and spiritually kindle the fire of resistance" (99). Although Phillips wrote these lines in 1987, and partly as commentary on the situation of writers in Poland in the aftermath of the Russian occupation, his words clearly resonate with his own experience and relationship with history and the role and responsibility felt by Caribbean writers. Carol Margaret Davison asked Phillips to comment on that statement in an interview in 1994, as did Sasha Panaram in another interview in 2020. On both occasions, Phillips continued to agree with the statement, adding that as part of the role and responsibility of the writer is the awareness and possibility to "perhaps do something about redressing the imbalance of some of the ills and falsehoods that have been perpetuated by others about your own history" (Davison 96–97). Equally, in 2020, Phillips added that people of African descent, Asian communities and Indigenous communities, among others, "have to write ourselves into visibility ... the experiences of people who looked like me, or made journeys that I have made, were wilfully absent. Literature to me is an engagement not just with the aesthetics of the sentence, the word, the rhythm of the sentence but it is also an engagement with history ... It's a responsibility, I think, to respond and grapple with that absence" ("Writing Oneself").

I would argue that aesthetics in Phillips' *oeuvre*, and in the work of the writers whose work is discussed in this chapter, communicates and carries that engagement. It is also in the layering, the rhythm, the breaks, and the call-and-response, where that engagement with history resides. Like Cozier, Philip, Danticat and Díaz; Bernard, Johnson, Kempadoo, Phillips, and Smartt have created, through their writing and performance, new critical approaches to the empty spaces and erasures of different archives, records, and modes of state memory. This crossroads between the archives' textuality, visuality, and performativity highlights the significance of understanding memory as multi-discursive, multi-generic, and interdisciplinary. The work of Bernard, Johnson, Kempadoo, Phillips, and Smartt makes historical erasure tangible; and brings continuities based on social inequity to the forefront. Their work conveys a strong visual and oral and aural component that facilitates a critical dialogue based on the *intersection* of different narratives. Such intersections generate a space of inquiry where the reader/viewer is able to question issues of readability, as well as their own interpretive role and responsibility in witnessing the stories and histories that are narrated. The juxtaposition of narrative voices from the past and the present, in the literature and artwork under discussion here, creates a space where the reader and viewer become more aware of the embodied and lived presence of memory, and how the past still resonates today. Moreover, their work reflects the rich cultural and artistic archival traditions where Caribbean and British histories have been actively recorded.

Notes

1. The lecture was one part of the 2018 MFA Fine Art & MFA Curating Lecture series, Goldsmiths University.

2. Anthony Joseph, "The Frequency of Magic." Goldsmiths College Department of Art MFA Lectures 2017–18, Series 3.2: Rhythm, 24 July 2018, www.youtube.com/watch?v=lexmeTirrfQ.
3. Although London is often the object of cultural histories around this period, moments of solidarity and activism took place nation-wide in places as diverse as Bristol, Birmingham, and Leeds (amongst other geographies) that illuminate aspects of how polit-ical activism and organising shaped diasporic communities in Britain.
4. The call for West Indian labour that took place before and after WWII happened as a means to palliate a moment of great economic necessity. Many West Indians migrated to Britain and enlisted to fight in the war. The docking of the famous *HMT Empire Windrush* in 1948, which arrived at Tilbury from Jamaica with 492 passengers on board from across the region, would become an emblem of Caribbean migration and diaspora formation.
5. The 1962 Commonwealth Immigrants Act introduced a new immigration policy in the United Kingdom that aimed to restrict migration from Commonwealth countries and initiated an insti-tutional culture of questioning Black peoples' citizenship rights, aggravated by the media and the police. A year later, the British West Indian Association complained about police brutality against racialised communities, which had increased since the passing of the Act.
6. Enoch Powell's famous 1968 incendiary speech "Rivers of Blood" marked the anti-immigrant rhetoric of British white nationalism which has had a lasting effect in providing a framework for that politics. Ironically, Powell was himself involved in the campaign to recruit nursing staff from the Caribbean for the National Health Service in Britain, indicating the extent of the conditionality of migration to Britain, and the expiry date of the welcome of West Indian migrants by conservative and right-wing sources.
7. Oluwale arrived to the city of Leeds in 1949 when he was 19 years old. After spending a sentence of 28 days in prison for travelling to Britain as a stowaway in a ship from Lagos, he started work at West Yorkshire Foundries during the day and would study in the evenings. However, Oluwale was regularly harassed by youth gangs and the local police, and regularly spent time in Leed's prison (Armley Gaol). In 1953 he was admitted to West Riding

Pauper Lunatic Asylum in Menston where he spent eight years and received strong sedatives and medication which, as Caryl Phillips points out, "radically changed the young man's personality and his sense of self" (Phillips and McLeod, "The City" 882). Oluwale confronted attempts at intimidation from the police; the system of regular incarceration eventually drove him to a situation of homelessness. He was often forcibly removed by the authorities from the city centre and taken to the outskirts, from where he would defiantly return again to the centre of Leeds. After his murder, Oluwale's body was found in Leeds' River Aire, "some three miles east of the city centre at a point near Knostrop Sewage Works" on 4 May 1969 ("The City" 882). The two police officers suspected of being responsible for his death were taken to trial in 1971 and were acquitted. When the details of the court case and Oluwale's story came out to the public arena, the story shook the public. *Remember Oluwale* is a charity (David Oluwale Memorial Association) and initiative created and supported by Caryl Phillips, Emily Zobel Marshall and Max Farrar, amongst other board members and patrons. Through collective organising, the work of *Remember Oluwale* has led to many initiatives including events of public and community outreach, as well the naming of the David Oluwale bridge (March 2022), a blue plaque (Apr. 2022), and garden project featuring a sculpture by artist Yinka Shonibare (the latter of which is to be unveiled in 2023).

8. A law, popularly referred to as 'sus' law (from "suspected person") that legally allowed police officers' 'stop and search' and potential detention of any individual suspected of being in breach of section 4 of the Vagrancy Act 1824.

9. Particularly from the 1970s, discrimination at an institutional level became widespread from education, the workplace (also with "high levels of unemployment, low pay and unsafe conditions") to irregular practices in the judicial, police and health care systems where women were also the target of unsafe birth control methods (Sudbury 327).

10. See *Institute of Race Relations* for a variety of resources, including reports on racism and race relations in the United Kingdom, including issues such as policy, migration, and surveillance, irr. org.uk.

11. Many of those affected by the hostile environment lost their jobs, and had their lives upended as a result of the indelible damage caused by the new governmental policy and resulting deportations that forcibly sent people "home", often to places they hadn't lived in for years.

12. See Amelia Gentleman, "Home Office Destroyed Windrush Landing Cards Says Ex-Staffer." *The Guardian*, 17 April 2018, www.theguardian.com/uk-news/2018/apr/17/home-off ice-destroyed-windrush-landing-cards-says-ex-staffer.

13. The Constitutional ruling of TC/0168–13 in the Dominican Republic (denying citizenship to Haitians and Dominicans of Haitian descent in the DR) and the 2014 and 2016 Immigration Act in the United Kingdom become examples and markers of a global turn towards a political alienation and criminalisation of immigrant and diasporic communities. Despite the rebranding of the hostile environment for the "compliant environment", the policies continue to affect citizens across Britain and deportations have continued, the most recent ones in the winter of 2020 which led to a public campaign and letter signed by more than 100 public figures including writers Benjamin Zephaniah and Bernardine Evaristo.

14. Reporting for *The Guardian*, Matta Busby covers the story of Osime Brown's planned deportation, a young man (twenty-two years old) who left Jamaica at age four. This, and other deportations, sparked public outrage and have mobilised the creation of the letter to Priti Patel, then Secretary of State for the Home Department (and self-proclaimed Thatcherite). Matta Busby, "More Than 100 Public Figures Call for Halt to Osime Brown Deportation." *The Guardian*, 12 Dec. 2020, www.theguardian.com/uk-news/2020/dec/12/public-fig ures-call-for-halt-osime-brown-deportation-priti-patel.

15. The activism and organising practices of Black women contributed significantly to the mobilisation of the term "Black" during the 1970s and 1980s as a political identity shaped through the dialogue and work of African, Caribbean, Asian and Middle Eastern women (Sudbury). According to Lola Okolosie, despite the fact that the term "black" as political identity "has become hotly contested", the spirit that made it possible carries on today in decolonial activism. (*The Heart of the Race* xi)

16. The films were contracted with the BBC and have been released on iPlayer, making viewing accessible to a wider audience in the United Kingdom which, in an interview for *The Guardian*, McQueen stressed was vital to him. See "Steve McQueen: "Black People Are Weirdly Missing from the Narrative." Interview conducted by various authors, *The Guardian*, 15 Nov. 2020, www.theguardian.com/tv-and-radio/2020/nov/15/steve-mcq ueen-black-people-are-weirdly-missing-from-the-narrative-small-axe-mangrove-viola-davis-idris-elba-bernardine-evaristo.

    The son of Grenadian and Trinidadian parents, McQueen has also expressed the long-held desire to create a film anthology like this and the need for the necessary distance to carry it out. McQueen's experience in historical adaptation is well-known for his Oscar-winning film *12 Years a Slave* (2013), an adaptation of Solomon Northup's 1853 slave narrative memoir. McQueen is also a video artist and recipient of a Turner Price and OBE for his role in the visual arts.

17. See also Franco Rosso and John La Rose's documentary film *The Mangrove Nine* (1973).

18. The Mangrove had become a meeting point socially connecting Black people in the neighbourhood and facilitating a space to organise politically and culturally. As the film shows, Howe's insistence to represent himself legally, propelling others to do the same, and the awareness of the historicity of that moment, were key to the unfolding of events and final verdict in favour of the "Mangrove nine".

19. This is the case in the next film in the anthology, *Lovers Rock* which focuses on a blues party night and recreates the intimate space, joy, and relationships between characters, some of whom are meeting each other for the first time. Other films in the anthology tell stories from other facets of life in Britain, from discrimination in education (*Education*), racism in the police (*Red, White and Blue*), and the life of writer of Jamaican descent Alex Wheatley and his time in prison after the Brixton Riots (*Alex Wheatley*).

20. Multimedia installations by Isaac Julien are structured around large screens that project various images at different times, moving the narrative focus and lens of the story across the space with the resulting effect of echoing sounds and narratives. This is the

case of various installations including *Ten Thousand Waves* (2013–2014) which toured across locations and is now in the permanent collection of Museum of Modern Art (MoMA), New York City.

21. Equally, both texts refer to the crossing(s) of the Middle Passage as a political marker of (inter)connection between the diasporic communities and the histories that shape them, connecting past, present, and future.

22. A markedly musical influence and sensibility characterises Phillips' *oeuvre*, particularly his fiction, an influence that plays a role in its relational aesthetics, present in works like *Crossing the River*, and in the thematic and narrative shifts of *In the Falling Snow* (2009), which resemble rhythmic structures of jazz composition, as Gerald D. Naughton argues in an interdisciplinary and comparative discussion of Phillips' novel and James Baldwin's "Sonny's Blues" (1957). Phillips has also written about the vital role of music in African diasporic literature. In "Literature: The New Jazz?", where Phillips reviews the 1996 *Norton Anthology of African American Literature*, he writes, "[t]he formal structures of music, its profound effect on the masses, and the individual talent of the performers, have obviously inspired the writers" (84). Phillips then goes on to stress the groundbreaking influence of music on literary genres and specifically on literary form (84).

23. Caryl Phillips, like Stuart Hall, has been greatly influenced by Black music, and particularly the jazz of Miles Davies. During an interview with Susheila Nasta at a symposium on the work of Caryl Phillips at the National Center for Writing (Norwich), Phillips spoke of his love of Miles Davies, and the influence of jazz in the compositional structure of his writing at a syntactic, narrative and overall aesthetic level. *Britain in the World, Day Symposium on the Work of Caryl Phillips*, National Centre for Writing, Norwich, 10 March 2018.

For instances of Stuart Hall describing the influence of jazz and other Black musics in his life and work, see his memoir *Familiar Stranger* (112; 127–131). John Akomfrah's documentary *The Stuart Hall Project* (2013) also provides insight into the influence of Jazz on Hall, particularly the music of Miles Davies.

24. The first letter from that location also contains intertextual references to Conrad's 1899 novel *Heart of Darkness*, as Nash states "[s]ince the passing of my wife and child, my wants are few, and of

course they are easily supplied in this land of darkness" (Phillips, *Crossing* 25).

25. After seven years as missionary, Nash disappears and Edward travels to Africa in a quest to find him. Nash writes, "We need to contend for our rights, stand our ground, and feel the love and liberty that can never be found in *your* America. Far from corrupting my soul, this Commonwealth of Liberia has provided me with the opportunity to open my eyes and cast off the garb of ignorance which has encompassed me all too securely the whole course of my life" (Phillips, *Crossing* 61; emphasis mine). Nash realises his own political relationship to an America that he doesn't recognise as his. Nash's journey to "the interior" of Liberia (which alludes to, and reverses, that of Charles Marlow in *Heart of Darkness*) marks his un-learning of the colonising project.

26. Similarly, the repetition of the word "prospecting" three times in nearby text to this excerpt equally demonstrates the extent and role of riff and repetition in the section "West" and, overall, in the novel.

27. Newton converted to evangelical Christianity but continued his role in the slave trade until he decided to stop his work transporting enslaved people to the Americas, and wrote *Thoughts Upon the African Slave Trade* (1778) and authored the hymn known popularly as "Amazing Grace" ("The Faith's Review and Expectation") in 1772, which has since become associated with liberation from enslavement. Although Newton became an active abolitionist campaigning with William Willberforce, taking this position after his direct role and benefit from the slave trade was also critiqued. A collection of copies of the letters of John Newton is held at the National Archives (920 MD 409), London, UK. Also see John Newton Letters 1767–1781, Frank Baker Collection of Wesleyana and British Methodism 1536–1996 (RL.00413) held at Duke University Library, Durham, NC, US. A selection of digitised writings by John Newton, held at various repositories, is available via the Digital Public Library of America, https://dp.la/search?utf8=✓&q=Newton,+John,+1725-1807.

28. This installation was commissioned by the City Art Gallery and the Peepul Centre in Leicester, UK (2004). It was part of the retrospective exhibition *Roshini Kempadoo: 1990–2004*, produced

by OVA: The Organization for Visual Arts, London. The installation was first exhibited at The City Center from 27 February to 3 April, 2004. Later, it toured with OVA after opening at the Pitzhanger Gallery in London on 15 July 2004.

29. In the 1990s, Kempadoo's artwork was featured in group exhibitions including *Transforming the Crown: African, Asian and Caribbean Artists in Britain 1966–1996* (1997–1998) and *Interrogating Identity* (1991), alongside the work of artists such as Althea McNish, Joy Gregory, Lubaina Himid, Sunil Gupta, Errol Lloyd, Ingrid Pollard, and others (Chambers 8, 236).

30. Kellie Jones situates Kempadoo's work as part of a tradition of Black British and American women whose use of text powerfully challenges the relationship between both mediums: visual and textual, which then stretch boundaries of each other (14–15; 332, 336). For an insightful discussion of the role of text in relationship to photography in the work of visual artists including Kempadoo, Lorna Simpson, Ingrid Pollard, and others, see Jones' "In Their Own Image" in *Eye Minded: Living and Writing Contemporary Art*, ed. Kellie Jones, 2011, pp. 319–340.

31. In *Black Artists in British Art: A History Since the 1950s*, Eddie Chambers historicises the work and context of Black artists in Britain and dedicates two chapters to the work and curatorial efforts of Black British women artists, highlighting their distinct position within the Black Arts Movement in Britain. Chambers marks three of the exhibitions curated in the 1980s by artist Lubaina Himid as vital to raising the profiles and visibility of other Black British women artists including Sonia Boyce and Maud Saulter (131–136). By historicising the three exhibitions organised by Himid and in which the three artists participated (*Five Black Women Artists*; *Black Women Time Now*, *The Thin Black Line*), Chambers revises and extends the canon of Black British art history (129–136).

32. The Blk Art group was formed in 1979 in Wolverhampton, in the West Midlands, England. Kempadoo was one of the artists associated with the group such as Eddie Chambers, Claudette Johnson, Keith Piper, Donald Rodney, Lubaina Himid, and others. The group questioned the space for Black artists within the larger art scene and market bringing to the forefront of the conversation

issues of racial discrimination shaping the nation and notions of belonging and exclusion.

33. For access to the full lecture, see Roshini Kempadoo, "State of Play: Photography, Multimedia and Memory." The Glasgow School of Art, 5 February 2010, vimeo.com/62421134.

34. Kempadoo's interest in documenting creole cultural histories is also linked to the influence of the documentary work of her father, the late Peter Kempadoo, Guyanese writer and journalist author of novels such as *Guyana Boy* (1960), who carried out extensive recording, through interviews, of cultural traditions in Guyana, particularly amongst the South Indian communities of indentureship, a methodology also used by Roshini Kempadoo in her artistic process. Kempadoo is also sister of scholar Kamala Kempadoo and writers Manghanita and Oonya Kempadoo, who all share artistic and scholarly interests such as the role of women in Caribbean societies and alternative ways of narrating histories.

35. In an account on the role and process of research in her lens-based photographic practice, Ingrid Pollard shares: "The enduring issues that I return to are landscape and people and ideas of hidden histories—the interactions and the outcomes about how the landscape influences people's behaviour and shapes the land through ownership, commerce, development, politics" ("Case Study: Ingrid Pollard", 1997, np. Ebook). See author's website at www.ingridpollard.com.

36. Archival research, such as the one carried by Gaiutra Bahadur in *Coolie Woman: The Odyssey of Indenture* (2013), has turned to both family and more official/formal archives to tell a fuller history of indentureship and family history simultaneously. Bahadur's research in the British Library has also uncovered the manuscript of a previously little-known text by an indentured migrant in Guyana, Lalbihari Sharma. The manuscript, was translated and published by poet Rajiv Mohabir. *I Even Regret Night: Holi Songs of Demerara* was originally published in India in a combination of Bhojpuri and Awadhi languages 1916. The influence of music, drumming and Indian literary traditions have shaped Sharma's *Holi Songs* in ways that also offer a vehicle for documenting life on a plantation of the region of Demerara. Sharma was a musician and singer who brought a musical sensibility and form to *Holi Songs of Demerara*, a collection of songs following the sixteenth-century tradition of

poems in Bhojpuri to be sang during the Holi festival celebrations in Guyana. *Holi Songs* is a rare text, as not many written records that speak of the experience of indentureship from the perspective of the indentured have been uncovered. As noted earlier, because of this, fiction has become a means to evoke the past, and imagine it as counterpoint to the silences, pushing the boundaries and possibilities of what is known and how it is being evoked through creative and artistic work. For example, through autobiographical fiction such as Peter Kempadoo's *Guyana Boy*, many of the traditions of South East Indians in Guyana have been recorded.

37. See Maria del Pilar Kaladeen's "'Those Not with Us Anymore': The Literary Archive of Indian Minorities in Guyanese Indenture and Beyond" (2021), pp. 26–35, for an engaging and insightful discussion of the ways in which literature of indenture in Guyana and Trinidad has confronted stereotypical representations, myths, and inaccuracies housed in colonial records.

38. Further, Reddock also frames this practice of division as the root to later tensions between African and Indian men. For a discussion of the various colonial policies and cultures of division see Reddock's "The Indentureship Experience" ([1998] 2020, e-book ed.).

CHAPTER 6

"A Genealogy of Resistance" in Works by Inés María Martiatu Terry, Mayra Santos-Febres, and Yolanda Arroyo Pizarro

In *Afrocubanas: historia, pensamiento y prácticas culturales* (2011), Daisy Rubiera Castillo frames the significance of this anthology as one that documents the central role of Black women in Cuban history, cultural practices, and processes of social justice. Rubiera Castillo notes how that role has been historically overlooked and silenced as shown in the accounts presented in the publication (35).[1] The book, recently translated into English, features contributions by 35 writers and scholars including Rubiera Castillo and Inés Maria Martiatu Terry (editors of the anthology), that confront and undo that process of erasure ("Introduction").[2] Rubiera Castillo also mentions schools and the university as vital spaces where knowledge by, and about Afro-Cuban women was then still largely absent, despite the state's commitment and work of anti-discrimination. In one of the articles in the anthology, journalist Yusimí Rodriguez López, points out that while the date 27 of November marks a national holiday in Cuba that honours the seven students of medicine who were murdered by the Spanish colonial army in 1871, official accounts and events did not commemorate the group of Black men, members of an Abakuá society who died in an attempt to stop the massacre ("La Revolución" 284–290). A similar situation takes place regarding education and memorialisation in the educational system of Puerto Rico, as

© The Author(s), under exclusive license to Springer Nature Switzerland AG 2023
M. Fernández Campa, *Memory and the Archival Turn in Caribbean Literature and Culture*, New Caribbean Studies,
https://doi.org/10.1007/978-3-030-72135-0_6

Yolanda Arroyo Pizarro explained in a Q&A session after a talk she delivered at Kelly Writers House in 2020.[3] Following a presentation on her work as director of the department of Afro-Puerto Rican Studies and founder of the Chair of Ancestral Black Women (*Cátedra de Mujeres Negras Ancestrales*) in 2015,[4] Arroyo Pizarro mentioned that despite the great interest in their educational work from schools, universities, and some politicians, the government (to date) does not implement anti-racist content in the school curriculum. As epigraph to her collection of poems *Afrofeministamente* (2020), Arroyo Pizarro includes the following quote from Afro-Puerto Rican historian Dr. Marie Ramos Rosado, "[s]e nos ha educado para negar todas las aportaciones africanas que existen en la cultura puertorriqueña" (np; we have been educated to negate all African contributions in Puerto Rican culture, translation mine).

Another essay in *Afrocubanas*, by Martiatu Terry, examines the history of the Black communities in Southern Spain, particularly in Seville, that existed prior to the arrival of Columbus in the Caribbean. She also discusses communities of enslaved Africans in the Iberian Peninsula from the sixteenth century, whose labour and cultural production were central to Spain's socio-economic growth, cultural expression, and the arts ("Los negros en España"). Similarly, her insights about how language in Siglo de Oro's drama racialised and marked hierarchies through the representation of Black and white characters' speech, a model later transported to the Cuban Bufo theatre, remains still largely unknown both in Spain and in Cuba, outside of certain academic and other specialist circles ("Los negros en el teatro del Siglo de Oro"). Within the context of the Dominican Republic, Lorgia García Peña also underscores the absence of a critical educational colonial history in schools (56–57). Equally, many aspects of the history of enslavement and liberation in Spain's former colonised territories have been largely absent from the educational curriculum and school programmes in Spain, and, when included, these have often incurred in reductionist and biased historiography, creating a pervasive knowledge gap that aims to sanitise the role of the Spanish crown and nation in what rarely gets acknowledged in textbooks or public discourse as genocide. The study of the silence and erasure of the history of Afro-descendants reveals strong hierarchies of knowledge and posits the question of what specific threat does that knowledge signify for the state? How does the answer or answers to that question redefine the relationship to former and present colonial powers such as Spain and the US? And how can we rethink the bias of traditional western historiography as constitutive of the project of whiteness? What would further acknowledgement of that amnesia, yield in the public sphere? Caribbean writers have been at the forefront of these discussions, and through their work, they have popularised and given space to further knowledge, imaginings, and documentation of suppressed histories in ways that account to how oppression continues to also be perpetuated through the control of national historical narratives.

Following the 1898 defeat of Spain as colonial power in the Spanish–American War, new socio-cultural concepts and imaginaries continued to develop in Cuba and Puerto Rico that were further centred around new localised and creolised identities, partly as a means to establish a cultural differentiation with the United States as new imperial power (and also colonial power in the case of Puerto Rico). In Puerto Rico, the trope of the *"gran familia puertoriqueña"* (the great Puerto Rican family), originated in the nineteenth century as a means to collectively organise against Spanish colonial powers, and re-emerged in the 1930s with the aim of uniting Puerto Ricans "against the threat of Americanization" and aimed to portray a harmonious coexistence of social groups with an idealised idea of the past under Spanish rule and other modes of Hispanophilia (Moreno 77, 78).[5] In an analysis of its influence on the Puerto Rican literary canon, Marisel C. Moreno argues how this metaphor as myth of national unity was "used to legitimize its 'silences' through three main tenets: social harmony and racial democracy, the glorification of the past, and the cult of patriarchy" (13). The process of idealising an imagined community and past in traditional configurations of *la familia puertoriqueña*, and particularly through a greater identification with Spanish language and cultural markers aimed to counter US imperialism. The concept of family as element of social cohesion already figures in canonical works from the nineteenth century such as Manuel Zeno Gandía's *La Charca* (1894), and later in the literature of the 1920s and 1930s with the aim of solidifying a strong sense of Puerto Rican identity, increasingly linked to patriotic ideas of national demarcation from US colonialism by the 1930s (Schmidt-Nowara, *Slavery* 35; Moreno 8). As Moreno emphasises, in women's writing from the 1970s onwards, this myth was increasingly challenged, especially in regard to its exclusionary attitude towards gender and race. The comparative approach of Moreno's study shows how diasporic refigurations of *la gran familia* trope facilitate critical spaces to address canon formation in relation to inequity and cultural erasure. In a parallel sense, another national imaginary in Cuba, that of *cubanidad* (Cubanness), invokes a vision of national unity based on ideas of racial harmony under the umbrella of cohesion. José Martí devised this concept's potential unifying force in the late nineteenth century, and it later became constitutive of the national project of Cuba and was refigured after the victory of the Cuban Revolution in 1959. However, scholars and writers have pointed out certain fissures between the premise of *cubanidad* and existing inequalities that Cubans of African and Chinese descent experience in Cuba (Bodenheimer; Casamayor-Cisneros "Imagining" 135–180; "Elogio" 303–327; Pacini Hernández 114; Spence Benson 12, 62, 78; López 209–213, 243). The aftermath of the Cuban revolution brought a series of groundbreaking policies and political reform that targeted racial discrimination and inequality. As Devyn Spence Benson points out, "the new government passed over 1,500 pieces of legislation during its first thirty months in power, including laws delivering land redistribution, free health care, and educational scholarship programs" (2). Through policy and an anti-discrimination campaign in March 1959, Fidel Castro dismantled many of the structural measures of inequality and segregation established by Fulgencio Batista's government, and by the 1980s Black and mulato Cubans had the same secondary education rates, life expectancy and percentage of professional positions than white Cubans (Spence Benson, 2). Following the victory of the revolution, the government also promoted the premise that national identity and kinship was a unifying element that should take precedence over racial identity (a discourse partly influenced by Jose Martí and encompassed in his essay "My Race", published in the newspaper *Patria* in 1893, only a few years before the Spanish–American War), where he claimed the emergence of an ultimate identity that transcends race: "Cubans are more than white, mulattoes or Negroes" (173). Martí saw the success of Cuban Independence as relying on racial and social cohesion, and twice in this short text, Martí asserts: "In Cuba, there will never be a racial war" (173, 174). For Martí, national identity should take precedence over any other identity constructs and experiences, in the expression of *cubanidad*. Although the government of Fidel Castro promoted African heritage and culture through different initiatives (Pacini Hernández 115), and the construct of *cubanidad* has historically been constructed in dialogue, and as inclusive in a multicultural nation, it has also proved malleable and exclusionary in some contexts. Kathleen López argues that *cubanidad* has both included the identity of the descendants of Chinese indentured labourers, and equally excluded their participation in a variety of contexts, as was also the case for Afro-Cubans (243). African cultural expression started to be celebrated, but also commodified, during the special period of the 1990s.[6] According to Myriam J. A. Chancy, "[w]hile Castro declared Cuba an 'African' state early in its regime, and the state has allied itself with pro-African causes in its history (the best known being its participation in the Angolan war of Independence), the state repressed expressions of African *cubanidad* from the 1950s until the period of dollarization which began in 1993 and ended in 2004 ..." (40). African cultural and religious practices including *regla de ocho* (*santería*) were partly promoted driven by interests of tourism (Chancy 40). Odette Casamayor-Cisneros similarly stresses that from the 1960s there has been a general consensus from the government that discussions of race or racial discrimination were unnecessary as it was declared that racial discrimination had been eliminated, a premise that started to be more fully challenged from the 1990s especially by activist artists including Sandra Alvarez Ramiro, Daisy Rubiera Castillo, Inés María Martiatu Terry, and Pedro Pérez Sarduy, amongst others ("Elogio" 304).[7]

The trope of the *gran familia puertorriqueña* bears the influence of *hispanismo* and *hispanofilia* and its legacies in Puerto Rico (Moreno 44–45), and similarly the concept of *cubanidad* reveals elements of national identity that have regulated the terms of its potential critique (Casamayor-Cisneros "Elogio"). I do not claim that all expressions and understanding of *cubanidad* and *la gran familia puertorriqueña* are exclusionary or experienced as such, for they are constructs of complex and even contradictory realities and experiences, but it remains important to this chapter's discussion to acknowledge how initially inclusive vocabularies and imaginaries can also reproduce hierarchies and occlude the perspectives of social groups. Although both terms equally depart from some of the tenets of Hispanism and its coloniality, there is a particular remnant in its emphasis on cohesion over social address. With its discursive solidification in the second half of the nineteenth century, Hispanism was promoted from Spain, as former imperial and colonial power, and from the conservative elite in Latin American and Caribbean countries following traditional visions for the future of former colonised territories and function also a means to negotiate the future influence of Spain over its former colonies (Schmidt-Nowara, "Spanish Origins" 34).[8] The roots of that colonial manifestation of Hispanism go back to the colonial project in Latin America and the Caribbean. Although Hispanism has different manifestations, understandings, and coinages, I am referring here to the geopolitical and cultural discourse at the core of Spanish colonialism through its *colonialidad del poder* (coloniality of power). When Aníbal Quijano theorised this concept, —also explored in the scholarship of Walter Mignolo, Sylvia Wynter, and others—he foregrounded the erasure of cultural heterogeneity amongst Indigenous groups and enslaved Africans and the configuration of racial categories and their colonial hierarchies as central to the machinery of colonial power (139–142).[9] Quijano connects that categorising drive that fixed and perpetuated socialisation and socio-economic classes according to race and colorism characteristic in the so-called New World with the contemporary ideology of the New World Order and globalisation in its continued aim of perpetuating hierarchies of gender and race. Ideologically grounded in Hispanophilia, this mode or strand of Hispanism, relied on monolingualism (and resulting monocultural hegemony) that Spain first imposed in the peninsula and a rhetoric exalting Spanish culture, uncritically centring its legacies in the Caribbean and Latin America.

The counter-archives of *afrodescendencia* embodied in the literature by Afro-Cuban and Afro-Puerto Rican women writers in this chapter, present historical memory from their perspective. Their storytelling ultimately challenges the notion of harmony embedded in concepts such as the *gran familia puertorriqueña* and *cubanidad*. They equally question and counter the legacy of *hispanidad* (Hispanicity) which I argue—borrowing from Trouillot's theorisation of archival silencing— can function as intimately bound with forms of silencing and controlling public discourse (*Silencing*). Trouillot underscored the discursive impact of Spain's promotion of *hispanismo* in Latin America from the nineteenth century (134), further arguing that "the Latin American rejection of Spain's political tutelage did not entail a rejection of *hispanismo*" (121). The three texts under discussion in this chapter: *Over the Waves*, *Negras* and *Fé en disfraz* all reflect a "geneaology of resistance". This phrase is used by M. NourbeSe Philip in the essay collection of the same title, where she identifies it as informing her understanding of memory and silence, and connecting her writing with her ancestors; a "geneaology of resistance" also highlights what is connecting the experience and memory of the protagonists in these literary texts by Arroyo Pizarro, Martiatu Terry, and Santos-Febres. In the opening essay,

Philip writes about her own genealogy and "[t]he silence of ancestors around whom we shape ourselves—their traces" ("A Genealogy" 9–30), engaging with "a genealogy" as "an account in a certain way of resistance by enumeration of intermediate persons" (14). Philip's notion of an Afrosporic consciousness also offers a helpful framework in this chapter. Philip coined the term "Afrosporic" to "describe the scattering of Africans around the world" (*Bla_k* 37). She further explains that Afrosporic "contains the roots of the place, Afro, and the idea of the spore which is scattered. It represents a continued drive on my part to develop words to speak the experience of Afrosporic people losing their original languages" (*Bla_k* 37). This critical concern with the configuration of other languages that speak to the experience of *afrodescendientes* (afrodescendants), extends to the poetics and storytelling strategies in the work of Yolanda Arroyo Pizarro, Inés Maria Martiatu Terry, and Mayra Santos-Febres. Their writing claims further the centrality of *otros saberes* (other knowledges) which Yomaira C. Figueroa-Vásquez coins and describes as "the epistemological break that occurs when devalued or othered knowledge comes to be understood as other ways of knowledge" (*Decolonizing Diasporas* 2). In all three texts by Arroyo Pizarro, Martiatu Terry, and Santos-Febres, historical, political, cultural, and religious knowledge of Afro-descendants is shared amongst characters, often intergenerationally and across time and space. It shapes a genealogy of resistance.

The collection *Over the Waves and other Stories* (2008), offers a heterogenous mosaic of stories mapping the history of Cuba and some of the key transnational connections of the African diaspora linking Cuba to other geographies like Jamaica, Trinidad, and Panama. Similarly, *Negras* (2012) and *Fe en Disfraz* (2009), introduce pathways for thinking and articulating the historical memory of enslaved women and *cimarronas* (maroon women). The works by Arroyo Pizarro, Martiatu Terry and Santos-Febres reflect a shared musical sensibility, and non-linear, relational poetics that is key to their revision of official histories and historical narratives of Cuba, Puerto Rico and the Americas. Focusing on literary works by Black Cuban and Puerto Rican women, this chapter establishes comparative links in articulations of African diasporic Caribbean memory and poetics and seeks to interrogate the significance and possibility of forms and poetics. It also asks, what possibilities do those stories and ways of retelling offer to rearticulations of the history and historiography in the Spanish-speaking Caribbean?

OVER THE WAVES: A POETICS
OF CONTRAPUNTO AND CLAVE

The Cuban literary landscape of the 1990s on the island was marked by the economic challenges of the "Special Period", felt particularly until 2006, and which had a strong impact on that decade's writing and literary culture. Miriam DeCosta-Willis points out the socio-economic impact on publishing, despite the initial institutional support through publishing houses such as *Ediciones Unión* and *Editorial Letras Cubanas*, the early works of Afro-Cuban writers such as Nancy Morejón, Soleida Ríos, Georgina Herrera, and Excilia Saldaña were no longer in print in the early 2000s (xix). The 1990s was also characterised by the very real "shortness of paper" of the special period (DeCosta-Willis xix), and to this date printing and the accessibility of books in Cuba is limited for economic reasons largely a result of the US economic blockade and series of embargos against Cuba since 1958. There was nevertheless a rich proliferation of writing in the 1990s, particularly by Afro-Cuban women writers, that underscores the role of Black women in the long history of political participation in Cuba, from the War of Independence to the Cuban Revolution. The formation of the Afro-Cubanas group and project in Havana in the mid-2000s (which animated Rubiera Castillo's and Martiatu Terry's anthology and who also featured as authors) created a vital critical space to address issues of race, and racism, gender, and feminism in Cuba. A similar initiative prior to the Afro-Cubanas project is the Centro Cultural Africano Fernando Ortiz founded by Rubiera Castillo in 1988 to form a space to debate social and historical issues in relation to racial discrimination (Rubiera Castillo, "Grupo" 204).[10] Around this time, Rubiera Castillo also engaged in bibliographic research around the socio-political context of Black women but found an absence in most books that led to her historiographical work in Cuban archives with the aim of researching and sharing knowledge to uncover lesser-known aspects of history.[11]

Several edited anthologies of writing by women authors were published in Cuba during the 1990s and were vital in illuminating new perspectives on the Caribbean experience and *cubanidad* as well as collecting and offering a sense of recent work of women writers. Still, the number of publications did not match the volume of literary production. Some were then translated and published in the United States; however, none of these collections (mentioned below) have included short stories by

Afro-Cuban women writers like Inés Maria Martiatu Terry and others. Although the international translation, publishing, and reception of Afro-Cuban writers, filmmakers, and visual artists outside of Cuba has been largely supported through the research interest and engagement of Cuban and US scholars who have invited writers to participate in author residencies and deliver lectures, and publishing in academic presses[12] (this is famously the case of the work and reception in the United States of Nancy Morejón), there has also been a striking absence of Black Cuban writers in some publications and US translated versions. In *Sugar's Secrets: Race and the Erotics of Cuban Nationalism* (1993) Vera M. Kutzinski addresses the 1990s' general absence in publications "of women in general and nonwhite women in particular", that reflect their "standing as self-conscious subjects in the national discourses of culture" (16). A little more than ten years later, in the critical essay that accompanies *Over the Waves*, Fernández De La Reguera Tayà draws attention to the fact that "Afro-Cuban women authors continue to be excluded, even in the most recent women's anthologies" (190). Two anthologies, from the late 1990s and early 2000s, where this imbalance in contributors is present are *Cubana: Contemporary Fiction by Cuban Women*, published in English in 1998 (an extended version of a previous anthology originally published in Cuba in 1996 as *Estatuas de sal*), and *Open Your Eyes and Soar: Cuban Women Writing Now*, translated and published in English in 2003. Some of the authors featured in *Cubana* also appear in *Open Your Eyes*, as is the case of Nancy Alonso, Aida Bahr, Marilyn Bobes, Adelaida Fernández de Juan, Ena Lucia Portela, and Mirta Yáñez, evidencing further their centrality in shaping a contemporary literary and publishing wave of women writers in Cuban literature. However, despite the imbalance, the cover of the book *Cubana* features artwork by Afro-Cuban visual artist María Magdalena Campos-Pons, whose art features on the cover of many literary and critical texts today and has received significant critical attention globally.[13]

As all other writers whose work is discussed in this book, Arroyo Pizarro, Martiatu Terry, and Santos-Febres have an active engagement with issues of cultural memory and social justice. Through education, cultural work, and activism, they have created spaces of dialogue and exchange that reflect many of the preoccupations in their work. Martiatu Terry was a pioneer critic and scholar of Cuban theatre and theatre studies, with a specific focus on the influence of Afro-Cuban rituals and myths in performance. African cultural influences, as well as her study of music in Havana, would play an important role in her writing, as evident in the formal and thematic concerns in *Over the Waves*. She graduated in History from the University of Havana where she was consultant to the Cátedra de Estudios Africanístas de Argeliers León and was a close collaborator with the Fundación Fernando Ortiz. Martiatu Terry was also a public intellectual and worked in various cultural and arts spaces of Havana.

In the bilingual edition and anthology of short stories *Over the Waves and Other Stories / Sobre las olas y otros cuentos* (2008), Martiatu Terry recentres the role of African Caribbean communities in leading and shaping historical processes and cultural memory and identity in Cuba and the region. The stories map a trans-Caribbean cartography that highlights the cross-cultural influences of migration within the region, and to and from the United States. The first story, "Follow Me", originally published in Spanish in 1993 with its title in English, highlights the weight of such transcultural markers, anticipating their role in linking the overall narrative. Tànit Fernández De La Reguera Tayà reads "Follow Me!" as the story that "establishes the ideological framework and the principal aesthetic interests of the book: the recovery of collective memory, the processes of forming Caribbean and Cuban culture and identity, and the role of black women as transmitters and creators in all of this" (195). "Follow Me!" tells the story of Lola (whose birth name is Wendolyn), a Jamaican woman who migrates with her mother from Jamaica to Camagüey, Cuba and who actively tries to succeed in the music industry, later touring the Caribbean and the United States in the 1920s. Victoria (Lola's mother) is proud to be named after Queen Victoria and to be a British subject. Disapproving of her daughter's life choices and pursuit of a career in music, Victoria forces Lola out of the family home since for her, music and dancing are "tools of the devil" (4). After moving to the city and starting employment singing and waitressing at a bar, Lola meets Armando with whom she later has a daughter, Virginia. When the child is three years old and their relationship is in crisis, Lola attempts to leave town with her daughter. However, Armando "managed to take the child from her mother in Ciego de Ávila, with the help of a bribed judge and the prejudices against Jamaican immigrants" ("FollowMe!" 6), highlighting some of the xenophobia and racism against *jamaiquinos* (Jamaicans or Cubans of Jamaican descent) in Cuba[14]. This is also in contrast with moments of solidarity amongst Jamaicans as when "a fellow countrymen", aware of Lola's interest in music, hands her the address of the bar where she later meets Armando (4).

After she leaves Cuba, Lola sends photos, letters, and postcards to her daughter from faraway "places like New York, Chicago and Washington D.C ... Greetings from Kingston or Montego Bay, salutations from St. Kitts or Barbados, ..." (3). In Jamaica, she meets Gilbert, born in the Canal Zone of Panama, the son of a Jamaican mother, like Lola, and a Barbadian father.[15] They travel together to Panama where they are exposed to the Pan-African ideas of Marcus Garvey. With Gilbert, Lola writes a song that celebrates Garveyism. The musical refrain in Lola and Gilbert's song: "Let's fight! Follow me!" becomes an important lyrical phrase in the story; it creates a vital bond between Lola and her daughter, and it simultaneously connects all stories in Martiatu's collection as it provides a thematic arc that extends throughout the collection. The title, *Over the Waves and Other Stories,* maps the journey of intra-Caribbean migration of the African diaspora, a journey marked by the shared historical context of slavery, colonialism, and economic migration as well as rebellion and political resistance. Through reading back issues of *Negro World*, the newspaper of UNIA (the United Negro Improvement Association), founded by Marcus Garvey and Amy Ashwood Garvey in 1914, Lola is able to connect to both Pan-African history and her daughter: "Lola discerned for the first time *the keys* to understand her firstborn; the works and dreams made sense in that everything was related to part of a huge drama that touched her and contained her at the same time" (emphasis mine 7). Motherhood for Lola heightens her awareness of ancestral and collective genealogy and the possibility of connection and healing through sharing knowledge. Writing postcards to her daughter becomes a means to communicate to her daughter, Jamaican and Caribbean political struggle. Interestingly, the word "*claves*" in the original Spanish (translated as "keys"), —as in English—evokes a central musical element in Afro-Cuban music. It marks syncopated rhythm patterns, the main two of which are son and rumba. *Clave* is also the name of the percussion instrument consisting of two wooden cylinder sticks, that played against each other serve to mark the underlying rhythm to which others join. Njoroge M. Njoroge describes clave as "the centrifugal force in Afro Cuban music [and as] a rhythm counterpoint, the central concept is that two cells that make up clave are held together in a binary structure generating a 'cycle of tension and release': unity in difference" (Ch. 2). This rhythmic pattern is marked narratively in this opening story of the collection (in the riff and motto of "let's fight, follow me!" and in the patterns of search in Lola's journey) as well as throughout the other stories where themes reappear in different keys, highlighting that variation in sameness or, as Njoroge puts it, "unity in difference" (Ch. 2).

The song will bring Lola and Virginia closer, as they continue to live their separate lives away from one another. As a girl, Virginia would hum and sing to herself the lyrics to her mother's song, spelt "Leta fight! Falla Me!" in one of the letters from Lola to phonetically facilitate a Jamaican patois reading. In the story, the song emerges from a consciousness nurtured by long conversations amongst Lola, Gilbert, and Patterson (another Jamaican in Panama who introduces them to Garvey), "their hope-filled conversations were wrought with old pains and the rage of a people that awakens and sees itself in grand histories and in a bright future. Let's Fight! Follow Me! Follow Me! They sang" (7). That Lola and Gilbert's homage to Garvey takes the form of song also signals the central role of Caribbean music in articulating a transnational political consciousness of Black liberation and social justice. In Panama, they inhabit a multi-Caribbean space with music at the centre of their cultural and political connections. Gilbert sings calypso and they both join Carnival every year, a time when,

> [t]he Antilleans tried to forget that they weren't anything more than silver and that everything was gold for the Americans. Silver homes, silver wages for the same work, silver life, silver, silver, silver. In one of the bars, with walls of pressed wood, Gilbert would sing that song composed for Garvey. (7)

The effect of the repetition of the word "silver", its counterpointed position to "gold" and the mention of the "Americans" indirectly evokes Trinidadian calypsos such as the Mighty Sparrow's "Jean and Dinah" and the exploitation of capitalist American interference in so many Caribbean and Latin American locations (and particularly so in Cuba). Further, the repetition of "silver" here emulates the tempo and political theme of calypso. In the story, calypso and the spaces available through Carnival, ultimately signal the kinship between Caribbean people from different islands. A type of Antillean kinship that Alaí Reyes-Santos defines as embodying a cultural and, perhaps most importantly, ethical and affective connection, through the possibility of imagining the other as kin, as one (14, 26).

"Follow Me!" also forms part of a literary canon in Cuban literature that engages with music, particularly singing, with attention to a characteristic trope of Cuban literature embedded in the bolero and nightclub scene. However, Martiatu's story revises and modifies that tradition which had often been dominated by the representation of the 'tragic mulata' in Cuban literature. This trope was famously popularised in Cirilo Villaverde's nineteenth-century novel *Cecilia Valdés* (1839), where Cecilia, a woman of mixed-race heritage and an illegitimate child, finds love with a young man that turns out to be her unknown brother, portraying symbolically the fears of miscegenation that informed Cuba and the non-viability of the marriage. A landmark of Cuban literature, the novel has been read both as critical of slavery and Spanish rule on the nation as well as weary of interracial love, kinship, and ultimately marriage (González Mandri 16). Afro-Cuban poet Nancy Morejón argues that Cecilia portrays racial self-rejection as she wishes not to be who she is (González Mandri 16).

Lola is described as having "a light complexion and the eyes of Bessie Smith" (3) and her performance at the bar where she meets Armando is described thus: "[s]ometimes, the young and visually striking mulatta sang and danced, which delighted the customers and caused envy among the other workers, who would watch the spectacle" (4). This portrayal does not, however, fix Lola, but departs from that exoticising tradition. The overall story shows how she resists external definitions of any type, but rather fashions her identity and her path. She is rather the one who renames herself as Lola, "the most exciting Latin name that she knew" (4) strategically taking ownership of her career through self-fashioning and aware of the marketability of a Latin name versus her anglophone one as a stage name. She leaves part of her old self behind, and the weight of a strict Anglican upbringing, but not her Jamaican heritage with which she reconnects through the ideas of Garvey and through music. Equally, she leaves her relationship with Armando when it brings her "anguish, postponements, abandonment and absence" (6). Although the description of her performances and the thematic focus on the hardships in her life, partially against the backdrop of the world of the music scene in Cuba, are characteristic of many texts that engage with the 'tragic mulata' trope, Lola's agency remains a central focus throughout the story. She resists limitations and expectations imposed on her and breaks away from social normativity. The narrator states: "[s]he took pleasure in moving from one place to another, in disappearing, and in sending notes from each city without *seeming* to care whether or not she received an answer or perhaps without wanting one" ("Follow Me!" 3, emphasis mine).

Like the Black woman in Nancy Morejón's famous poem "Mujer Negra", Lola's vision is both individual *and* collective. "Follow Me!" centres around Lola's story and her specific life circumstances but it also speaks about Pan-Caribbean connections through anti-colonial struggle that are channelled through cultural expression. The brief lines between stanzas in "Mujer Negra" record Black women's history of rebellion in Cuba. A history that extends to the whole Caribbean; "I rebelled" / "I walked" / "I rose up" / "I walked on and on" / "I left for the hills" / "I came down from the Sierra" (200–203). Initially, these lines function as counterpoint to the stanzas in the poem, which chart the history of racial terror and genocide in the region. Moreover, the stanzas also progressively stress throughout the poem the formation of a new culture in the Americas "I strengthened the foundations of my millenary song and my hope. Here I built my world" (200–202). Writing about the poetry of Morejón, Martiatu Terry highlights how it marked a significant shift in the representation of Black women in Cuban poetry, whom authors from earlier generations such as José Zacarías Tallet had exoticised and sexualised in their writing. According to Martiatu Terry, their writing exoticised women's bodies often in connection with dancing, as in the poem "La rumba" where Zacarías Tallet presents a hyperbolic rendition of the movement of a Black woman dancing rumba drawing from a stereotypical image of excessive sexuality ("La Poesía" 409). In contrast, the portrayal of Lola and the narration of her story departs from those representations of mulata and Black women in Cuban literature and repositions a relationship to music (and the Afro-Cuban literary canon) as a powerful outlet of political consciousness and articulation. The character of Lola echoes the process of voicing agency in Morejón's "Mujer negra". Mayra Santos-Febres's *Sirena Selena, vestida de pena* (2000), translated into English as *Sirena Selena*, similarly rewrites that trope through the character of Selena, a Puerto Rican young travesti singer whose dream is to start a new life singing boleros in the Dominican Republic. As an immigrant living in precarity, Selena seeks opportunities through music. For Selena, performing boleros expands the possibilities of queerness, and challenges the genre's own traditional heteronormativity.

Music is a major unifying element connecting the stories in *Over the Waves*. In "The Re is Green" and "A Subtle and Electric Sensation", where it plays a more explicit role, "music stands out as a stylistic resource in the telling of the story and as a motif in the plot so as to represent the cultural and identitary learning and formation of the female protagonists" (Fernández De La Reguera Tayà 202). In "The Re is Green", the fascination that Fe, a middle-class Black girl from Havana, feels toward the conversations and interactions of a group of Black men in her street is conveyed through a language filled with musical references. In the communication amongst this group, through speech and song, she identifies a musicality that she starts to translate into the rhythms and patterns of her life in the neighbourhood where she lives. Fe plays the piano and studies music theory. She "has the ability to sing and produce melodies, to capture the rhythm and immediately notice when any one of her accompanists was off pitch or made a mistake" (10), but she sometimes struggles to sight-read music sheets. However, by closely observing the language and speech patterns of this group of men, she is able to capture and interiorise an Afro-Cuban musical sensibility and ultimately taps into a different sense of musical rhythm herself, widening her musical repertoire and ability to identify and reproduce polyphonic rhythms.

> When they saw each other, *"Mi sangre!"* When they greeted each other, *"Mi social!"* The words intertwined in a difficult and staccato rhythm in which all of them spoke. They rhymed, they repeated, or they found amusing phrases that came out of nowhere. One person began, another would join in, they would interrupt, interweave, and even guess the thoughts of the other in an *"Official!"* in unison that would leave her dumbstruck ... They whispered at times, rhythmically recalling a musical phrase they knew or improvised only to end up singing it softly, ... (11)

In the form of counterpoint, the next paragraph in the story opens with an image of Fe attempting, but struggling, to play Bach's Minuet No. 1. Later in the story a newfound musical sensibility enables Fe to experience rhythm differently, similarly to how the character of Lola in "Follow Me!" experiences her first encounter with the Cuban dance style *danzón*, when Lola was "enraptured by its stimulating tension whose rhythms promised liberation" in contrast with the "tunes derived from marches that had Anglo-saxon influences" with which she had grown up (4). A musical style of an older generation, *danzón* is an example of the transculturation of elements from African, Chinese and European origin that Fernando Ortíz wrote about. When Ortíz defined the concept of transculturation in his discussion of the Cuban counterpoint, in the eponymous 1940 seminal publication, he suggested it as an alternative to acculturation, "the process of transition of one culture to another" (98). Transculturation describes instead a process of a new culture emerging from the contact and interaction of two or more cultures in a dialectical, and dialogic dynamic akin to the one musically marked by counterpoint. Martiatu Terry has engaged with Ortíz's theories in her critical work and was also, as previously mentioned, a student of music as a child. The references to music in "The Re is Green", through European classical music and Afro-Cuban rhythms, point to both that process of transculturation and the counterpoint dynamic distinctive of Baroque music, exemplified in Bach's style, which Edward Said identifies as "fully contrapuntal", that is "regularly composed of several equal lines, sinuously interwoven, working themselves out according to stringent rules" (*Music at the Limits* 66). Bach was also a master of the fugue in all its complexity, which as seen in Chapter 3, is a musical composition where the contrapuntality reaches a maximum. However, the strictures of Bach's counterpoint, the "stringent rules" that Said notes (ch. 1), are only accessible to Fe via the call-and-response experienced outside of Bach's harmonies. After hearing the rhythm whilst observing the men in her neighbourhood, Fe then tries to play Bach's Minuet No. 1 one more time, and is surprised to be able to play it and enjoy "[t]he pleasure of variation" (12), and because the musical phrase stays in her memory, she is also able to translate and reproduce that rhythm as she skates on the sidewalk or plays yo-yo in the street. Then as she plays, she feels "the tempo of minuet joining the rhythm of their speech" (13).

A description of music in "A Subtle and Electric Sensation" also blends in contrapuntal elements and equally refers to a young girl discovering the connection to music through dancing on her father's feet whilst listening to the chords in an orchestra playing, and grieving for the death of her mother.

Distinguishing the nearly imperceptible distances of the semitones that ascend and descend only a little, forcing you to lend your five senses and leaving you softly slipping into an uncertain sea. Startling you before the unforeseen dissonances that explode and force the ears into acute agreement. ... The girl, little by little, felt in her chest, in her feet, in her hands, that a mystery was being revealed to her. (17)

This evocative rendering of the appreciation of music and the effect of cadence and dissonance, highlight the emotive and affective role of the discrepant notes. It also points toward an element that is repeated here in variation, that is the revelation embodied in the significant moment of musical enjoyment and realisation which is also present in "The Re is Green", where Fe admires the interactions and kinship of the group of men from whom she learns dissonance and counterpoint (13). The *claves* in these stories take the form of secrecy and mystery which allude also to the cultural and religious ceremony from the Abakuá's secret societies[16] referenced in "The Re is Green". The Abakuá religious societies were formed in 1836[17] by captive Africans from the Calabar nation as a means to fight, and support each other, against enslavement[18] and have preserved and transformed their culture and language based on the African language *Efik*, as well as songs, dress, and drums (Sublette 199–205). Comprised only of men, they have had a great influence in Cuban music, particularly in *rumba*, and in linguistic structure as well as key words of Cuban Spanish such as "asere" (now used to mean "brother/comrade" in salute, from the Efik meaning "I salute you"). The greeting is used by the men that Fe observes in the story (9, 11).[19] The members of Cuban secret societies such as Abakuá have historically fought actively in the struggle against slavery, Spanish colonial rule, in labour unions and against US intervention and aggression (Ishemo 266–269), and although initially a secret society only open to Black men, in time, it offered membership to men of all racial identities and ethnicities on the island, while, in contrast, Black male members of the societies continued to be segregated and discriminated against in Cuba (Moret Miranda 29). Martiatu Terry's story reveals the cultural influence of the Abakuá in an effort to document their significance, and the discrimination and misrepresentation they faced, partly encoded through the discourse of middle-class respectability and a national suppression.[20] The interest and fascination that Fe feels toward the group is also marked by a class gap, as hers is a middle-class Afro-Cuban family. Fe's grandmother's use of the term "gibberish" to refer to the men's speech (13), embodies the types of stereotypes also held amongst some Black Cubans of different classes and mostly directed at Abakuá societies and their members who have traditionally been "object of much defamatory propaganda" (Sublette 99). Abakuá societies are referenced in the description of an initiation in "The Re is Green": "Indecipherable secrets foreshadowed the preparation of a grand event, a huge fiesta in which some of them, the youngest, would take part for the first time" (12). The use of the word *misterio* (mystery) in the story alludes to initiation rites in Abakuá societies.[21] In both "The Re is Green" and "A Subtle and Electric Sensation" the *misterio* also symbolically alludes to a kind of initiation that the young characters experience into a new and heightened musical sensibility and sense of belonging to various familial and wider communities (affirming a sense of belonging to one's sense of self and local space).

Other stories in Martiatu Terry's collection such as "The Senator", "Doubt", and "Trillo Park" reflect further the contribution and role of Afro-Cubans in shaping the nation's history and collective memory whilst stressing the obstacles faced and the mechanisms in which state memory has at times occluded or marginalised those contributions. "Trillo Park", for instance, shows the changes undergone by an iconic park in the Afro-Cuban community in the neighbourhood of Cayo Hueso in central Havana, where Martiatu Terry and other friends such as filmmaker Sara Gómez Yera, grew up. The social and spatial description of the park reflects the unequal historical recognition of Afro-Cubans in forms of state memory through the focus on the statue of General Quintín Bandera (1837–1906). José Quintín Bandera Betancourt fought in the Cuban War of Independence but was nevertheless denied the rank he deserved in the army due to racial discrimination, and was brutally killed by a rural army under presidential orders years after the war, and then denied official burial. The physical description of the park in the opening section denotes signs of neglect during the 1950s government of Batista when the story is set, as well as the fact that Quintín Bandera's statue is not standing in the middle of the park, and the first model of the statue "wasn't done to the liking of the black veterans of the war of Independence" who could not see "the resemblance and dignity of the hero with whom some had fought in the hills" (*Over the Waves* 43). The figure of Bandera represents the decisive role of Afro-Cubans and the Mambi army of liberation in the victory against Spanish forces in the Cuban War of Independence. In the story, his figure and history also marks the ways in which the government and state memory marginalised Bandera's role in public narratives, evident in the poetics of place and space in the story. Bandera was removed from office and was later killed by the new government. The position of the statue in the story echoes that mistreatment, as does the policing in Trillo Park. The description of the park presents it as a busy one with local commerce of the weekly market where *marijuana* is also sold and smoked, as well as a place of political meetings, worker and student protests. One of the many stories of frequent visitors to "Trillo Park", is that of an unnamed character, a Black boxer who had enjoyed great success and fortune and then lost it all. Talking to friends in the park, he would reminisce about his past. In one of the regular raids from the police, he finds shelter in the house of an elderly woman who beckons him to come and hide inside, aware of the implications of an arrest for him as a Black man, and as a famous person. As others in *Over the Waves*, this story documents a series of dissonances between local life and experience and national imaginaries. Local forms of kinship and community-based belonging emerge as providing a space for counter-narratives.

The syncretism that, as Antonio Benítez Rojo argues, characterises Cuban cultural expression through processes of transculturation (*The Repeating Island*), has meant that the contrapuntal and non-linear modes of storytelling characteristic of African diasporic aesthetics have informed the writing of Cuban authors from different ethnicities and cultural backgrounds. One example of this is the fragmentariness of a truly contrapuntal novel, Guillermo Cabrera Infante's *Tres Tristes Tigres* (1965) (*Three Trapped Tigers*), where the different fragments in the narrative disrupt, connect, disconnect and reconnect the storyline(s). It is also present in historical literature by Cuban women writers such as Daína Chaviano, based in Miami, whose novel *La isla de los amores infinitos* (2006) (*The Island of Eternal Love*, in its translation) reconstructs the story of three families in Cuba during slavery, the later migration of Spaniards seeking fortune, Chinese indentureship and economic migration. The interrelationships between different members of the descendants of these families, narrated through a series of counterpoints, equally reveal the inequality in their relationships to the national project in which belonging can be rhetorically granted, but not equally accessed by all. Other texts of non-linear fiction such as Wendy Guerra's *Nunca fui Primera Dama* (2017), attempt to recuperate the historical role of women in the revolution through a fictionalised narrative. In *Nunca fui Primera dama* this is enacted through an account based on Celia Sánchez Mandulay who played a vital role in the revolution and its aftermath not only as secretary of Fidel but also as activist and archivist preserving the historical record. Guerra's narrative is intertwined with letters, journal entries, lists, radio script, lyrics, and ongoing references to songs that archive a nostalgic playlist with some *desencanto* (disenchantment), capturing the potential and memory of the revolution, and featuring the likes of Carlos Varela, Carlos Puebla, Silvio Rodriguez, and Pablo Milanés whose music offers a socio-political and historical soundtrack to those years. Although highly influential, African diasporic aesthetics is not the only influence or tradition that is shaping the fragmentariness of Cuban texts; as Benítez Rojo notes, the Caribbean powerfully embodies a postmodern Caribbean perspective and poetics of fragmentation that draws from its many cultural influences.

A Genealogy of Resistance: *Negras* and *Fe en disfraz*

Mayra Santos-Febres' *Fe en disfraz* (2009) and Yolanda Arroyo Pizarro's *Negras* (2012) re-examine the historical narrative around enslavement in the Americas and challenge the ways in which Euro- and US Anglocentric historiography has erased the resistance of captive Africans.[22] Their focus in rethinking official histories and creating a record of the imagined past is carried from an Afro-feminist perspective that excavates stories of enslaved women and their descendants. As Edgar J. Nieves López argues, both texts rehistoricise through fiction what is not found in historical documents and what historians have relegated to oblivion (48). Amarilis Hidalgo de Jesús underscores the scarce fiction and historiography in the past that deals with female slavery in the Spanish-speaking Caribbean, especially in Puerto Rico, and particularly in contrast with the critical studies and literature on the subject in the Anglophone Caribbean (23). Similarly, Zaira Rivera Casellas discusses *Fe en drisfraz* and *Negras* within a tradition of contemporary fiction by Puerto Rican women writers that finds a creative source in slave narratives from the United States and neighbouring Caribbean islands like Cuba, where there are—contrary to Puerto Rico—some slave narratives such as *Autobiografía de un esclavo* (1886) by Juan Francisco Manzano and Esteban Montejo's narrative *Cimarrón: Historia de un esclavo* (1967), recorded and transcribed by Miguel Barnet. *Fe en disfraz* and *Negras* aim to counter the absence of written slave narratives in Puerto Rico. Arroyo Pizarro and Santos-Febres reference this gap in Puerto Rican history and literature in the texts' dedication, epigraphs and writer's note, respectively. The erasure of Africans and their descendants in the historiography of the Caribbean is captured in the satiric dedication of Arroyo Pizarro in *Negras*, "To the historians, for leaving us out" (np). Critics like Marie Ramos Rosado and Edgar J. Nieves López have pointed out that in *Negras* "dedications, citations and epigraphs reveal the author's intentions" (Ramos Rosado, "Foreword", *Las Negras* 17; Nieves López 55).

The 1960s brought a change in Caribbean historiography that turned to study the role of women in historical processes, and in the 1970s this started to influence and redefine historical narratives in the region. The historiographical focus widened with further research and the unearthing of the significant role of women in history, towards also considering gender and gender relations, the impact of masculinity and non-normative gender identities, resulting in what Jean Stubbs describes as an "engendering of Caribbean history and historiography" (3).[23] The work of Caribbean women writers was equally influenced by these critical shifts, as evident in the essays of the 1990 publication of *Caribbean Women Writers: Essays from the First International Conference,* with contributions (mostly) from the Anglophone Caribbean and three articles representing the literary ecology of women writers in the Spanish, French, and the Dutch speaking Caribbean. This new approach was also a response to a shared context across the region and globally, as for centuries those writing the history of the region "were overwhelmingly male historians for whom women were largely 'invisible'" (Stubbs 3). In the Spanish-speaking Caribbean, the new revisionist approach was also influenced by the socio-political context of various key moments, including the post-WWII plans of industrialising Puerto Rico with Operation Bootstrap; the social unrest that led to, and followed, the end of the Trujillo era in 1961 in the Dominican Republic; and the victory of the 1959 Cuban Revolution (Stubbs 5). This shift in studies of the Caribbean has been importantly shaped by Caribbean women historians and scholars across disciplines including sociology and anthropology, cultural studies, linguistics as well as literature and visual art; they have also challenged and corrected the ethnocentric failures in feminism that excluded intersectionality.[24]

Arroyo Pizarro and Santos-Febres turn to a Caribbean based historiography. Both writers mention *Slave Revolts in Puerto Rico. Conspiracies and Uprisings 1795–1873* (1982, 2007), by Puerto Rican historian Guillermo A. Baralt, as an important source and creative influence, amongst other texts. In various paratextual comments, both Arroyo

Pizarro and Santos-Febres address the situation, and situate their narratives as repositories of histories largely untold. The rest of the dedication in *Negras* states the determination to resist erasure: "Here we go again ... bodies present, color in full force, defying invisibility, refusing to be erased" (5). Opening a series of three epigraphs is a citation from the introduction in Baralt's book:

> Until very recently, only a limited number of nineteenth century slave conspiracies and rebellion were known of. The present research, however, mainly based on historical documents from several municipalities in Puerto Rico, shows that, contrary to what has always been deemed true, slaves on the island did rebel frequently. The number of known conspiracies to take over towns or even the entire island, and attempts to kill whites, particularly overseers, adds up to more than forty. Furthermore, if we consider the secret, clandestine nature of these movements, the number undoubtedly rises. (*Negras* 11; Baralt, "Introduction," 1)

This citation from Baralt's historical study is particularly telling. Its stress on the previously scarce knowledge of slave rebellion in Puerto Rico, despite the frequency of revolts and, equally, the stress on the recent focus on that history at the time Baralt's book was published in 1982, is revealing of the predicament of a traditional historiographical tradition that had previously overlooked (and silenced) vital parts of colonial history. These omissions include the resistance and rebellion of Indigenous and African enslaved population. Whilst acknowledging the revisionist trend of the *Nueva Historia* generation of Puerto Rican historians in the 1970s, who started to focus more on the study of colonial enslavement and the structure of the plantation, Francisco Scarano also points out knowledge gaps in their approach which he argues have been addressed by new historical critical studies from 1984 onwards. According to Scarano, one of the shortcomings of the New History of agrarian Puerto Rico lies in the focus on slavery as system rather than on enslaved people as individuals: "although claiming to write the history of workers, peasants, slaves, and women, it in fact did so primarily in the idiom of statistics and other forms of aggregate representation, all the while registering the lives of people in dominant positions on a more individual and first-name basis" (16). However, in the same article from 2020 where he revisits his own 1984 publication *Sugar and Slavery in Puerto Rico: the Plantation Economy of Ponce, 1800–1850* in order to address a series of "meaningful gaps and silences" (4), Scarano identifies a space for new research possibilities and knowledge, particularly of the histories of enslaved women, the intersectionality of race, gender and sexuality as well as the contributions of the enslaved to "proto-peasant" agriculture, forms of regular resistance, religious and cultural processes ("Revisiting" 5, 8, 14, 22). However, it has especially been Eurocentric historiographical approaches that have overwhelmingly silenced and overlooked subaltern histories. Such approaches are rooted in the tradition of early modern chronicles of *conquistadores*, as novelist and philosopher Rafael Sánchez Ferlosio argues in *Esas Yndias equivocadas y malditas: Comentarios a la historia* (1994). The way in which early colonial travel diaries and chronicles describe the land and Indigenous people through a language of possession and superiority, and the assumption to be writing them into history and "civilisation", affirms how in the genealogy of the coloniality of power, the control of the narrative has always been an a priori principle (even before their arrival of *conquistadores*).

In "(Des)memorias en torno a la esclavitud negra y la abolición: Puerto Rico, siglo XIX", María Margarita Flores Collazo speaks of a deafening silencing regarding the experience of enslavement and fugitive captives in the nineteenth century Puerto Rican public sphere, promoted by planters who aimed to control and erase the memory of enslaved Africans and their rebellion. Through a discursive analysis of the rhetoric used in poetry, newspapers, and political speeches of the time, Flores Collazo pinpoints a voice that rhetorically exalts the figure of the abolitionist whilst reinforcing colonial hierarchies and linguistically reproducing the discursive violence of the institution of slavery. Citing a poem by G. R. de San Germán, published in the newspaper *La Razón* on 25 April 1873, a month after the abolition of slavery in Puerto Rico was proclaimed, Flores Collazo illustrates the conflation of the abolitionist's and the planter's voice expecting redemption and setting its terms. The poem "Upon Graciously Freeing my Slave Zacarías", "Al darle la libertad graciosamente a mi esclavo Zacarías", reads as follows:

> Go with God, be merry
> You are now free, you are now man
> Now you have a name in the world
> Raise your neck, young man
> And tell the people
> How loose your yoke was
> That never did I squeeze

Your poor humanity out
Say that freedom
Is felt in the heart
That reason is its temple
And heaven its truth
Tell the people
That those who speak of equality
When chains still suffocate the slave, his brother
Lie needlessly
Tell, alas, my dear friend,
That my sin dissipates
Once I offer you a good life
As we embrace. (translation mine)[25]

This rhetorical turn with its tension on controlling the discourse around the moment of (post)abolition reveals the fears of the plantocracy. The loss of power, the poem shows, lies also in the uncertainty over the historical narrative of that system after the end of slavery. The Black person is simultaneously written about and erased. In the poem, an enslaved man named Zacarías is pressured to relate his experiences under the language and representation of colonial powers. The poetic personae, imposes a silence by controlling the terms of public debate and demarcating the law of what can and cannot be said, which Foucault identities as one of the quintessential characteristics of the Archive (*The Archaeology* 129). This text reveals a latent anxiety in the planters community around the way in which the reality of slavery might be further known and remembered. The way in which its discourse pushes for a rewriting of the memory of enslavement illustrates that careful negotiation of silencing. Records like de San Germán's poem are often held and preserved in archives. This is the case, for example, of abolitionist speeches once delivered at the Asamblea Nacional Española in Madrid in 1873, today digitised and held at the Biblioteca Nacional de España, many of which reveal similar fears and rhetoric of the plantocracy on the island.[26] Although access to most national repositories is available to the general public, these documents remain largely the domain of academics and writers. Yet, the silences that some of these documents once encouraged, as manifest in the poem, have prevailed in the public sphere, particularly of former colonial powers such as Spain where the debate around the history of the nation's past as a slaveholding society has been largely absent in the contemporary moment. On the other hand, as Raphael Dalleo notes, abolitionist discourse once circulated predominantly, and almost exclusively, in the public sphere of the European metropolis as planters controlled the circulation of any written means in the colonies that would challenge their status quo. As Dalleo points out "[i]n the Spanish islands, antislavery advocacy was for the most part forbidden and punished by the colonial authorities" (32). Therefore, a more representative Caribbean public sphere did not take shape in the region until the twentieth century, particularly during the various anti-colonial movements. The 1970s particularly marked this shift in Puerto Rican historiography. Its assessment of the role of the enslaved in the economic and political structure of the plantation, as well as significantly their resistance, broke further a silence and knowledge gap, equally addressed in literary representations of that history from the 1970s and especially from the last decade of the twentieth century to the present moment.

Memory Work in Mayra Santos-Febres and Yolanda Arroyo Pizarro

By centring their narratives around the largely unrecorded stories of enslaved women, Arroyo Pizarro and Santos-Febres invite readers to consider the implications of imagining the history of female rebellion for which there are scarce and often no records written by its protagonists. However, oral traditions of storytelling and music convey memories from that history of resistance and figure in both texts. The second citation in *Negras* is by Gabriela Sonya from October 1998 and it focuses specifically on women who "actively played central roles in actual insurrections and revolts, in a pure manifestation of their rebelliousness" (13). Finally, the third citation by Gloria Steinem exalts women whom "with no history to guide them, and with the courage to make themselves vulnerable" are "exploring the outer edge of human possibility" (Steinem qtd. in Arroyo Pizarro 15).

Zaira Rivera Casellas interrogates whether a number of literary texts by contemporary Black Puerto Rican women writers, including Arroyo Pizarro's *Negras* and Santos-Febres' *Fe en disfraz*, can be set in conversation with the representations of race in Cuban and American literature during and after the abolitionist period (*Bajo la sombra*). Following a discussion of Carmen M. Colón Pellot's *Ambar Mulato: (ritmos) y otros poemas* (1938)—which refigures the trope of the 'tragic mulata' in works such as *Cecilia Valdés* (1839) by Cirilo Villaverde (Cuba), and a critical analysis of Beatriz Berrocal's *Memorias de Lucila: una esclava rebelde* (1996), Rivera Casellas situates *Negras* and *Fe en disfraz* as texts that continue a 'genealogy of resistance' shaped by Colón Pellot and Berrocal and push forward the limits of the historical knowledge and representation of enslaved and Black women in Puerto Rico and in Latin America. There is a critical dialogue between *Negras* and *Fe in disfraz* as, in the original Spanish version of *Negras,* Arroyo Pizarro mentions *Fe in disfraz* in a final section dedicated to works that inspired the stories (*Las negras* 147).[27] Remarking on the epigraphic subtext and references to the silences in the official record, Marie Ramos Rosado notes how the citation from Baralt's *Slave Revolts in Puerto Rico* "highlights the importance of slave uprisings in the nineteenth century and the disinformation that exists in the official record regarding slave rebellions" ("Exordio" *Las negras* 17).

The title *Negras* (Black women) is also an affirmation of blackness, which has historically been controlled and at times silenced in the official public sphere of Puerto Rico and further erased also in the public sphere in Spain. As Puerto Rican historian Illeana M. Rodriguez-Silva points out, "*Negro* underscored a certain purity of blackness and links to slavery, a past many were invested in erasing" (5). The three stories in *Negras*: "Wanwe", "Midwives", and "Arrowhead", tell the stories in the lives of three captive African women who exercise various acts of resistance and attempt to subvert the power mechanisms imposed on them. There are significant echoes and threads connecting the three stories but each conveys a variety of narrative approaches and voices that reflect forms of access to power and participation against the system of slavery marked by the use and knowledge of African languages, medicine, and combat. Edgar J. Nieves López reads *Negras* as embodying various forms of self-definition and subversion ("Autodefinición" 48–61). Several events and acts of resistance in the three short stories echo those recorded in slave narratives, historical documents, and literature from the African diaspora creating and expanding an archive of a 'genealogy of resistance'. Based upon an Afrosporic consciousness theorised by Philip as emerging from the collective work of Black peoples to find new languages to articulate their experience ("Jammin'" *Bl_k* 24, 36, n24), this critical archive and geneaology looks for new articulations of not only the experience of historical erasure and amnesia but also of resistance and struggle. In an interview with Melanie Pérez Ortiz, Santos-Febres speaks of an Afro-diasporic identification and kinship, asserting "black authors, … we were always thinking about diasporic gatherings", adding "for me, Toni Morrison is just as much a writer of mine as José Luis González" (Santos-Febres and Perez Ortiz qtd. in Rivera Casellas, "La Poética" ("El Lugar") *Bajo la Sombra*, translation mine).[28]

Brief epigraphs by Toni Morrison and Audre Lorde in the opening and final stories of *Negras*, reinforce and expand the genealogy of Black women's resistance, emphasising notions of fuelling imaginative work. The reference to Morrison's line, "I get angry about things, then go on and work", frames the pain and anger out of which the act of remembrance and work of creation grows. This allusion to the transformative power of anger implicitly connects with Lorde's essays "Uses of Anger: Women responding to Racism" and "The Transformation of Silence into Language and Action", which anticipate the epigraph by Lorde before the closing section "Arrowhead": "Even the smallest victory is never to be taken for granted. Each victory must be applauded" (*Negras* 101). Connecting all stories are the multilayered ways in which enslaved women in the Caribbean have actively fought oppression, whose stories are celebrated and historicised in Arroyo Pizarro's writing.

Narrated in the third person, the opening story "Wanwe" offers an account of the Middle Passage from the moment when Wanwe and other members of her community are captured and forced into the journey across the Atlantic. Wanwe is transported to the coast and from there onto the slave ship (*owba cocoo*), in a canoe with women from other tribes. Acts of insurrection take place early on in the story. One of the women, silently and "shrewdly unties the ropes that bind her hands and legs, and suddenly jumps out of the canoe" (26). She is later captured and tortured as a result in an attempt to impose fear on the rest of the women. A reference to a very similar episode in the following story "Midwives", opens the possibility that Ndizi, the protagonist in that story may also have, as Wanwe, witnessed that and had therefore travelled together in the same ship. In her account, Ndizi mentions that Undraá, a woman "who was forced to cohabit with the white men on the ship had waited until the ship reached the open sea, near the sharks' nests. Then she jumped into the water" (78). This horrific death connecting both stories, points to the ways in which death by drowning became a frequent episode in the traumatic memory on the enslaved, as happened in the massacre aboard the *Zong* and the *Duke of York* (as seen in Chapters 2 and 4), and countless others recorded and unrecorded in official histories. There are several phrases of conjecture in "Wanwe" that obliquely establish a critique of colonial historiography. The opening sentences of several sections speculate on the historicity of a series of moments that both acknowledge the impossibility of knowing that history with precision the fragility of memory in the aftermath and ongoing experience of trauma. The first line in the story opens thus: "Her first memory *might* be the ship" (25 emphasis mine). Then, the fifth section starts with, "Her first memory *could* also be her village" (emphasis mine 35) and the eighth section notes: "It is *also possible* that her first memory is the day of the kidnapping" (emphasis mine 43). These phrases of speculation become an important riff in the story that highlights the ruptures with the original homeland and the challenges to accessing Wanwe's own story.

Wanwe's *espiritu cimarron* (maroon spirit) is another key connecting thread that links with all the other women portrayed in the collection. The second story, "Midwives" ("Saeta" in the original Spanish), is narrated in the first person using the confessional mode of slave narratives like that of Harriet Ann Jacobs, which Arroyo Pizarro describes as one of the texts that influences the collection (*Las negras* 147). Through Ndizi's account, readers learn about her story and the events that have led to her arrest in the town's dungeon of an unnamed island in the Spanish-speaking Caribbean. Ndizi is a "witch doctor, herbalist, bone healer, midwife" (89). She offers assistance to a group of Mandingo runaway captives that had managed to escape the ship before it docked and with whom Ndizi flees to the hills where she is made captive one more time. Once back in the dungeon, she re-encounters Petro, a Catholic friar who aims to convince her to confide in him.

> All he wants is to know, "to document violence spreading all over humankind," he explains, "all this historical bestiality." There are friars in other islands writing chronicles about these events; I want to tell your story … . (83)

Despite not fully trusting Petro, Ndizi decides to share with him her story. This testimony, however, only complements the main narrative, already in Ndizi's voice and already addressing an implied audience (us readers). It is her voice that orders (and centres her in) the narrative. Its authorial position locates the meta-narrative element of "confession" (as Petro once terms Ndizi's testimonial account prior to her execution), as secondary to Ndizi's main account in the story. She is already narrating her story and this retelling to Petro becomes only a partial moment in the overall account. The readers' access to the story is not through Petro or his voice but always through Ndizi's. This testimony figures predominantly as a means to retell and historicise some of Ndizi's account whilst pointing to a different type of record held in the local religious buildings and municipalities of Puerto Rico. It is also helpful in showing her awareness of Petro's motivations and strategic negotiation of her own narrative in their exchange.

From the beginning, Ndizi's narration in "Midwives" hints at her use of medicinal knowledge to end the life of the babies of enslaved women she delivers and is confirmed in her account to Petro. Ndizi would often do so following their mothers' request who, like Sethe in Toni Morrison's *Beloved* (1987), aimed in this way to save their offspring from a life of enslavement and trauma. The knowledge of herbal medicine and ancestral healing, as well as religious ceremonies, constitutes one of the ways in which Africans and Afro descendants in the Caribbean, particularly women, participated in acts of resistance and survival. This knowledge and its transmission established a vital link of connection with some matrilineal cultures in Africa. In the story, Ndizi evokes that 'genealogy of resistance' through the memory of her grandmothers: "I had many grandmothers, and they taught me how to make potions" (71). Some of the archival records that historian Fe Verdejo unearths in Santos-Febres' *Fe en disfraz* also reveal the ways in which enslaved women used herbal medicine as a means of agency across Latin American geographies, including Brazil, Costa Rica, Colombia, and Venezuela in the seventeenth and eighteenth centuries. These fictional archival records in the novel are all summaries from complaints brought by enslaved women to governors in their respective colonies. In one of them, Francisca da Silva—also known as Chica da Silva (based on a real-life person)—denounces to the governor, Alonso de Pires, the verbal and physical abuse at the hands of the wife of the planter in Aldea de Tejuco, Minas Gerais, Brazil. Diamantina (how Chica da Silva was also popularly known) asks to be transferred to a different plantation with her five children. The record also documents how a month after the declaration, the planter's wife fell ill.[29] This infers the possibility that the planter's wife may have been poisoned by Chica da Silva.

Historians have pointed out that active resistance and rebellion was a regular and a defining aspect of life in the Caribbean plantation (Bush 193). As Barbara Bush argues, resistance took on many forms, "from outright revolt to more subtle forms of everyday resistance. Evidence indicates that women were no less prominent than men in such resistance, and they may have been in the vanguard, particularly in cultural resistance" (83). The control of reproduction through plant medicine was one of the ways in which women avoided unwanted pregnancies, often the result of planters' and overseers' rape. Another means of resistance, as *las negras* and *Fe en disfraz* capture, was the use of herbal medicine to enact justice by way of covertly poisoning oppressors and secretly undermining the system of slavery as well as taking the life of babies of enslaved women to protect them. Arroyo Pizarro's short stories thus historicise the fact that "[s]uicide, abortion, and infanticide were widespread among the slaves, even though these acts were severely punished" (Munro, *Different Drummers* 19).

Compassionate death as means of resistance in a system such as slavery in which forms of extreme physical and psychological violence relied on the constant threat of death, became a powerful form to fight that violence. After Ndizi escapes the *hacienda* with the group of maroons, they all consider and then discard the unlikely plan of crossing the Atlantic to return home. They finally decide on compassionate suicide and share stories from others who had left behind as legacy, the knowledge of how to carry this out. Ndizi recalls "we talk about some of our brothers who were experts in compassionate suicide; they had done it, and had left instructions as their legacy" (77–78). That plan is never carried out as they are apprehended by the authorities. Back in the dungeon, Ndizi also tells Petro, the Catholic friar, about midwives and healers who, like her, carefully and strategically gained whites' confidence and access to their babies. Although Petro understands and refers to Ndizi's account as a confession of her sins before her public hanging, ordered by the Spanish authorities on the island, for her, the account remains her story and that of a community and new culture. Petro's oral to scribal means of archiving becomes only *another* record. Aware as Ndizi is of the filtered historiographical position of the friar's voice and lens, the story nevertheless becomes the closest thing there might be to a written record of the events. But the central legacy in the story remains in the transmission of knowledge amongst women forged across the different linguistic and cultural groups from Africa forced into slavery. Ndizi states:

> *Nous allons reproduire une armeé, kite a kwanza yon lame.* That is what we set out to do. That is what we women set out to do, and we spread the

word through the beating of our drums. *Hebu kuzaliana jeshi*. We repeated it at music gatherings to the Wolof, Touareg, Bakongo, Malinbo and Egba. The news continued to spread in chant to the Balimbe, Ovimbundu, and the rest. Those of us from Congo, those of us from Ibibio, and those of us from Seke or Cabinda, all of us women responded. *Hagámonos un ejército*. Let us breed an army. (85)

As in the fictional preface opening *Crossing the River*, in this account of *Negras* (and in the collection's overall narrativity), the drum and its rhythm become vehicles for connection, creating community and communicating resistance. During slavery, the drum was key in transmitting and consolidating cultural memory, and the organising of rebellion in religious and music gatherings across the Caribbean. As Martin Munro points out, "slave dances were not simply means of escaping and forgetting the deadening rhythms of everyday life ... the memory of slavery, at least in Maya Deren's interpretation, is not excluded from the ritualistic dance but is instead integral to its continuing purgative functions" (*Different Drummers* 21). One example, as Munro notes, is the way in which the use and sound of the cracking whip was used in Haitian Vodou Petro ceremonies as a means to process and work through the painful memory of daily experience in the plantation. The whip can also be heard and seen today being used by the Blue Devils in Trinidad and Tobago's Carnival. The various forms of repression and devaluation of drumming in the Anglophone, Francophone, and Spanish-speaking Caribbean throughout the eighteenth and nineteenth centuries, confirm how powerful and threatening it was perceived to be by colonial governments in the Americas.[30] As well as political, drums have historically been vital to the development of philosophical thought. For example, in Cuba, drums are considered sacred in Orisha ceremonies and the talking drums are endowed with properties not only through music and religion, but also in their contribution to philosophy and complex cosmogonies (Villepastour 3–32).

Like the beating of drums, the sounds in religious and cultural practices mark rhythms with important communicative properties and vibrational impact. As the previous citation from "Midwives" demonstrates, it was in those gatherings too that rebellion was invoked both through the vibration and reverberation of the drum's rhythms as well as through the messages sang and shared, at times in code form, to spread the message of insurgence. The spiritual and cosmogonic relevance of the

African drum transcends the communicative power of song and speech meaning. Musicologists Meki Nzewi, Israel Anyahuru, and Tom Ohiaraumunna describe drum-talking as "a metaspeech concept of instrumental music" with rhythmic communicative characteristics that extend beyond the lingual, and are sometimes accompanied by drummed-dialogue, that is "spontaneous drum versus vocal discourse" (91). As well as highlighting the role of music gatherings as spaces where enslaved people created and shaped resistance, the text in the above passage reflects one of the main characteristics found in African rhythms; the repetition of a musical phrase in variation of key. In the text, the invocation of an army of women is first uttered in Haitian creole (kreyòl ayisyen), then in Swahili, in English and finally in Spanish at different points. These sentences both create breaks in the narrative through their alternation yet reinforce the original key and idea of female revolt (symbolically uttered in kréyol). This variation of the same sentence and idea, through its placing in different languages throughout the description of forms of organising functions as chorus—and a form of kalinda in a call-and-response dynamic. The African cultural and rhythmic remittances, in musical forms in the Spanish-speaking Caribbean, are very significant and have preserved much of the Afro-Caribbean memory and identity in the region. For example, the music and dance expression of *bomba* in Puerto Rico originated in the sixteenth century and although it is argued that it also has Taíno and some Spanish influences, its main cultural influence is the fusion of African music and dance from tribal groups of West Africa forced into slavery.

The stories of *marronage* in *Negras* portray life in captivity from a variety of angles and moments in that history of diasporic dislocation and display differing ways of resistance, widening readers' appreciation of their irreducibility. The three women whose stories are captured in the collection: Wanwe, Ndizi, and Tshanwe, all share similar experiences of violence, in particular sexual violence, and are simultaneously tormented and relieved by memories from their past lives in Africa. Yet their distinct individual circumstances are acknowledged, variously connected and contrasted with the lives of other women in the plantation. Wanwe's and Tshanwe's stories are narrated in the third person whilst Ndizi's is a first-person account, and her linguistic proficiency in various Creole languages and African ones, disguised from the white gaze, is something she uses strategically to access various spaces in the plantation. There are literal moments of marronage in *Negras*, as there are in all three texts by Arroyo Pizarro, Martiatu Terry, and Santos-Febres, figurative and philosophical marronage. Drawing from Audre Lorde's theorising on the futility to fight oppression with the tools and language of the oppressors, Odette Casamayor-Cisneros identifies in the concept of *cimarronaje* (marronage) that practice of seeking and creating new means and vocabularies ("Elogio" 308–309). It is the creation of new ways of existence (individual and social), Casamayor-Cisneros argues, that guarantees the survival of the enslaved person (309). To a great extent, despite their circumstances of real captivity, the women in *Negras* both seek and create opportunities where they (to varying degrees) push the boundaries of their captivity and configure that 'genealogy of resistance' that Philip theorises (as described earlier). They further archive this through their awareness and connection with their own bodies and communities (connecting self and multitude).

The *cimarrona* (maroon woman) figures predominantly in the literature of Arroyo Pizarro, including the short story collection *Ojos de luna* (2007) where "Saeta" introduces the characters that would later appear in *Las negras* (the original text in Spanish, later entitled *Negras* in its English translation) and the poetry collection *Saeta, the poems* (2011). These characters have fled enslavement, and other times they have rebelled and resisted with the means available to them in the plantation. Arroyo Pizarro also describes herself in public appearances—as does Santos-Febres—as a *cimarrona*. This becomes a central element to their decolonial feminism, and it shares characteristics with Casamayor-Cisneros' notion and discussion of *apalencamiento*, as resulting in a "reinvención identitaria como sujetos libres" (an identity reinvention as free subjects) that centres self-determination in its most radical form, completely outside the boundaries of the imposed sociality and enforced racial identity categories of enslavement ("Elogio" 309). In the first article for her column *Tinta Negra* in the online magazine *On Cuba News*, Casamayor-Cisneros proposes the act of allowing oneself to be oneself. Something that she argues would necessarily lead to accepting one's deep complexity thus rendering categorisations futile (2021). The characters in Arroyo Pizarro's writing—as in that by Martiatu Terry and Santos-Febres—explore, and engage in, those possibilities, beyond the constrictions of imposed categories. The literature of Arroyo Pizarro challenges the identities dictated and imposed by heteronormativity and patriarchal structures. As a lesbian *cuir* (queer) writer and activist, or rather "artivist" (as she describes herself), Arroyo

Pizarro writes also articles in her blog *Boreales* on all topics from an Afro-cuir (queer) perspective ("Cuiring Black Genders").[31]

Within the range of Caribbean neo-slave narratives, *Negras* offers a unique and distinctive archive of African rites and memory, that is also present in historical novels such as *Daughters of the Stone* (2009) by Puerto Rican author Dahlma Llanos-Figueroa, where a stone carrying the essence of her unborn child travels with Fela across the Middle Passage and is inherited by her daughter, Mati, born in slavery. The stone is handed down across generations connecting all women back to Fela. Ancestral memories are equally central to the storytelling in both novels, as is the connection with the past from both material and spiritual contact with objects of inheritance. Equally, in *Negras*, for Wanwe, the act of remembering the African *ureoré* ceremony during the heightened state of stress and trauma whilst crossing the Middle Passage brings comfort. The sensorial elements such as smell and touch that activate memory evoke thoughts of this ceremony:

> First, the girls stand the boys next to them, right beside them, and come close, arm to arm. Usually, a girl stands next to the boy she likes. Closeness reveals which of the boys smell nice, how soft their skin is when they touch, how their heartbeats become one, because both feel it like a drumming in their chest. (35–36)

The allusions to (and pulse of) drumming can be read through the stories in *Negras* as a conduit of memory in Africa and in the Americas, connecting the various accounts. It also figures in some of the poems in *Saeta: the poems* as in "Tamborera" where the poetic personae, an enslaved woman and drummer, for whom the identity of *tamborera* (drummer) connects her experiences and memories in Africa and in Puerto Rico. Many neo-slave narratives in the wider Caribbean, including Dionne Brand's *At the Full and Change of the Moon* (1999) or Marlon James' *The Book of Night Women* (2009), start their account in the Caribbean, and although there are references to knowledge and cultural traditions brought from Africa, they generally explore the experiences of women in the plantation and often also of those born into the system of slavery. Arroyo Pizarro's exploration of the lived realities of enslaved women extends to different moments in the historical process of enslavement. In *Negras*, "to portray the struggle of the female slaves, Arroyo Pizarro values and recovers the historical memory of the female slaves during the intermediate step between freedom, future captivity and enslavement" (Hidalgo de Jesús 33). *Negras* reimagines the moment of capture and forced migration to the Caribbean in "Wanwe", and subversive resistance in the form of marronage and medicinal knowledge and use in "Midwives", the violence of renaming the enslaved and spiritual righting in the afterlife in "Arrowhead". *Negras* archives different moments of rebellion and survival that have shaped the history of the Caribbean and the Americas at large. M. NourbeSe Philip describes how the enforcing of cultural erasure through various practices, including the separation of Africans into different linguistic groups to avoid rebellion would culminate in the acquisition of another colonial "language that was not only experientially foreign, but also epistemologically hostile and expressive of the non-being of the African.[32] To speak another language is to enter another consciousness" (*A Genealogy of Resistance* 46). Although these prohibitions extended also to music, Philip argues that language was the main site of struggle. *Negras* documents the process of forced acculturation and its resistance, highlighting the value and existence of that cultural knowledge and its centrality to survival. *Negras* shows the loss of the original languages of the enslaved, enforced by the laws of the colonial powers and how, at the centre, resistance was the determined retention of knowledge, culture, philosophy, and religion. A retention of languages that is also manifest across the Caribbean in lexicon, expression, syntactical structures, and linguistic preservation in religious practices of Ekpe groups in Cuba or Haiti.

FÉ EN DISFRAZ: ARCHIVE AND THE BODY AS A SITE OF MEMORY

The work of Mayra Santos-Febres has been widely translated. She has been writing from the 1990s, first publishing poetry (three collections) and short fiction, with influential titles such as *Pez de vidrio* (1994) published in English as *Urban Oracles* (1997), and novels like *Sirena Selena, vestida de pena* (2000) (translated as *Sirena Selena*); *Nuestra señora de la noche* (2006) (published in English as *Our Lady of the Night*); *Fe en disfraz* (2009) and *La amante de Gardel* (2015), and non-fiction including *Antes que llegue la luz* (2021). Santos-Febres graduated from the University of Puerto Rico where she now teaches. She also holds an M.A. and PhD from Cornell University, where she has been visiting professor. She has spoken about the special precarity of Black women in academia, an issue that features in *Fe en disfraz*. In an interview with the University of Maryland's Dresher Center for the Humanities, Santos-Febres speaks about how, in her four historical novels (*Sirena Selena vestida de pena*, *Nuestra señora de la noche*, *Fe en disfraz* and *La amante de Gardel*), she aims to recuperate stories that remain untold. She speaks of her interest in "bring[ing] them to life through fiction".[33] Toward the end of the interview, Santos-Febres, with a smile, highlights "writers are agitators and dreamers ... we've always had this incredible job which is imagining what is impossible so that it can become possible. It's like a magician that conjures a reality". As part of her research for the novel, Santos-Febres consulted a variety of historical sources by women including Júnia Ferreiro Furtado's *Chica da Silva e o contratador dos diamantes: o outro lado do mito*; María de los Ángeles Acuña's MA Thesis in History from SUNY (Albany), *Slave Women in Costa Rica During the Eighteenth-Century* and Digna Castañeda Fuertes' "Demandas judiciales de las mujeres del siglo cubano" (Peñaranda-Angulo 98–116).

As in *Negras*, in Santos-Febres' *Fe en Disfraz*, the paratextual elements that precede and follow the text are in close dialogue with the fiction, as part of a shared critical intervention of revisionary nature. The paratextual in both novels address the erasure of Black women's histories and responds with fictional accounts that problematise conventional narratives to historicise the lived experience of enslaved women and their descendants. Similarly, the archival records in *Fe en disfraz* contrapuntally connect with the present-day narrative of the novel in that they interrupt, or rather intersect with it, connecting Fe's past and present with the past of the historical subjects of her research into slavery in the Americas. This counterpoint results in an expanding notion of the temporality of slavery and its aftermath as the ongoing legacy of institutional racism continues to impact on the lives of Black people globally.

Fe en disfraz is narrated in the first person by Martín Tirado, a white historian from Puerto Rico who has recently joined the department of Latin American Studies at the University of Chicago to digitise historical records from the period of slavery, in order to preserve and safeguard them. It is in the history research group that he meets Venezuelan-born historian Fe Verdejo, his line manager and director of the group. In his account, Martín describes her as being in a position of influence and success in academia, which, as he notes, is an industry where Black women have historically faced multiple barriers and serious discrimination. It is also clear that Fe has reached a position of leadership in the field, in the

face of a lack of support and resources, particularly at the beginning of
her career as a historian:

> Fe Verdejo, alone, got to work determined to achieve the impossible. She
> decided to save the research group. She started to catalogue documents,
> digitize those which were deteriorating, and ponder the possibility of an
> innovative historic exhibition. (translation mine, ch. 2)[34]

The intense sexual relationship that unfolds between Fe and Martín is
marked by history and parallels the relationship between oppressor and
oppressed/master and enslaved which is at times blurred and complicated in the various power dynamics at stake in their relationship, some of
which are determined by the historical accounts of enslaved women that
Fe sends to Martín for digitisation. He starts to experience sexual arousal
whilst reading the accounts. This portrayal offers further insight into the
violence of the white male gaze embedded not only in the narrativity
of the texts but also in their reception and the system of representation that emerged from that archival violence. In the different types of
archival records referenced in the novel, the experiences and voices of
enslaved women are highly mediated by the scribal tradition of white
supremacy which Martín's own contemporary account both embodies,
and departs from.

In the historical accounts about enslaved women that Fe finds in her
research, women seek justice and carry out acts of denunciation and
strategic resistance. This is reflected in the first record to appear in the
novel, dated from 1785 and concerning Xica da Silva, a non-fictional, real
historical figure. Enslaved women in Brazil, especially in the state of Minas
Gerais during the eighteenth century managed to acquire a great deal of
autonomy in positions of power and owning land, sometimes finding the
opportunity to access freedom for themselves and their children (Schmidt-
Nowara *Slavery*). Christopher Schmidt-Nowara mentions Chica (Xica)
da Silva as an example of someone with that access to freedom and
land ownership. The 1774 census of the Tejuco area (today known as
Diamantina) "reported that free or freed women headed almost half
of the households; 86 per cent of them were black" (Schmidt-Nowara,
Slavery 88). Schmidt-Nowara attributes their negotiation of the complex
dynamics of sexual and intimate ties with men from the planter class as a
factor in their manumission (87–89). Framing such negotiations in the

context of the violence of slavery and the slave trade in various locations (Senegal, French Saint-Domingue, Cuba, and the US Gulf Coast), Jessica Marie Johnson underscores the pursuit of "safety from intimate violence, and insecurity" as lying "at the heart of the decisions to secure or reject patrons, partners, lovers, and other kin" (3). "Black women's intimacy with individuals", Johnson points out, "ranged along the spectrum of coerced to strategic, from fraternal to sexual" in attempts to "safeguard their bodies and legacies" (3). Gaining the status of "free" did not mean freedom as Black women remained implicated in the power structure of the plantation economy and, as Schmidt-Nowara puts it, "freedom from slavery in slave societies was a cramped and confined condition" (J. M. Johnson 2; Schmidt-Nowara, *Slavery* 42, Sheller, *Citizenship* "Introduction"). Social dynamics after manumission were further complicated by the fact that some previously enslaved women later legally owned the enslaved people labouring the land they acquired: "Safety and security for some women included exploiting enslaved labor" (J. M. Johnson 3).

Form in *Fe en disfraz* plays a central part in connecting the experience of the enslaved women mentioned in the legal records and Fe, for, as Helene C. Weldt points out, the two chapters that appear as accounts of Fe's past (otherwise minimally present in the narrative) appear in Fe's own voice (1939–1941). They are introduced similarly to the interjecting texts emulating archival records and their descriptive language is similar to them. They indicate the place of the event, name of the subject, and date following that record keeping style. For example, Xica de Silva's fictionalised legal record: "Statement before the Governor Alonso de Pires, Town of Tejuco. Historical Archive of Mias Gerais. Case: Diamantina. Status: slave, 1785" ("Declaración ante el gobernador Alonso de Pires, Aldea de Tejuco. Archivo Histórico de Minas Gerais. Caso: Diamantina. Condición: esclava, 1785" ch. 3). The filing metadata of the record shows parallelisms in form with the document describing Fe's rape that Fe sends to Martín in one of her emails: "Ciudad de Maracaibo. Fe Verdejo. Circa 1985" (ch. 18). The similar narrative form of the accounts connects them more immediately with the accounts and memories of enslaved and freed Black women in Brazil and Venezuela during the eighteenth century. Weldt further positions this formal choice as a means to highlight the continuation of (sexual) violence in the colonial and postcolonial context. By refiguring the archival documents and connecting them to new testimonies, including the digital account that Martín is creating, the novel interrogates the possibilities and ethical limitations in engagements with the Archive, pointing with particular poignancy to the academy and universities as spaces were exclusionary practices and racial hierarchies have historically regulated access to knowledge and safety/(un)safe spaces.

For Fe, the embodiment of the historical memory in the recovered records, and its many gaps of knowledge, takes place in material objects that conjure both the absence and life of the enslaved women she studies. An example of this is Chica da Silva's dress, which Fe finds during her research in a convent's attic after discovering documents written by her, including letters. Fe asks the nuns for permission to exhibit the dress at the upcoming exhibition *Esclavas Manumisas en Latinoamerica* that she is curating in Chicago. They agree, to Fe's surprise, with the condition and promise that she did not return the dress. They imply it might be cursed or haunted by the spirit of the original owner. The evening prior to the opening of the exhibition, on All Hallow's Eve, Fe undresses herself in the empty museum and slips into the intricate dress, described now as *disfraz* (outfit/disguise): "Entonces, bajo aquel disfraz, la museógrafa Fe Verdejo se tiró a la calle y no regresó al seminario hasta la madrugada, con la piel hecha un rasguño y un ardor" (Then, under that disguise, the museographer Fe Verdejo left for the streets and didn't return until the late hours of the night, with scratched and burning skin, ch. 24). The performative and ritual-based character of the sexual encounters between Fe and Martín, their masochistic nature and the way in which they mirror and counter dynamics of master and enslaved, reveals the legacy of violence enacted on racialised bodies. The dress also enables a re-enactment that allows Fe to connect further with her ancestors through the act of masking (wearing Chica da Silva's dress and its harness). Although their sexual relationship is consensual, it is tainted by the past trauma and violence exerted on both the body and the mind which thus complicates however issues of autonomy and choice. Throughout the novel, Martín presents his own process of uncovering the effects of the violence that he has inherited, and of which he also participates as a white man. He identifies the way it manifests in erotic desire and commoditisation of the bodies of Black women in contexts of sexual coercion and violation, and also identifies another form of violence in the formation of silencing epistemologies and historiographies. When Fe and Martín discuss the presentation of their digital archive project for a university in Germany, Martín suggests that a multimedia presentation with music, video and the inclusion of images of enslaved and freed women, could perhaps include an engraving or drawing to make it more appealing to audiences (ch. 9). To this suggestion, Fe points out the fact that there are no existing visual records for them, apart from images taken when they were imprisoned, sold or featured in pornographic photographs (but only from the nineteenth century) (ch. 9). These are all visual records that mark the Black female body as inscribed within a visual grammar and politics of policing and objectification potentially perpetuated through Martín's suggested approach. Martín also admits to have never considered the fact that Fe's research subject is so close to her own skin and body (ch. 9), thus revealing an unawareness stemming from his own privilege and positionality as a white person with a different relationship to the colonial past of slavery in his native Puerto Rico. The distance through which he dissects and examines the various elements of the presentation to make it more interesting and appealing for academic consumption, mark his own relationship to history and to notions of ethical responsibility in the digital humanities that he engages with as *web master*. All these dynamics confirm how, as Saidiya V. Hartman describes,

> the fungibility of the commodity makes the captive body an abstract and empty vessel to the projection of other's feelings, ideas, desires, and values … Thus the desire to don, occupy, or possess blackness or the black body as a sentimental resource and/or locus of excess enjoyment is both founded upon and enabled by the material relations of chattel slavery. (*Scenes of Subjection* 21)

Fe en disfraz highlights a series of continuities between slavery and the present of its aftermath in ways that bring visibility to some of those remnants in the contemporary moment. Localising the body as "empty vessel", in Hartman's words (21), Martín projects various desires, fantasies and fears that echo the gaze and authorship of many of the historical records in the colonial archive. Toward the end of the novel, the relationship between Fe and Martín breaks a kind of bond, through ritual. On a trip to Spain for a conference, Fe gifts Martín a "navaja toledana", a knife from the city of Toledo, which plays a role in their sexual ritual during that trip, and again when Martín cuts the constricting harness in Xica da Silva's dress worn by Fe on the third night of Hallows' Eve. He does so following Fe's directions (ch. 24). Although it is Martín who cuts the harness, the emphasis lies on how Fe directs him to do so, which is reinforced various times in that final chapter through the phrase "sácame de aquí" (get me out of here), acting as riff. Parallelisms through the physical enactment and embodiment of Fe's historical subjects is further marked by connection to that history and shared experience of anti-blackness. The relationship between Fe and Martín further reveals the different relationships of each to the records of slavery in the Archive.

Scholars underscore important differences and singularities between slavery in the various territories of Latin America and the Caribbean.[35] Brazil was the nation where abolition came latest, in 1888, and it was also a place with "relatively high rates of manumission" during slavery (Cowling 3). Camillia Cowling's analysis of legal records regarding the claims made by Black women in Brazil reveals the ways in which they actively formulated a variety of legal arguments to free themselves and often also to demand freedom for, and to protect, their children (32, 88–94). For example, the case of Josepha Gonçalves de Moraes shows how she was able to argue legally for her own freedom and request the freedom of her daughter Maria, arguing that Maria had been abused and neglected by José Gonçalves de Pinho, the household's owner. The trial took two years under two different judges in Rio de Janeiro and, as Cowling notes, it involved a mobilising of witnesses including "neighbours, friends, fellow ex-slaves", all organised by Josepha (9). Some of the fictionalised records included in *Fe in disfraz* are inspired by the archives and underscore this strategic use of the restricted agency of (formerly) enslaved women. The novel's reproduction of the historical account featuring Chica da Silva is illustrative of this. The record, a legal summary, details Chica da Silva's petition to be removed from the current household where she labours on the grounds of the physical abuse and torture enacted by *doña* Antonia de la Granda y Balbín, whose hatred and obsession with da Silva, whom she accuses of seducing her husband and fathering five children: "Justo, Isidro, Joaquín, Fernando y Ricardo" (157). In her statement, da Silva states having previously claimed protection before another judge, Alonso Pires, thus leaving record of the ongoing nature of the issue and her own previous legal exercise. She also makes the claim on behalf of her children, thus mobilising some notions of motherhood which were at times referenced by enslaved and freed women in legal testimony to rhetorically affect cases (Cowley 76–77).[36] Schmidt-Nowara asks "[w]hy were women more likely to become free and to become property owners than were men in Minas Gerais? Ties of affection, formal and informal, were important in shaping these dynamics" (88). Similarly, through archival and historical comparative scholarship, J. M. Johnson offers a transnational history that demonstrates the complex ways in which for freed, formerly enslaved women "[i]ntimacy and kinship became key strategies in their bids for freedom and were central to how and what freedom looked like on a quotidian basis" (3). By representing this reality through interjecting fictionalised accounts about formerly enslaved women, *Fe en disfraz*, Rivera Casellas points out, shows readers the omissions and silences in official historical records and insists on resisting the acceptance of totalising representations of slavery (*Bajo La Sombra del Texto*). The way in which those archival records disrupt and engage with the narrative storyline in *Fe* configures a historical poetics closely in conversation with the work of historians today. As J. M. Johnson argues, "any history of women of African descent, during the period of slavery must build a narrative using fragments of sources and disparate materials" and require that historians also ethically address gender and racial biases whilst engaging with existing records creatively (5).

Although the geographical settings of both *Negras* and *Fe en disfraz* are more focused on a variety of locations in the Caribbean and Latin America (Brazil and Venezuela), the backdrop of the coloniality of Puerto Rico is important to those narratives as it encompasses the continued legacy of colonialism. As free-associated state of the United States, and deeply marked by the neocolonial history that binds both geographies, Puerto Rico has a historically complex and multilayered relationship to notions of community and national belonging. Further, the worsening of neocolonial economic and political measures and "punitive solutions to societal problems" of the Puerto Rican government from the late twentieth century has increased inequality (Lebrón, "Introduction"). These realities became further evident after the governmental corruption scandals including the response in the aftermath of Hurricane Maria that led to massive protests and finally led to the resignation of president Ricardo A. Roselló. In *Antes que llegue la Luz* (2021), Mayra Santos-Febres interweaves her account of the aftermath of hurricanes with those of other Puerto Ricans after collecting oral histories during cultural response activities in a number of communities across the island. These accounts, especially those by Santos-Febres offer an insight into how racism, colourism, and white privilege have perpetuated social hierarchies in Puerto Rico, fostered by what the writer describes in an interview as the intersection between the racism of Spanish Hispanophilia and US *gringo* racism (Santos-Febres, Perez Ortiz 76).

Negras and *Fe en disfraz* reference Baralt's *Slave Revolts in Puerto Rico* as an important critical and historical source where the organising and resistance of enslaved Afro-Puerto Ricans are centred. Both texts complement Baralt's study by exploring imaginatively and creatively (also inspired by their own historical research) the active role played by women in that history of resistance and insurrection. *Slave Revolts in Puerto Rico* makes reference to a few instances where the names of enslaved women participants in acts of insurrections appear in official records. However, it is known that many women were also involved in insurrections as well as other forms of resistance despite their comparatively minor presence in the official record, already very carefully controlled and suppressed by colonial authorities. One of these forms of resistance was medicinal poisoning, related in various Caribbean novels including Dionne Brand's *At the Full and Change of the Moon* where Marie Ursule leads a collective suicide by poisoning in Trinidad in 1824. Another example is Marlon James' *The Book of Night Women* which focuses on a secret society of enslaved women practitioners of Obeah in eighteenth-century Jamaica. *Negras* and *Fe en disfraz* centre the medicinal and religious knowledge of the ancestors as both literal and spiritual means of survival. Similarly, Inés María Martiatu Terry's *Over the Waves and Other Stories* highlights the ways in which music conveys a medium of cultural memory that constantly negotiates and establishes not only collective connections but also a greater sense of individuality within that collective and shared cultural experience. For the Black women protagonists in stories such as "Follow Me!", "The Re is Green", and "A Subtle and Electric Sensation", music of African diasporic influence enables transformative connections to sense of self and autonomy as Black women; music provides a language to connect with their history, legacy, and their own relationship to place and space in Cuba and the wider Caribbean. According to Myriam J. A. Chancy, to better grasp the intersection and interrelation of race, gender, and history in the work of Cuban writers and artists, it is essential to consider how that intersection also takes place in the Dominican Republic and Haiti; "we might be better able to think of Haiti, the D.R. and Cuba in simultaneity" (*From Sugar* "Preface" xx). That simultaneity in Chancy's critical discussion allows for connections that point beyond each geography's national boundary, to transnationally and diasporically explore legacies and systems of oppression and coloniality and their investment in signification and exclusion. With that spirit of simultaneity in mind, this chapter's critical discussion of the interrelation of history, race, and gender in literature from Cuba and Puerto Rico, also aims to establish a relational view of the ways in which women across the geographies explored in all these literary texts have refigured a series of archives and historical narratives.

Diana Taylor's notion of the repertoire as performative acts that archive knowledge in non-normative ways, understood as an assemblage of mediums (written, visual, and oral), suits the more ephemeral archives shaping the narratives in *Over the Waves, Negras* and *Fe en disfraz*. For Taylor, repertoires document the memory of an experience in performative ways, which emphasises and further highlights the connection between the past and the present in processes of memorialisation, allowing a preservation through praxis of the embodied memory of ancestral and Indigenous knowledges (*The Archive*). These literary texts by Inés Maria Terry Martiatu, Yolanda Arroyo Pizarro, and Mayra Santos-Febres, capture how acts and gestures of kinship, solidarity, and survival have constituted a powerful, lasting archive of Black women's histories across the American hemisphere, from Cuba and Puerto Rico to Brazil and Venezuela.

NOTES

1. Original in Spanish: "cuestionar la sistemática ausencia que el discurso oficial nos ofrece, y el deliberado o no, olvido académico—salvo algunas excepciones—no solo de las mujeres negras que se desenvolvieron durante los siglos XVI al XVIII, sino de las que vivieron en la sociedad cubana durante el siglo XIX y el XX y que formaron parte tanto de las capas pobres, como de las clases media y alta" (*Afro Cubanas* "Introduction").
2. *Afro Cubanas: History, Thought and Cultural Practices* (2020) is the English translation of the anthology. Devyn Spence Benson edited this translation by Karina Alma, and wrote its introduction which contextualises the cultural relevance of the text, particularly in its documentation of the historiographic and intellectual labour of the Afro-Cubanas project and network.
3. Yolanda Arroyo Pizarro, "Calle de la Resistencia: Narrative, Poetry and Perreo Combativo from an Afrolesbian Boricua." The Kelly Writers House, University of Pennsylvania, 2 March 2020, https://www.youtube.com/watch?v=tDjg4p_ul8w.
4. Arroyo Pizarro works at the University of Puerto Rico, Rio Piedras.

5. The exclusionary nature of the concept of 'the great Puerto Rican family' through its emphasis on claiming Spanish language as elevated and of greater literary value, also excluded Puerto Ricans living in the US diaspora, as well as women, LGBTQI* and Black writers who were generally not included in a canon that privileged the writing of white creole male writers (Moreno 78–80).

6. See Pacini Hernández's "Dancing with the Enemy: Cuban Popular Music, Race for a discussion of the various measures, including governmental cultural support and promotion of African based musics, pp. 110–125.

7. In her article, "Elogio del 'apalencamiento'", Casamayor-Cisneros argues that although the government of Raul Castro has publicly acknowledged existing racial inequalities in Cuba, and introduced some changes in terms of increased representation of Black Cubans in government and the media, the lack of specific policy to tackle such inequality proves, as Casamayor-Cisneros notes, the unlikely delivery of such promise, pp. 303–307.

8. However, even though Spain made all attempts at reinforcing its cultural and identity ties with the ex-colonies through the republication of colonial chronicles and the construction of monuments celebrating Spain's colonial past, ex-colonies like Puerto Rico continued to explore and develop their own cultural and national identities. (Schmidt-Nowara, "Spanish Origins" 36). However, as this chapter argues, these expressions continue to carry the remnants of Iberian coloniality. See also Frederick B. Pike's *Hispanismo, 1889–1936: Spanish Conservatives and Liberals and Their Relations to Spanish America* (1971), p. 2.

9. For the English article where Quijano explores the coloniality of power see "Coloniality of Power, Eurocentrism, and Latin America." (2000), pp. 533–580.

10. Rubiera Castillo has explained that the group activities and meetings were sometimes met with racist comments and attitudes by academics, artists, and intellectuals in acts of dismissal ("Grupo Afrocubanas" 204).

11. In "Afrocubanas" (2019), Rubiera Castillo also stresses the key role of oral history, particularly the conversations with her mother, Maria de los Reyes Castillo Bueno, about racial discrimination in her lifetime, which resulted in the publication *Reyita, sencillamente: Testimonio de una negra cubana nonagenaria* (1996). The

book centres the role of oral histories and the family record in contesting and complementing gaps in the official historiography or the larger public sphere. The self-reflexive voice in Reyita's own construction of self in this text, reveals an "autobiographical "I"", using Sandra Pouchet Paquet's concept, through which Castillo Bueno narrates her life against impositions on her own racialised identity, from her family to fellow Cubans. An English translation by Anne McLean was published in 2002, as *Reyita: The Life of a Black Cuban Woman in the Twentieth Century*, with an introduction by Elizabeth Dore.

12. Out of one of these collaborations emerged also the bilingual publication of *Over the Waves and Other Stories* ("Introduction"), as well as Spence Benson's efforts to publish the translation of the anthology *Afrocubanas*, edited by Castillo Rubiera and Martiatu Terry.

13. See Flora González Mandri's *Guarding Cultural Memory: Afro-Cuban Women in Literature and Art* (2006), and Myriam A. J. Chancy's *From Sugar to Revolution: Women's Visions of Haiti, Cuba and the Dominican Republic* (2013) for discussions of the art of Maria Magdalena Campos-Pons. Interestingly, both critical texts discuss Campos-Pon's art in conversation with literature, which attests to the productive contemporary interdisciplinary shifts in the study of both Caribbean literature and visual art.

14. The reference to Ciego de Ávila in the story also maps a history of intra-Caribbean migration, as this is an area home to communities from other parts of the (Anglophone) Caribbean, mostly from Jamaica but also from Antigua, Barbados, Grenada, St. Vincent and Nevis, as well as some migration from Haiti and the Dominican Republic. Especially concentrated in the town of Baraguá, these communities have continued to communicate in English, celebrate festivities such as Emancipation Day on 1 August and retain typical dishes and drinks including ackee, black cake, or sorrel.

15. See *Dying to Better Themselves: West Indians and the Building of the Panama Canal* (University of the West Indies Press, 2014), by Jamaican writer and critic Olive Senior. Senior traces a history of the perils faced by Caribbean workers in the building of the canal and the many contributions (cultural, political, and socio-economic) that they made. The book draws from a great variety

of historical sources including newspapers, historical records, literature and oral histories.

16. Abakuá secret societies have famously been documented by Fernando Ortíz and Lydia Cabrera.

17. Although the 6 January 1836 is considered officially as the date when the first *potencia* (group/lodge) was formed in the neighbourhood of Regla, scholars point to an earlier date. Karo Moret Miranda notes that it is possible that they were first formed in the sixteenth century with the arrival of the first enslaved Africans from the Calabar region (29), and Shubi L. Ishemo suggests that it could possibly date back to the eighteenth century (253).

18. The Calabar nation originated from a geographic area encompassing part of what today is Nigeria and Cameroon.

19. Originally membership to the societies was only open to Black men, and over time Chinese and mulato men were also allowed into Abakuá societies (Ishemo 254), later including white creole men.

20. The iconographic, religious, and spiritual influence of the Abakuá on Cuban art is perhaps most notable in the work of visual artists Belkis Ayón and José Bedia. For Bedia, the integration of elements of palo monte and Abakuá epistemologies was central to his *oeuvre*, as was the influence of Lydia Cabrera's writings on Andrés Petit (1830–1878), and the figure of Petit himself as founder of a Kimbisa branch of palo monte, and as someone who bridged epistemologies of Afro-Cuban based religions (Bettelheim and Berlo 126–127). Abakuá societies were Ayón's main source of inspiration and through the iconic black and white figures of her intricate printmaking, she reinscribed history and religion. For example in *La Cena* (1991) which alludes to the Christian scene of the Last Supper, Ayón "cleverly disrupts the exclusion of women by replacing the Jesus figure with the Abakuá princess, Sikán" (Mohammed, *Imaging* 21).

21. There is a secret language only available for Abakuá initiates, that communicates the Mystery through the Ekio, or ancestors. Historically, transmission has been key to their functioning for centuries. Lydia Cabrera, in her anthropological work and documentation writes, "the internal functions of Abakuá—judicial, legislative, and religious—were meant to preserve the beliefs, music, language, and oral literature of the ancestors by passing it on to the lodge

members" (3). *Misterio* is also an important concept in Afro-Cuban religious practice. For example, despite having incorporated influences from Catholicism (and partly to guarantee its continued practice in the face of colonial law; Moret Miranda 29), La Regla de Ocha-Ifá/La Regla Lucumí, have historically guarded their own practice and knowledge from the control of Spanish colonial forces and, to varying degrees, secrecy in religious practice became important as a means of preservation.

22. The original title in Spanish is *Las negras.*

23. Some landmark publications that appeared in later decades and that are linked to (and emerge from) this shift are the 1995 anthology *Engendering History: Caribbean Women in Perspective* edited by Verene Shepherd, Bridget Brereton and Barbara Bailey, as well as *Gender in Caribbean Development* (1988) edited by Patricia Mohammed and Catherine Shepperd.

24. See Jean Stubbs, "Gender in Caribbean History." *Engendering Caribbean History: Cross-Cultural Perspectives, a Reader*, edited by Vere Shepperd (2011), pp. 3–37.

25. Original text in Spanish:

> Vete con Dios, sé feliz
> Ya eres libre, ya eres hombre,
> Ya en el mundo tienes nombre,
> Alza, joven, la cerviz;
> Y dile a la sociedad
> Lo blando que fue tu yugo
> Que nunca le saqué el *jugo*
> A tu pobre humanidad;
> Dile que la libertad
> Se siente en el corazón,
> Que su templo es la razón,
> Y su cielo es la verdad.
> Dile, que mienten en vano
> Los que la igualdad invocan,
> Si con cadenas sofocan
> Al esclavo, que es su hermano;
> Dile, en fin, querido amigo,
> Que mi pecado se dilata
> Al darte una vida grata,

Y al abrazarme contigo. (poem by G. R. de San Germán qtd. in
Flores Collazo 23)

26. *Biblioteca Nacional de España*, https://datos.bne.es/entidad/XX9
    2384.html. The digital portal of the Biblioteca Nacional de España
    offers access to digitised records including documents from the
    Spanish Abolitionist Society. In one of their reports on the situ-
    ation in Puerto Rico after the passing of the law abolishing
    slavery on 22 March 1873, the Society contradicts malign rumours
    and fears of insurrection. They also critique the role of two Spanish
    newspapers (unnamed in the report) in silence relating to events on
    the island (arson fires and attacks) that reflect rather unrest from
    the planter class ("La abolición en Puerto Rico; primers effects de
    la led de 22 de Marzo de 1873" VC/2612/25, Salon General,
    Sala de Recoletos).
27. This reference does not appear in the First English edition, 2012.
28. Original in Spanish: "Los escritores negros ... siempre pensamos
    en unas reuniones diaspóricas ... Para mí, Toni Morrison es
    tan escritora mía como lo es José Luis González" (Santos-
    Febres interviewed by Melanie Pérez Ortiz [76–77], qtd. in
    Rivera Casellas *Bajo la Sombra del Texto* (2015). Ebook edition,
    translation in text mine.
29. From original: "Al cabo de un mes, Doña Antonia se vió aquejada
    por una fulminante enfermedad" ("After a month, Doña Antonia
    suffered from a sudden illness"; *Féeen Disfraz* ch. 3).
30. See Martin Munro, *Different Drummers: Rhythm and Race in the
    Americas* (2010).
31. In her post "*Cuiring* Black genders and sexualities in the Ameri-
    cas" (25 Aug. 2020), advertising a series of talks in her blog *Bore-
    ales*, Arroyo Pizarro writes "Black scholars and artivists have been
    producing theory to help all of us better understand our position-
    ality as racialized, gendered and sexualized subjects", thus offering
    a sense of the intersection of identity constructs and lived expe-
    riences in that intersectionality. See http://narrativadeyolanda.blo
    gspot.com/2020/08/aula-do-curso-afrocuiridades-yolanda.html.
32. Karo Moret Miranda discusses that process of calculated strategic
    separation of the various ethnicities and African nations in Cuba,
    with the aim to avoid insurrection and promote discordance rather

than union. However, various aspects favoured the communication of ethnicities on the island (21).

33. Mayra Santos-Febres, Dresher Conversations, Dresher Center for the Humanities, University of Baltimore. Interview conducted by Jessica Berman, 12 Sept. 2019, https://www.youtube.com/watch?v=HpA0ulvvO2I.

34. Original text in Spanish: "Fe Verdejo, sola, se dio a la tarea de lograr lo imposible. Decidió salvar el seminario. Comenzó a catalogar documentos, a digitalizar los que ya estaban deshaciéndose en el papel y a ponderar la posibilidad de montar una vistosa exposición histórica" (ch. 2).

35. See Marrietta Morrissey, "Women in New World Slavery." *Engendering Caribbean History: Cross-Cultural Perspectives, a Reader*, edited by Verene Shepherd, 2011, pp. 298–310.

36. In her fictionalised account in *Fe en disfraz*, Chica da Silva mentions how Antonia de la Granda y Balbín would physically attack her with a stick in her pregnant belly. However, the legal text presents a series of silences or gaps, as 10 days after her declaration in court doña Antonia, accompanied by the local priest, returns to correct her initial statement and admit to its inaccuracy. A month later, Antonia falls very ill and writes in her will the wish that Chica da Silva (Diamantina) is sold to pay for her own funeral. However, after her passing, her husband, Tomás de Angueira, decides to grant Chica da Silva her freedom instead and, as the legal text conveys, she would then return to the courthouse with the will signed by Tomás in which he bequeaths his possessions to his five children, whom he officially acknowledges as his (*Fe en disfraz* ch. 3). The mysterious month-apart deaths of Antonia and Tomás that result in Diamantina/Chica da Silva's extended unofficial ownership of the estate through her sons' inheritance suggests the possible intervention of herbal poisoning.

CHAPTER 7

Coda

In *Silencing the Past: Power and the Production of History*, Haitian anthropologist and historian Michel-Rolph Trouillot distinguishes between two different types of silences; on one hand, there are the "[s]ilences [that] are inherent in history because any single event enters history with some of its constituting parts missing. Something is always left out whilst something else is recorded" (49). However, as Trouillot underscores, there is another type of active silencing caused by an "uneven power in the production of sources, archives, and narratives" as is the case in the Western historiographical dismissal of the Haitian Revolution (27). *Memory and the Archival Turn in Caribbean Literature and Culture* explores how dynamics of silencing have influenced (colonial) historiographical and narrative traditions in the Caribbean, Europe, and the United States, and examines the multilayered ways in which Caribbean contemporary writers and visual artists are addressing those silences in their work by engaging critically with a variety of historical narratives and archival materials in the Caribbean region and diasporic locations. The work of the writers and visual artists included in this book is concerned with an ethical engagement and representation of historical memory, and ancestral and contemporary memory work. The varied artistic expressions that I discuss here, ultimately challenge readers and viewers to consider non-linear, circuitous paths to engaging with distant and recent

© The Author(s), under exclusive license to Springer Nature 273
Switzerland AG 2023
M. Fernández Campa, *Memory and the Archival Turn in Caribbean
Literature and Culture*, New Caribbean Studies,
https://doi.org/10.1007/978-3-030-72135-0_7

episodes of Caribbean history. Such challenges epitomise a postcolonial sense of plurivocality and heterogeneity that can confront the authoritative nature of colonial, national, or state archives. The archiving of counter-memory and the creation of counter-archives moves beyond the postcolonial emphasis on rewriting history (where the reader or viewer gains access to a wider variety of perspectives and experiences of memory) by emphasising artists' investment in interrogating and actively challenging our viewing and reading of history. Mourning also figures in many of these texts. Not only does it signal a process of critical engagement, seeking to know more about particular histories, and stimulating dialogue around suppressed historical events or individuals; mourning is enacted through aesthetic configurations of remembering, and the ethical considerations they express, generating in the process conversations on multiple scales within local and global communities of readers and viewers.

The contrapuntal poetics of fragmentation enacted in artists' literary and artistic work is an invitation at engaging with the fragments, and establishing connections in the speculative ways in which they themselves operate. All the works, in differing ways, stress the notion of process and praxis of engagement. That aesthetic fragmentation beckons the reader and the viewer to look closer, to listen more deeply and tune critically into the work's polyrhythms. For example, the peera situated in front of *Tropical Night*, invites viewers to sit down and look closer at the composition, and the effect of the fragments, both as a whole and in isolation, which can feel as if they moved across the composition. By looking closer, viewers can also appreciate the details of the mixed media and the moving iconography of the series which evokes the rhythm and musical pattern of call-and-response in calypso and soca, similarly present in the fragmentariness of Cozier's *Wait Dorothy Wait*, where the interrelation of fragments brings in the memory tradition of calypso with its language of picong. The warri board in *Ghosting* also marks the multiplicity of pathways of memory it can activate or not, all depending on the viewers' level of engagement with it. Both the peera and the warri are wooden objects that came to the Caribbean, first encoded in the memory of the enslaved and indentured person, and later materially, physically reconstructed. Their materiality is also connected to a poetics of place that Puri describes as operating in the daily and ongoing negotiation of cultural practice and remembrance (*The Grenada Revolution*). This relationship to place offers the potentiality of accounting for both the collective shared experience of place and the personal. Puri, in the context of the Grenada Revolution and its aftermath privileges "a poetics of the land, vernacular idioms, and local knowledges", and I identify that poetics also in the work of the writers and artists included here (23). Through their poetics, the works under discussion in this book, equally place focus and value on the detail and the gesture, the personal account as necessarily irreducible and as political in its co-existing with multiple forms of belonging and their contribution to collective identities and solidarities.

This book engages with conceptualisations of the archive by Caribbean thinkers and artists that, I argue, significantly expand those made by Jacques Derrida and Michel Foucault. By identifying and dissecting the general principles of the Archive within the domain of the law, discursive hegemony, and the status quo of state memory, Derrida's and Foucault's theorisation of the Archive offers helpful understandings of its inclusionary and exclusionary practices and the consequences, as well as the archival drive and logics in societies, aiming to organise and control knowledge, and thus power. Foucault, in particular, suggests links in the modus operandi of the Archive within the space of the public sphere in its regulatory dynamics of controlling what is favourably included or not. However, Derrida's and Foucault's description of the Archive, in the abstract and categorial sense (not the plural), as "the archive" risks conflation of the actual singularities in archives in terms of their own geographic and cultural specificities, production, and of the nuances that are stored within them. Not all archives are guided by the same agendas and structures. Since their conceptualisation of the Archive (that I place with capital A for emphasis) emerges from the French and European historical traditions and understanding, Derrida and Foucault remain critically grounded in those. Despite their interest in the power and reach of archives, neither assessed in depth the archive as (neo)colonial machinery fundamental to the success of the colonial project. The chapters in this book have dealt with, and addressed, a series of questions that emerged partly from this notion of the archive as discursive regulatory tool. By focusing on the contributions of Caribbean scholars, and artists (writers, performers and visual artists) to wider archival understandings and configurations, this book contextualises the vital role that they have also played in popularising (and complicating narrative accounts of) lesser known histories. This project was activated by a series of questions and problematics. How do forms of state memory reproduce that archival law of inclusion and exclusion? What has the legacy of silencing in the aftermath of slavery and colonialism been reproducing throughout the postcolonial "moment"? And what might be the impact of key regulatory forces operating in key moments such as abolition, emancipation and independence look like? What is their relationship to imposed silences? How can we consider those forces (and the silences they created) as constitutive of other narratives such as Hispanism, or those in current forms of neoimperialism, fascism, and white supremacy in Europe, United Kingdom, the United States, and across global networks of the extreme right?

The works I have explored and discussed here reveal some of the ways in which states, individuals, and social groups have practised and enforced silencing (as both a practice and a legacy of colonialism) to gain control of the narrative in the public sphere, enacting an overt/covert policing of that which can be said and that which cannot (which Foucault identified as one of the main tenets of archival logic). For example, the celebratory rhetoric around British abolitionists during the 2007 bicentennial anniversary of the abolition of the slave trade in Britain—as well as the resistance to voice responsibility and apology, address and action reparations, or acknowledge any critical stance, serves as equal reminder. Discussing Black unfreedom, Rinaldo Walcott speaks of "a long emancipation" (1). He writes: "Emancipation is commonly understood as the "freeing of the slaves" in the post-Columbus world, but emancipation is a legal process and term that I will argue marks continued unfreedom, not the freedom that is supposedly ushered in" (1). In *The Long Emancipation: Moving Toward Freedom* (2021), Walcott articulates the long emancipation as a yet-to-arrive moment, which exists rather as a potentiality. Freedom and emancipation, he argues, continue to be closely interlinked with the past as "the "discovery" of the Americas inaugurates a relation to Black nonhumanness that we still live in the present" (9). Thus, the continued epistemic and real lived violence of unfreedom blurs the temporality of colonialism, which remains in "discontinuous continuum of Euro-Western ethno-domination" (R. Walcott, *The Long Emancipation* 29). Movement, R. Walcott suggests, becomes a central element in the process of liberation (14). Movement marks the limits to freedom, but at the same time movement (actual and metaphorical) also happens "within and across borders, it is dancing, it is style, it is language, it is all the ways in which Black People attempt to express autonomy and freedom" (*The Long Emancipation* 14). Drawing from Nathaniel Mackey's notions on language and performativity, in a another essay, R. Walcott discusses the centrality of movement and action through verb/verbing in creativity (from Nathaniel Mackey's play on Amiri Baraka's essay "Other: from noun to verb"). Discussing the poetry of Dionne Brand and M. NourbeSe Philip, Walcott sees the "continuity of verbing (doing)" as the space of possibility and argues that, as Mackey notes, "the performativity of black language" is a site of possibility as "a continued verbing of resistance is practiced by engaged diasporic poets and musicians (re)write and (re)invent form(s)" (*Black Like Who?* 76). This verbing, and movement is at stake in the writing, performance and mixed media, installation, and multimedia art that I have discussed in this book. The formal fragmentation in this literature and art requires a dynamic contrapuntal reading because it is an aesthetics in movement, marking patterns of call-and-response through rhythmicity, and in relation. For example, as discussed throughout the chapters, the instrument of the drum and drumming figures literally and figuratively as a means of disrupting the silence and the censorship, that control over the conversation and discourse. Mackey sees this disruption as making noise, that is, embracing and allowing dissonance and "[o]pen form [which] is a gesture in the direction of noise" (*Discrepant Engagement* 20). In this sense, conceptually, through a disruption of discourses and silences, the works by Arroyo Pizarro, Bernard, Cozier, Danticat, Díaz, Kempadoo, Martiatu Terry, Santos-Febres, Smartt, Philip, and Phillips confront that logic in a series of (post)colonial creative archives.

The field of postcolonial studies has both opened up and complicated in rich and productive ways those critical conversations initiated by Derrida, Foucault, and others, particularly when it comes to the boundaries of official and national archives and the complex ways in which they have also occluded and obscured histories as well as knowledge in certain geographies (particularly, but not exclusively, in the 'West'). In this sense, for example, the theoretical work and legacy of Michel-Rolph Trouillot centres the issue of the unequal power in the production and holding of sources in the historical archive as necessary to any discussion of archival studies. Trouillot's work unveils the multiple ways in which the documents in the archives can in themselves, when obscured or not consulted, examined and challenged, contribute to a process of "silencing the past". Trouillot also points to the knowledge that exists outside those archives, that are their own repositories. In *The Grenada Revolution in the Caribbean Present: Operation Urgent Memory* (2014), Puri addresses the fractured narratives and silences around the Grenada Revolution in order to understand and revisit its impact on the nation and relevance to the region. Puri's study of the Grenada Revolution foregrounds "several genres of remembrance", through a discussion of a series of individual and collective accounts that provide a varied archive (9), which is particularly significant considering the precarity and inaccessibility of historical records remaining that relate to the revolution. Sensitive national documents were burnt by the People's Revolutionary Government right before the US invasion and, as a result of the United States bombing, many others were destroyed. Another 35,000 documents were airlifted by the US government and have only later been returned to Grenada but are in poor condition stored in the National Archives. Additionally, the stark differences in institutional and national memorialisation of the revolution generally favour US narratives (9). Puri stresses the need to acknowledge and consider the economic factors conditioning forms and acts of remembrance and the revealing impact of capitalist policies, as she states: "Any account of the Grenada Revolution's collapse needs to address not only conflicts in ideology or personality but the structural difficulties in economic transformation" (275). It is in the arts and cultural expression that Puri identifies essential records that contain in themselves the tensions of remembering that period in Grenada's history. The register is incredibly rich and wide, it includes poems; novels; calypsos; films; cartoons; comics; pamphlets; graffiti; and different forms of testimony. In their research process, many of the writers and visual artists whose work I have discussed in this book, turn to official archives for research yet simultaneously move away from them and from the fixity and categorising structures within them, in an attempt to explore instead other forms of memory and archival records including family and photographic archives, oral histories, the journal and the notebook where the speculative, in all its generative power, prevails and where ancestral memory and forms of resistance are indirectly documented and explored. The authors featured here have been highly influenced by, and have drawn from, the work of Caribbean and Caribbeanist historians, critics and scholars whose work in archives yield other knowledges and perspectives with attention to the dialogic. The legacy and work of Guillermo Baralt, Juan Bosch, Kamau Brathwaite, Bridget Brereton, C. L. R. James, Rhoda Reddock, Michel-Rolph Trouillot and many others, grapple with issues around erasure and omission that artists equally confront in their work.

The work of the writers and artists included in this book is concerned with an ethical engagement and representation of historical memory, and ancestral and contemporary memory work. The contrapuntal poetics of fragmentation that is enacted in their literary and artistic work is an invitation at engaging with the fragments, and establishing connections in the speculative ways in which they themselves operate. All the works, in differing ways, stress the notion of process and praxis of engagement. In turn, engagement is further connected to a poetics of place that Puri describes as operating in the daily and ongoing negotiation of cultural practice and remembrance. This relationship to place offers the potentiality of accounting for both the collective shared experience of place and the personal. Puri, in the context of the Grenada Revolution and its aftermath, privileges "a poetics of the land, vernacular idioms, and local knowledges" (23), and I identify that poetics also in the work of the writers and artists included here. The poetics of place and location at work in Cozier's practice as artist and curator, makes spaces for creation possible, such as Alice Yard in Trinidad, which offers alternatives that help imagine new forms of supporting and engaging with the arts and the work of artists. But it is ultimately people, organising together, that make these spaces possible and the vision of Cozier, Chen, Laughlin and Leonard who have primarily imagined and facilitated this space. Alice Yard has greatly influenced Caribbean contemporary art and, together with other local art spaces in the region including Beta Local in Puerto Rico, Fresh Milk in Barbados, New Local Space in Jamaica, and others, has been instrumental in the formation of an international network and ecosystem of Caribbean arts.

These archival dynamics apply to the assemblages through bricolage, montage, contrapuntal, and fugal techniques, configured in the work of Christopher Cozier, Edwidge Danticat, Jay Bernard, Junot Díaz, Inés Maria Martiatu Terry, Roshini Kempadoo, Mayra Santos-Febres, M. NourbeSe Philip, Caryl Phillips, and Yolanda Arroyo Pizarro. The fragmentation in their work interconnects, the way in which fragments relate to each other, encourages that archival engagement, reveals the gaps in history and reflects on them, but rather points to the non-recoverability of those losses and many of those memories. Puri speaks of the fragmentation in the poetics of Grenada as "micropoetic fragments and telling details"; one of their functions is that "they embody or trigger insight. Another is that they evoke an intense awareness of how much is still missing from the story, and form a montage from which connections might yet emerge" (*The Grenada Revolution* 25). This dynamic is at stake in the memory work of the literature I discuss in this book, and that awareness of what is missing is critical to the very process of counter-archiving they engage in. The literary texts, artwork, and performance discussed here, embody a turn to the archive that is simultaneous with a turn to affect; the combination of both reveals new counter-archives. The intersection of personal experience and its assemblage adjacent to other colonial archival documents (of erasure) challenges the silences in official forms of memory but also their epistemic violence. The inclusion of the notebook, the letter, or the family album in this memory work heightens the affective potentiality of these new counter-archives within their critical dimension, but moreover this intervention centres and grounds the archival possibilities of those other records and how they generate other personal and collective knowledges, a repertoire (in Diana Taylor's understanding of the term) of local, regional, and diasporic knowledges (*The Archive*). The literary and visual art included in this book explores languages of memory that challenge and pull apart Eurocentric discourses and constructs of race with their genesis in early colonial discourse. In the works under discussion, the various aesthetics and poetics highlight colonial and neo-colonial processes that through legislation and discourse have historically mobilised and promoted division across race and ethnicity, and through those constructs. The close entanglement between the forms of silencing and narrative control of coloniality, and colonial racialisation is evident in the language and rhetoric of colonial records in the Archive. The project of whiteness and white supremacy relies heavily on that archival silencing, present in the colonial records and also in the public sphere and institutions of power. In "Managing the Unmanageable", M. NourbeSe Philip emphasises the power of language in the context of the slave trade and colonial history as a managing tool. This idea runs through her work and is also more directly and indirectly addressed in the writing, artwork, and performance assembled for discussion in this book. This emphasis on imagining and creating vocabularies of experience and aesthetics that challenge the logic and management of coloniality through simultaneity and relationality, has resulted in generative forms of counter-memory in the archival turn of the last few decades.

Bibliography

Aching, Gerard. *Masking and Power: Carnival and Popular Culture in the Caribbean.* U of Minnesota P, 2002.

Adichie, Chimamanda Ngozi. "The Danger of a Single Story", *TED: Ideas Worth Spreading*, Oct. 2009, www.ted.com/talks/chimamanda_ngozi_adichie_the_danger_of_a_single_story?language=en.

Afro Modern: Journeys Through the Black Atlantic. 29 Jan.–25 Apr. 2010, Tate Liverpool, Liverpool, www.tate.org.uk/whats-on/tate-liverpool/exhibition/afro-modern-journeys-through-black-atlantic.

Afro Modern: Journeys Through the Black Atlantic. 16 July–10 Oct. 2010, Centro Galego de Arte Contemporánea, Santiago de Compostela, cgac.xunta.gal/gl/exposicions/afro-modern-journeys-through-black-atlantic.

After Mas. Directed by Karen Martinez. Riposte Pictures, 2013.

Akomfrah, John. "Why History Matters." *TateShots.* YouTube, uploaded by Tate, 2 July 2025, www.youtube.com/watch?v=jDJYyG7jKV0.

———. *The Stuart Hall Project.* Directed y John Akomfrah, Creation Rebel Films, 2013.

Alexander, Claire E., et al. *The Bengal Diaspora: Rethinking Muslim Migration.* Routledge, 2016.

Alexis, Jacques Stephen. *General Sun, My Brother.* 1955. Translated by Carrol F. Coates. U P of Virginia, 1999.

Ali, Shereen. "The Madman's Rant." *Repeating Islands*, 21 Feb. 2018, repeatingislands.com/2018/02/21/the-madmans-rant/.

Alvarez, Julia. *In The Time of the Butterflies.* 1994. Plume/Penguin, 1995.

M. Fernández Campa, *Memory and the Archival Turn in Caribbean Literature and Culture*, New Caribbean Studies, https://doi.org/10.1007/978-3-030-72135-0

Anderson, Benedict. *Imagined Communities: Reflections on the Origin and Spread of Nationalism*. 1983. Verso, 2006.

André, Richard. "The Dominican Republic and Haiti: A Shared View from the Diaspora." Interview with Edwidge Danticat and Junot Díaz, *Americas Quarterly*, 28 July, 2014, www.americasquarterly.org/fulltextarticle/the-dom inican-republic-and-haiti-a-shared-view-from-the-diaspora/.

Anim-Adoo, Joan and Yasmin Gunaratnam. "Secrets and Lies: Narrative Methods and the Limits of Research." *Journal of Creative Practice*, vol. 5, no. 3, 2013, pp. 383–396.

Aponte Alsina, Marta. *Somos Islas. Ensayos de Camino*. Editora Educación Emergente, 2015.

Arana, R. Victoria. *Black British Aesthetics Today*. Cambridge Scholars Pub., 2009.

Araujo, Ana Lucia. *Brazil Through French Eyes: A Nineteenth-Century Artist in the Tropics*. U of New Mexico P, 2015, *EBSCOhost*, eds.a.ebscohost. com/eds/ebookviewer/ebook/bmxlYmtfXzk4MjQ4OV9fQU41?sid=241 60e37-b65d-4b03-bcdb-5d6052df8dfe@sessionmgr4006&vid=1&format= EB&rid=9.

Archer, Melanie and Mariel Brown. *Pictures from Paradise: A Survey in Caribbean Contemporary Photography*. Robert and Christopher Publishers, 2013.

Armistead, Claire. "Speaking Out: Ted Hughes Winner Jay Bernard on Exploring the New Cross Fire in a One-Off Performance." *Guardian*, 5 Apr. 2018, www.theguardian.com/books/2018/apr/05/speaking-out-jay-bernard-surge-side-a-poet.

Arroyo Pizarro, Yolanda. "A Reading by Yolanda Arroyo Pizarro." Kelly Writers House, 2 Mar. 2020, *YouTube*, uploaded by Kelly Writers House, 2 Mar. 2020, www.youtube.com/watch?v=tDjg4p_ul8w.

———. *Afrofeministamente*. E-book ed., Editorial EDP, 2020.

———. "Cuiring Black Genders and Sexualities in the Americas." *Blog Boreales*. *La Narrativa de Yolanda*, 25 Aug. 2021, narrativadeyolanda.blogspot.com.

———. "Calle de la Resistencia: Narrative, Poetry and Perreo Combativo from an Afrolesbian Boricua." The Kelly Writers House, University of Pennsylvania, 2 Mar. 2020, www.youtube.com/watch?v=tDjg4p_ul8w.

———. *Negras: Stories of Puerto Rican Slave Women*. Translated by Alejandro Álvarez Nieves. Amazon, 2012.

———. *Saeta, The Poems*. Boreales, 2011.

Assing, Tracy. "Unaccounted For." *So Many Islands: Stories from the Caribbean, Mediterranean, Indian and Pacific Ocean*. 2017. Edited by Nicholas Laughlin and Nailah Folami Imojah, introduction by Marlon James, Telegram, 2018, pp. 135–144.

Bagoo, Andre. *The Undiscovered Country*. Leeds: Peepal Tree, 2020.

Bahadur, Gaiutra. *Coolie Woman: The Odyssey of Indenture*. Hurst & Company, 2013.

Balaguer, Joaquín. *La isla al revés: Haiti y el destino dominicano*. 1983. Editorial Corripio, 1994.

Ballester Panelli, José Arturo. *Caribe Fractal / Fractal Caribbean*. Nov. 2020. RCAH Lookout Gallery, Michigan State University, 2021.

Baralt, Guillermo A. *Slave Revolts in Puerto Rico: Conspiracies and Uprisings, 1795–1873*. 1982. Translated by Christine Ayorinde. Marcus Wiener, 2015.

Barnet, Miguel and Estaban Montejo. *Cimarrón: Historia de un esclavo*. 1967. Siruela, 2002.

Bastian, Jeannette A., et al. *Decolonizing the Caribbean Record: An Archives Reader*. Library Juice Press, 2018.

Batson, Dawn K. "Voices of Steel: A Historical Perspective." *Carnival. Culture in Action: The Trinidad Experience*, edited by Milla Cozart Riggio, Routledge, 2004, pp. 195–203, *EBSCOhost*, search.ebscohost.com/login.aspx? direct=true&AuthType=sso&db=cat07845a&AN=uea.57120332&authtype= sso&custid=s8993828&site=eds-live&scope=site.

Baucom, Ian. *Specters of the Atlantic: Finance Capital, Slavery, and the Philosophy of History*. Duke U P, 2005.

Bayer, Osvaldo. "Los Indios Son Anarquistas." *Pagina/12:Ultimas Noticias*. 31 Mar. 2013, www.pagina12.com.ar/diario/contratapa/13-26560-2003-10-11. html.

Benítez-Rojo, Antonio. "Three Words Towards Creolization." *Caribbean Creolization: Reflections on the Cultural Dynamics of Language, Literature and Identity*, edited by Kathleen M. Balutanski and Marie-Agnés Sourieau. Translated by James Maraniss, Library Press U of Florida, 2017, pp. 53–61, https://ufdcimages.uflib.ufl.edu/AA/00/06/13/74/00001/AA00061374_00001.pdf.

———. *The Repeating Island: The Caribbean and the Postmodern Perspective*. Duke U P, 1996.

Benson, Devyn Spence, et al. *Afrocubanas History, Thought, and Cultural Practices*. Rowman &. Littlefield International, 2020.

Berg, Mary G, Karla Suárez, et al. *Open Your Eyes and Soar: Cuban Women Writing Now*. Translated by Pamella Carmell. White Pine Press, 2003.

Bernard, Jay. *Surge*. Chatto & Windus, 2019.

———. "Surge." *New Beacon in Poetry and Prose. Beacon of Hope*. New Beacon, 2016, pp. 49–59.

Berrocal, Beatriz. *Memorias de Lucila: una esclava rebelde*. Taller nacional de Creación, 1996.

Best, Curwen. "Sounding Calypso's Muted Tracks, Past and Present: Barbados & St. Lucia." *Culture at the Cutting Edge: Caribbean Popular Music. Kingston*. U of West Indies P, 2004, pp. 10–53.

Best, Tamara. "The Artist Sheena Rose Is Reaching Beyond Barbados." *The New York Times*, 31 May 2017, www.nytimes.com/2017/05/31/arts/design/she ena-rose-contemporary-artist-barbados.html.

Bettelheim, Judith and Janet Catherine Berlo, editors. "Transgressive Heroes; Painting An Alternative Caribbean History." *Transcultural Pilgrim. Three Decades of Work by José Bedia*. Fowler Museum at UCLA, 2012.

Billy, Dizanne. "Madman's Rant: David Rudder", *Write it Down*, 15 July 2016, dizzannebillyblog.wordpress.com/2016/07/15/madmans-rant-david-rudder/.

Birth, Kevin. *Bacchanalian Sentiments: Musical Experiences and Political Counterpoints in Trinidad*. Duke U P, 2008.

Black Stalin. (Artistic name). Leroy Calliste. "Wait Dorothy Wait." *Roots Rock Soca*, © 1985, 1991. Rounder Records, Compact Disc.

Blevins, Steven. *Living Cargo: How Black Britain Performs Its Past*. U of Minnesota P, 2016.

Blouin, Francis X. Jr. and William G. Rosenberg. *Archives, Documentation, and Institutions of Social Memory: Essays from the Sawyer Seminar*. U of Michigan P, 2007.

Bodenheimer, Rebecca M. *Geographies of Cubanidad: Place, Race and Musical Performance in Contemporary Cuba*. E-book ed., U P of Mississippi, 2015.

Boehmer, Elleke. "Postcolonial Poetics. A Score for Reading." *Postcolonial Poetics: 21st Century Critical Readings*. E-book ed., Palgrave Macmillan, 2018, pp. 22–59.

Bouhchichi, M'barek and Sasha Huber. Interview. Feb. 2021, *Institut Finlandais*, www.institut-finlandais.fr/en/blog/2021/02/10/interview-sasha-huber-and-mbarek-bouhchichi/.

Brathwaite, E. Kamau. *Ancestors: A Reinvention of Mother Poem, Sun Poem and X/Self*. New Directions, 2001.

———. "Caribbean Man in Space and Time," *Savacou*, nos. 11–12, Sept. 1975.

———. *Contradictory Omens: Cultural Diversity and Integration in the Caribbean*. Savacou, 1974.

———. *History of the Voice: The Development of Nation Language in Anglophone Caribbean Poetry*. New Beacon Books, 1984.

———. "History, the Caribbean Writer and *X/Self*." *Crisis and Creativity in the New Literatures in English*, edited by Geoffrey V. Davis and Hena Maes-Jelink. Rodopi Press, 1990, pp. 23–47.

———. "Kamau Brathwaite." Interview. *Talk Yuh Talk! Interviews with Anglophone Caribbean Poets*, by Kwame Dawes, editor. U P of Virginia, 2001, pp. 22–37.

———. *The Zea Mexican Diary, 7 Sept. 1926–7 Sept. 1986*. U of Winsconsin P, 1993.

Brereton, Bridget. *A History of Modern Trinidad 1783–1962*. Heinemann, 1981.

———. *Race Relations in Colonial Trinidad 1870–1900*. Cambridge U P, 1979.

Bridgens, Richard. *West Indian Scenery with Illustrations of Negro Character*. R. Jennings, 1836.

Bryan, Beverley, Stella Dadzie and Suzanne Scafe. *Heart of the Race. Black Women's Lives in Britain*. 1985. Verso, 2018.

Buchhart, Dieter and Tricia Laughlin Bloom, editors. *Basquiat: The Unknown Notebooks*. Brooklyn Museum & Skira Rizzoli, 2015.

Busby, Matta. "More Than 100 Public Figures Call for Halt to Osime Brown Deportation." *The Guardian*, 12 Dec. 2020, www.theguardian.com/uk-news/2020/dec/12/public-figures-call-for-halt-osime-brown-deportation-priti-patel.

Bush, Barbara. "Hard Labor: Women, Childbirth and Resistance in British Caribbean Slave Societies." *Moran Than Chattel: Black Women and Slavery in the Americas*, edited by David Barry Gaspar and Darlene Clark Hine, Indiana U P, 1996, pp. 193–217.

Bush, Ruth. "New Beacon Books—The Pioneering Years." *New Beacon in Poetry and Prose. Beacon of Hope*. New Beacon, 2016, pp. 1–48.

Cabrera, Lydia. *The Sacred Language of the Abakuá*. 1988. Edited and translated by Ivor L. Miller and P. González Gómes-Cásseres. The U P of Mississippi, 2020.

Cabrera Infante, Guillermo. 1967. *Tres Tristes Tigres*. Catedra, 2017.

Campt, Tina. *Image Matters: Archive, Photography, and the African Diaspora in Europe*. Duke U P, 2012.

Carby, Hazel V. *Imperial Intimacies: A Tale of Two Islands*. Verso, 2019.

Caruth, Cathy. *Unclaimed Experience: Trauma, Narrative and History*. The John Hopkins U P, 1996.

Casamayor-Cisneros, Odette. "Elogio al 'apalencamiento.'" *Cuban Studies*, no. 48, Special Issue dedicated to the Afro-Cuban movement, 2019, pp. 303–327, www.jstor.org/stable/pdf/26725397.pdf?refreqid=excelsior%3A698f97f0752152448c5a5ac2986a5c69.

———. "Imagining the "New Black Subject": Ethical Transformations and Raciality in the Post-Revolutionary Cuban Nation." *Black Writing, Culture and the State in Latin America*, edited by Jerome Branch. E-book ed., Vanderbilt U P, 2015, pp. 135–180.

———. "¡Reto Aceptado!" *Con Tinta Negra, OnCuba News*, 12 Sept. 2021, https://oncubanews.com/opinion/columnas/con-tinta-negra/reto-aceptado/.

Castillo Bueno, María de los Reyes and Daisy Rubiera Castillo. *Reyita, sencillamente: testimonio de una negra cubana nonagenaria*. Instituto Cubano del Libro, 1996.

Cayonne, Bruce, *Fete Sign*, by *Toof*, Granderson Lab, Port of Spain, 2021, https://fetesign.com.

Chambers, Eddie. *Black Artists in British Art: A History from 1950 to the Present*. I.B. Tauris & co. Ltd., 2014. *EBSCOhost*, https://search-ebscohost-com.uea.idm.oclc.org/login.aspx?direct=true&db=e000xww&AN=838362& site=ehost-live.

Chamoiseau, Patrick. *Texaco*. 1992. Vintage, 1998.

Chancy, Myriam A. J. *From Sugar to Revolution: Women's Visions of Haiti, Cuba and the Dominican Republic*. E-book ed., Wilfrid Laurier U P. 2013, ebookc entral.proquest.com/lib/uea/reader.action?docID=3282132&ppg=1.

Chaviano, Daina. *The Island of Eternal Love*. 2006. Translated by Andrea G. Labinger. Riverhead Books, 2009.

Chen, Willi. "How She Go Look." *Chutney Power and Other Stories*. Macmillan Caribbean, 2006, pp. 100–104.

Chinee Girl. Directed by Natalie E. Wei, Natalie Wei Productions, 2011, *Vimeo*, uploaded by Natalie E. Wei, Sept. 13, 2011, vimeo.com/28971743.

"Christopher Cozier." *Kentucky Museum of Arts and Craft*, 2011, www.kmacmu seum.org/christopher-cozier.

Colón Pellot, Carmen. *Ámbar mulato (Ritmos) y Otros Poemas*. 1938. Los libros de La Iguana, 2014.

Conrad, Joseph. *Heart of Darkness*. 1899. Penguin Classics, 2007.

Copeland, Huey and Krista A. Thompson, "New World Slavery and the Matter of the Visual." *Representations*, vol. 113, no. 1, Feb. 2011, pp. 1–5. *EBSCOhost*, https://doi.org/10.1525/rep.2011.113.1.1.

Cowling, Camillia. *Conceiving Freedom: Women of Color, Gender, and the Abolition of Slavery in Havana and Rio De Janeiro*. E-book., The U of North Carolina Press, 2013, *EBSCOhost*, search.ebscohost.com/login.aspx?direct= true&AuthType=sso&db=cat07845a&AN=uea.861692793&authtype=sso& custid=s8993828&site=eds-live&scope=site.

Cozart Riggio, Milla. "We Jamming It: Introduction to Part II." *Carnival: Culture in Action—The Trinidad Experience*, edited by Milla Cozart Riggio. Ebook ed., Routledge, 2004, pp. 183–186, *EBSCOhost*, search.ebscohost. com/login.aspx?direct=true&AuthType=sso&db=cat07845a&AN=uea.571 20332&authtype=sso&custid=s8993828&site=eds-live&scope=site.

Cozier, Christopher. "All around us – elsewhere are beginnings and endings." *Dig and fly*, single channel video, *Look for the All Around You*, Sharjah Biennial, 2019.

———. *Art and Nation: Things You Should Learn from Day 1*, multimedia installation, 1998.

———. *Blue Soap*. 1994. Video Performance. VHS.

———. "Christopher Cozier." Interview by Annie Paul. *Bomb Magazine*, no. 82, Dec. 2002/2003, pp. 66–73, *EBSCOhost*, search.ebscohost.com/ login.aspx?direct=true&AuthType=sso&db=edsjsr&AN=edsjsr.40426862&aut htype=sso&custid=s8993828&site=eds-live&scope=site.

———. "Christopher Cozier." *One Month after Being Known in that Island*, edited by Alanna Stang and Well Said, Hatje Cantz, 2020, pp. 66–71.

———. *Christopher Cozier: In Development*. Mixed Media Drawing on Paper, Monotype, Linotype. David Krut Projects, 2013, New York City, https://davidkrutprojects.com/artworks/27124/in-development-instal lation-view-by-christopher-cozier-2.

———. "Christopher Cozier in Development: A Collaborative Project." 2013-Ongoing, dpatterns2013.wordpress.com/category/dpatterns/.

———. *Conversation with a Shirt Jac*. 1990. Performance. Central Bank lobby (1990); Aquarella Galleries, 1991, Port of Spain, Trinidad and Tobago.

———. *Dark Circles,* ink on paper, 2014-ongoing.

———. *Entanglement series*, ink on paper, 2014–15.

———. *Gas Men,* video, 2014.

———. Interview conducted by Marta Fernández Campa, August 2012, Port of Spain.

———. "Laocoon." *Laocoon (triptych), In Development* series, mixed media, 2012.

———. *Madman's Rant*. Collaboration with David Rudder. Multi-Panelled Artwork, Drawing, Dimensions Variable, 1997.

———. *New Level Head(s)*. *Relational Undercurrents: Contemporary Art of the Caribbean Archipelago*, 16 Sept. 2017–25 Feb. 2018, Museum of Latin American Art, Long Beach.

———. "No More Than an Backyard on a Small Island." Interview by Claire Tancons, *Fillip*, no. 16, May 2012, pp. 42–51, *EBSCOhost*, search.ebscohost.com/login.aspx?direct=true&AuthType=sso&db=edb&AN=76589718&authtype=sso&custid=s8993828&site=eds-live&scope=site.

———. "One Narrative Thread." *Tropical Night* weblog. 10 May 2010, tropic alnightblogspot.com.

———. "Terrastories (Notes)." *Small Axe*, vol. 7, no. 2, 2003, pp. 120–126. *EBSCOhost*, search.ebscohost.com/login.aspx?direct=true&AuthType=sso&db=edspmu&AN=edspmu.S1534671403201208&authtype=sso&custid=s89 93828&site=eds-live&scope=site.

———. *The arrest: hands up, hands out*. Pen and ink on paper, lightbox installation, 2013, Art Basil, Betsy Hotel, Miami.

———. *The Whip*. 1991. Performance. Port of Spain, Trinidad and Tobago.

———. *Three Stains on Paper*. *Cultural Autopsy Series*. 1995. Mixed Media on Paper.

———. "Topicality, Flexibility, Fluidity: Visual Negotiations from Port of Spain." Wesley Gallery, University of Miami. 10 Nov. 2008, scholar.library.miami.edu.

———. *Tropical Night* (2006–present). Mixed Media Drawing (Installation).

———. *turbulence 2019–2021*, mixed media installation, ink on paper. *The Stomach and the Port*, Liverpool Biennial, 2021.

———. "Uniform and Weapon." *Interrogating Caribbean Masculinities: Theoretical and Empirical Analyses*, edited by Rhoda E. Reddock, U of the West Indies P, 2004, pp. 404–417.

———. *Wait Dorothy Wait*. 1991. Mixed Media. Collection of the Late Jeoffrey Stanford.

Cozier, Christopher and Nicholas Laughlin. "Tropical Night: Random Notes 06." 4 May 2007. *Tropical Night,* www.tropicalnight.blogspot.com.

Cruz, Angie. *Dominicana*. Flatiron Books, 2019.

———. *Let it Rain Coffee*. Simon & Schuster, 2005.

Cudjoe, Selwyn R. *Caribbean Women Writers: Essays from the First International Conference*. Calaloux Publications, 1990.

Cuello, José Israel. *Documentos del conflicto dominico-haitiano de 1937*. Editora Taller, 1985.

Dabydeen, David and Maria del Pilar Kaladeen. *The Other Windrush: Legacies of Indenture in Britain's Caribbean Empire*. Pluto Press, 2021.

Dabydeen, David, John Gilmore and Cecily Jones, editors. *Oxford Companion to Black British History*, Oxford U P, 2010.

DaCosta-Willis, Miriam. "Introduction: 'This Voyage Toward Words': Mapping the Routes of the Writers." *Daughters of the Diaspora: Afra-Hispanic Writers*, edited by Miriam DaCosta-Willis. Ian Randle, 2003, pp. xvi–xlii.

Dalleo, Raphael. *Caribbean Literature and the Public Sphere: From the Plantation to the Postcolonial*. U of Virginia P, 2011.

Danticat, Edwidge. *Brother, I'm Dying*. Alfred A. Knopf, 2007.

———. *Create Dangerously: The Immigrant Artist at Work*. 2010. Vintage Books, 2011.

———. *Krik? Krak!*. Soho Press, 1995.

———. "Nature has no Memory" *Border of Lights,* borderoflights.org/edwidge-danticat.

———. *The Art of Death: Writing the Final Story*. Graywolf Press, 2017.

———. *The Dew Breaker*. Vintage Books, 2004.

———. *The Farming of Bones*. 1998. Penguin, 1999.

———. "Recovering History by the Bone: Conversation with Edwidge Danticat." Interview by Myriam J. A. Chancy. *Calabash: A Journal of Caribbean Arts and Letters*, vol. 1, no. 2, 2001, pp. 15–38, https://doi.org/10.33682/jagt-nk9v.

Davies, Miles. *Sketches of Spain*, Columbia Records, 1960.

Davison, Carol Margaret. "Crisscrossing the River: An Interview with Caryl Phillips." *Ariel*, vol. 25, no. 4, 1994, pp. 91–99.

Dawes, Kwame. *Natural Mysticism: Towards a New Reggae Aesthetic*. 1999. Peepal Tree Press, 2008.

———. *Talk Yuh Talk! Interviews with Anglophone Caribbean*. U of Virginia P, 2001.

de Ferrari, Guillermina. "A Caribbean Hauntology: The Sensorial Art of Joscelyn Gardner and M. NourbeSe Philip." *Journal of Latin American Cultural Studies*, vol. 27, no. 3, 2018, pp. 271–293, Academic Search, https://search.ebscohost.com/login.aspx?direct=true&AuthType=sso&db=asn&AN=133694691&authtype=sso&custid=s8993828&site=eds-live&scope=site.

deCaires Narain, Denise. *Contemporary Caribbean Women's Poetry: Making Style.* 2001. Routledge, 2002.

Derby, Lauren. *The Dictator's Seduction: Politics and the Popular Imagination in the Era of Trujillo.* Duke U P, 2009.

Derrida, Jacques. *Archive Fever: A Freudian Impression.* The U of Chicago P, 1009.

Díaz, Junot. "A Conversation with Junot Díaz." Interview by Achy Obejas. *Review: Literature and Arts of the Americas*, 42.1, 2009, pp. 42–47, *EBSCOhost*, https://doi.org/10.1080/08905760902815941.

———. *Drown.* New York: Riverhead Books, 1996.

———. *The Brief Wondrous Life of Oscar Wao.* Riverhead Books, 2007.

Douglas, Marcia. *The Marvellous Equations of the Dread: A Novel in Bass Riddim.* Peepal Tree Press, 2016.

Edmondson, Belinda J. "Introduction: The Caribbean; Myths, Tropes, Discourses." *Caribbean Romances: The Politics of Regional Representation*, edited by Belinda J. Edmonson. U of Virginia P, 1999, pp. 1–11.

Eleison, Keyna and Manuela Moscoso, editors. "Teatime." *Reader The Stomach and the Port*, Liverpool Biennial, 2021, pp. 132–138.

Emery, Mary Lou. *Modernism: The Visual, and Caribbean Literature.* Cambridge U P, 2007.

Espinet, Ramabai. *The Swinging Bridge.* Harper Collins, 2004.

Evans, Lucy. *Communities in Contemporary Anglophone Caribbean Short Stories.* Liverpool University Press, 2014. *EBSCOhost*, search.ebscohost.com/login.aspx?direct=true&AuthType=sso&db=cat07845a&AN=uea.911019134&authtype=sso&custid=s8993828&site=eds-live&scope=site.

Fehskens. Erin M. "Accounts Unpaid, Accounts Untold: M. NourbeSe Philip's *Zong!* and the Catalogue." *Callaloo*, vol. 35, no. 2, 2012, pp. 407–24, *EBSCOhost*, https://doi.org/10.1353/cal.2012.0043.

Fernández Campa, Marta. "Caribbean Art in Dialogue: Connecting Narratives in Wrestling with the Image." *Anthurium: A Caribbean Studies Journal*, vol. 9, no. 1, 2012, pp. 1–12, https://doi.org/10.33596/anth.219.

Fernández De La Reguera Tayà, Tànit. "Inés María Martiatu and Her Stories: A Critical Assessment." *Over the Waves and Other Stories / Sobre las olas y otros cuentos.* Translated by Emmanuel Harris II. Swan Isle Press, 2008, pp. 189–204.

Figueroa-Vásquez, Yomaira C. *Decolonizing Diasporas: Radical Mappings of Afro-Atlantic Literature.* Northwestern U P, 2020.

Fischer, Sibylle. *Modernity Disavowed: Haiti and the Cultures of Slavery in the Age of Revolution*. Duke U P, 2004.

Flores Collazo, María Margarita. "(Des)memorias en torno a la esclavitud negra y la abolición: Puerto Rico, siglo XIX." *Cincinnatiti Romance Review*, vol. 30, 2011, pp. 17–38, *Scholar @ UC*, scholar.uc.edu/show/8w32r6982.

Fofana, Lamin. *Life and Death by Water. The Stomach and the Port*, Liverpool Biennial, Liverpool, 2021.

Foster, Hal. "Introduction." *The Anti-Aesthetic: Essays on Postmodern Culture*. 1983, edited by Hal Foster. The New Press, 1998, pp. ix–xvii.

Foucault, Michel. *The Archaeology of Knowledge*. 1969. London: Routledge, 1989.

Francisco, Slinger (Mighty Sparrow). "Jean and Dinah." 1956. *Volume One*, Ice Records, 1992.

Franco, Daniela. "Dominican Consul Calls Author Junot Díaz 'Anti-Dominican', Revokes Medal." *Abc News*, Oct. 23 2015, www.nbcnews.com/news/latino/dominican-consul-author-junot-diaz-anti-dominican-n450441.

Fryer, Peter. *Staying Power*, Pluto Press, 2018.

Fuentes, Marisa J.M. *Dispossessed Lives: Enslaved Women, Violence and the Archive*. U of Pennsylvania P, 2016.

Fumagalli, Maria Cristina. "Before and After Ovid: Metamorphoses in Marlene Nourbese Philip and Gabriel García Márquez." *Caribbean Perspectives on Modernity: Returning Medusa's* Gaze. U of Virginia P, 2009, 73–86.

———. *On the Edge: Writing the Border between Haiti and the Dominican Republic*. U of Liverpool P, 2017.

Fusco, Coco. "The Other History of Intercultural Performance." *The Drama Review*, 38.1, Spring 1994, pp. 143–167, *JSTOR*, https://doi.org/10.2307/1146361.

———. "Still in the Cage: Thoughts on "Two Undiscovered Indians, 20 Years Later," February 2012, *Modern Painters*, https://www.alexandergray.com/attachment/en/594a3c935a4091cd008b4568/Press/594a5dcb5a4091cd008b9284.

Fusco, Coco and Guillermo Gómez Peña. *The Couple in the Cage: Two Undiscovered Amerindians Visit The West*. Performance, 1992–1993, Seville (and Various Locations).

García, Scherezade. *Postcard Project*, painting and installation, 2012.

García, Scherezade and Edward Paulino. "The 1937 Haitian Massacre and Border of Lights" *Afro Hispanic Review*, vol. 32, no. 2, Oct. 2013, pp. 111–118, *EBSCOhost*, https://search.ebscohost.com/login.aspx?direct=true&AuthType=sso&db=edsjsr&AN=edsjsr.24585148&authtype=sso&custid=s8993828&site=eds-live&scope=site.

García Peña, Lorgia. *The Borders of Dominicanidad: Race, Nation, and Archives of Contradiction*. Duke U P, 2016.

Garder, Joscelyn. *omi ebora*. Video installation, 2014.

Gay, Roxane. "In the Manner of Water or Light." *Ayti*. Artistically Declined Press, 2011, pp. 57–83.

Gaye, Marvin. "Mercy, Mercy, Me (The Ecology)." *What's Going On*. Tamla, 1971.

Gayle, Dennis J. "Trade Policies and the Hemispheric Integration Process." *Globalization and Neoliberalism: The Caribbean Context*, ed. by Thomas Klak. Rowman & Littlefield, 1998.

Gen Doy. *Black Visual Culture: Modernity and* Postmodernity. I.B. Taurus, 2000.

Gentleman, Amelia. "Home Office Destroyed Windrush Landing Cards says Ex-Staffer." *The Guardian*, 17 Apr. 2018. www.theguardian.com/uk-news/2018/apr/17/home-office-destroyed-windrush-landing-cards-says-ex-staffer.

Gikandi, Simon. *Slavery and the Culture of Taste*. E-book ed., Princeton U P, 2011.

———. *Writing in Limbo. Modernism and Caribbean Literature*. Cornell U P, 1992.

Gilroy, Paul. *The Black Atlantic: Modernity and Double Consciousness*. Harvard U P, 1993.

———. *There Ain't No Black in the Union Jack: The Cultural Politics of Race and Nation*. 1987. Routledge, 2002.

Glissant, Édouard. *Caribbean Discourse: Selected Essays*. 1981. Introduction and Translation by J. Michael Dash. U of Virginia P, 1999.

———. *Poetics of Relation*. 1990. Translated by Betty Wing. The U of Michigan P, 1997.

Glover, Kaiama L. *Haiti Unbound: A Spiralist Challenge to the Post-Colonial Canon*. Liverpool: Liverpool U P, 2010.

González Mandri, Flora. *Guarding Cultural Memory: Afro-Cuban Women in Literature and the Arts*. U of Virginia P, 2006.

Goodfellow, Maya. *Hostile Environment: How Immigrants Became Scapegoats*. 2019. Verso, 2020.

Gregson v. Gilbert. "Documents relating to the ship Zong." National Maritime Museum. REC/19, Box 89–folder 90.

Gregson v. Gilbert. Zong! as Told to the Author by Setaey Adamu Boateng, by M. NourbeSe Philip. Wesleyan U P, 2008, pp. 210–211.

Guerra, Wendy. *Nunca fui primera dama*. Alfaguara, 2017.

Gugolati, Maica. "A detergent artwork in Trinidad and Tobago: Christopher Cozier's Blue Soap" *Esclavages & Post-Esclavages*, vol. 5, 2021, pp. 2–20, *Open Edition Journals*, https://doi.org/10.4000/slaveries.5352.

Hadchity, Therese Kaspersen. *The Making of a Caribbean Avant-Garde: Postmodernism as Post-nationalism*. E-book ed., Purdue U P, 2020.

Hall, Catherine. "Britain's Massive Debt to Slavery." *The Guardian*, 27 Feb. 2013, www.guardian.co.uk/commentisfree/2013/feb/27/britain-debt-slavery-made-public.

———. "Remembering 1807: Histories of the Slave Trade, Slavery and Abolition. Introduction." *History Workshop Journal*, vol. 64, Autumn 2007, pp. 1–5m, *EBSCOhost*, https://doi.org/10.1093/hwj/dbm064.

Hall, Stuart. "Black Diaspora Artists in Britain: Three 'Moments' in Post-War History." *History Workshop Journal*, vol. 61, 2006, pp. 1–24, EBSCOhost, https://doi.org/10.1093/hwj/dbi074.

———. "On Postmodernism and Articulation: An Interview with Stuart Hall by Lawrence Grossberg and Others." *Essential Essays, Volume 1: Foundations of Cultural Studies*, edited by David Morley. Duke U P, 2019, pp. 222–246. ProQuest Ebook Central, http://ebookcentral.proquest.com/lib/uea/detail.action?docID05609562.

Hall, Stuart and Bill Schwarz. *Familiar Stranger: A Life Between Islands*. Allen Lane, 2017.

———. "New Ethnicities." *Black British Cultural Studies: A Reader*, edited by Houston A. Baker, Jr., Manthia Diawara and Ruth H. Lindeborg. The U of Chicago P, 1996, pp. 163–172.

Hamilton, Carolyn, Verne Harris, et al. "Introduction." *Refiguring the Archive*. David Philip, 2002, pp. 7–18.

Hamilton, Njelle W. *Phonographic Memories: Popular Music and the Contemporary Caribbean Novel*. Rutgers U P, 2019.

Handsworth Songs. Directed by John Akomfrah, Black Audio Film Collective, 1986.

Hanna, Monica. "'Reassembling the Fragments': Battling Historiographies, Caribbean Discourse, and Nerd Genres in Junot Díaz's *The Brief Wondrous Life of Oscar Wao*." *Callaloo*, vol. 32, no. 2, 2010, pp. 398–520, *EBSCOhost*, search.ebscohost.com/login.aspx?direct=true&AuthType=sso&db=edsjsr&AN=edsjsr.40732888&authtype=sso&custid=s8993828&site=eds-live&scope=site.

Hartman, Saidiya V. *Wayward Lives, Beautiful Experiments: Intimate Histories of Social Upheaval*. Serpent's Tail, 2019.

———. *Scenes of Subjection: Terror, Slavery, and Self-Making in Nineteenth-Century America*. Oxford U P, 1997, *EBSCOhost*, search.ebscohost.com/login.aspx?direct=true&db=cat07845a&AN=uea.36417797&authtype=sso&custid=s8993828&site=eds-live&scope=site.

Hernández, Rita Indiana. *Tentacle*. 2015. Translated by Achy Obejas. And Other Stories, 2018.

Hernández, Rita Indiana and Los Misterios. "Da Pa Lo Do." *El Juidero*, Sonic Music Latin, 2011.

Hewett, Heather. "At the Crossroads: Disability and Trauma in *The Farming of Bones.*" *MELUS*, vol. 31, no. 3, 2006, pp. 123–145, *EBSCOhost*, search. ebscohost.com/login.aspx?direct=true&AuthType=sso&db=edsjsr&AN=eds jsr.30029654&authtype=sso&custid=s8993828&site=eds-live&scope=site.

Hidalgo de Jesús, Amarilis. "Images of Afro-Caribbean Female Slaves in the Works of Yolanda Arroyo Pizarro." *Twenty-First Century Latin American Narrative and Postmodern Feminism*, edited by Gina Ponce de León, Cambridge Scholars Publishing, 2014, pp. 23–37, *EBSCOhost*, search.ebs cohost.com/login.aspx?direct=true&AuthType=sso&db=mzh&AN=201432 1807&authtype=sso&custid=s8993828&site=eds-live&scope=site.

Hughes, Langston. "The Weary Blues." *Selected Poems*. 1959. *Serpents Tail*, 1999, pp. 33–34.

Ishelmo, Shubi L. "From Africa to Cuba: An Historical Analysis of the Sociedad Secreta Abakuá (Ñañiguismo)." *Review of African Political Economy*, 29.92, 2002, pp. 253–272, *JSTOR*, www-jstor-org.uea.idm.oclc.org/stable/pdf/400 6814.pdf?refreqid=excelsior%3A7b79b6548bf394982365ec63c3eacae4.

Jain, Shobhita and Rhoda Reddock, "Introduction." 1998. *Women Plantation Workers: International Experiences*. E-book ed., edited by Shobhita Jain and Rhoda Reddock, Routledge, 2020.

James, C.L.R. *The Black Jacobins. Toussaint L' Ouverture and the San Domingo Revolution*. 1938. Vintage Books, 1989.

James, Marlon. *A Brief History of Seven Killings*. Riverhead Books, 2014.

Johnson, Linton Kwesi. "New Craas Massahkah." *Mi Revalueshanary Fren. Selected Poems*. Ausable Press, 2006, pp. 52–57.

Jones, Kellie, editor. *Eyeminded: Living and Writing Contemporary Art*, Duke U P, 2011.

Jones, LeRoy (Amiri Baraka). *Black Music*. Da Capo Press, 1968.

Joseph, Anthony. *Kitch. A Fictional Biography of a Calypso Icon*. Peepal Tree, 2018.

———. *The Frequency of Magic*. Peepal Tree, 2019.

———. "The Frequency of Magic." Goldsmiths College Department of Art MFA Lectures 2017–2018 Series 3.2: Rhythm, *YouTube*, uploaded by Gold-smiths Art, 24 July 2018, www.youtube.com/watch?v=lexmeTirrfQ.

Kaladeen, María del Pilar. "'Those Not with Us Anymore': The Literary Archive of Indian Minorities in Guyanese Indenture and Beyond." *Journal of West Indian Literature*, vol. 29, no. 1, April 2021, pp. 26–35, *EBSCOhost*, search. ebscohost.com/login.aspx?direct=true&AuthType=sso&db=mzh&AN=202 122344908&authtype=sso&custid=s8993828&site=eds-live&scope=site.

———. "Windrushed." *Wasafiri*, vol. 33, no. 2, 2018, pp. 22–25, https://doi. org/10.1080/02690055.2018.1431099.

Kambon, Khafra. *The Black Revolution 1970: A Retrospective*. Edited by Selwyn Ryan and Taimoon Stewart. ISER, UWI, 1995, pp. 215–243.

Katz, Jonathan M. "What Happened When a Nation Erased Birthright Citizenship." *The Atlantic*, 18 Nov. 2018, www.theatlantic.com/ideas/archive/2018/11/dominican-republic-erased-birthright-citizenship/575527/.

Kempadoo, Peter. *Guyana Boy*. 1960. Peepal Tree, 2001.

Kempadoo, Roshini. "An Interview with Roshini Kempadoo." Interview by Nalini Mohabir. *Ex Plus Ultra. The Postgraduate Ejournal of the WUN International Network in Colonial and Postcolonial Studies*. vol. 2, Dec. 2010, exp lusultra.wun.ac.uk/images/issue2/Interview_with_Roshini.pdf.

———. *Creole in the Archive. Imagery, Presence and the Location of the Caribbean Figure*. Rowman & Littlefield, 2014.

———. *Creole in the Archive: Imagery, Presence and Location of the Plantation Worker of Two Plantations, Nearby Villages and Towns in Trinidad (1838–1938)*. 2008. Goldsmiths College, University of London, PhD dissertation. *EBSCOhost*, search.ebscohost.com/login.aspx?direct=true&AuthType=sso&db=edsble&AN=edsble.498379&authtype=sso&custid=s8993828&site=eds-live&scope=site.

———. "Digital Media Practice as Critique: Roshini Kempadoo." *Black British Aesthetics Today*, edited by R. Victoria Arana, Cambridge Scholars, 2009.

———. *Ghosting*. 2004. Multimedia Installation. The City Gallery, Leicester (2004); PM Gallery & House, London, 2004.

———. "'Ghosting's (In)visibility and Absence of Racialized Caribbean Landscapes." *Feminist Review*, vol. 77, *Labour Migrations: Women on the Move*, 2004, pp. 125–128, *EBSCOhost*, https://doi.org/10.1057/palgrave.fr.9400173.

———. "Interpolating Screen Bytes: Critical Commentary in Multimedia Artworks." *Journal of Media Practice*, vol. 11, no. 1, 2010, pp. 59–79, *EBSCOhost*, search.ebscohost.com/login.aspx?direct=true&AuthType=sso&db=edb&AN=48642984&authtype=sso&custid=s8993828&site=eds-live&scope=site.

———. "State of Play: Photography, Multimedia and Memory." The Glasgow School of Art, *Vimeo*, uploaded by The Glasgow School of Art, 5 Feb. 2010, vimeo.com/62421134.

Kennedy, Joyce Bourne and Michael Kennedy. "Counterpoint." *The Concise Oxford Dictionary of Music*, Oxford U P, 2007.

Kester, Grant H. *Conversation Pieces: Community and Communication in Modern Art*. U of California P, 2004.

Kutzinski, Vera M. *Sugar's Secrets: Race and the Erotics of Cuban Nationalism*. Charlottesville: U of Virginia P, 1993.

LaCapra, Dominick. *Writing History, Writing Trauma*. Johns Hopkins U P, 2001.

Ladoo, Harold Sonny. *No Pain Like This Body*. 1971. 2003. Introduction by David Chariandy. A List, 2013.

Lambert, Laurie R. "Poetics of Reparation in M. NourbeSe Philip's *Zong!*" *Global South*, vol. 10, no. 1, 2016, pp. 107–129, *EBSCOhost*, search.ebs cohost.com/login.aspx?direct=true&AuthType=sso&db=edspmu&AN=eds pmu.S1932865616100051&authtype=sso&custid=s8993828&site=eds-live& scope=site.

———. *Sister Comrade. Caribbean Feminist Revisions of the Grenada Revolution.* Ebook ed., U of Virginia P, 2020.

Lammy, David. "Foreword." *Mother Country: Real Stories of the Windrush Children*, edited by Charlie Brinkhurst-Cuff. London: Headline 2018.

Laughlin, Nicholas. "Notebook." *The Caribbean Review of Books*, 9, 2006, pp. 21–26.

———. "Taking Note." *The Caribbean Review of Books.* Aug. 2005, http://car ibbeanreviewofbooks.com/crb-archive/9-august-2006/taking-note/.

———. *Work in Process.* Johannesburg: David Krut Publishing, 2013.

———. *Working Notes: On Christopher Cozier's Tropical Night Drawings.* Capital Offset Company, 2007.

LeBron, Marisol. *Policing Life and Death: Race, Violence and Resistance in Puerto Rico.* E-book ed., U of California P, 2019.

Ledent, Bénédicte. *Caryl Phillips,* Manchester U P, 2002.

———. "Caryl Phillips's *Crossing the River* and the Chorus of Archival Memory." *Commonwealth Essays and Studies*, vol. 40, no. 1, Autumn 2017, pp. 11–20, *Open Edition Journals*, https://doi.org/10.4000/ces.4438.

Ledent, Bénédicte and Daria Tunca. "Introduction." *Caryl Phillips: Writing in the Key of Life.* Rodopi, 2012, pp. xi–xxi.

Lezama Lima, José. "La Curiosidad Barroca." *La expresión americana.* Fondo de Cultura Económica, 1993, pp. 79–106.

Levy, Andrea. *Small Island.* 2004. Headline, 2009.

Lima, Maria Helena. "Dorothea Smartt." *Twenty-first Century "Black" British Writers*, edited by Victoria Arana, *Dictionary of Literary Biography.* Vol. 347, e-book ed., Gale, 2009, pp. 302–307.

Lipsitz, George. "History, Myth and Counter-Memory." *Time Passages: Collective Memory and American Popular Culture.* E-book ed., U of Minnesota P, 1990.

Llanos-Figueroa, Dahlma. *Daughters of the Stone.* Thomas Dunes Books, 2009.

Lockward, Alanna. *Marassá and the Nothingness.* Translated by Amari Barash. E-book ed., Partridge, 2016.

López, Kathleen. *Chinese Cubans: A Transnational History.* The U of North Carolina P, 2013.

Lorde, Audre. "The Transformation of Silence into Language and Action." *Audre Lorde: Your Silence Will Not Protect You.* Preface by Reni Eddo-Lodge and Introduction by Sar Ahmed, Silver Press, 2017, pp. 1–6.

———. "Uses of Anger: Women Responding to Racism." *Audre Lorde: Your Silence Will Not Protect You.* Preface by Reni Eddo-Lodge and Introduction by Sar Ahmed, Silver Press, 2017, pp. 107–118.

Lovelace, Earl. *The Dragon Can't Dance: A Novel.* 1979. Persea Books, 1998.

———. *Salt.* Faber & Faber, 1996.

Lowe, Hannah. *Ormonde.* Hercules Editions, 2014.

Lowney, John. *Jazz Internationalism. Literary Afro-Modernism ad the Cultural Politics of Black Music.* U of Illinois P, 2017.

Mackey, Nathaniel. "Breath and Precarity: The Inaugural Robert Creeley Lecture in Poetry and Poetics." *Poetics and Precarity*, edited by Myung Mi Kim and Cristanne Miller. SUNY Press, 2018, pp. 1–30.

———. "Other: From Noun to Verb." *Discrepant Engagement: Dissonance, Cross-Culturality and Experimental Writing.* Cambridge U P, 2013.

Mahabir, Joy. *Jouvert.* Author House, 2006.

Manzano, Juan F. and Iván A. Schulman. *Autobiografía de un Esclavo.* Guadarrama, 1975.

Martí, José. "La Raza." *José Martí Reader: Writings on the Americas*, edited by Deborah Shnookal and Mirta Muñiz, Ocean Press, 2007, pp. 172–174.

Martiatu Terry, Inés María. "El tema negro en el teatro cubano del XIX." *Afrocubanas: historia, pensamiento y prácticas culturales*, edited by Inés María Martiatu Terry and Daisy Rubiera Castillo. E-book ed., Editorial de Ciencias Sociales, 2015.

———. "Los negros en Sevilla." *Afrocubanas: historia, pensamiento y prácticas culturales*, edited by Inés María Martiatu Terry and Daisy Rubiera Castillo, e-book ed., Editorial de Ciencias Sociales, 2015.

———. *Over the Waves and Other Stories / Sobre las olas y otros cuentos.* Translated by Emmanuel Harris II. Swan Isle Press, 2008.

Martínez-San Miguel, Yolanda. "Rethinking the Colonial Latinx Literary Imaginary: A Comparative and Decolonial Research Agenda." *The Cambridge History of Latina/o American Culture*, edited by John Morán González and Laura Lomas, Cambridge U P, 2018, pp. 93–118. https://doi.org/10.1017/9781316869468.006.

Martínez-San Miguel, Yolanda and Michelle Stevens. "Introduction. Isolated Above, but Connected Below": Toward New, Global Archipelagic Thinking." *Contemporary Archipelagic Thinking. Toward New Comparative Methodologies and Disciplinary Formations*, edited by Yolanda Martínez-San Miguel and Michelle Stevens. E-book ed., Rowman & Littlefield, 2020.

Mascoli, Giulia. "'The River That Does Not Know Its Own Source Will Dry Up': Caryl Phillips's Musicalized Fiction." *Commonwealth: Essays and Studies*, vol. 40, no. 1, 2017, pp. 81–94. ProQuest. https://www.proquest.com/scholarly-journals/river-that-does-not-know-own-source-will-dry-up/docview/2214889182/se-2?accountid=10637.

———. "Remembering Beyond Words. Jazz and Musicality in Caryl Philip's *Crossing the River.*" *Lamar Journal of the Humanities*, XLII.1, Spring 2017, pp. 5–22, https://orbi.uliege.be/handle/2268/214221.

Matibag, Eduardo. *Haitian-Dominican Counterpoint: Nation, State and Race on Hispaniola.* Palgrave Macmillan, 2003.

Mbembe, Achille. "The Power of the Archive and its Limits." *Refiguring the Archive*, edited by Carolyn Hamilton, Verne Harris and Graeme Reid. Kluwer Academic Publishers, 2002, pp. 19–27.

McLeod, John and Caryl Phillips. "The City by the Water: Caryl Phillips in Conversation with John McLeod." *Interventions*, vol. 17, no. 6, pp. 879–892, *EBSCOhost*, https://doi.org/10.1080/1369801X.2014.998258.

McQueen, Steve. *Small Axe*. BBC, 2020.

McWatt, Tessa. *Shame on Me: An Anatomy of Race and Belonging.* Scribe, 2019.

Mignolo, Walter. *Local Histories, Global Designs.* Princeton U P, 2000.

Miller, Kei. *Augustown*. Weidenfeld & Nicholson, 2016.

———. "Recognizing the Spirit. Indigenous Spirituality and Caribbean Literature." *The Routledge Companion to Anglophone Caribbean Literature*, edited by Michael Bucknor and Alison Donnell. Routledge, 2011, pp. 450–459.

Mirzoeff, Nicholas. *The Right to Look: A Counter-History of Visuality.* Duke U P, 2011.

Mohammed, Patricia. "Belkis Ayón." *A to Z of Caribbean Art*, edited by Melanie Archer and Mariel Brown. Robert & Christopher, 2019, p. 21.

———. "Decoding the Image as Method for Researching Culture." *Methodologies in Caribbean Research on Gender and Sexuality*, edited by Kamala Kempadoo and Halimah A. F. DeShong. E-book ed., Ian Randle Publishers, 2021.

———. *Imaging the Caribbean: Culture and Visual Translation.* Macmillan, 2009.

Moïse, Myriam. "Grasping the Ungraspable in M. NourbeSe Philip's Poetry." *Commonwealth: Essays and Studies*, vol. 33, no. 1, 2010, pp. 23–33, *EBSCOhost*, search.ebscohost.com/login.aspx?direct=true&AuthType=sso&db=mzh&AN=2011383957&authtype=sso&custid=s8993828&site=eds-live&scope=site.

Moore, Alexandra Schultheis. "'Disspossessions within the Law': Human Rights and the Ec-Static Subject in M. NourbeSe Philip's *Zong!*" *Feminist Formations*, 28.1, Spring 2016, pp. 166–189, *EBSCOhost*, https://doi.org/10.1353/ff.2016.0020.

Morejón, Nancy. "Mujer Negra." *Looking Within. Mirar Adentro: Selected Poems.* Bilingual Edition. Introduction and Translation by Juanamaría Cordones Cook. Detroit Wayne State U P, 2003.

Moreno, Marisel, C. *Family Matters: Puerto Rican Women Authors on the Island and the Mainland*. U of Virginia P, 2012, *EBSCOhost*, search.ebscohost. com/login.aspx?direct=true&AuthType=sso&db=cat07845a&AN=uea.811 411339&authtype=sso&custid=s8993828&site=eds-live&scope=site.

Moret Miranda, Karo. "Apercepciones de la africanía: Instituciones afrodescendientes en la Cuba del XIX." *Crear Mundos*, vol. 12, 2014, pp. 27–31, www. crearmundos.net/asociacion/as/revista_files/Crearmundos_12_2014.pdf.

Morgan, Paula. "With a Tassa Blending: Calypso and Cultural Identity in Indo-Caribbean Fiction." *Music, Memory and Resistance: Calypso and the Caribbean Literary Imagination*, edited by Sandra Pouchet Paquet, Patricia J. Saunders et al. Ian Randle, 2007, pp. 224–251.

Morrison, Toni. "Harlem on My Mind: Contesting Memory—Meditation on Museums, Culture and Integration." 2006. *Mouth Full of Blood: Essays, Speeches, Meditations*. 2019. Vintage, 2020. pp. 79–86.

———. *Beloved*. 1987. Vintage, 2016.

Mosaka, Tumelo, Annie Paul, and Nicollette Ramirez. *Infinite Island: Contemporary Caribbean Art*. Philip Wilson Publishers, 2007.

Munasinghe, Viranjini. *Callaloo or Tossed Salad?: East Indians and the Cultural Politics of Identity in Trinidad*. Cornell U P, 2001.

Munro, Martin. *Different Drummers: Race and Rhythm in the Americas*. U of California P, 2010.

———. "Trauma, Memory, and History in Edwidge Danticat's *The Farming of Bones*." *Ethnologies*, vol. 28, no. 1, 2006, pp. 81–98, https://doi.org/10. 7202/014149ar.

Naipaul, V.S. *A House for Mr. Biswas*. 1961. Picador, 2003.

Naughton, Gerald David. "'The Whole Root Is Somewhere in the Music': Jazz, Soul, and Literary Influence in James Baldwin and Caryl Phillips." *Ariel: A Review of International English Literature*, vol. 44, no. 2, pp. 113–139, *EBSCOhost*, https://doi.org/10.1353/ari.2013.0020.

Nichols, Grace. *Startling the Flying Fish*. Virago Press, 2005.

Nieves López, Edgar J. "Autodefinición y Subversión en Fe en Disfraz de Mayra Santos-Febres y Las Negras de Yolanda Arroyo Pizarro." *Afro-Hispanic Review*, vol. 37, no. 1, Spring 2018, pp. 48–61, *EBSCOhost*, https://search. ebscohost.com/login.aspx?direct=true&AuthType=sso&db=asn&AN=134 235558&authtype=sso&custid=s8993828&site=eds-live&scope=site.

Nixon, Angelique V. *Resisting Paradise: Tourism, Diaspora and Sexuality in Caribbean Culture*. E-book ed., U P of Mississippi, 2015.

Njoroge, Njoroge M. *Chocolate Surrealism: Music, Movement, Memory and History in the Circum Caribbean*. E-book ed., U P of Mississippi, 2016.

Novack, Amy. "A Marred Testament: Cultural Trauma and Narrative in Danticat's *The Farming of Bones*." *Arizona Quarterly*, vol. 62, no. 4, Winter 2006, pp. 93–120, *EBSCOhost*, https://doi.org/10.1353/arq.2006.0027.

Okolosie, Lola. "Foreword." *Heart of the Race: Black Women's Lives in Britain*, edited by Beverly Bryan, Stella Dadzie and Suzanne Scafe. Verso 2018, pp. ix–xi.

Ortíz, Fernando. *Cuban Counterpoint. Tobacco and Sugar*. 1940. Translated by Harriet de Onís, Duke U P, 1995.

Ovid. *The Metamorphoses*. Translated by David Raeburn, Penguin Books, 2004.

Pacini Hernandez, Deborah. "Dancing with the Enemy: Cuban Popular Music, Race, Authenticity, and the World-Music Landscape." *Latin American Perspectives*, vol. 25, no. 3, May 1998, pp. 110–125. *EBSCOhost*, search. ebscohost.com/login.aspx?direct=true&db=edsjsr&AN=edsjsr.2634169&aut htype=sso&custid=s8993828&site=eds-live&scope=site.

Panaram, Sasha Ann and Caryl Phillips. *Left of Black | Caryl Phillips on Writing Oneself Into Visibility*. Duke University. *YouTube*, uploaded by John Hope Franklin Center at Duke U, 20 June 2020, www.youtube.com/watch?v=asq 8T3SyE7Y.

———. "Afrosporic Intimacies: Breath, Song, and Wind in M. NourbeSe Philip's *Zong!*" *Black Scholar*, 49.3, July 2019, pp. 21–35, *EBSCOhost*, https://doi. org/10.1080/00064246.2019.1619119.

Pasley, Victoria. "The Black Power Movement in Trinidad: An Exploration of Gender and Cultural Changes and the Development of a Feminist Consciousness." *Journal of International Women's Studies*, vol. 3, no. 1, 2001, pp. 24–40, *EBSCOhost*, search.ebscohost.com/login.aspx?direct= true&AuthType=sso&db=mzh&AN=2005873505&authtype=sso&custid= s8993828&site=eds-live&scope=site.

Paul, Annie. "Chris Cozier: A State of Independence." *Caribbean Beat*, issue 50, July/Aug., 2001, www.caribbean-beat.com/issue-50/chris-cozier-state-of-ind ependence#axzz7XKPDcmrL.

———. "The Enigma of Survival: Travelling Beyond the Expat Gaze." *Art Journal*, vol. 62, no. 1, Spring 2003, pp. 48–65, *EBSCOhost*, https://doi. org/10.1080/00043249.2003.10792148.

Paulino, Edward. "Anti-Haitianism, Historical Memory, and the Potential for Genocidal Violence in the Dominican Republic." *Genocide Studies and Prevention*, vol. 1, no. 3, July 2011, pp. 265–288, *EBSCOhost*, https://doi.org/10. 1353/gsp.2011.0072.

———. *Dividing Hispaniola: The Dominican Republic's Border Campaign Against Haiti, 1930–1961*. E-book ed., Pittsburgh: U of Pittsburgh P, 2016.

Pearce, Marsha. "Playing in the Yard." *Trinidad Guardian*, 10 Nov. 2010, www. guardian.co.tt/article-6.2.434476.9b97ac788b.

Peñaranda-Angulo, Verónica. "La Historia Femenina Negra o La Herstory Negra: Fe En Disfraz De Mayra Santos-Febres, Lectura y Reescritura De La Historia Desde y Para Las Mujeres Afrodescendientes." *Perífrasis: Revista De*

Literatura, Teoría y Crítica, vol. 9, no. 19, 1 July 2018, pp. 98–116. Directory of Open Access Journals, *EBSCOhost*, https://doi.org/10.25025/perifrasis20189.18.06.

Pérez, David. *Línea fronteriza*. Video installation, 2008.

Pérez Ortiz, Melanie. *Palabras encontradas: Antología personal de escritores puertorriqueños de los últimos 20 años (Conversaciones)*. Ediciones Callejón, 2008.

Persaud, Ingrid. *Love After Love*. Faber, 2020.

Persaud, Lakshmi. *Butterfly in the Wind*. 1990. Peepal Tree Press, 2008.

Petermann, Emily. *The Musical Novel: Imitation of Musical Structure, Performance and Reception in Contemporary Fiction*. E-book ed., Camden House, 2014.

Petty, Sheila. "CyberRace Constructs: Transnational Identities in Roshini Kempadoo's Ghosting." *Media Art Histories Archive*, Refresh! Conference, 2005, http://95.216.75.113:8080/xmlui/handle/123456789/285.

Philip, NourbeSe M. "A Poet of Place: Interview with M. NourbeSe Philip." Interview by Kristen Mahlis, *Callaloo*, vol. 27, no. 3, 2004, pp. 682–697, *EBSCOhost*, https://doi.org/10.1353/cal.2004.0127.

———. *A Genealogy of Resistance: And Other Essays*. Toronto: Mercury Press, 1997.

———. "A Travelogue of Sorts: Transatlantic Trafficking in Silence and Erasure." *Anthurium: A Caribbean Studies Journal*, vol. 6, no. 1, art. 3, 2008, pp. 1–30, https://doi.org/10.33596/anth.110.

———. *Bla_k: Essays and Interviews*. BookThug, 2017.

———. *Coups and Calypsos*. The Mercury Press, 2001.

———. "Defending the Dead, Confronting the Archive: A Conversation with M. NourbeSe Philip", by Patricia Joan Saunders, *Small Axe: A Caribbean Journal of Criticism*, vol. 26, June 2008, pp. 63–79, *EBSCOhost*, https://doi.org/10.2979/SAX.2008.-.26.63.

———. "Fugues, Fragments and Fissures—A Work in Progress." *Music, Memory and Resistance: Calypso and the Caribbean Literary Imagination*, edited by Sandra Pouchet Paquet, Patricia J. Saunders and Stephen Stuempfle. Ian Randle, 2007, pp. 75–96.

———. "GA(S)P: Experiments in Radical Hospitality." 2020 Hammed Shahidian Lecture, Women and Gender Studies Institute, *YouTube*, uploaded by Women and Gender Studies, 28 Oct. 2020, www.youtube.com/watch?v=KqfX6HPAVaw.

———. "In Conversation with History: An Interview with M. NourbeSe Philip." Interview by Marta Fernandez Campa, *Small Axe: A Caribbean Journal of Criticism*, vol. 26, no. 1, Mar. 2022, pp. 85–100, *EBSCOhost*, https://doi.org/10.1215/07990537-9724079.

———. "The Ga(s)p." *Poetics and Precarity*, edited by Myung Mi Kim and Cristanne Miller, State U of New York P, 2018, pp. 31–40.

———. "The Habit of: Poetry, Rats and Cats." *A Genealogy of Resistance and Other Essays*. Mercury Press, 1997, pp. 113–119.

———. "Managing the Unmanageable." *Caribbean Women Writers: Essays from the First International Conference*. Edited by Selwyn R. Cudjoe, Callaloux Publications, 1990, pp. 295–300.

———. *She Tries Her Tongue; Her Silence Softly Breaks*. 1988. The Women's Press, 1993.

Phillips, Caryl. *Crossing the River*. 1993. London: Vintage, 2006.

———. *Dancing in the Dark*. Secker & Warburg, 2005.

———. *Foreigners: Three English Lives*. Harvill Secker, 2007.

———. "Literature: The New Jazz." *Color Me English. Migration and Belonging. Before and After 9/11*. The New Press, 2011, pp. 81–85.

———. *The European Tribe*. 1987. Vintage Books, 2000.

———. *The Final Passage*. Vintage, 2004.

———. *The Lost Child*. Oneworld, 2015.

Philoctète, René. *Massacre River*. 1989. Translated by Linda Coverdale. A New Directions Book, 2005.

Pike, Frederick B. *Hispanismo, 1989–1936: Spanish Conservatives and Liberals and Their Relations to Spanish America*, Notre Dame, 1971.

Pilgrim, Chike, editor. *Power. Interviews: T&T 1970, Part 1*. E-book ed., self-published work, 2020.

Pollard, Ingrid. "Case Study: Ingrid Pollard." *Photographers and Research: The Role of Research in Contemporary Photographic Practice*. Routledge, 2017, *EBSCOhost*, learning.oreilly.com/library/view/photographers-and-res earch/9781317549055/xhtml/Ch0108.xhtml.

Poupeye, Veerle. *Caribbean Art*. Thames and Hudson, 1998.

Power, Kevin, editor. *Diciendo lo que me pasa por la mente*. Marlborough Gallery, Madrid, 2005, pp. 2–21.

Pressure. Directed by Horace Ové. British Film Institute, 1976.

Puri, Shalini. "Finding the Field: Notes on Caribbean Cultural Criticism, Area Studies, and the Forms of Engagement." *Theorizing Fieldwork in the Humanities: Methods, Reflections, and Approaches*, edited by Shalini Puri. Palgrave, 2016, pp. 29–49.

———. *The Caribbean Postcolonial: Social Equality, Post-Nationalism and Cultural Hibridity*. Palgrave Macmillan, 2004.

———. *The Grenada Revolution in the Caribbean Present: Operation Urgent Memory*. Palgrave Macmillan, 2014.

Quijano, Aníbal. "Colonialidad del poder, cultura y conocimiento en América Latina." *Crítica Cultural en Latinoamérica: Paradigmas globales y enunciaciones locales*, 24.51, 1999, pp. 137–148, *JSTOR*, www.jstor.org/stable/pdf/41491587.pdf?refreqid=excelsior%3A555c00d6ff1473cc3fcc95ac9eb93659.

———. "Coloniality of Power, Eurocentrism, and Latin America." *Nepantla: Views from the South*, vol. 1, no. 3, Nov. 2000, pp. 533–580. *EBSCOhost*, eds.b.ebscohost.com/eds/pdfviewer/pdfviewer?vid=3&sid=fe6cb84a-e6cb-4718-b54d-9a4c25dff83d%40pdc-v-sessmgr01.

Ramazani, Jahan. *A Transnational Poetics*. 2009. E-book ed., The U of Chicago P, 2015.

Ramos Rosado, Marie. "Exordio a *Las Negras*." *Las Negras*, Yolanda Arroyo Pizarro, 4ta Edición. Boreales, 2016, pp. 17–18.

———. "Foreword." *Negras: Stories of Puerto Rican Slave Women*. Yolanda Arroyo Pizarro, Amazon, 2012.

Rankine, Claudia. *Citizen: An American Lyric*. Penguin, 2014.

Reckin, Anna. "Tidalectic Lectures: Kamau Brathwaite's Prose/Poetry as Sound-Space." *Anthurium: A Caribbean Studies Journal*, vol. 1, no. 1, art.5, 2003, pp. 1–16, https://doi.org/10.33596/anth.4.

Reddock, Rhoda. "Freedom Denied: Indian Women and Indentureship in Trinidad and Tobago, 1845–1917." 1985. *Caribbean Quarterly*, vol. 4, no. 54, Dec. 2008, pp. 41–68, *EBSCOhost*, earch.ebscohost.com/login.aspx?direct=true&AuthType=sso&db=edsjsr&AN=edsjsr.40654698&authtype=sso&custid=s8993828&site=eds-live&scope=site.

———. "Jahaji Bhai: The Emergence of a Dougla Poetics in Trinidad and Tobago." *Global Studies in Culture and Power*, vol. 5, no. 4, 1999, pp. 569–601, https://doi.org/10.1080/1070289X.1999.9962630.

———. "The Indentureship Experience: Indian Women in Trinidad and Tobago 1845–1917." 1998. *Women Plantation Workers: International Experiences*. E-book ed., edited by Shobhita Jain and Rhoda Reddock, Routledge, 2020.

Reed, Anthony. *Freedom Time: The Poetics and Politics of Black Experimental Writing*. John Hopkins U P, 2014.

Regis, Louanne Ferne. The Trinidad Dougla: Identity and Lexical Choice. Cambridge Scholars Publishing, 2016, *EBSCOhost*, search.ebscohost.com/login.aspx?direct=true&AuthType=sso&db=cat07845a&AN=uea.956991420&authtype=sso&custid=s8993828&site=eds-live&scope=site.

Relational Undercurrents: Contemporary Art of the Caribbean Archipelago, 16 Sept. 2017–25 Feb. 2018, Museum of Latin American Art, Long Beach.

República Dominicana, Tribunal Constitucional. Sentence TC/0168–13, 2013, https://www.refworld.org.es/pdfid/5d7fcd99a.pdf.

Reyes-Santos, Alaí. *Our Caribbean Kin: Race and Nation in the Neoliberal Antilles*. Rutgers U P, 2015, *EBSCOhost*, search.ebscohost.com/login. aspx?direct=true&AuthType=sso&db=cat07845a&AN=uea.918984101&aut htype=sso&custid=s8993828&site=eds-live&scope=site.

Rich, Adrienne. "When We Dead Awaken: Writing as Re-vision." *The Norton Anthology of Literature by Women*, edited by Sandra M. Gilbert and Susan Gubar, vol. 2, third edition, W. W. Norton & Company, 2007, pp. 982–993.

Ricoeur, Paul. *Memory, History, Forgetting*. The U of Chicago P, 2004.

Ricourt, Milagros. *The Dominican Racial Imaginary: Surveying the Landscape of Race and Nation in Hispaniola*. E-book ed., Rutgers U P, 2016.

Riddell, Barry. "A Tale of Contestation, Disciples, and Damned: The Lessons of the Spread of Globalization into Trinidad and Tobago." *Environment and Planning A*, vol. 35. no. 4, 2003, pp. 659–78, *EBSCOhost*, https://doi.org/ 10.1068/a35199.

Riggio, Milla Cozart, editor. "We jamming it: introduction to part III." *Carnival. Culture in Action: The Trinidad Experience*, Routledge, 2004, *EBSCOhost*,   search.ebscohost.com/login.aspx?direct=true&AuthType=sso& db=cat07845a&AN=uea.57120332&authtype=sso&custid=s8993828&site= eds-live&scope=site.

Rivera Casellas, Zaira. *Bajo la Sombra del Texto. La crítica y el silencio en el discurso racial en Puerto Rico*. E-book ed., Terranova Editores, 2015.

———. "La Poética de la Esclavitud (Silenciada) en la Literatura Puertorriqueña: Carmen Colón Pellot, Betraiz Berrocal, Yolanda Arroyo Pizarro y Mayra Santos Febres." *Cincinnati Romance Review*, vol. 30, 2011, pp. 99–116, *Scholar @ UC*, https://scholar.uc.edu/concern/articles/r207tq90h.

Robert W. Rudnicki. *Percyscapes: The Fugue State in Twentieth-Century Southern Fiction*. Louisiana State UP, 1999.

Rodríguez López, Yusimí. "La Revolución hizo a los negros personas." *Afrocubanas: historia, pensamiento y prácticas culturales*, edited by Inés María Martiatu Terry and Daisy Rubiera Castillo, e-book ed., Editorial de Ciencias Sociales, 2015.

Rodríguez-Silva, Illeana M. *Silencing Race: Disentangling Blackness, Colonialism and National Identities in Puerto Rico*. E-book ed., Palgrave, 2012.

Rohlehr, Gordon. "Black Sycorax, My Mother." *The Geography of a Soul: Emerging Perspectives on Kamau Brathwaite*, edited by Timothy Reiss. Africa World Press, 2001, pp. 277–295.

———. "We Getting the Kaiso that We Deserve: Calypso and the World Music Market." *The Drama Review*, vol. 42, no. 3, 1998, pp. 82–95, *EBSCOhost*, search.ebscohost.com/login.aspx?direct=true&AuthType=sso&db=edsjsr& AN=edsjsr.1146683&authtype=sso&custid=s8993828&site=eds-live&scope= site.

Roorda, Eric. *The Dictator Next Door: the Good Neighbor Policy and the Trujillo Regime in the Dominican Republic, 1930–1945*. Duke U P, 1998.

Rose, Sheena. Photo of Rose's notebooks displayed at *The Other Side of Now* exhibition. *Instagram*, 9 Nov. 2018, www.instagram.com/p/Bp9GDB sgvXL/.

Roshini Kempadoo: Works 1990–2004. Directed by Sunil Gupta. Ova Production, 2004. *Vimeo*, uploaded by Autograph, 10 Oct. 2012, vimeo.com/51149469.

Roumain, Jacques. *Masters of the Dew*. Translated by Langston Hughes and Mercer Cook. Heinemann, 1987.

Rubiera Castillo, Daisy. "Grupo Afrocubanas: ¿Por Qué y Para Qué?" *Cuban Studies*, no. 48, Jan. 2019, pp. 202–13. *EBSCOhost*, search.ebscohost.com/ login.aspx?direct=true&AuthType=sso&db=edsjsr&AN=edsjsr.26725390&aut htype=sso&custid=s8993828&site=eds-live&scope=site.

———. "Introducción. Avivar la memoria, desterrar el olvido." *Afrocubanas: historia, pensamiento y prácticas culturales*. 2011, edited by Diasy Rubiera Castillo and Inés María Martiatu Terry. E-book ed., Editorial de Ciencias Sociales, 2015.

Rudder, David. "A Madman's Rant." *Tales from A Strange Land*. Lipsoland, 1996.

Rusell, Heather. *Legba's Crossing: Narratology in the African Atlantic*. U of Georgia P, 2009, *EBSCOhost*, search.ebscohost.com/login.aspx?direct=true& AuthType=sso&db=nlebk&AN=311009&authtype=sso&custid=s8993828& site=eds-live&scope=site.

Said, Edward W. *Culture and Imperialism*, Vintage 1994.

———. *Music at the Limits: Three decades of Essays and Articles on Music*. E-book ed., London: Bloomsbury, 2009.

San Germán, G. R. de. "Al darle la libertad graciosamente a mi esclavo Zacarías." *La Razón*, 25 April 1873, *La Colección Puertorriqueña*. issuu.com/coleccion puertorriquena/docs/la_razon_mayaguez_18730425.

Sánchez Ferlosio, Rafael. *Esas Yndias equivocadas y malditas: Comentarios a la historia*. Ediciones Destino, 1994.

Sander, Philip. "Galvanize: Talking It Through." *Caribbean Beat Magazine*, 83, Jan.–Feb. 2007, www.caribbean-beat.com/issue-83/galvanize-talking-it-through#ixzz6aNPOVW00.

Santos-Febres, Mayra. *Antes que llegue la luz*. Planeta, 2021.

———. *Fe en disfraz*. Alfaguara, 2009.

———. *La amante de Gardel*. Planeta, 2015.

———. *Our Lady of the Night*. Harper Perennial, 2001.

———. *Sirena Selena*. 2000. Translated by Stephen Lytle. Picador, 2000.

———. *Urban Oracles*. Brookline Books, 1997.

Scarano, Francisco. "Revisiting Puerto Rico's Nineteenth- Century Sugar-and-Slavery History." *Centro Journal*, vol. 32, no. 1, 2020, pp. 4–32.

Academic Search Ultimate, *EBSCOhost*, search.ebscohost.com/login.aspx?dir ect=true&AuthType=sso&db=asn&AN=143243128&authtype=sso&custid= s8993828&site=eds-live&scope=site. Accessed 26 June 2022.

Schmidt-Nowara, Christopher. *Slavery, Freedom, and Abolition in Latin America and the Atlantic World*. U of New Mexico P, 2011, *EBSCOhost*, search. ebscohost.com/login.aspx?direct=true&AuthType=sso&db=cat07845a&AN= uea.957636053&authtype=sso&custid=s8993828&site=eds-live&scope=site.

———. "Spanish Origins of American Empire: Hispanism, History, and Commemoration, 1898–1915." *The International History Review*, vol. 30, no. 1, Mar. 2008, pp. 32–51. *EBSCOhost*, search.ebscohost.com/login. aspx?direct=true&db=edsjsr&AN=edsjsr.40109956&authtype=sso&custid= s8993828&site=eds-live&scope=site.

Scott, Lawrence. *Night Calypso*. Allison and Busby, 2004.

———. *Witchbroom*. 1992. Papillote Press, 2017.

Selvon, Sam. *The Lonely Londoners*. 1956. Longman, 1979.

———. *Ways of Sunlight*. 1957. Hodder Education, 2015.

Senior, Olive. *Dying to Better Themselves: West Indians and the Building of the Panama Canal*. U of the West Indies P, 2014.

Sharpe, Christina Elizabeth. *In the Wake: On Blackness and Being*. Duke University Press, 2016.

Sharpe, Granville. "Letter to William Baker re: Zong Incident." 23 May 1783, D3549 13/1/B1, Gloucestershire Archives.

Sharpe, Jenny. *Immaterial Archives: An African Diaspora Poetics of Loss*. Northwestern U P, 2020.

Sheller, Mimi. *Citizenship from Below: Erotic Agency and Caribbean Freedom*. Duke U P, 2012.

———. *Consuming the Caribbean: From Arawaks to Zombies*. Routledge, 2003.

Shemak, April. *Asylum Speakers: Caribbean Refugees and Testimonial Discourse*. Fordham U P, 2011.

———. "Re-membering Hispaniola: Edwidge Danticat's *The Farming of Bones*." *Modern Fiction Studies*, vol. 48, no. 1, Spring 2002, pp. 83–112, *EBSCOhost*, https://doi.org/10.1353/mfs.2002.0010.

Shepherd, Verene. *Engendering Caribbean History: Cross-Cultural Perspectives, a Reader*. Ian Randle Publishers, 2011. *EBSCOhost*, search.ebscohost.com/ login.aspx?direct=true&db=e000xww&AN=668405&authtype=sso&custid= s8993828&site=eds-live&scope=site.

Siklosi, Kate. "The Absolute / of Water": The Submarine Poetic of M. NourbeSe Philip's Zong!" *Canadian Literature*, 228/229 Spring/Summer 2016, pp. 111–130, *EBSCOhost*, search.ebscohost.com/login.aspx?direct= true&AuthType=sso&db=mzh&AN=2017700691&authtype=sso&custid= s8993828&site=eds-live&scope=site.

Smartt, Dorothea. *Connecting Medium*. Peepal Tree, 2001.

————. *Ship Shape*. Peepal Tree, 2009.

Smith, Zadie. *White Teeth*. Penguin, 2001.

Stoler, Ann Laura. *Along the Archival Grain: Epistemic Anxieties and Colonial Common Sense*. Princeton U P, 2009.

————. "Colonial Archives and the Arts of Governance: On the Content in the Form." *Refiguring the Archive*, edited by Carolyn Hamilton, Verne Harris at al. Springer, 2002, pp. 83–102.

Strongman, Roberto. "Reading through the Bloody Borderlands of Hispaniola: Fictionalizing the 1937 Massacre of Sugarcane Workers in the Dominican Republic." *Journal of Haitian Studies*, vol. 12, no. 2, Oct. 2006, pp. 22–46, *EBSCOhost*, https://search.ebscohost.com/login.aspx?direct=true&AuthType=sso&db=edsjsr&AN=edsjsr.41715327&authtype=sso&custid=s8993828&site=eds-live&scope=site.

Stubbs, Jean. "Gender in Caribbean History." *Engendering Caribbean History: Cross-Cultural Perspectives, a Reader*, edited by Vere Shepperd. Ian Randle Publishers, 2011, pp. 3–37. *EBSCOhost*, search.ebscohost.com/login.aspx?direct=true&db=e000xww&AN=668405&authtype=sso&custid=s8993828&site=eds-live&scope=site.

Stuempfle, Stephen. *The Steelband Movement: The Forging of a National Art in Trinidad and Tobago*. U of Pennsylvania P, 1995.

Subirats, Eduardo. "Seven Thesis against Hispanism." *Border Interrogations: Questioning Spanish Frontiers. Edited by Benita San Pedro Vizcaya and Simon Doubleday*. Bergham Books, 2008, pp. 246–259.

Sublette, Ned. *Cuba and Its Music. From the First Drums to the Mambo*. 1st, ed., Chicago Review Press, 2004, *EBSCOhost*, search.ebscohost.com/login.aspx?direct=true&AuthType=sso&db=cat07845a&AN=uea.753486044&authtype=sso&custid=s8993828&site=eds-live&scope=site.

Subramanian, Shreerekha. "Blood, Memory and Nation: Massacre and Mourning in Edwidge Danticat's The Farming of Bones." *The Masters and the Slaves: Plantation Relations and Mestizaje in American Imaginaries*, edited by Alexandra Isfahani-Hammond, Palgrave, 2005, pp. 149–161.

Sudbury, Julia. *'Other Kinds of Dreams' Black Women's Organisations and the Politics of Transformation*. 1998. E-book ed., Routledge, 2005.

Sullivan, Marek. "Jay Bernard's Explosive Poetry and the Long Shadow of Racism in Britain." *Frieze*, 23 Sept. 2019, www.frieze.com/article/jay-bernards-explosive-poetry-and-long-shadow-racism-britain.

Tapia y Rivera, Alejandro. *La cuarterona. Drama original en tres actos*. 1867. Instituto de Cultura Puertorriqueña/Editorial de la Universidad de Puerto Rico, 2007.

Taylor, Diana. *The Archive and the Repertoire: Performing Cultural Memory in the Americas*. Duke U P, 2003.

Taylor, Paul C. *Black Is Beautiful: A Philosophy of Black Aesthetics*. E-book ed., Wiley, 2016.

The Other Side of Now: Foresight in Contemporary Caribbean Art. 18 July 2019– 7 June 2020, Pérez Art Museum, Miami, www.pamm.org/exhibitions/other-side-now-foresight-contemporary-caribbean-art.

The Sea is History: Discourses on the Poetics of Relation, Mar. 7–Aug. 18, Museum of Cultural History, University of Oslo, 2019.

Thompson, Krista A. *An Eye For The Tropics: Tourism, Photography, and Framing the Caribbean Picturesque*. Duke U P, 2006.

———. "No Abstract Art Here?: The Problem of the Visual in Contemporary Anglo-Caribbean Art." *Small Axe: A Caribbean Journal of Criticism*, vol. 23, no. 23, 2007, pp. 119–137, *EBSCOhost*, search.ebscohost.com/login. aspx?direct=true&AuthType=sso&db=edspmu&AN=edspmu.S15346714071 01191&authtype=sso&custid=s8993828&site=eds-live&scope=site.

Thompson, Robert Farris. *Flash of the Spirit: African and Afro-American Art and Philosophy*. Vintage Books, 1984.

Torres-Saillant, Silvio. *Caribbean Poetics: Towards an Aesthetic of West Indian Caribbean Literature*. 1997. second ed., Peepal Tree, 2013.

Torres Zayanas, Ramón. *La Sociedad Abakuá. Los Hijos del Èkpè*. E-book ed., Ciencias Sociales, 2017.

Trotz, D. Alissa. "Behind the Banner of Culture? Gender, 'Race,' and the Family in Guyana." *New West Indian Guide / Nieuwe West-Indische Gids*, vol. 77, no. 1–2, 2003, pp. 5–29, *EBSCOhost*, search.ebscohost.com/login.aspx?dir ect=true&AuthType=sso&db=edsjsr&AN=edsjsr.41850226&authtype=sso& custid=s8993828&site=eds-live&scope=site..

Trouillot, Michel-Rolph. *Silencing the Past: Power and the Production of History*. Beacon Press, 1995.

Turits, Richard Lee. "A World Destroyed, a Nation Imposed: The 1937 Haitian Massacre in the Dominican Republic." *Hispanic American Historical Review*, vol. 82. no. 3, Aug. 2002, pp. 589–635, *EBSCOhost*, https://doi.org/10. 1215/00182168-82-3-589.

Ulmer, Gregory L. "The Object of Post-criticism." *The Anti-Aesthetic: Essays on Post-modern Culture*, edited by Hal Foster. The New Press, 1998, pp. 93–126.

"Uncomfortable: The Art of Christopher Cozier." Directed by Richard Fung, Video Data Bank, 2005.

Vargas Llosa, Mario. *La fiesta del chivo*. Círculo de Lectores, 2000.

Vega, Bernardo. *Trujillo y Haiti*. Vol. 2. Fundación Cultural Dominicana, 1988.

Villaverde, Cirilo. *Cecilia Valdés or El Angel Hill*. Translated by Helen Lane, Oxford U P, 2005.

Villepastour, Amanda, ed. "Introduction." *The Yorùbá God of Drumming: Transatlantic Perspectives on the Wood that Talks*, U P of Mississippi, 2015, pp. 3–34.

Vous Êtes Ici. 29 Oct.–5 Dec. 2010, Fondation Clément, Martinique.

Wahab, Amar. *Colonial Inventions: Landscape, Power and Representation in Nineteenth-Century Trinidad*. E-book ed., Cambridge Scholars Publishing, 2010.

Wahab, Amar and Cecily Jones. *Free at Last? Reflections on Freedom and the Abolition of the British Slave Trade*. Cambridge Scholars, 2011, *EBSCOhost*, search.ebscohost.com/login.aspx?direct=true&db=cat07845a&AN=uea. 823720923&authtype=sso&custid=s8993828&site=eds-live&scope=site.

Wainwright, Leon. *Timed Out: Art and the Transnational Caribbean*. Manchester U P, 2011.

Walcott, Derek. *Selected Poems*. Straus and Giroux, 2007.

———. "The Antilles: Fragments of Epic Memory." *What the Twilight Says: Essays*. Farrar, Straus and Grioux, 1998, pp. 65–84.

———. "The Schooner Flight." 1979. *Collected Poems*, Farrar, Straus and Giroux, 1986, pp. 345–361.

Walcott, Rinaldo. *The Long Emancipation. Moving Toward Black Freedom*. Duke U P, 2021.

———. ""No Language is Neutral": The Politics of Performativity in M. NourbeSe Philip's and Dionne Brand's Poetry." *Black Like Who? Writing Black Canada*, Insomniac Press, 2003, pp. 73–88.

Wallace, Michelle. "Modernism, Postmodernism and the Problem of the Visual in Afro-American Culture." *Dark Designs in Visual Culture*. Duke U P, 2004.

Walsh, John Patrick. *Migration and Refuge. An Echo Archive of Haitian Literature, 1962–2017*. Liverpool U P, 2020, *EBSCOhost*, https://search.ebscohost.com/login.aspx?direct=true&AuthType=sso&db=cat07845a&AN=uea.1090812920&authtype=sso&custid=s8993828&site=eds-live&scope=site.

Warsh, Larry, ed. *Jean Michel Basquiat: The Notebooks*. Princetown U P, 2015.

Watkin, William. *On Mourning: Theories of Loss in Modern Literature*. Edinburgh U P, 2004.

Watson, Tim. *Caribbean Culture and British Fiction in the Atlantic World, 1780–1870*. Cambridge U P, 2008.

Weir-Soley, Donna. "Voudoun Symbolism in *The Farming of Bones*." *Obsidian*. vol. 6/7, no. 1/2, 2005, pp. 167–84, *EBSCOhost*, search.ebscohost.com/login.aspx?direct=true&AuthType=sso&db=edo&AN=21684206&authtype=sso&custid=s8993828&site=eds-live&scope=site.

Weldt-Basson, Helene C. "Memoria Cultural Versus Olvido Histórico: Las Voces de las Esclavas en Fe en disfraz de Mayra Santos-Febres y Cielo de tambores de Ana Gloria Moya." *Hispanofila*, vol. 179, no. 1, January 2017, pp. 187–201, *EBSCOhost*, https://doi.org/10.1353/hsf.2017.0017.

Windrush Years. Directed by David Upshall, produced by Mike Phillips, *BBC 2*, 2018.

Winer, Lise. *Dictionary of the English/Creole of Trinidad & Tobago: on Historical Principles.* McGill-Queen's U P, 2009. *EBSCOhost*, search.ebscohost.com/login.aspx?direct=true&AuthType=sso&db=cat07845a&AN=uea.759157066&authtype=sso&custid=s8993828&site=eds-live&scope=site.

Wood, Marcus. *Blind Memory: Visual Representations of Slavery in England and America.* Routledge, 2000.

Wucker, Michelle. "Race and Massacre in Hispaniola." *Tikkun*, vol. 13, no. 6, Nov./Dec., 1998, pp. 61–63.

———. *Why The Cocks Fight: Dominicans, Haitians, and The Struggle for Hispaniola.* Hill and Wang, 1999.

Yáñez, Mirta, editor. *Cubana: Contemporary Fiction by Cuban Women.* 1996. Foreword by Ruth Behar, translated by Dick Cluster and Cindy Schuster, Beacon Press, 1998.

Yúdice, George. "Testimonio and Postmodernism." *The Real Thing: Testimonial Discourse and Latin America*, edited by Georg M. Gugelberger, Duke U P, 1996, pp. 42–57.

Zacarías Tallet, José. "La Rumba." *Órbita de la poesía afrocubana, 1928–1937*, edited by Ramón Guirao, Úcar García y Cia., 1938, p. 37.

Zeno García, Manuel. *La Charca.* 1894. Editorial Dictatorial, 2013.

INDEX